DATE DUE

FEB 24 2013			

WELFARE REFORM AND ITS LONG-TERM
CONSEQUENCES FOR AMERICA'S POOR

Two decades of federal- and state-level demonstration projects and experiments concerning cash welfare in the United States culminated with the passage of the Personal Responsibility and Work Opportunity Reconciliation Act of 1996, better known as "welfare reform." Ten years after reform, there remain a host of unanswered questions on the well-being of low-income families. In *Welfare Reform and Its Long-Term Consequences for America's Poor*, many of the nation's leading poverty experts come together in a single volume to assess the longer-term effects of welfare reform. A diverse array of survey and administrative data are brought to bear to examine the effects of welfare reform and the concomitant expansions of the Earned Income Tax Credit on the level and distribution of income, the composition of consumption, employment, public versus private health insurance coverage, health and education outcomes of children, marriage, and social service delivery.

James P. Ziliak holds the Carol Martin Gatton Endowed Chair in Micro-economics in the Department of Economics at the University of Kentucky, and he is the Founding Director of the University of Kentucky Center for Poverty Research. He is a research affiliate with the National Poverty Center at the University of Michigan and with the Institute for Research on Poverty at the University of Wisconsin. Professor Ziliak received his Ph.D. in economics from Indiana University in 1993. From 1993 to 2002 he served as assistant and associate professor of economics at the University of Oregon. He has held visiting positions at the Brookings Institution, University of Michigan, University of Wisconsin, and University College London. Professor Ziliak's research expertise is in the areas of labor economics, poverty policy, and tax policy. He has published in leading academic journals of economics, including the *American Economic Review* and the *Journal of Political Economy*. Most recently, he coedited the book *Income Volatility and Food Assistance in the United States* (2008).

Welfare Reform and Its Long-Term Consequences for America's Poor

Edited by

JAMES P. ZILIAK

 **CAMBRIDGE**
UNIVERSITY PRESS

CAMBRIDGE UNIVERSITY PRESS
Cambridge, New York, Melbourne, Madrid, Cape Town, Singapore,
São Paulo, Delhi, Dubai, Tokyo

Cambridge University Press
32 Avenue of the Americas, New York, NY 10013–2473, USA

www.cambridge.org
Information on this title: www.cambridge.org/9780521764254

First published 2009

Printed in the United States of America

A catalog record for this publication is available from the British Library.

Library of Congress Cataloging in Publication data

Welfare reform and its long-term consequences for America's poor / James P. Ziliak, editor.
p.   cm.
Includes bibliographical references and index.
ISBN 978-0-521-76425-4 (Hardback)
1. Public welfare–United States.   2. Poor–United States.
I. Ziliak, James Patrick.   II. Title.
HV91.W4694 2009
362.5'5680973–dc22   2009004015

ISBN 978-0-521-76425-4 Hardback

Contents

Contributors

Scott W. Allard is associate professor in the School of Social Service Administration, University of Chicago.

Rebecca M. Blank is Robert V. Kerr Senior Fellow in the Economic Studies Program, Brookings Institution.

Christopher Bollinger is Gatton Endowed Professor of Economics in the Department of Economics, University of Kentucky.

Greg J. Duncan is Distinguished Professor of Education in the School of Education, University of California at Irvine.

Bianca Frogner is a postdoctoral Fellow in the Health Policy and Administration Department, University of Illinois at Chicago.

Qin Gao is assistant professor in the Graduate School of Social Service, Fordham University.

Irv Garfinkel is Mitchell I. Ginsberg Professor of Contemporary Urban Problems in the School of Social Work, Columbia University.

Lisa A. Gennetian is senior research director in the Policy Evaluation Project, Brookings Institution.

Luis Gonzalez is a graduate student in the Department of Economics, University of Kentucky.

John C. Ham is professor in the Department of Economics, University of Maryland.

Aletha C. Huston is Pricilla Pond Flawn Regents Professor of Child Development in the School of Human Ecology, University of Texas at Austin.

Ariel Kalil is associate professor in the Harris School of Public Policy, University of Chicago.

Neeraj Kaushal is associate professor in the School of Social Work, Columbia University, and a faculty research Fellow at the National Bureau of Economic Research.

Jean Knab is a researcher at Mathematica Policy Research, Inc.

Xianghong Li is assistant professor in the Department of Economics, York University.

Sara McLanahan is William S. Tod Professor of Sociology and Public Affairs in the Department of Sociology, Princeton University.

Robert Moffitt is Krieger-Eisenhower Professor of Economics in the Department of Economics, Johns Hopkins University.

Emily Moiduddin is a researcher at Mathematica Policy Research, Inc.

Pamela Morris is codirector of the Family Well-Being and Children's Development Policy Area, MDRC.

Peter R. Mueser is professor in the Department of Economics, University of Missouri at Columbia.

Cynthia Osborne is assistant professor in the LBJ School of Public Affairs, University of Texas at Austin.

David C. Ribar is professor in the Department of Economics, University of North Carolina at Greensboro.

Lara Shore-Sheppard is associate professor in the Department of Economics, Williams College.

David W. Stevens is executive director of the Jacob France Institute, University of Baltimore.

Kenneth R. Troske is the William B. Sturgill Professor of Economics in the Department of Economics, University of Kentucky.

Jane Waldfogel is professor in the School of Social Work, Columbia University.

James P. Ziliak is Gatton Endowed Chair in Microeconomics and Director of the Center for Poverty Research in the Department of Economics, University of Kentucky.

Kathleen M. Ziol-Guest is assistant director for research at the Institute for Children and Poverty.

Preface

Taking stock of the research on the effects of the 1996 welfare reform in the fall of 2005, it became abundantly clear that as we neared the tenth anniversary of its passage, we knew comparatively little about the longer-term consequences of the reform for America's poor. The lucid surveys by Blank (2002) and Moffitt (2003), followed by the meta-analysis by Grogger and Karoly (2005), summarized the research using experimental and non-experimental data from the "welfare waiver" era spanning 1990 to 1995 and data from the first four years postreform through 2000. The late 1990s was a period of great prosperity and relative peace for the nation, and thus many of the gains of the poor uncovered in the research were undoubtedly fostered by the strong economy. Since the business cycle peak of 2000, the country has experienced a recession, the 9/11 terrorist attacks, two ongoing wars in Afghanistan and Iraq, rising poverty, declining health insurance coverage, a series of devastating hurricanes, and stagnant real wages. As this book goes to press, the world is in the midst of the greatest financial crisis since the Great Depression. How these developments interact with public policies such as welfare reform and the Earned Income Tax Credit to affect the lives of the poor had not been explored nearly to the extent that the pre-2000 experience would dictate. This realization was the genesis for the present book.

In the spring of 2006, I commissioned the authors represented here to conduct new research on the effects of welfare reform using up-to-date data a decade after passage of the legislation. In April 2007 I invited the authors, formal discussants, and other guests from the research and policy communities to Lexington, Kentucky, for a two-day conference to discuss preliminary results and suggest revisions. I am particularly grateful to the discussants Peter Gottschalk, Sarah Hamersma, Julia Henly, Harry Holzer, Lynn Karoly, Robert LaLonde, Dan Lichter, Donna Pavetti, Bob Plotnick,

Seth Sanders, Tim Smeeding, and Jim Sullivan for their many helpful comments on earlier versions of the chapters.

The project was made possible by financial support from the University of Kentucky Center for Poverty Research, which is underwritten by a grant from the Office of the Assistant Secretary of Planning and Evaluation in the U.S. Department of Health and Human Services. I owe a special debt of gratitude to Donald Oellerich for his support and encouragement; to Sheldon Danziger and Don Winstead, whose early insights helped shape the project; and to Scott Parris, Adam Levine, and Helen Greenberg at Cambridge University Press for their editorial support and assistance. I also thank Jeff Spradling for his many hours and good cheer spent organizing the working conference. Three anonymous reviewers recruited by the Press also provided valuable feedback on the initial draft of the book. The views expressed herein are solely those of the authors and do not necessarily reflect the views of the federal government, the reviewers, or any sponsoring agency.

Much of my research energy over the past decade leading up to the publication of this volume has been spent on understanding the effects of welfare reform on low-income families in the United States. Along the way, I have benefited from fruitful conversations with many individuals but wish to extend a special thanks to my collaborators David Figlio, Craig Gundersen, and Erik Hurst, whose numerous insights have informed and challenged my thinking on the most significant piece of legislation to affect the poor since the New Deal. Finally, to my wife, Gena, for her love and support throughout.

References

Blank, Rebecca. 2002. "Evaluating Welfare Reform in the United States." *Journal of Economic Literature*, 40(4): 1105–1166.

Grogger, Jeffrey, and Lynn A. Karoly. 2005. *Welfare Reform: Effects of a Decade of Change.* Cambridge, MA: Harvard University Press.

Moffitt, Robert, ed. 2003. *Means-Tested Transfer Programs in the United States.* Chicago: University of Chicago Press.

Introduction

James P. Ziliak

Two decades of federal and state demonstration projects and experiments with cash welfare in the United States culminated with the passage of the Personal Responsibility and Work Opportunity Reconciliation Act of 1996 (PRWORA). PRWORA, aka welfare reform, is widely viewed as the most fundamental reform to the U.S. social safety net since the New Deal by its dismantling of the major cash entitlement program Aid to Families with Dependent Children (AFDC) and replacement with the nonentitlement block grant program Temporary Assistance for Needy Families (TANF). Ten years after reform, a host of unanswered questions remain on the well-being of low-income families: Are labor-market earnings and total incomes higher, and are the effects of the reform the same across the income distribution? Did welfare reform and the concomitant expansions in the Earned Income Tax Credit (EITC) foster lasting transitions from welfare to work? What impact did these policy reforms have on household consumption and child outcomes? Did welfare reform affect health insurance and health outcomes for adults and children, and were there differential effects between immigrant and native populations? Did welfare reform, which encouraged the formation of two-parent families, succeed in increasing marriage? The 10 chapters in this book bring together leading poverty scholars to address these and many related questions on the longer-term consequences of welfare reform for America's poor.

I. Setting the Context: The Pre–Welfare Reform Era

Momentum for welfare reform had been building for the better part of two decades prior to its passage.[1] Conservative commentators, alarmed at the

---

[1] For comprehensive treatments of the issues leading up to welfare reform see Bane and Ellwood (1996), Blank (1997), DeParle (2004), and Haskins (2006).

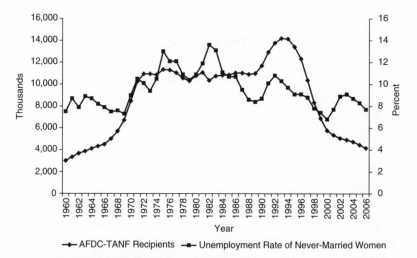

Figure I.1. Trends in Welfare Recipiency and Unemployment Rates, 1960–2006
Source: Author's calculations from HHS and BLS data.

growth of AFDC in the 1960s and early 1970s (see Figure I.1), saw welfare
as the source of a variety of the nation's social ills (Murray 1984). With
the election of Ronald Reagan in 1980, the retrenchment of AFDC was set
in motion.[2] Early in his first year, President Reagan signed the Omnibus
Budget Reconciliation Act (OBRA) of 1981, which, among other things,
increased the implicit tax rate on earnings and reduced the liquid asset level
required to qualify for benefits, each of which reduced the potential pool of
recipients. At the same time, the macroeconomy went into a severe slump
and unemployment rates shot up across the board, as seen in Figure I.1,
including the primary group of never-married women who are at greatest
risk of receiving welfare. As an entitlement program, AFDC participation
normally would have been expected to rise with the recession of the early
1980s, but the reforms in OBRA 1981 counteracted the anticipated increase;
in fact, welfare participation declined between 1981 and 1982.

Aggregate welfare levels remained steady throughout the remaining
1980s, in part because of the countervailing influences of strong regional
business cycles involving a recession in oil-producing states that pushed
welfare up and an expansion in states with high concentrations of defense-
related industries that pulled welfare down (Ziliak 2002). But beginning

---

[2] The TANF data in Figure I.1 do not contain those recipients of the TANF State Supplemental
Program. If those data are included, then the total number of recipients is fairly constant
after 2001; that is, states are picking up the full cost for an increasing number of welfare
cases, now close to 10 percent of the total number of cases.

in 1990, participation in AFDC surged in all states and the District of Columbia. This was a surprising development, as the recession of 1991 was mild compared to the deep recession of 1981–1982. Unemployment among never-married women (see Figure I.1) increased by just over 2 percentage points between 1989 and 1991, compared to a 4 percentage point increase in the early 1980s. The increase in caseloads was also surprising because, at the end of his second term, Reagan signed the Family Support Act of 1988, which required most welfare mothers without a child under age three to engage in education, work, or training under the Job Opportunities and Basic Skills Training Program (JOBS). If anything, the formal work require-ment was expected to deter entry into AFDC. In spite of these reforms, welfare participation in the early 1990s accelerated at a pace unseen since the 1960s.

The timing of the surge in welfare caseloads could not have been worse from a state budgetary perspective because tax revenues plummeted with the recession. Funding for the AFDC program came from a federal-state matching formula that was set as a progressive function of the state's per-sonal income (the same formula as the current Medicaid program); that is, poorer states had a larger fraction of their AFDC expenditure covered by the federal match. With the across-the-board increase in participation, state budgets were strained to meet the higher need. In search of relief, many states applied for waivers from federal program rules under Section 1115 of the Social Security Act in order to experiment (usually via demonstration projects) with their welfare programs. A total of 12 states were authorized to receive waivers under President George H. W. Bush's administration. During his 1992 campaign for president, Bill Clinton vowed to "end welfare as we know it," and by 1996, 43 states had received approval of waiver requests.

The waivers, which are described in detail in Grogger and Karoly (2005), varied in scope, ranging from work requirements to stringent sanctions for failing to work or participate in a training program to a time limit on benefit receipt. Not all waiver requests were "sticks" designed to deter par-ticipation; some were "carrots" designed to encourage work (e.g., higher earnings disregards) and asset accumulation (e.g., expanded liquid asset and vehicle equity limits). Many of the waivers were significant departures from post–New Deal thinking about entitlements, especially those waivers that time-limited benefit receipt and those that placed a cap on family size benefit adjustments. Probably more than any aspect of welfare, the ability to receive benefits year after year (assuming that a dependent child under age 18 was present in the family) undermined support for AFDC not only among detractors of government-sponsored assistance, but also among

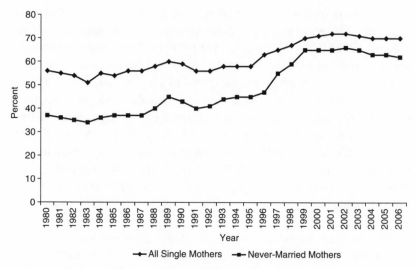

Figure I.2. Current Employment Rates of Single Mothers Ages 16–54, 1980–2006
Source: Author's calculations with March CPS data.

many inclined to provide prima facie support for such programs. Although most spells on AFDC were completed in less than a year, a sizable minority of recipients remained on it for a decade or more (Blank 1997). Time-limit waivers were thus designed to break long-term spells on AFDC. Likewise, notions of horizontal equity—the equal treatment of equals—led states to raise the size of the welfare check as the number of persons in the recipient family increased. However, some believed that more generous welfare benefits created incentives to have more children out of wedlock. Thus, family cap waivers were designed to eliminate these perverse incentives, even though the social science evidence supporting such claims has never been strong (Moffitt 1992).

From the perspective of states, the waivers seemed to be working. As seen in Figure I.1, AFDC caseloads peaked in 1993, and by 1996 they had already fallen below their 1991 level. However, there were simultaneously other important forces at work, most notably a growing macroeconomy and expansions in the refundable EITC. The nation's economy emerged from the recession at a rapid clip, driving down unemployment rates. Although some states recovered sooner than others, by 1995 unemployment was dropping in all states. At the same time, the OBRA of 1993 increased the maximum first-dollar subsidy rate of the EITC from 14 percent to 40 percent over the ensuing three years. Figure I.2, which depicts current employment rates of all single mothers ages 16–54 as well as those of never-married mothers,

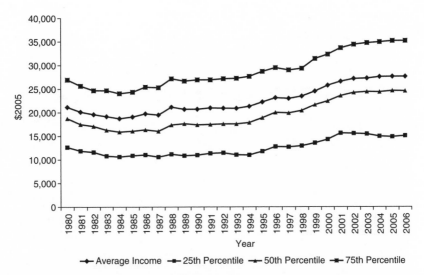

Figure I.3. After-Tax Incomes of Single Mothers Ages 16–54, 1980–2006
Source: Author's calculations with March CPS data.

shows that the primary population of welfare recipients responded to the economic and policy developments by increasing employment. Figure I.3 shows that after-tax incomes of single mothers started to rise, even in the first quartile of the distribution, and poverty rates fell (Figure I.4).[3]

A flurry of research emerged in the wake of these changes, primarily focused on the decline in welfare participation, the key policy outcome of interest at the time. In particular, the studies attempted to quantify whether the decline in caseloads between 1993 and 1996 was largely due to the welfare waivers, the macroeconomy, or other policies such as the EITC. The three most prominent papers in the group (Blank 2001; Council of Economic Advisers 1997; Ziliak et al. 2000) reached broad agreement that the macroeconomy was a critical determinant, but they disagreed on the amount and on whether welfare waivers had anything to do with the declines. The Council of Economic Advisers found that about one-half was due to the growing economy, while Ziliak et al. (2000) found that about

---

[3] The estimates in Figures I.2–I.4 come from the 1980–2006 Annual Social and Economic Study (March) of the Current Population Survey. In Figure I.2 employment rates refer to the month of the interview, whereas the income and poverty data in Figures I.3 and I.4 refer to the prior year. After-tax income in Figure I.3 is defined as gross income (the definition used in census poverty calculations), plus the dollar value of food stamps and school breakfast and lunch programs, less federal, state, and payroll tax payments (inclusive of the state and federal EITC). Poverty rates in Figure I.4 are based on the official census definition of income poverty.

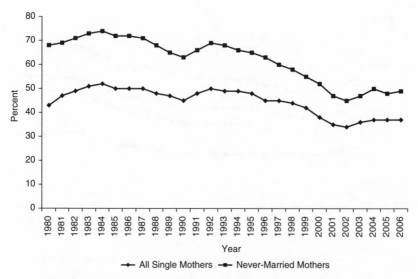

Figure I.4. Poverty Rates of Single Mothers Ages 16–54, 1980–2006
Source: Author's calculations with March CPS data.

three-fourths was due to the economy. The Council attributed about one-third of the decline in welfare caseloads to state waiver policies; Ziliak et al. attributed none of it to waivers. (Blank's estimates fell in between on both counts.) The difference in results stemmed from modeling choices, in particular whether explicit dynamics in caseloads were incorporated into the model (this is the approach of Ziliak et al.). Presumably the unexplained residual contributor to the caseload declines in all the papers was the expanding EITC, which made work relatively attractive. Indeed, Meyer and Rosenbaum (2001) attribute up to 60 percent of the rise in employment of single mothers between 1984 and 1996 to the expanded EITC.

II. Setting the Context: The Post–Welfare Reform Era

By 1996 the consensus in Washington was that welfare reform was a winning proposition at the federal level. To be sure, there were substantive differences over the content of the legislation across party lines, and between Congress and the Clinton administration, especially with regard to time limits and provisions restricting immigrants' access to programs. However, with the looming presidential election and the desire to fulfill his 1992 campaign pledge to end welfare, President Clinton signed PRWORA on August 22, 1996, thereby closing the final chapter on the AFDC program.

In addition to eliminating AFDC and creating the state block grant program TANF, PRWORA greatly expanded state authority over welfare program design. For example, under TANF, the new federal rules included a five-year lifetime limit on benefit receipt, but states had the option of lowering the limit to as little as two years, and many states chose that option (Grogger and Karoly 2005). States also had broad leeway on the amount of earnings that they could disregard prior to reducing the benefit, on the amount of liquid assets and vehicle equity they could exempt prior to losing eligibility, and on the stringency of work requirements and sanctions for failing to fulfill those requirements, among other factors. In some respects, PRWORA simply codified into federal legislation what many states were already implementing through the waiver process. Indeed, states that implemented a wide array of waivers left their welfare programs substantively unchanged after passage of the 1996 legislation. In other respects, PRWORA opened a completely new chapter in the development of the social safety net through the elimination of entitlement to cash welfare. In fact, the only remaining program in the safety net that resembles an entitlement is the Food Stamp Program. However, welfare reform did not leave food stamps untouched, as it removed many immigrants from eligibility and restricted benefits among healthy childless adults.

PRWORA had four main goals, not the least of which was to promote work and to end dependence on welfare. Based on the trends shown in Figures I.1–I.4, the first five years of the reform appear to have been a smashing success. The number of TANF recipients fell 55 percent between 1996 and 2000 to levels comparable to those of the late 1960s, and the employment rate of never-married single mothers soared nearly 40 percent. At the same time, after-tax incomes rose over 10 percent at the 25th percentile and higher, and poverty rates among all mothers as well as never-married mothers fell over 15 percent in the first five years after passage of PRWORA. These changes came as a surprise to many in the policy and research communities, some of whom had predicted dire consequences and others of whom had not predicted such large reductions in welfare use and poverty based on historic experience.

The social science research covering the waiver period and the first few years after the passage of PRWORA is comprehensively reviewed in Blank (2002), Moffitt (2003), and Karoly and Grogger (2005) and thus will not be reexamined here. Because the early research focused primarily on welfare caseloads, employment, and earnings, the three surveys necessarily emphasized those outcomes. But as Figures I.1–I.4 make clear, the employment gains, income gains, and poverty reduction came to a halt in the next five

years after reform. From 2000 to 2005 there was a recession, the 9/11 terrorist attacks, two wars in Afghanistan and Iraq, major natural disasters such
as Hurricanes Katrina and Rita, rising poverty, declining private health
insurance coverage, and stagnant household incomes. How each of these
macroeconomic and political forces interacts with welfare reform and the
EITC to affect the lives of the poor over the longer term is not well understood and thus serves as the starting point for this book.

III. The Longer-Term Consequences of Welfare Reform

At the beginning of this decade, researchers started to shift their attention
from caseloads and employment to a broader set of outcomes not covered
in the earlier literature reviews, including health, marriage, fertility, consumption, and saving, among others. In Chapter One, Rebecca Blank provides a critical survey of this research, bringing the literature up-to-date on
what we know about welfare reform leading up to the new work presented
in the remaining nine chapters of the volume.

Blank's survey demonstrates that the expanded research shows highly
mixed effects of welfare reform. Blank concludes that these studies show
that welfare reform reduced access to health insurance, both public and
private, but with little corresponding change in health outcomes. TANF
did cause welfare caseloads to fall (accounting for about 20 percent of the
drop in the few years after 1996) and employment to rise, but Blank also
points out that the macroeconomy was the primary driver of the caseload
decline even in the TANF period and that the EITC expansion had more to
do with employment growth, much as it did in the waiver period. Welfare
reform had little significant effect on child outcomes, some positive effects
for toddlers and some negative effects for adolescents, but it did have a
significant positive effect on the take-up of center-based child care. This is
likely a direct result of the expansion of the Child Care and Development
Fund that was included as part of PRWORA. Even though three of the
four goals of welfare reform focused on marriage and fertility, the studies reviewed by Blank continue to reveal little effect of welfare on marriage and fertility choices, which is consistent with the historical evidence.
Welfare reform also had little effect on consumption and saving, with the
possible exception of increasing vehicle wealth.

Blank also discusses a key methodological challenge facing researchers
using nonexperimental survey data after the 1996 reform, including some
of the work contained herein, namely, that identification of TANF effects
is greatly inhibited by the fact that the policy was implemented across all

states within a relatively short period of time (roughly 18 months). In addition, while the bundle of policies differs in stringency (e.g., full benefit sanctions versus partial or no sanctions), the overall set of policies is basically congruent across states. This is in sharp contrast to the research on the welfare waiver period, when only a subset of states were adopting different waivers at different times over a four-year time horizon. The latter offered wide cross-state over-time variation in policy implementation to identify welfare waiver effects. Blank notes that some researchers have attempted to incorporate qualitative aspects of TANF programs as part of their empirical strategy, but most of them utilize a simple indicator variable that "turns on" in the month or year (or fraction of the year) when the TANF plan was implemented. Others have attempted to buy greater variation by interacting the TANF variable with other observed variables such as education, nativity status, and/or the business cycle. This is the strategy used by the authors of Chapters Two, Six, and Nine of this book to identify the effect of TANF.

Although the topical coverage expanded greatly in the early part of the decade, the work summarized by Blank is based primarily on survey data obtained no more than five years after passage of welfare reform. Only recently have enough postreform data become available, coupled with a complete business cycle, to address more comprehensively the effects of welfare reform over the long run. The remaining nine chapters are thematically linked in their focus on the intended and unintended consequences of welfare reform for single-mother families. A diverse array of survey and administrative data is brought to bear on varied outcomes including income, consumption, welfare and employment dynamics, health insurance, child well-being, and marriage. The chapters draw from major survey datasets such as the Current Population Survey (CPS), the Consumer Expenditure Survey (CE), and the Survey of Income Program Participation (SIPP); from two recent longitudinal surveys designed to follow low-income families after welfare reform (the Three-City Study and the Fragile Families Study); from random assignment experimental data; from a survey of social service providers in urban and rural areas; and from state-level administrative data. The use of multiple data sources offers a panoramic view of how welfare reform has affected low-income families across a number of outcomes, regions, and populations.

IV. How Has Welfare Reform Affected Income and Consumption?

There was general agreement that welfare waivers had a modest positive effect, and the EITC an even larger effect, on the earnings of single-mother families during the mid- to late 1990s. However, most of the research focused on average impacts, which limits our understanding of program effects at other points of the distribution, and none of it spanned a full decade after TANF was introduced. The latter is critical to a better understanding of welfare reform because, with the downturn and subsequent recovery of the macroeconomy in the early 2000s, it is now possible to examine whether the economy interacted with welfare reform to affect the economic status of families. In Chapter Two, Christopher Bollinger, Luis Gonzalez, and James Ziliak tackle these and related issues by estimating the effect of waivers, TANF and the EITC, and interactions of each with the business cycle and the education status of the mother, on earnings and after-tax incomes. They use 26 years of data from the March CPS to examine effects of policy and the economy at both the means and at several quantiles of the earnings and income distributions.

Bollinger et al. find that TANF and the EITC expansions raised the earnings of single mothers, but that both policies contributed to declines in after-tax income, especially among the low-skilled in the bottom half of the earnings and income distributions. They also show that strong local economies in the mid-1990s interacted with waivers to boost income and earnings gains among the less skilled. The estimates in Chapter Two suggest that the earnings gains among the low-skilled a decade after the implementation of TANF and expansions of the EITC have been more than offset by losses in transfer income and have left the most vulnerable single mothers behind. Some of the "claw-back" of transfer benefits is automatic as labor-market earnings increase, but the reduced after-tax income after the policy changes may also reflect the fact that some mothers are no longer receiving benefits even though they remain eligible. This seems to corroborate the findings of recent work by Blank (2007) on the growing ranks of "disconnected" single mothers who are neither working nor on welfare, and it raises the concern that deep poverty is not only expanding but has been exacerbated by recent policy changes.

It is well known that family income in a given year may not be an ideal indicator of the family's permanent economic status because job loss, illness, and a variety of other factors can make incomes volatile, a factor that is especially acute among low-income families (Jolliffe and Ziliak 2008). Consumption, on the other hand, often reflects a family's so-called permanent income; thus, an analysis of expenditures offers the opportunity to examine the longer-term impacts of reform on family well-being. In Chapter Three, Qin Gao, Neeraj Kaushal, and Jane Waldfogel examine the effects of social policy reforms, with a particular focus on the EITC, on expenditure and debt patterns of mothers. The focus on the EITC is particularly relevant for the welfare reform era because as mothers substituted labor-market earnings for government transfers, the EITC offered the family the opportunity to make durable goods purchases and/or pay down debt that they otherwise could not afford.

Gao et al. use 11 years of data from the CE for their analysis, and find that among mothers with a high school diploma or some college education, the EITC expansions resulted in increased spending on food (both at home and away from home), alcohol and tobacco, and clothing. Interestingly, there is strong evidence of a "month of receipt" effect among this group; that is, expenditures spike in the month of February, which suggests that the EITC is viewed as a forced saving mechanism by this group of mothers, who use their tax refund to make large purchases rather than smooth consumption over the year with the refund. Gao et al. also find evidence that more generous EITCs lowered debt levels, especially among high school dropouts. Paying down debt clearly improves the family's financial balance sheet, but if this group faces challenges in meeting regular expenses, the fact that they still opt for the lump-sum EITC tax refund rather than the Advanced EITC that can be received monthly remains unexplained and an area in need of additional research.

V. Has Welfare Reform Fostered Lasting Transitions from Welfare to Work?

Early studies on the AFDC program found that most spells on welfare were short (less than a year), but there was a considerable amount of cycling on and off of the rolls (Blank 1997; Moffitt 1992). Exits from welfare were affected by several factors, but the most prominent reason was the start of a new spell of employment. However, the employment spells were often short as well, and given the rules governing unemployment insurance eligibility, these women rarely qualified for unemployment insurance and thus returned to AFDC. A key goal of welfare reform was to make sure that the transition to employment endured; thus, many states poured a sizable fraction of their TANF block grant into job readiness, transportation, and child care subsidy programs. Indeed, nearly 70 percent of all TANF funds are spent on in-kind programs today. This is just the opposite of the AFDC program, where 70 percent were spent on cash grants.

In Chapter Four, Bianca Frogner, Robert Moffitt, and David Ribar use the Three-City Study to examine welfare and employment dynamics, as well as the levels and composition of incomes, the latter of which provides a focused longitudinal counterweight to the repeated cross-sectional CPS data used in Chapter Two by Bollinger et al. In the wake of welfare reform, several entrepreneurial scholars embarked on major longitudinal survey data collection efforts, and this book contains results from the two most ambitious surveys—the Three-City Study and the Fragile Families Study. The Three-City Study is ideally suited to examine welfare and employment transitions, as it follows the same families living in Boston, Chicago, and San Antonio in 1999, 2001, and 2005. Although the three cities are not necessarily representative of the nation as a whole in terms of demographics and economic activity, the economic and welfare caseload trends in the three cities mirror those in the country and thus the analysis in the chapter is instructive for the wider population of low-income families.

Frogner et al. find that exit rates from TANF were very high (consistent with national data) and that entry and reentry rates were very low, which differs from experience under the former AFDC program. Families leaving welfare saw increases in their household incomes that are largely attributed to increases in the earnings of spouses and partners, the latter of which occurred partly because marriage and cohabitation rates increased and partly because more spouses and partners with earnings were in the household after leaving welfare. However, when Frogner et al. combine employed and nonemployed leavers together, they find that increases in average own-earnings are completely offset by declines in TANF and food stamp benefits, corroborating the findings from the CPS by Bollinger et al. Their estimates underscore a number of policy challenges facing a work-based safety net; namely, the system of in-kind transfers, especially food stamps, remains very important for these families and needs to better accommodate the often nonstandard work schedules of single-parent families.

In Chapter Five, Peter Mueser, David Stevens, and Kenneth Troske address some of the same issues of welfare and employment dynamics covered in Chapter Four, but instead rely on detailed administrative datasets from Missouri and Maryland. Their analysis is also distinct in that they examine the demographic composition, employment, and welfare recidivism of three cohorts of welfare leavers: those leaving welfare in fiscal year 1993, those leaving welfare in fiscal year 1997, and those leaving in fiscal year 2002. Using the three separate cohorts permits the authors to compare welfare recipients before welfare reform, during its implementation, and six years later. As with the Three-City Study, the data from Missouri and Maryland are not nationally representative, but again the trends are strikingly similar to national trends in welfare, employment, and economic growth.

Mueser et al. find little change in the demographic composition of the caseload across cohorts, but employment rose and persisted even into the most recent downturn not only among leavers but also among current recipients and new entrants, the latter pattern consistent with work requirements. Paralleling Frogner et al., they find scant evidence of earnings gains among post–welfare reform leavers compared to prereform leavers (recall that the earnings gains reported in Chapter Four come mostly from other adults in the family). Mueser et al. also find that the types of firms employing welfare leavers did not change much after welfare reform. Thus, recipients are no more likely to work for employers paying low wages or in industries with unstable employment, nor are they more likely to be in industries offering upward mobility. The latter results, while not entirely surprising, are nonetheless discouraging because for welfare reform to make a long-run positive change in the lives of the poor, former recipients (and potential new entrants) must find gainful employment with wage growth.

A corollary to employment and welfare transitions is health insurance coverage of the family. A concern raised during debates on the TANF bill was whether or not single-mother families would retain health coverage after leaving welfare. Recipients of AFDC were adjunctively eligible for Medicaid, the health insurance program for low-income Americans. However, its successor, TANF, has no direct link to Medicaid, but those who meet AFDC eligibility standards that existed in 1996 are eligible for Medicaid. Those women who leave welfare for work and whose earnings place them above Medicaid eligibility thresholds have access to transitional medical assistance for up to 12 months. But after that point, health insurance coverage ends unless they are covered by their employer or purchase it on private markets. It is possible that their children will remain covered under either Medicaid or the State Children's Health Insurance Program, depending on the age of child, state of residence, and income. In short, there is ample opportunity for health insurance coverage of single-mother families to fall through the cracks in the postwelfare world.

In Chapter Six, John Ham, Xianghong Li, and Lara Shore-Sheppard use data from the Survey of Income and Program Participation to estimate the effect of welfare reform on health insurance coverage among single-mother families. As highlighted by Rebecca Blank in Chapter One, there has been some disagreement in the literature on the importance of reform for health care coverage, in part because of differences in the population used as the comparison group to the "treated" single mothers. Ham et al. conduct a battery of tests and actually reject the use of all previously adopted comparison groups—single childless women and married women either with or without children. This has important implications for many nonexperimental studies adopting the differences-in-differences estimation strategy, as most use the comparison group approach without verifying whether or not the treatment and comparison groups have similar pretreatment trends in the outcomes of interest. Ham et al. thus estimate their models separately for each group, but they also admit heterogeneity in the effect of reform on insurance coverage by the education level of the mother and whether the mother is an immigrant or a native. The authors find evidence that welfare reform reduced Medicaid coverage among less skilled single mothers, though this loss was somewhat offset by a rise in private coverage. These effects were heavily concentrated among the Hispanic immigrant population, perhaps reflecting the so-called chilling hypothesis discussed in Chapter Nine by Ariel Kalil and Kathleen Ziol-Guest. Although for some groups the loss of public insurance was offset by gains in private coverage (e.g., among more highly educated mothers), a recurring theme across the first six chapters is that the most disadvantaged groups of single mothers appear to be worse off a decade after welfare reform.

VI. What Has Been the Effect of Welfare Reform on Child and Family Well-Being?

As noted previously, much of the policy focus and attendant research on welfare reform was concentrated on caseload reductions and employment gains at the expense of more global issues of child and family well-being. One of the reasons for the creation of the Aid to Dependent Children program in the 1930s was to allow widows to care for their dependent children at home, under the assumption that a stay-at-home mother was better for the well-being of her children. In the 1980s such women were often labeled "welfare queens," and by the time PRWORA was passed, it was clear that the notion of a welfare mother had been rejected in favor of that of a working mother and, better still, a married mother. This change in thinking was not necessarily grounded in research; rather, it reflected social and political preferences. Chapters Seven to Nine explore in detail the ramifications of welfare reform on measures of child academic achievement and health, as well as marriage and cohabitation.

In Chapter Seven, Pamela Morris, Lisa Gennetian, Greg Duncan, and Aletha Huston synthesize results on child outcomes from seven random assignment experiments covering more than 30,000 children as part of (MDRC's) Next Generation Project and then extend the literature by exploiting the experimental nature of the data to test how welfare policies designed to discourage welfare and encourage work affect children's achievement and school performance. The focus on child achievement is timely given the burgeoning push for expansion of pre-K programs throughout the nation. Morris et al. find that programs with earnings supplements that boost both maternal employment and income improve preschool children's achievement, but if the program only raises employment and not income, then there are no discernible effects on pre-K children. Moreover, programs that support center-based child care also result in improved achievement for pre-K children relative to children in home-based or other care. Adolescents ages 11 and older, on the other hand, experience worse academic outcomes relative to children in control groups; no conclusive pattern of effects is found among children ages 6–10. The worse outcomes for older adolescents seem to be linked to maternal employment and the attendant increase in home responsibilities for the older child. This raises a number of policy challenges because there are few programs that offer care for children over age 10, and solving the problem of "kids taking care of kids" has received scant attention to date. A disturbing trend over the past decade, however, is the rise in high school dropouts (Heckman and LaFontaine 2007). Whether or not this trend is linked to increased home responsibilities and maternal employment is unknown.

One of the four key goals of PRWORA was to encourage the formation and maintenance of two-parent families. The legislation set out to accomplish this by time-limiting benefits (which raises the cost of long-term single motherhood), relaxing restrictions on two-parent families qualifying for benefits, and enhancing child support enforcement policies. In Chapter Eight, Jean Knab, Irv Garfinkel, Sara McLanahan, Emily Moiduddin, and Cynthia Osborne employ data from the Fragile Families Project to test whether the policy reforms affected the likelihood of marriage following a nonmarital birth. The Fragile Families Study is a longitudinal study of births that occurred in 20 large urban areas between 1998 and 2000, with follow-up interviews when the children were ages one, three, and five.

Knab et al. advance the literature in several ways, in particular by distinguishing marriage from cohabitation and by identifying policy heterogeneity based on whether the father has engaged in multiple-partner fertility. The authors find that the marriage behavior of unwed parents is strongly influenced by the facets of the post-PRWORA welfare environment, particularly for certain subgroups. Included in their findings are that welfare generosity (i.e., higher cash benefits and more lenient sanctions) is associated with lower rates of marriage, especially among cohabitors and low-skilled parents. Stronger child support enforcement is also associated with lower rates of marriage, particularly for cohabiting couples and those where the father has children from multiple partners. Although some of their estimates are not robust to the inclusion of controls for time-invariant and state-specific unobserved heterogeneity, overall the estimates suggest that child support obligations to prior children in stronger enforcement states deter marriage from the mother's perspective.

Many advocates for immigrant groups were concerned not only about the direct effect of new restrictions on eligibility for welfare among immigrants after enactment of PRWORA, but also on the indirect chilling effect on benefit take-up even among eligible immigrant families who may have feared being stereotyped as illegal and possibly subject to deportation. In Chapter Nine, Ariel Kalil and Kathleen Ziol-Guest use data from the SIPP to examine the consequences of the so-called chilling hypothesis on the heretofore unstudied health outcomes of low-income young children of immigrants versus natives over the period spanning welfare reform. They find that the gap between low-income children of noncitizens versus natives in terms of children's health and family access to care widened substantially after welfare reform. In terms of poor health among children, the gaps widened up to 30 percent between children of immigrants and children of natives over the baseline, suggesting that immigrant families face barriers, whether real or perceived, to health care after enactment of PRWORA. This unintended consequence of welfare reform has been addressed by outreach efforts in some states, but such efforts remain the exception to the rule.

VII. How Has Welfare Reform Affected Social Services Delivery?

The book concludes with Chapter Ten by Scott Allard on how services actually get delivered in the new world of welfare. Under the AFDC program, about $0.70 of every dollar spent went to the family as cash assistance, and the remaining $0.30 was spent on various social services such as education and training. Under PRWORA, the allocation of resources has been reversed; now $0.70 of every dollar is spent on services, which have greatly expanded in scope to cover mental health and substance abuse, as well as more traditional education and training. Moreover, PRWORA enhanced opportunities for nongovernmental organizations (NGOs), including faith-based groups, to participate in the delivery of services with federal and state financial support. In other words, welfare today has a very different meaning than it did two decades ago. The move toward in-kind provision of assistance, whether it is food stamps, Medicaid, or TANF, is consistent with paternalistic social preferences that target relief to key priority areas rather than lump-sum cash grants to be used at the discretion of recipients.

Allard conducted a survey of over 2,000 social service providers in selected urban and rural areas to examine issues of proximity of the poor to service provision (i.e., whether there is spatial mismatch) and issues of funding volatility among service agencies. He finds considerable evidence of spatial mismatch between the location of the poor and the location of services for the poor in both urban and rural areas. Moreover, he finds substantial volatility in funding and service operations from year to year, which compromises the ability of NGOs to deliver reliable assistance to those in need. The combination of poor access to services and uncertainty over funding poses a double jeopardy for the many single mothers facing multiple barriers to employment. The new delivery model of welfare is likely to face its most serious test under the dire global economic climate as this book goes to press, and the results presented in Allard's chapter suggest that much need will be unmet because many service providers are likely to be forced to close operations just as demand for services peaks.

VIII. Lessons Learned and Unmet Challenges of Welfare Reform

Has welfare reform been a positive long-term change for single-mother families in the United States? Based on the research presented in this book, the answer is both yes and no. A nuanced answer is less likely to grab headlines than if things turned out strongly negative or positive, but with a complex piece of legislation serving a heterogeneous population, perhaps nuance should be expected. On the plus side, long-term dependence on welfare has been cut substantially, if not altogether eliminated for the majority of recipients, and the number of new recipients has been slashed. Aggregate employment rose to historic highs, and while it stopped rising after the first five years after the passage of PRWORA, it fell only slightly in the next five years. TANF and the expanded EITC lifted the earnings of single mothers (and other adult earners in the household) across the earnings distribution, suggesting greater economic self-reliance 10 years later. Extrapolating from the results of the random assignment experiments, it is not unreasonable to assume that higher earnings and the EITC had a positive spillover effect on the academic achievement of young children. The EITC also allowed some groups of mothers to pay down debt and other groups to increase expenditures on transportation services, which likely assisted the welfare-to-work transition. Welfare reform also spurred states and local agencies to introduce new and innovative services and service delivery methods to better target assistance for the new cohort of low-income working single mothers.

On the negative side, welfare reform and the EITC led to reduced after-tax income for low-skilled single mothers (i.e., those with less than 12 years of schooling) in the bottom half of the income distribution. Even though both policies increased the earnings of these families, the loss of benefits more than offset earnings gains, and on net they fell deeper into poverty. This finding is buttressed by the evidence from CPS data in Chapter Two, Three-City Study data in Chapter Four, and administrative data in Chapter Five. In addition, these low-skilled families experienced a net loss of insurance coverage; the decline of public Medicaid insurance exceeded the gain of private insurance from employers and personal policies. The latter was particularly acute among Hispanic immigrant women. The children of these immigrant parents were much more likely to be in poor health and their medical treatment to be delayed relative to the children of native-born parents in the years after welfare reform. Children aged 11 and older experienced worse academic outcomes as their mothers transitioned to work, possibly because of reduced supervision during critical developmental stages of puberty and/or because of enhanced home responsibilities such as doing more chores or caring for younger siblings. And for many of the poorest families in need of additional assistance, the post–welfare reform legacy has left them displaced from the very services they need to succeed.

Whether or not welfare reform has been a net positive or negative development for America's poor hinges critically on the weight placed on the different segments of the single-mother population. If the greatest weight is placed on those with at least a high school diploma and only young children, then welfare reform has been a force for good. These mothers are likely to be employed, to have higher after-tax incomes, to have public or private insurance, and to have healthy children in good academic standing. On the other hand, if the greatest weight is placed on single mothers who are high school dropouts with older adolescents or teens in the household, then welfare reform has left them worse off. They are more likely to be working than previous cohorts, but with less total income, they are less likely to be insured, more likely to have unhealthy children in poor academic standing, more likely to be in poor health themselves, and no more likely to be married. This group is what Rebecca Blank calls "disconnected mothers," and their number seems to be growing.

My personal bias is to give more weight to the well-being of those facing greater disadvantage. In doing so, my interpretation of the research in this book is that the net effect of welfare reform a decade after passage has been somewhat negative. This does not mean that I believe that the 1996 reform has been a failure of intent; citizens and policymakers were justified in their desire to change the rules of the game of the former AFDC program. Rather, I believe the failure of welfare reform is one of direction.

At one level, welfare reform was groundbreaking in its transformation of the program from an entitlement to a block grant. But at the same time, the legislation was silent on the broader issue of poverty reduction and eradication. Rather than supplementing the goal of reducing welfare dependence and encouraging work with the more ambitious goal of combating poverty, the legislation was diverted into issues of marriage and fertility, even though the research evidence that policy can affect the latter outcomes has always been weak. I believe that the failure to tackle the bigger issue of long-term economic mobility is now being played out in the worse outcomes among those facing the greatest ex ante disadvantage—the less skilled, those facing multiple barriers to employment, and those with work-limiting disabilities. The reauthorization of TANF in 2006 is unlikely to ameliorate the latter situation because it increased work requirements to qualify for benefits and reduced the scope of education and training programs that count toward the work requirement; in other words, it is more difficult for mothers to invest in human capital while on welfare, even though increased human capital is the surest road to long-run success. Self-reliance through employment does not correspond one-to-one with economic security when employment offers low wages and unstable hours, and the recurring finding throughout this book that a sizable fraction of less skilled single mothers are falling through the cracks is troubling.

The promise going forward is that whatever PRWORA lacked in addressing persistent poverty can be redirected toward new policies affecting both children and adults. On this front, there is a growing national movement in favor of expanding pre-K programs. The random assignment experiments discussed in Chapter Seven showed that young children in center-based care did better than those in alternative care settings, and the long-term evaluations of preschool experiments such as those of Perry and Abecedarian showed that children in high-quality pre-K programs did much better than those in the randomized control group on a host of social and labor market outcomes (Karoly, Kilburn, and Cannon 2005). These programs are most likely to be successful if they are targeted to the disadvantaged such as the children of low-skilled single mothers. The hope is that early human capital investments will pay off in the long run by increasing high school completion and lowering crime and out-of-wedlock childbirth, among other risky behaviors. However, the pre-K programs must be supplemented with new after-school and summer-based programs for older adolescents and teenagers. The problem with placing all resources in pre-K programs is that it may take a generation or more for the positive outcomes of these programs to appear. In the meantime the nation is facing a dropout crisis, which could be exacerbated in the aftermath of welfare reform, as indicated by the worse outcomes among older adolescents found by Morris et al. Comparatively little policy attention has been given to this group, and the area is in sore need of innovative thinking.

For less-skilled single mothers, the anti–human capital investment aspects of the 2006 TANF reauthorization should be rolled back and pro-education elements incorporated. Hotz, Imbens, and Klerman (2006) present strong evidence that the so-called Riverside Miracle of a work-first strategy for welfare recipients was transitory, and the California counties that invested in the human capital of the mothers showed better long-term outcomes in terms of earnings and employment. Better training should be supplemented with work supports that reduce poverty. In this vein, expanding the EITC at both the federal and state levels is an obvious avenue, as is expanding child care subsidies. The positive employment effects of child care subsidies for single mothers are backed by scores of studies, yet the United States lags well behind other industrialized nations in providing child care assistance. For example, Canada has implemented over the past decade an aggressive child care subsidy program to foster the transition to work for families with young children. A single mother with one infant less than 18 months old earning $25,000 per year in Toronto pays only $1.92 per day for child care—an effective subsidy of over $50 per day.[4]

Other key work supports in need of policy revision includes the Food Stamp Program, Unemployment Insurance, and, perhaps most important of all, health insurance. Food Stamps is the only entitlement program in the safety net, and while the Agriculture Department has expanded its outreach of benefits in recent years, it still remains a challenge for many working families to recertify. New approaches such as online recertification, adopted by several states, could be a promising mechanism to maintain food assistance to the working poor. It is widely agreed that the current experience-rated Unemployment Insurance system is long overdue for reform and also needs to expand coverage to part-time and seasonal workers—a group in which single mothers are overrepresented. There is also a near-universal consensus that the provision of health insurance and health care is in need of fundamental reform, and low-income mothers would greatly benefit from such efforts.

Whether the decade after welfare reform is just a pothole in the road to lasting economic security for America's poor or eventually becomes a sinkhole remains to be seen. We have the policy tools to ensure that the pothole gets filled before the road is washed out completely.

---

[4]   http://www.toronto.ca/children/fee_calculator.html. In the fall of 2008, $25,000 Canadian (CAD) was approximately equal to $25,000 (USD).

References

Bane, Mary Jo, and David R. Ellwood. 1996. *Welfare Realities: From Rhetoric to Reform*. Cambridge, MA: Harvard University Press.

Blank, Rebecca. 1997. *It Takes a Nation: A New Agenda for Fighting Poverty*. Princeton, NJ: Princeton University Press.

2001. "What Causes Public Assistance Caseloads to Grow?" *Journal of Human Resources*, 36: 85–118.

2002. "Evaluating Welfare Reform in the United States." *Journal of Economic Literature*, 40(4): 1105–1166.

2007. "Improving the Safety Net for Single Mothers Who Face Serious Barriers to Work." *Future of Children*, 17: 183–197.

Council of Economic Advisers. 1997. *Technical Report: Explaining the Decline in Welfare Receipt, 1993–1996*. Washington, DC: Executive Office of the President.

DeParle, Jason. 2004. *American Dream: Three Women, Ten Kids, and a Nation's Drive to End Welfare*. New York: Penguin Group.

Grogger, Jeffrey. 2003. "The Effects of Time Limits, the EITC, and Other Policy Changes on Welfare Use, Work, and Income Among Female-Headed Families." *Review of Economics and Statistics*, 85(2): 394–408.

Grogger, Jeffrey, and Lynn A. Karoly. 2005. *Welfare Reform: Effects of a Decade of Change*. Cambridge, MA: Harvard University Press.

Haskins, Ronald. 2006. *Work Over Welfare: The Inside Story of the 1996 Welfare Reform Law*. Washington, DC: Brookings Institution Press.

Heckman, James, and Paul LaFontaine. 2007. "The American High School Graduation Rate: Trends and Levels." National Bureau of Economic Research Working Paper 13670.

Hotz, V. Joseph, Guido Imbens, and Jacob Klerman. 2006. "Evaluating the Differential Effects of Alternative Welfare-to-Work Training Components: A Re-evaluation of the California GAIN Program." *Journal of Labor Economics*, 24(3): 521–566.

Jolliffe, Dean, and James P. Ziliak. 2008. *Income Volatility and Food Assistance in the United States*. Kalamazoo, MI: W. E. Upjohn Institute for Employment Research.

Karoly, Lynn, Rebecca Kilburn, and Jill Cannon. 2005. *Early Childhood Interventions: Proven Results, Future Promise*. Santa Monica , CA: Rand Corporation.

Meyer, Bruce, and Dan Rosenbaum. 2001. "Welfare, the Earned Income Tax Credit, and the Labor Supply of Single Mothers." *Quarterly Journal of Economics*, 116(3): 1063–1114.

Moffitt, Robert. 1992. "Incentive Effects of the U.S. Welfare System: A Review." *Journal of Economic Literature*, 30(1): 1–61.

Moffitt, Robert, ed. 2003. *Means-Tested Programs in the United States*. Chicago: University of Chicago Press.

Murray, Charles. 1984. *Losing Ground: American Social Policy, 1950–1980*. New York: Basic Books.

Ziliak, James P. 2002. "Social Policy and the Macroeconomy: What Drives Welfare Caseloads?" *Focus*, 22(1): 29–34.

Ziliak, James P., David N. Figlio, Elizabeth E. Davis, and Laura S. Connoly. 2000. "Accounting for the Decline in AFDC Caseloads." *Journal of Human Resources*, 35(Summer): 570–586.

ONE

What We Know, What We Don't Know, and What We Need to Know about Welfare Reform

Rebecca M. Blank

It has been more than a decade since major national legislation passed in August 1996, changing the structure of public assistance programs in the United States. During that time period, researchers from many fields have tried to evaluate the various effects of these changes on the behavior and well-being of low-income families. These policy changes have been among the most thoroughly evaluated public policies in history. Yet, it is striking how many questions about the effects of these changes remain unanswered. This chapter summarizes the state of this literature, discussing what we know and what we don't know about the effects of welfare reform.

"Welfare reform" refers primarily to the changes in public assistance programs that were enacted in 1996, particularly the creation of the Temporary Assistance for Needy Families (TANF) block grant. TANF dollars were used by states (along with their own dollars) to fund redesigned cash assistance programs for low-income families that provided much stronger work incentives among recipients. Poor single-mother families were the group predominantly affected by these changes.

But the term welfare reform also is used loosely to refer to a broader set of policy changes. These include the demonstration projects on welfare-to-work efforts within specific states that replaced the then-existing Aid to Families with Dependent Children (AFDC) program. States received federal waivers to enact these programs, which are known as "waiver demonstration projects." Other policy changes include a variety of "make-work-pay" policies that were enacted very close to the time of welfare reform. Most notably, significant increases in the Earned Income Tax Credit (EITC) helped subsidize low-wage workers in low-income families; ongoing expansions in Medicaid helped cover children in low-income families; and expansions in child care subsidies and in child support requirements also particularly assisted single-mother families. I shall be careful to clarify which aspects of welfare reform are analyzed in various parts of the literature.

The first section of this chapter summarizes the research literature in a variety of key areas, with particular attention to more recent studies that were not covered in already published literature reviews. While I mention a few of the methodological issues that these papers confront, I discuss these issues in more detail in the second section, which lays out some of the methodological and data issues that limit our ability to evaluate welfare reform. The third section discusses some key issues that remain open questions and where further research is likely to be fruitful.

I. What We Know: Existing Research on Welfare Reform

A couple of very good summaries of the welfare reform evaluation research exist that cite papers available through the early 2000s, including Blank (2002) and Grogger and Karoly (2005). Moffitt (2003) also provides an extended discussion of welfare reforms and the structure of the new state programs. I will not repeat the extensive literature discussion provided by these publications. Instead, I will focus on the literature that has emerged in the past few years, indicating what it adds to our understanding.

Since this is a shorter chapter and not a comprehensive literature review, I am somewhat selective in the research I discuss. In particular, I've given attention primarily to papers written more recently that include data from the year 2000 or later and to papers that were not discussed in earlier research reviews. Hence, I do not discuss recent papers that reanalyze the waiver demonstration project data of the 1990s, but I do include papers that utilize new or more recent datasets. I also focus on studies that analyze the effects of welfare reform on a set of behaviors that the earlier literature did not investigate. A hallmark of the more recent literature, as exemplified in the chapters in this volume, is that it encompasses a broader set of effects, looking at the impact of welfare reform on outcomes, such as child achievement or consumption patterns. This is far beyond the questions that dominated the earlier literature, which focused on welfare participation and employment. I will briefly review the literature in five topical areas.

A. Work and Welfare Participation

Almost all early evaluation literature on welfare reform focused on its effects on welfare participation and on employment, and earlier literature reviews focused extensively on these topics. Table 1.1 lists some of the more recent

Table 1.1. *Recent research on welfare reform, welfare participation, and employment*

Authors and date	Data and sample	Dependent variable	Key issue	Key findings
Dyke et al. (2006)	Missouri and North Carolina administrative data, spanning 1997–2002, single mothers, ages 18–64, entering welfare in 1997–1999	Quarterly earnings	How job assessment, training, and search programs affect earnings	Initial negative effects of program participation, but positive over time. More intensive training linked to eventual larger earnings gains
Fang and Keane (2004)	March CPS microdata, 1980–2002, single mothers	Welfare use and employment	Effects of specific policy components within states on welfare use and employment	Primary causes of decreasing welfare and increased work are work requirements, EITC changes, time limits, and economic conditions
Fitzgerald and Ribar (2004)	SIPP panels, spanning 1990–1999, women ages 15–55 ever observed as single mothers	Transitions into and out of female family headship and welfare participation	Effects of welfare and EITC policies on female family headship and welfare participation	Welfare reform had little effect on transitions to female family headship or welfare use; EITC changes led to less welfare use and more female headship
Grogger (2004a)	March CPS microdata, 1978–1999, single mothers	Welfare use	Time limits and welfare use among female-headed families	Time limits reduce welfare use, especially among young families with young children

Grogger (2004b)	SIPP panels, spanning 1986–1999, less-skilled women ages 18–54	Entry into and exits from welfare	Effect of welfare reform and EITC on entry into and exit from welfare	Economy, welfare reform, benefit levels, and EITC all affect transitions
Haider et al. (2004)	CPS microdata, 1993–2001, all households	Public assistance program use by immigrants	Effect of welfare reform on participation among immigrants	Immigrant and native public assistance trends are similar; difference due to greater economic cyclicality among immigrants
Huang et al. (2004)	State administrative data and CPS, 1980–1999, single mothers ages 18–54	Welfare caseloads	Effect of child support enforcement (CSE) on welfare caseloads	Greater CSE associated with decreased caseloads
Johnson and Corcoran (2003)	Women's Employment Survey and MI Employment Survey, spanning 1997–2002, women ages 18–54 on welfare in 1997	Job quality index and job transitions	Job and personal characteristics associated with job quality and job change	Job history and lower skills limit job quality and stability among welfare leavers
Looney (2005)	SIPP panels spanning 1990–1999, single mothers ages 15–55	Welfare use and employment	Effects of welfare reform, EITC, and Medicaid on welfare use and work among single mothers	Welfare policies, EITC, and economic conditions linked with welfare use and employment

(continued)

Table 1.1. *Continued*

Authors and date	Data and sample	Dependent variable	Key issue	Key findings
Meara and Frank (2006)	Three-City Study: Boston, Chicago, San Antonio, 1999–2001, low-income women	Welfare use and employment	Effects of barriers to work: mental health, drug/alcohol abuse, child under age three, and children's behavior	Poor mental health, drug use, and alcohol use associated with lower work participation and more sanctioning
Seefeldt and Orzol (2005)	Women's Employment Survey, spanning 1997–2001, women ages 18–54 on welfare in 1997	Months of TANF receipt	Factors associated with TANF accumulation	Those with more barriers to work stay on TANF longer
Wu et al. (2006)	Wisconsin administrative data, 1997–2003, women on welfare	Frequency, length, and severity of sanctioning	Factors that explain sanctioning dynamics	Those with most barriers are most prone to sanctioning; race/ethnicity and location are also factors

papers in this genre, which look at the impact of the new policy configurations on work and welfare.

The earlier literature in this area relied heavily on state panel data analysis, trying to explain changes in work and welfare participation based on changing policies within states over time during the 1990s. The conclusions generally suggest that welfare reform had an impact both on declines in welfare participation and on increases in work effort, although the magnitude of this effect varies across studies. Most studies that attempt to measure the overall impact of TANF suggest that it caused about a 20 percent decline in caseloads (Grogger and Karoly 2005, table 5.8) and about a 4 percent increase in employment (Grogger and Karoly 2005, table 6.8). The earliest study that looks at the effects of both EITC and welfare reform finds the EITC has a larger effect than welfare reform (Meyer and Rosenbaum 2001), but it only utilizes data through 1996 on state waiver efforts. More recent literature using updated data finds significant and large effects from both the implementation of TANF and EITC expansion. Grogger (2004b) uses the Survey of Income and Program Participation (SIPP) data to look at entry into and exit from welfare. He finds that both policies are highly important in reducing entry into welfare, while TANF also has a substantial effect on increasing exit from welfare. Looney (2005) also uses SIPP data but focuses on welfare participation, not entry and exits. He finds that welfare reform was slightly more important than the EITC over the 1990s in reducing caseloads.

While more recent research generally identifies effects in the same way, by considering changes in state policies over time, the variety of data sources is much greater. Some studies rely on self-collected survey data like the Women's Employment Survey, which provides multiple waves of information on a group of women receiving welfare in 1997 in a Midwestern city (Johnson and Corcoran 2003); some utilize administrative data from specific states (Dyke et al. 2006; Wu et al. 2006); and a number utilize the SIPP panels (Fitzgerald and Ribar 2004; Looney 2005).

Recent studies tend to focus on more detailed questions than the earlier literature, which generally just asked whether the policy changes affected work or welfare usage. For instance, Johnson and Corcoran (2003) look at personal attributes that affect employment and wages among less-skilled single mothers, finding that lower skills, higher unemployment rates, and greater personal problems increase job change and reduce job quality. Meara and Frank (2006) find that mental health and drug use affect welfare and employment changes among ex-welfare recipients. Other researchers have focused on more specific aspects of policy. Dyke et al. (2006) indicate that specific types of assessment, job search assistance, and skill train-ing programs can lead to greater earnings gains. Huang, Garfinkel, and Waldfogel (2004) find that better child-support enforcement, along with welfare reform, reduces welfare usage. Wu et al. (2006) find that sanction-ing policies can affect benefit usage. Grogger (2004a) finds that time limits can reduce welfare use.

At least two of these more recent studies conclude that changes in welfare policy had only a limited effect. Fitzgerald and Ribar (2004) find that wel-fare reform seems to have had little effect on welfare participation, except through changes in benefit levels. This result is somewhat puzzling, since their paper uses a dataset virtually identical to that of Looney (2005) and similar variables describing welfare reform. Fitzgerald and Ribar approach the problem quite differently, however, estimating hazard models of welfare participation, while Looney estimates a state panel data model. Reconciling these results would be interesting. Haider et al. (2004) find that most changes in welfare usage among adult immigrants were due to economic factors, not welfare reform. This is a very specific population, however, that was largely ineligible for many public assistance programs prior to welfare reform. (Kalil and Ziol-Guest, in Chapter Nine of this volume, review the literature on immigrant use of public assistance.)

In contrast, one newer study claims that welfare reform policies and EITC changes can explain virtually 100 percent of the changes in welfare use and employment over the 1990s. Fang and Keane (2004) use a very complicated specification, with substantial numbers of leads and lags of policy compo-nents. The two published discussant comments that follow this paper (one of which I wrote) raise doubts about the specification and its interpretation. Other more recent studies that evaluate the overall effects of welfare reform on employment and welfare participation (Grogger 2004b; Looney 2005) find results consistent with those of most of the earlier literature. Like that litera-ture, their results indicate that welfare reform had a significant effect on case-loads and employment but did not explain the majority of these changes.

Most of the newer studies, however, focus on refining our knowledge about specific program details rather than evaluating overall TANF changes. They indicate that some specific policies seem to have had larger effects than others and that some particular individual attributes allow women moving into work to be more (or less) successful. In general, this litera-ture makes it clear that state and national policy choices have influenced welfare and work participation. It is hard, however, to distill many overall policy lessons, perhaps because most papers focus on a particular policy without comparing it to other options. While we learn that job assessment and search programs can promote higher employment or that child support enforcement can reduce welfare usage faster, at this point there is little here that would allow us to make comparative statements about the value of different policy components or the priorities that states should follow as they review their policies to determine which have the most impact.

B. Health and Health Insurance

A second strand of the recent welfare reform literature focuses on the effects of these reforms on health insurance coverage and on health outcomes. A review of this literature is recently available in Bitler and Hoynes (2008), and I will say only a little about this area since they have already provided a very good discussion. Table 1.2 lists some of the recent papers that look at the effect of welfare reforms on health outcomes and health insurance. In Table 1.2, I distinguish between the papers that focus on welfare reform and health insurance coverage (part A) and those that look at health outcomes more generally (part B).

Because of the variety of outcomes they examine, these papers utilize many data sources. Some make use of data from the Current Population Survey (CPS) (DeLeire, Levine, and Levy 2006). Others use information from the Behavior Risk Factor Surveillance System (Bitler, Gelbach, and Hoynes 2005; Kaestner and Tarlov 2006), the Fragile Families Study (Knab, McLanahan, and Garfinkel 2008), the National Natality Files (Kaestner and Lee 2005), or state administrative data (Holl, Slack, and Stevens 2005).

As the summaries in part A of Table 1.2 indicate, in most recent studies welfare reform appears to reduce health insurance coverage (Bitler et al. 2005; Cawley, Schroeder, and Simon 2005; Kaestner and Kaushal 2003). Bitler and Hoynes's (2008) review of the literature, which includes earlier studies from welfare demonstration programs, confirms this result. Ham, Li, and Shore-Sheppard (Chapter Six, this volume) find that declines in public coverage are especially pronounced among Hispanic mothers. Furthermore, health insurance coverage appears to be unstable, with frequent spells of noninsurance (Holl et al. 2005) among low-wage single mothers. In the one paper with a different set of results, DeLeire et al. (2006) claim that welfare reform was not correlated with declines in Medicaid use and was correlated with increased private health coverage.

Because of this different conclusion, these authors extensively compare their paper with other papers. They estimate the impact of welfare reform among all women, and their positive effects come largely from an estimated positive effect of welfare on insurance among married women. Their

Table 1.2. *Recent research on welfare reform, health insurance, and health outcomes*

| | | | A. Welfare reform and health insurance | |
Authors and date	Data and sample	Dependent variable	Key issue	Key findings
Bitler et al. (2005)	Behavior Risk Factor Surveillance System, state panel data, 1990–2000, women ages 20–45	Health insurance coverage, health care utilization, health status	Impact of welfare reform on health insurance, health care utilization, and health of single women	Welfare reform associated with decrease in health insurance and care utilization, little effect on outcomes
Cawley et al. (2005)	SIPP panels spanning 1984–1999, mothers ages 16–44	Health insurance coverage, Medicaid participation, private health coverage	Effect of welfare reform on health insurance coverage of single mothers	Welfare reform reduced health insurance coverage, primarily through a drop in Medicaid coverage
DeLeire et al. (2006)	March CPS microdata, 1988–2000, women ages 18–64	Health insurance coverage by education group	Effect of welfare reform on health insurance coverage among low-skilled women	Waivers and TANF correlated with increases in private health insurance, little effect on use of Medicaid
Holl et al. (2005)	Illinois Family Study, 1999–2002, welfare recipients in 1998 with young children	Health insurance coverage and type, length of coverage gap	Effect of welfare reform on stability of health insurance among parents transitioning from welfare to work	Leaving welfare leads to significant instability of coverage, higher probability of being uninsured

Kaestner and Kaushal (2003)	March CPS microdata 1992–1999, low-skilled single mothers ages 18–44	Medicaid participation, private health coverage, number uninsured	Effect of welfare reform on health insurance coverage among low-income single mothers and their children	Welfare reform associated with decrease in health insurance coverage, but effects are relatively small
		B. Welfare reform and health outcomes		
Cawley and Danziger (2005)	Women's Employment Survey, spanning 1997–2004, women ages 18–54 on welfare in 1997	Employment status, months on welfare, earnings	Whether obesity is a barrier to employment and earnings for current and former welfare recipients	Morbid obesity is correlated with decreased work and earnings, primarily among white women
Haider et al. (2003)	Ross Laboratories Mothers Survey and state panel data, 1990–2000, new mothers	Breast-feeding in the hospital and six months after birth	Effects of welfare work requirements on breast-feeding	Welfare work requirements associated with significant decrease in breast-feeding six months after birth
Kaestner and Lee (2005)	National Natality Files, 1992–2000, births to less-educated women ages 19–39	Prenatal care, birth weight	Effect of welfare reform on infant health	Small negative effects on prenatal care and birth weight
Kaestner and Tarlov (2006)	Behavior Risk Factor Surveillance System and state panel data, 1993–2001, low-skilled women	Various health-related behaviors and health outcomes	Effect of welfare reforms on health and health behavior of low-educated single mothers	Welfare reform associated with less binge drinking, little effect on other indicators

(continued)

Table 1.2. *Continued*

Authors and date	Data and sample	Dependent variable	Key issue	Key findings
Knab et al. (2008)	Fragile Families Survey, spanning 1998–2003, single mothers who gave birth in 1998–2000	Various health-related behaviors and health outcomes	Effects of welfare policies on maternal health	Greater welfare generosity correlated with negative effects on maternal health, reductions in smoking
Slack et al. (2007)	Illinois Family Study, 2001–2004, welfare recipients in 1998 with young child	Indicators of children's physical health	Effects of welfare and work outcomes on children's health	No correlation between child health and whether mother is on welfare or working. Children whose mothers report no welfare or work have best health outcomes

estimates of the effects of welfare reform on single women are quite small, similar to those of the other studies in Table 1.2 that focus on single women and find insignificant (or negative) effects. It is problematic to find a result that is driven by estimated welfare reform effects among married women since these effects—if they exist—should be substantially smaller than among single mothers. This suggests that there may be omitted variables affecting the married women that are correlated with the timing of welfare reform. This concern is buttressed by the results discussed later showing that welfare reform has had relatively little effect on marriage behavior.

Part B of Table 1.2 suggests that the impact of these changes in health insurance on health outcomes is limited, however, at least over the period that these studies investigate. Kaestner and Tarlov (2006) find few effects of welfare reform on a range of health-related behaviors. Their only significant result is a small decrease in the likelihood of binge drinking. Knab et al. (2008) actually find somewhat perverse effects, with greater welfare generosity correlated with declines in maternal health. Kaestner and Lee (2005) find very small negative effects on infant health. Slack, Holl, et al. (2007) find no correlations between child health outcomes and welfare or work patterns among former welfare recipients. The strongest evidence of health-related problems comes from Haider, Jacknowitz, and Schoeni (2003), who find significant declines in breast-feeding due to welfare reform, and from Kalil and Ziol-Guest (Chapter Nine, this volume), who find that children of immigrants are at increased risk of poor health and more likely to postpone care.

It is possible, of course, that evidence of health effects will emerge only over time. Declines in health insurance coverage may not have an immediate health effect; health problems (or benefits) often cumulate over time. Hence, long-term research results could be different from these short-term results, which are based largely on no more than three to five years' data after the policy change. It remains an open question, however, whether the long-term effects will appear any larger or more significant than the short-term effects.

Health-related impacts of welfare reform will continue to draw researchers' interest, I suspect. In part, this is because a growing body of studies has shown that health problems create barriers to work (Blank 2007 provides multiple citations). For instance, Cawley and Danziger (2005) indicate that morbid obesity is associated with greater difficulty in leaving welfare and finding a job. The incidence of depression among low-income single mothers is often cited as a particularly acute problem (Danziger et al. 2000). Health problems that affect work include not only the direct mental or physical health problems experienced by the mother, but also health problems among children or other adults for whom the mother is providing care. Hence, I expect that future research will continue to focus on the interrelationships between health insurance and health outcomes, access to services that alleviate health problems, and work and economic well-being among less-skilled single mothers.

C. Child Outcomes and Child Care Usage

Several earlier demonstration programs invested significantly in studying the effects of welfare-to-work programs on the children in the family. Grogger and Karoly (2005) provide a review of this evidence, and Smolensky and Grootman (2003) summarize the models and the literature. Morris, Gennetian, Duncan, and Huston (Chapter Seven, this volume) also discuss the results from these demonstration programs on child outcomes. These earlier programs showed few large positive or negative effects of parental welfare-to-work programs on children, although the evidence seems to indicate that young children did slightly better, particularly if child care subsidies allowed newly working parents to place their children in formal child care settings. There was also some evidence of negative effects on adolescent behavior.

More recent research has tried to estimate the effects of national welfare reform on child outcomes. Table 1.3 summarizes some of these studies in part A. This research is quite heterogeneous, both in the questions it studies and in the data it utilizes.

One of the most detailed studies is that of Dunifon, Kalil, and Bajracharya (2005), who attempt to measure the specific attributes of low-wage work that might affect children's behavioral problems. They find that only lengthy commute times seem to have negative effects; various other aspects of low-wage work appear to have no impact on children's behavior. Chase-Lansdale et al. (2003) find that mothers' transition from welfare to employment has no effect on younger children's cognitive achievement, and they find some positive effects among adolescents. Coley et al. (2007) find that mothers' movement from welfare to employment improves their economic status and psychological well-being but has little effect on parenting. In contrast, Osborne and Knab (2007) find that the children of employed mothers have better behavioral outcomes, but this is explained entirely by the selectivity of mothers who move into employment following welfare reform. Miller and Zhang (2007) find that low-income children's math scores improve relative to those of higher-income children over the time period that welfare reform is implemented, but this study provides only correlations, with no attempt to link these changes to specific welfare reforms.

In short, much of the recent research evidence indicates that children's outcomes do not appear to be significantly affected by welfare reform, similar to findings from the earlier research. The exception to this is a paper by Bennett, Lu, and Song (2004) that looks not at children's outcomes but at family income. While they find that most families did not experience declines in income following welfare reform, they do find income declines over the welfare reform period among families that were poorer and less educated. This result is consistent with other research that suggests that some share of the most disadvantaged single-mother families may be worse off after leaving welfare, with difficulty in finding and holding a stable job (Blank 2007). So far as I am aware, there is no research to date that investigates specific child outcomes in these most disadvantaged families.

If welfare has had little effect on child outcomes, it appears to have had a clear effect on child care options and choices. Part B of Table 1.3 lists two recent papers on child care changes related to welfare reform. Both Witte and Queralt (2003) and Tekin (2005) find that child care subsidies from welfare reform had a substantial effect on the usage of center-based care. This is consistent with similar findings from the earlier welfare-to-work demonstration projects (Gennetian et al. 2004).

One of the motivations behind welfare reform was the hope that moving mothers into work would change their children's perspective. More children would understand the value of education and the need to prepare for the world of work. So far, there is little evidence to support or refute these claims. In fact, I believe that many have been surprised by the lack of effects—positive or negative—that welfare-to-work programs have had on children. The strongest evidence to emerge from the literature on welfare reform and children is the growing body of research studies that demonstrate the value of child care subsidies for low-income working women that allow them to place their young children in formal preschool settings. Children's school readiness and their behavior appear to improve as a result of these programs.

D. Family Composition and Fertility

At least some supporters of welfare reform were less concerned about its impact on work than its impact on marriage and out-of-wedlock childbearing. Earlier demonstration project evidence suggested that mandatory welfare-to-work programs had little effect on marriage (Grogger and Karoly 2005). In Grogger and Karoly's words, the earlier studies are "inconclusive," with some positive and some negative results.

Table 1.4 lists some of the more recent studies on the effects of welfare reform on marriage and living arrangements in part A. Bitler et al. (2004) find that welfare reform does little to increase the rate of marriage, but

Table 1.3. *Recent research in child well-being and child care following welfare reform*

		A. Welfare reform and child well-being		
Authors and date	Data and sample	Dependent variable	Key issue	Key findings
Bennett et al. (2004)	Matched March CPS state panel data, 1987–2000, families with children	Family income-to-needs ratios	Effects of welfare reform on family income	Welfare implementation has a negative effect on incomes among those who were initially poorer and less educated
Chase-Lansdale et al. (2003)	Three-City Study: Boston, Chicago, San Antonio, 1999–2001, low-income mothers and children	Children's cognitive achievement and behavioral outcomes	How welfare-to-work transitions affect children's development	No effects among preschoolers; some evidence of positive effects among adolescents
Coley et al. (2007)	Three-City Study: Boston, Chicago, San Antonio, 1999–2001, low-income mothers and children	Economic well-being, maternal functioning, and parenting practices	How welfare-to-work transitions affect mothers' well-being and behavior toward their children	Sustained employment is correlated with higher incomes, less hardship, and improved maternal psychological outcomes; little relationship between these changes and parenting quality
Dunifon et al. (2005)	Women's Employment Survey, spanning 1997–2002, women ages 18–54 on welfare in 1997	Children's behavioral outcomes	How maternal work conditions affect children's well-being	Lengthy commute time correlated with behavioral problems; other job stress factors have few effects

Miller and Zhang (2007)	NAEP state panel data, 1996, 2000, 2003, 2005, fourth and eighth graders	Fourth- and eighth-grade math scores	How children in low-income families fared academically after welfare reform	Children in low-income families improve math achievement relative to other students
Osborne and Knab (2007)	Fragile Families Survey, spanning 1998–2003, single mothers who gave birth in 1998–2000	Children's emotional and behavioral outcomes	Effects of welfare receipt and employment on children's outcomes	Children of working women have fewer behavioral problems; most of this effect due to selectivity of mothers who are employed
B. Welfare reform and childcare				
Tekin (2005)	NSAF, 1999, families with children	Employment and child care choices	Effect of child care subsidies on joint work and care provider choices	Large effects of subsidy on employment and center-based care usage
Witte and Queralt (2003)	Rhode Island administrative data, 1996–2000, single mothers ages 18–60 with some cash assistance between 1996 and 2000	Use of child care subsidy, welfare and work participation	Whether expansion of Rhode Island's child care subsidies affected welfare or work behavior	Policy change associated with more subsidy use and increased work

Table 1.4. *Recent research on welfare reform, family composition, and fertility*

	A. Welfare reform and marriage and living arrangements			
Authors and date	Data and sample	Dependent variable	Key issue	Key findings
Bitler et al. (2004)	Vital statistics marriage and divorce state panel data, 1989–1990	Rate of new marriages and divorces	Effect of welfare reform on marriage and divorce rates	Welfare reform associated with fewer new divorces and fewer new marriages
Bitler et al. (2006)	March CPS microdata, 1989–2000, all children ages 16 or less	Children's living arrangements	How welfare reform affected children's living arrangements	Little effect of welfare reform. Waivers associated with fewer children living with unmarried parents, more living with married parents or no parents
Cherlin and Fomby (2004)	Three-City Study: Boston, Chicago, San Antonio, 1999–2001, low-income families	Marital/cohabitation status	Factors determining changes in cohabitation and marriage	Small increase in children living with two adults, mostly due to increased cohabitation; no increase in children living with biological fathers

B. Welfare reform and fertility

Study	Data/Sample	Outcome	Research question	Findings
Hao and Cherlin (2004)	NLSY97, women born in 1980 vs. 1982–1983	Teen pregnancy and birth rates, school dropout rates	Impact of welfare reform on teen behaviors	No effect of welfare reform on fertility; some evidence of increases in school dropout rates
Joyce et al. (2003)	Vital Statistics births and state panel data 1990–1999, women ages 19–39	Nonmarital childbearing	Effect of welfare reform on births among less-educated unmarried women	Little effect of welfare on nonmarital births; some declines in nonmarital births among Hispanics
Kaestner et al. (2003)	NLSY79 and NLSY97, women ages 17–19 in 1979–1984 vs. 1997–1999	Welfare use, school dropout, marriage, and fertility rates	Effect of welfare reform on welfare use, marriage, fertility, and schooling among teenage girls after welfare reform in high-risk families	Welfare reform associated with decreased welfare use, decreased fertility and marriage rates
Lopoo and DeLeire (2006)	NCHS births, state panel data, 1992–1999, females age 19 or less	Teen fertility rates	Effects of "living arrangement rule" and "stay in school rule" on teenage fertility	Implementation of these rules associated with decreased fertility

it does appear to reduce the likelihood of divorce among those who are already married. Cherlin and Fomby (2004) note that more low-income children lived with two adults in 2001 versus 1999, but this trend is largely due to the increase in cohabitation. There is no increase in the share of women living with the biological fathers of their children. Bitler, Gelbach, and Hoynes (2006) are also concerned with children's living arrangements. They find that welfare reform has few effects, while the earlier state waiver welfare-to-work demonstration projects had stronger effects. These projects appeared to increase the number of children living either with married parents or with adults who were not their parents.

In short, the evidence of any substantial marriage effects as a result of welfare reform is quite weak. A growing number of studies show increased cohabitation (almost surely because of the need for greater income sharing). The effects of this increase on the children, especially when the man is not their biological father, are not obviously positive.

Part B of Table 1.4 describes recent studies on the link between welfare reform and fertility outcomes. Two of these studies find no effects of reform on fertility (Hao and Cherlin 2004; Joyce, Kaestner, and Korenman 2003). In contrast, a third study (Kaestner, Korenman, and O'Neill 2003) finds that welfare reform reduced teenage births (and reduced marriage rates). This last study compares births among teenagers in the early 1980s to those among teens in the late 1990s, and the possibility for omitted variables is greater with their specification. Hence, its conclusions about the impact of welfare reform are less clearly causal than those of studies that utilize more specific welfare reform–related variables. A fourth study finds that two specific rules aimed at teenage mothers as part of welfare reform—requiring teens to stay in school and to continue living with relatives in order to be eligible for welfare—both reduced teen fertility (Lopoo and DeLeire 2006). This is not necessarily inconsistent with results that show no overall effect of welfare reform implementation on nonmarital fertility. One would expect that these more narrowly focused requirements would have effects within their targeted population.

My reading of the literature on the impact of welfare reform on fertility is that it continues to show relatively minor effects. Unlike work behavior and welfare participation, both of which changed dramatically in the years after welfare reform, the trends in fertility and marriage did not change much in the mid-1990s. So far, the effects of welfare reform on marriage arrangements and on fertility appear to have been small. Of course, it is possible that there are multiple policy effects that offset each other; for instance, Knab et al. (Chapter Eight, this volume) indicate that stricter child support enforcement reduces the probability of marriage, while less generous welfare payments increase marriage.

It is possible that the impact of these reforms on fertility and marriage will be larger over time as women (and particularly younger women) become aware of the policy changes and learn that there are fewer supports for single mothers who do not work. None of the studies cited here use data later than 2001, which is only three to four years after welfare reform was implemented in all states. This is clearly an area where it may be fruitful to give ongoing attention to changing trends in marriage and fertility and their correlation with different state policy approaches.

E. Consumption Changes

One new strand of the welfare reform literature that has emerged in the past five years focuses on the impact of welfare reform on patterns of consumption. Current research clearly indicates that poverty fell in the 1990s, partly due to economic growth and partly due to policy changes (Gundersen and Ziliak 2004). Others have also documented income increases among some single mothers (Blank 2006; Bollinger, Gonzalez, and Ziliak, Chapter Two, this volume). Frogner, Moffitt, and Ribar (Chapter Four, this volume) document income changes among ex-welfare recipients, showing that income growth is particularly strong among those who are steadily employed.

A criticism of earlier studies that focused just on income is that income levels provide only very limited information about changes in well-being. Increased work means increased work expenses for child care, transportation, and clothing. Even those who experienced income increases as a result of increased work may have spent all their extra income on work-related items, leaving them no better off with regard to other forms of consumption. Consumption data therefore provide an alternative, and potentially more useful, measure of well-being. Table 1.5 identifies a number of studies that focus on consumption changes following welfare reform.

The most extended investigation of changes in consumption following welfare reform has been done by Meyer and Sullivan (2006). They study changes in consumption across a wide variety of measures before and after the implementation of welfare reform using several datasets; they compare consumption and income changes; and they look at time-use trends as well. Their general conclusion is that consumption changes are less dramatic than income changes following welfare reform. Consumption among single mothers shows neither the sharp declines at the bottom of the distribution nor the significant increases at the top that are visible within the income

Table 1.5. *Recent research in consumption and well-being following welfare reform*

Authors and date	Data and sample	Dependent variable	Key issue	Key findings
Cancian and Meyer (2004)	Wisconsin administrative data and survey, 1999 data, single mothers on welfare in 1997–1998	Public assistance use, work, hardship, and poverty	Comparing alternative measures of economic well-being among welfare recipients following welfare reform	Families are leaving poverty and working more; few achieve independence from all forms of public assistance.
Kaushal et al. (2007)	CES, 1990–1995 vs. 1998–2003, families with children, mothers ages 18–54	Total expenditures and spending patterns among less-educated single mothers	Changes in spending patterns after welfare reform among single mothers	No effect on total expenditures; increased spending on transportation, food away from home, adult clothing.
Meyer and Sullivan (2006)	CES, PSID, CPS, AHS, NTUS, and ATUS, 1993–2003, single mothers ages 18–54	Income, consumption, and housing characteristics	Comparative changes in income and consumption among female-headed households following welfare reform	Consumption changes after welfare reform are less than income changes; increases in housing and transportation spending; declines in nonmarket time.
Slack et al. (2007)	Women's Employment Study, Illinois Family Study, Milwaukee TANF Applicant Study, Fragile Families Study, Three-City Study; 1997–2003 (differs by study), single mothers	Various measures of hardship and economic well-being	Descriptive trends over time in well-being among women who were welfare recipients in the past	No clear pattern of change in hardship measures across these datasets; some improve a little, some decline a little.

42

distribution. Meyer and Sullivan suggest that this consumption–income difference is due to measurement issues in income.

Consumption does increase for 90 percent of single-mother families over this time period. These increases in consumption are largely concentrated in transportation spending (not surprising as work increases) and in housing (perhaps the result of the rising housing and rental prices of the 1990s). The changes in time use are consistent with the data on growing employment, showing large declines in nonmarket work.

While Meyer and Sullivan focus on comparative trends, Kaushal, Gao, and Waldfogel (2007) regress consumption trends on a variety of variables, with particular attention to the effects of welfare reform. They find few effects of welfare reform on overall expenditures, but they do find an effect on certain types of expenditure. They find that welfare reform appears to have increased spending on transportation, on food eaten away from home, and on adult clothing, all effects that might be expected as a result of increases in women's employment. It is interesting to compare these results to those of the study by Gregg, Waldfogel, and Washbrook (2006), which looks at consumption changes among low-income British families over the same time period. Under Tony Blair's leadership in the late 1990s, Britain implemented a variety of policy changes designed to reduce child poverty, which ultimately produced very large declines in child poverty rates. This increase in income is mirrored in increased consumption among these families, and much of this increased consumption is focused on child-related goods. In contrast, the U.S. work-focused reforms seemed to have fewer overall consumption-related effects and no impact on expenditures on children. Waldfogel (2007) provides a more detailed U.S./U.K. comparison. Gao, Kaushal and Waldfogel (Chapter Three, this volume) provide further evidence of U.S. expenditure changes, focusing particularly on the effect of EITC expansions.

Cancian and Meyer (2004) look at hardship and poverty in the state of Wisconsin immediately after welfare reform. They find increases in income, but few families achieve full independence from all public assistance programs. They do find that a majority of single mothers avoid hardship. The hardship and the poverty measures overlap but are far from perfectly correlated. They conclude that consumption and hardship measures provide valuable and different information from poverty and income measures.

A final paper documents trends in various hardship measures (Slack, Magnuson, et al. 2007) among five datasets, each of which tracks a cohort of low-income women after welfare reform. The authors find no consistent trend in hardship measures over time, but the results are somewhat hard to interpret across surveys since they come from quite differently sampled datasets.

F. Other Studies

Most of the more recent work on the effects of welfare reform has focused on the topics summarized in Tables 1.1 through 1.5. There are, however, a few other issues that have been taken up by researchers.

Several papers have looked at the impact of welfare reform on programs other than AFDC/TANF participation. For instance, two recent papers indicate that the policy changes made in the Food Stamp Program in the 1990s matter. Hanratty (2006) and Danielson and Klerman (2006) both indicate that welfare reform was correlated with the drop in food stamp caseloads in the mid-1990s and that other policy changes in the Food Stamp Program designed to increase access for working low-income families led to subsequent rises in caseloads. Schmidt and Sevak (2004) indicate that changes in welfare reform spilled over into Supplemental Security Income (SSI) caseload changes, with significant increases in SSI caseloads that are correlated with declines in welfare caseloads.

Others have looked at the effect of welfare reform on savings. Hurst and Ziliak (2006) study whether increases in allowable assets for welfare participants led to increases in household savings. They find no effects on savings but small effects on vehicle ownership. Similarly, Sullivan (2006) finds no effect of increases in the allowable value of vehicles owned by welfare recipients on asset holdings among this population.

II. What Don't We Know?

Almost 11 years following welfare reform, the limits on what we can and can't learn about the effects of this set of policy changes are becoming clear. In particular, there are two major issues that limit our knowledge. The first is the problem of identifying and estimating the effects of welfare reform in a way that is clearly causal. The second is our limited data on certain aspects of welfare reform programs within states.

A. Limitations to Our Evaluation Ability

The research summarized in Tables 1.1 to 1.5 takes a variety of approaches. The vast majority of papers estimate some sort of over-time regression, typically using annual survey data from multiple years to measure the dependent variable of interest. In some cases, the data are at the individual level; in others, they are at the state level. These regressions typically include state and year fixed effects. Welfare reform is often specified as the point at which states implement either waivers or TANF programs. In some cases, welfare reform is not described by an aggregate implementation variable but rather by program components in each state, so that provisions like state time limits, sanctions, or teenage stay-in-school rules are specified.

As has been discussed elsewhere (Blank 2002), these approaches provide relatively weak identification. Welfare reforms were implemented across all states within one and a half years. Since much of the data are annual, there is limited variance in implementation dates across states. One might expect that coding the components of specific state policies would provide more effective identification, but this specification rarely provides much additional power. In some cases, there is small variance in these policies across states, or only a few states implement the policy in a markedly different way (and if those happen to be small-population states, then national surveys have few observations from these states). In other cases, our information about these policies is limited, as I discuss more fully later.

In addition, a variety of other important changes were occurring at exactly the same time as welfare reform. Just as TANF programs were being implemented, minimum wage increases and expansions in the EITC were also being put in place. In these same years, a very strong economic expansion also reduced unemployment rates and created jobs in almost all parts of the country. Untangling these effects from each other has been extremely difficult. Including extensive lags or leads for policy effects or for economic effects can substantively change the comparative effects of different variables (for instance, see Fang and Keane 2004 and the two comments that follow by Blank and by Grogger.) But with low-frequency data, such lags or leads may start proxying for omitted variables and not provide a satisfying causal interpretation.

In my mind, the best papers that utilize this approach gain additional power by comparing the effects on women who are likely to be welfare-eligible and on a comparison group. Often researchers use women with high levels of education as a comparison group for women with low levels of education; occasionally, researchers use married women as a comparison group for single mothers. The result is a difference-in-difference approach that estimates the differences before and after welfare reform and between the two groups. Even this approach, however, cannot absolutely nail down the effects of welfare reform. Omitted variables are a troubling issue for virtually all of the research cited in this chapter and prevent strong causal conclusions. (Ham, Li, and Shore-Shephard, Chapter Six, this volume, discuss this concern in the context of studying the effects of welfare reform on health insurance coverage.) In many cases, when describing a paper's result in Tables 1.1 to 1.5, I note that a paper indicates correlations between the timing of welfare reform and a specific outcome; this is the strongest statement that one can typically make in this literature.

A few papers manage to be more causally convincing. These typically look at the impact of one or two very specific policy changes that are clearly targeted to a specific population. In this case, one can compare the effects on this population with the effects on other low-income single-mother families. For instance, Grogger's (2004a) work on time limits is of this sort. So is Lopoo and DeLeire's (2006) paper on the impact of teen living arrangement and stay-in-school rules on teen fertility.

Some of the papers cited previously do not attempt causal analysis. They simply focus on trends over time during the period when welfare reform was being implemented or on changes immediately after welfare reform was enacted. For example, Meara and Frank (2006), Holl et al. (2005), and Miller and Zhang (2007) use this approach.

These identification problems are inherent in the welfare reform literature. We will not be able to nail down the final causal effect of these changes in state-level welfare programs in a fully convincing way, although we may be able to say something more certain about a few components of welfare reform. The fact that this literature has flourished even in the absence of a fully convincing methodological approach is testimony to how intensely interested people are in the effects of welfare reform.

The most convincing evidence we have comes from accumulating evidence from multiple studies. Results that appear to be robust to different datasets, different specifications, and across multiple papers are more believable than results that are more dependent upon a particular dataset or a particular methodological approach. For instance, the conclusion that child care subsidies have increased the use of formal day care is found in the results from waiver experiments as well as from a variety of empirical studies of the post–welfare reform era. There are no studies that find the opposite. Hence, this is a conclusion that I find more persuasive, whereas I am more cautious about other results where the impacts are smaller and more variable across studies.

B. Limits to Our Data

The data problems in studying welfare reform are also significant. At the national level, we continue to have limited data with which to specify either individual program eligibility or state program parameters. For instance, with the CPS data, the most commonly used dataset in this literature, prior to 2001 there was no information on whether an individual was subject to work requirements, had gone through any job search assistance, had experienced sanctions or time limits, or was receiving child care assistance. A welfare reform supplement has asked some of these questions since 2001, but response accuracy is a concern. Without this information, estimating the causal effects of program components is quite difficult. Other national survey datasets have similar limitations. For instance, a variety of short papers in Besharov (2003) discuss the limitations in the data on child and family well-being following welfare reform.

Administrative data on individuals can provide much more complete information on program history and involvement, but they often have limited information on postprogram outcomes, family demographics, or key recipient characteristics such as education levels. Some of the most detailed analysis is based on longitudinal field surveys specifically designed to collect both program and family information (the Women's Employment Study, the Fragile Families Study, and the Three-City Study come to mind), but such studies are necessarily limited in scope and representativeness.

The result of these data limits is that it is hard (if not impossible) to estimate the specific effects of program components implemented by states, that is, to estimate the impact of specific training, welfare-to-work requirements, or sanction policies. Much of the best research on the impact of specific program components is based on the results of the demonstration projects from the early 1990s, which were often more limited in scope and design than the TANF programs states enacted in the late 1990s.

Another problem is that there is only limited state-based reporting of program information to any central national unit. Fortunately, the Department of Health and Human Services has continued to fund the Welfare Research Database (WRD) at the Urban Institute, which collects annual information on state program parameters. This information, collected in a consistent way across states and over time, is absolutely mandatory for ongoing and effective research. Yet even this dataset lacks some key variables, such as details about the job training and welfare-to-work requirements within a state. Admittedly, this information is lacking in part because there is no simple way to describe these requirements; they vary among individuals and are affected by caseworkers' discretion.

Beyond the WRD data, there is no other good central source of program information. States do report some program items to the Department of Health and Human Services, including such things as the percentage of the caseload in a work-related program or the percentage of the caseload subject to sanctions. There is limited consistency across states in exactly how they define various groups, however, so cross-state numbers are not always comparable. And, with the end of quality-control data collection, there is very little monitoring of state-reported data.

These data and methodological limitations make evaluation of certain aspects of welfare reform difficult, and they make almost all welfare reform research open to question by those who are skeptical of the results. Virtually every welfare reform study has some data and methodological issues that are open to criticism.

III. What Do We Need to Know?

The history of welfare reform has made it clear that the effects of a policy are affected by the particular time in which it happens to be implemented. If welfare reform had been implemented immediately before a major recession hit the U.S. economy, the story could have turned out quite differently. As I have noted elsewhere (Blank 2006), the economic expansion gave states the ability to focus on the details of implementing a new program without worrying about whether jobs would be available for those who were given job search assistance. Almost surely, this expansion in the late 1990s meant that more women found jobs, found them more rapidly, kept them longer, and found their next job more quickly than would have happened in a slower labor market.

In part because of this unusual economic environment when welfare reform was being implemented, the long-term evaluation of welfare reform will hinge on more than just the results from these early years (1997–2001 is the postreform period available in most of the current research), when caseloads plummeted and employment rose. I think there are at least three crucial research questions related to the impact of welfare reform that will need to be answered over a longer time period.

A. Will the Current Program Configuration Survive
a Major Recession?

In the years since 2001, the labor market has been more sluggish. Employment has gone down among single mothers, although (as of 2008, when this was written) it remains above the level of the early 1990s. Caseloads, however, have not risen. Blank (2006) discusses some of the reasons why caseloads continued to fall even through the mild recession of the early 2000s. Most notably, the industries where many less-skilled women were employed did not experience a recession over the past decade. Retail sales, health care, other services, and consumer-spending-related industries remained strong even through the recession of the early 2000s.

The long-run evaluation of welfare reform will depend upon how the revised public assistance system works when (inevitably) we hit a downturn in the economic cycle that leads to much greater job scarcity in these industries. It is possible that single mothers will access food stamps and receive Unemployment Insurance and that state TANF programs will provide support. (One could even imagine a special federal appropriation in a time of high unemployment to state TANF programs, something like the "Extended Benefits" appropriations in the Unemployment Insurance system.) But it is also possible that economic need could rise sharply among mothers and children if women are not able to find support or to locate another job quickly.

In the long run, the viability of the current configuration of state welfare programs and federal funding requirements depends upon this system's surviving intact through a major economic slowdown that affects the jobs single mothers are most likely to hold. While the new work-centered public assistance system solves some of the previous work-disincentive problems embedded in cash public assistance programs, it provides a much less effective safety net when jobs become scarce. Single mothers and their children remain a vulnerable and publicly sympathetic population; demands for increased federally funded cash assistance could increase if it appeared that children and women were experiencing serious economic deprivation in the face of ongoing but unsuccessful attempts to find employment in the midst of a recession.

Of course, this concern only underscores the fact that macroeconomic policy has become more important for low-income families than ever before. While job availability has always been important to the poor, the advent of work-focused welfare reform has made a growing number of low-income families—especially single mothers—more reliant on labor market earnings. The most important antipoverty policies in the decades ahead may be those that focus on preventing a major economic recession and ensuring strong employment demand for less-skilled workers.

B. What's Happening to Disconnected Women?

There appears to be a growing segment of single mothers who report themselves as neither working nor on welfare, often referred to as "disconnected" women. It is statistically inevitable that this group would grow, given that employment levels among single mothers fell over the 2000s and caseloads did not rise. My own calculations of the size of this group over time indicate that it doubled between the mid-1990s and the mid-2000s, with 20 to 25 percent of all low-income single mothers reporting themselves with no or extremely low levels of welfare assistance and earnings (Blank 2007, table 1).

The rapid growth in this population is visible across a variety of datasets and has been a growing concern among those who follow these data (Turner, Danziger, and Seefeldt 2006).

While some disconnected women are living with other adults, about half of these low-income single mothers report themselves as the only adult in the household. The group of disconnected single mothers is very poor; 73 percent are in households below the poverty line, and median household income is less than $13,000 per year (Blank 2007; Blank and Kovak 2009, forthcoming).

Quite a bit of research has tried to describe which women are unsuccessful at finding or keeping stable work after leaving welfare. The evidence suggests that many of these women face multiple barriers to work, including physical health problems, mental health problems such as depression, low skills, a history of domestic violence, and substance abuse. This population is also disproportionately likely to leave welfare through sanctions or time limits. These women face barriers to participating in welfare-to-work programs, just as they face barriers to working steadily (Seefeldt and Orzol 2005).

Why has the number of disconnected women been rising in the 2000s? One possibility is that the slower economy means that more single mothers struggle harder to keep and maintain employment. Furthermore, these problems may be enhanced by the growing number of women who cannot readily return to welfare due to sanctions or time limits. Entry into welfare has fallen substantially, so even those who are still eligible for welfare may have received the message that welfare is no longer readily available and could be reluctant to apply.

Understanding exactly what this trend means is important. If these women experience a year of difficult times but then are able to find a job, perhaps the problem is not too serious. But we know little about the dynamics of these families. We do know that children do not do well in families with sustained low income levels, nor do they do well in families where parents are dealing with serious personal problems that may limit their parenting skills (Duncan and Brooks-Gunn 1997).

Research is needed on how these families are surviving, what their prospects are over time, and how children are faring. Much of this research will require small-sample in-depth interviews or surveys.

C. What Is the Impact of Time Limits and Sanctions?

Closely related to the concerns about disconnected women are concerns about how states are utilizing time limits and sanctions. We have very limited information on the ways in which these policies are actually being implemented. In almost all states, there is discretion about who faces time limits or sanctions and who receives assistance to help them avoid these problems.

The evidence on women who have faced sanctions indicates that they are a more disadvantaged population (Kalil, Seefeldt, and Wang 2002; Pavetti, Derr, and Hesketh 2003). Lee, Slack, and Lewis (2004) indicate that those who are sanctioned are more likely to work in informal and occasional jobs and earn less than those who leave welfare in other ways. Of course, the problems that limit women's ability to hold a stable job might also make it difficult for them to comply with the rules of public assistance programs. Indeed, one reason many believe that the overall level of disadvantage has not increased among those on welfare is that more disadvantaged women are being sanctioned, while less disadvantaged women are leaving through welfare-to-work programs.

Time limits began to bite during the early 2000s. Studying their impact has been difficult, since the share of the population that actually hits time limits has grown slowly over time. Furthermore, many states report relatively few women who have been time-limited off welfare. It is not clear if this is because few women actually hit time limits in these states, because the states have poor caseload records that make it hard to identify persons subject to time limits, or because caseworkers are finding ways to provide ongoing assistance to these women.

Some good implementation studies of time limits and sanctions in the mid-2000s would be very useful, particularly if done in several different states with different program approaches. One example of such research is that of Fording, Schram, and Soss (2007), who look at variation in sanctioning outcomes across Florida counties. There are a variety of interesting issues that need to be better understood. How much discretion do caseworkers have in applying these policies? Which women face these sanctions and which women are able to avoid them? Research on disconnected women, as described previously, will prove evidence from another angle, indicating how women who have been sanctioned or time-limited are managing to get by if they are not successful in finding work. A fine example of useful research of this sort is the paper by Pavetti and Kauff (2006), which describes the problems faced by families who are hitting time limits in a county in Minnesota.

An important policy question is whether there are "best practices" with regard to time limits and sanctions. Are there some states that are more effective in determining who should face time limits or sanctions? Are there some states that are more effective in helping women avoid these penalties?

Are there some states that find ways to assist women who are forced off TANF to continue using the services still available to themselves and their children? For instance, Allard (Chapter Ten, this volume) suggests that there is a spatial mismatch between the location of potential recipients and local services. Answers to these questions are important for state policy analysts who want to understand the impact of their policy choices, as well as for researchers who want to draw conclusions about the overall effects of welfare program changes.

The rising share of disconnected women and the link between this population and the sanction/time limit policies of states make it important to understand how these policies are functioning. These policies were designed to create strong incentives for women to seek work and leave welfare through welfare-to-work assistance. If, however, these policies are primarily targeting women who are unable to hold a steady job, then we need to reevaluate the costs of these policies and the benefits that they provide.

IV. Conclusions

The welfare reforms of the mid-1990s were a rare example of major legislative reform. Every state fundamentally altered the ways in which it delivered public assistance by changing the parameters and policies regarding eligibility and work requirements, retraining caseworkers, and providing a very different mix of incentives and opportunities to recipients and applicants in the welfare system. Given these sweeping changes, it is not surprising that researchers have been so interested in measuring the effects of welfare reform.

In the years following welfare reform, the dramatic changes in welfare participation, in work behavior, and in income and poverty measures were also important in generating great interest among researchers in these issues. If these policy changes produced such dramatic results, we wanted to understand why and how this occurred.

My own reading of the research literature to date leads me to conclude that these major changes in policy had substantial effects on work and welfare recipiency. There appears to be good evidence that these changes were one of the primary causes behind falling caseloads, rising employment, and growing earnings among single mothers. But other forces, such as the growing EITC and the strong economy, were at least as important and in many studies appear to be more important than the public assistance policy changes. All of these factors together did lead to unexpectedly large declines in welfare usage and a big increase in work and earnings.

It is perhaps surprising that these very large changes in welfare use, work, and earnings have had at best small effects on other domains of family life among single-mother families. The evidence suggests that these large changes in work and welfare behavior had relatively small effects on marriage and fertility behavior, children's behavior or school achievement, consumption patterns, or health outcomes. It is possible that these other domains will show effects only over time, with longer-term cumulative effects on health, child outcomes, or fertility that are simply not yet visible in the data. At this moment, however, these other areas appear to be much less affected by welfare reform or by the changes in behavior and work that occurred concurrently with welfare reform.

Thus, I find myself struck by the following conundrum: On the one hand, the movement off public assistance and into work was far greater than I would have guessed possible in such a short period of time. Even with multiple synergies between welfare reform, EITC expansion, economic expansion, and other changes, I would not have guessed that such rapid behavioral change would have occurred among single mothers. On the other hand, given that such dramatic changes did occur, I am surprised at how little they have affected other domains of life for these women. I would have guessed that such dramatic labor market changes would have led to greater changes in other behaviors. Certainly, there is continuing grist for the research mill of social scientists in all disciplines to understand why one set of behaviors was so responsive in the past decade, while other behaviors have been relatively unchanged.

Those who supported welfare reform because it promised greater work and less welfare usage should find their expectations more than met. Many low-skilled single mothers have become much more involved with the labor force, which led to significant gains in earnings, and at least prior to some of the studies in this volume, there was limited evidence of negative effects in other domains. Of course, as Bollinger, Gonzalez, and Ziliak (Chapter Two, this volume) find, some of the least skilled women lost more in benefits than they gained in earnings, so not everyone was better off.

Those who expected welfare reform to truly transform the lives of low-income mothers should be more disappointed. Despite dramatic changes in work behavior and welfare reliance, so far there is little evidence that marriage or fertility patterns have changed much as a result of welfare reform, nor is there evidence that the children of low-skilled working mothers are doing better than the children of welfare recipients a decade ago.

References

Bennett, Neil G., Hsien-Hen Lu, and Younghwan Song. 2004. "Welfare Reform and Changes in the Economic Well-Being of Children." *Population Research and Policy Review*, 23:671–699.

Besharov, Douglas J. 2003. *Family and Child Well-Being After Welfare Reform*. New Brunswick, NJ: Transaction Publishers.

Bitler, Marianne P., Jonah B. Gelbach, and Hilary W. Hoynes. 2005. "Welfare Reform and Health." *Journal of Human Resources*, 40:309–334.

2006. "Welfare Reform and Children's Living Arrangements." *Journal of Human Resources*, 41:1–27.

Bitler, Marianne P., Jonah B. Gelbach, Hilary W. Hoynes, and Madeline Zavodny. 2004. "The Impact of Welfare Reform on Marriage and Divorce." *Demography*, 41:213–236.

Bitler, Marianne P., and Hilary W. Hoynes. 2008. "Welfare Reform and Indirect Impacts on Health," in *Making Americans Healthier: Social and Economic Policy as Health Policy*. Robert F. Schoeni, James S. House, George A. Kaplan, and Harold Pollack, eds. New York: Russell Sage, 231–280.

Blank, Rebecca M. 2002. "Evaluating Welfare Reform in the United States." *Journal of Economic Literature*, 40:1105–1166.

2006. "What Did the 1990s Welfare Reforms Accomplish?" in *Public Policy and the Income Distribution*. Alan J. Auerbach, David Card, and John M. Quigley, eds. New York: Russell Sage, 33–79.

2007. "Improving the Safety Net for Single Mothers Who Face Serious Barriers to Work." *Future of Children*, 17:183–197.

Blank, Rebecca M., and Brian Kovak. 2009, forthcoming. "The Growing Problem of Disconnected Single Mothers." in *Making the Work-Based Safety Net Work Better*. Carolyn J. Heinrich and John Karl Scholz, eds. New York: Russell Sage.

Cancian, Maria, and Daniel R. Meyer. 2004. "Alternative Measures of Economic Success Among TANF Participants: Avoiding Poverty, Hardship, and Dependence on Public Assistance." *Journal of Policy Analysis and Management*, 23:531–548.

Cawley, John, and Sheldon Danziger. 2005. "Morbid Obesity and the Transition from Welfare to Work." *Journal of Policy Analysis and Management*, 24:727–743.

Cawley, John H., Mathis Schroeder, and Kosali I. Simon. 2005. "Welfare Reform and the Health Insurance Coverage of Women and Children." *Frontiers in Health Policy Research*, 8. Berkeley Electronic Press. Available at http://www.bepress.com/fhep/8/5/.

Chase-Lansdale, P. Lindsay, Robert A. Moffitt, Brenda J. Lohman, Andrew J. Cherlin, Rebekah Levine Coley, Laura D. Pittman, Jennifer Roff,and Elizabeth Votruba-Drzal. 2003. "Mothers' Transitions from Welfare to Work and the Well-Being of Preschoolers and Adolescents." *Science*, 299:1548–1552.

Cherlin, Andrew J., and Paula Fomby. 2004. "Welfare, Work and Changes in Mothers' Living Arrangements in Low-Income Families." *Population Research and Policy Review*, 23:543–565.

Coley, Rebekah Levine, Brenda J. Lohman, Elizabeth Votruba-Drzal, Laura D. Pittman, and P. Lindsay Chase-Lansdale. 2007. "Maternal Functioning, Time, and Money: The World of Work and Welfare." *Children and Youth Services Review*, 29:721–741.

Danielson, Caroline, and Jacob Alex Klerman. 2006. "Why Did the Food Stamp Caseload Decline (and Rise)? Effects of Policies and the Economy." Institute for Research on Poverty Discussion Paper #1316–06. Madison, WI: IRP.

Danziger, Sandra K., Mary Corcoran, Sheldon Danziger, Colleen Heflin, Ariel Kalil, Judith Levine, Daniel Rosen, Kristin Seefeldt, Kristine Siefert, and Richard Tolman. 2000. "Barriers to the Employment of Welfare Recipients," in *Prosperity for All? The Economic Boom and African Americans*. Robert Cherry and William Rogers, eds. New York: Russell Sage, 239–272.

DeLeire, Thomas, Judith A. Levine, and Helen Levy. 2006. "Is Welfare Reform Responsible for Low-Skilled Women's Declining Health Insurance Coverage in the 1990s?" *Journal of Human Resources*, 41:495–528.

Duncan, Greg J., and Jeanne Brooks-Gunn. 1997. *Consequences of Growing Up Poor*. New York: Russell Sage.

Dunifon, Rachel, Ariel Kalil, and Ashish Bajracharya. 2005. "Maternal Working Conditions and Child Well-Being in Welfare-Leaving Families." *Developmental Psychology*, 41:851–859.

Dyke, Andrew, Carolyn J. Heinrich, Peter R. Mueser, Kenneth R. Troske, and Kyung-Seong Jeon. 2006. "The Effects of Welfare-to-Work Program Activities on Labor Market Outcomes." *Journal of Labor Economics*, 24:567–607.

Fang, Hanming, and Michael P. Keane. 2004. "Assessing the Impact of Welfare Reform on Single Mothers." *Brookings Papers on Economic Activity*, 1–116.

Fitzgerald, John M., and David C. Ribar. 2004. "Transitions in Welfare Participation and Female Headship." *Population Research and Policy Review*, 23:641–670.

Fording, Richard, Sanford F. Schram, and Joe Soss. 2007. "Devolution, Discretion, and Effect of Local Political Values on TANF Sanctioning." *Social Service Review*, 81:285–316.

Gennetian, Lisa A., Danielle A. Crosby, Aletha C. Huston, and Edward D. Lowe. 2004. "Can Child Care Assistance in Welfare and Employment Programs Support the Employment of Low-Income Families?" *Journal of Policy Analysis and Management*, 23:723–743.

Gregg, Paul, Jane Waldfogel, and Elizabeth Washbrook. 2006. "Expenditure Patterns Post–Welfare Reform in the UK: Are Low-Income Families Starting to Catch Up?" *Labour Economics*, 13:721–746.

Grogger, Jeffrey. 2004a. "Time Limits and Welfare Use." *Journal of Human Resources*, 39:405–424.

———. 2004b. "Welfare Transitions in the 1990s: The Economy, Welfare Policy and the EITC." *Journal of Policy Analysis and Management*, 23:671–695.

Grogger, Jeffrey, and Lynn A. Karoly. 2005. *Welfare Reform: Effects of a Decade of Change*. Cambridge, MA: Harvard University Press.

Gundersen, Craig, and James P. Ziliak. 2004. "Poverty and Macroeconomic Performance Across Space, Race, and Family Structure." *Demography*, 41:61–86.

Haider, Steven J., Alison Jacknowitz, and Robert F. Schoeni. 2003. "Welfare Work Requirements and Child Well-Being: Evidence from the Effects on Breast-Feeding." *Demography*, 40:479–497.

Haider, Steven J., Robert F. Schoeni, Yuhua Bao, and Caroline Danielson. 2004. "Immigrants, Welfare Reform, and the Economy." *Journal of Policy Analysis and Management*, 23:745–764.

Hanratty, Maria J. 2006. "Has the Food Stamp Program Become More Accessible? Impacts of Recent Changes in Report Requirements and Asset Eligibility Limits." *Journal of Policy Analysis and Management*, 25:603–621.

Hao, Lingxin, and Andrew J. Cherlin. 2004. "Welfare Reform and Teenage Pregnancy, Childbirth, and School Dropout." *Journal of Marriage and the Family*, 66:179–194.

Holl, Jane L., Kristin Shook Slack, and Amy Bush Stevens. 2005. "Welfare Reform and Health Insurance: Consequences for Parents." *American Journal of Public Health*, 95:279–285.

Huang, Chien-Chung, Irwin Garfinkel, and Jane Waldfogel. 2004. "Child Support Enforcement and Welfare Caseloads." *Journal of Human Resources*, 39:108–134.

Hurst, Erik, and James P. Ziliak. 2006. "Do Welfare Asset Limits Affect Household Saving? Evidence from Welfare Reform." *Journal of Human Resources*, 41:46–71.

Johnson, Rucker C., and Mary E. Corcoran. 2003. "The Road to Economic Self-Sufficiency: Job Quality and Job Transition Patterns after Welfare Reform." *Journal of Policy Analysis and Management*, 22:616–639.

Joyce, Theodore, Robert Kaestner, and Sanders Korenman. 2003. "Welfare Reform and Non-Marital Fertility in the 1990s: Evidence from Birth Records." *Advances in Economic Analysis and Policy*, 3. Available at http://www.bepress.com/bejeap/advances.

Kaestner, Robert, and Neeraj Kaushal. 2003. "Welfare Reform and Health Insurance Coverage of Low-Income Families." *Journal of Health Economics*, 22:959–981.

Kaestner, Robert, Sanders Korenman, and June O'Neill. 2003. "Has Welfare Reform Changed Teenage Behaviors?" *Journal of Policy Analysis and Management*, 22:225–248.

Kaestner, Robert, and Won Chan Lee. 2005. "The Effect of Welfare Reform on Prenatal Care and Birth Weight." *Health Economics*, 14:497–511.

Kaestner, Robert, and Elizabeth Tarlov. 2006. "Changes in the Welfare Caseload and the Health of Low-Educated Mothers." *Journal of Policy Analysis and Management*, 25:623–643.

Kalil, Ariel, Kristin S. Seefeldt, and Hui-chen Wang. 2002. "Sanctions and Material Hardship Under TANF." *Social Service Review*, 76:642–662.

Kaushal, Neeraj, Qin Gao, and Jane Waldfogel. 2007. "Welfare Reform and Family Expenditures on Children." *Social Service Review*, 81: 369–396.

Knab, Jean Tansy, Sarah McLanahan, and Irv Garfinkel. 2008. "The Effects of Welfare and Child Support Policies on Maternal Health and Wellbeing," in *Making Americans Healthier: Social and Economic Policy as Health Policy*. Robert F. Schoeni, James S. House, George A. Kaplan, and Harold Pollack, eds. New York: Russell Sage, 281–306.

Lee, Bong Joo, Kristen S. Slack, and Dan A. Lewis. 2004. "Are Welfare Sanctions Working as Intended? Welfare Receipt, Work Activity, and Material Hardship among TANF-Recipient Families." *Social Service Review*, 78:370–403.

Looney, Adam. 2005. "The Effects of Welfare Reform and Related Policies on Single Mothers' Welfare Use and Employment." Federal Reserve Board of Governors, Finance and Economics Discussion Series 2004–45, Washington, DC: Federal Reserve Board.

Lopoo, Leonard M., and Thomas DeLeire. 2006. "Did Welfare Reform Influence the Fertility of Young Teens?" *Journal of Policy Analysis and Management*, 25:275–295.

Meara, Ellen, and Richard G. Frank. 2006. "Welfare Reform, Work Requirements, and Employment Barriers." National Bureau of Economic Research Working Paper 12480. Cambridge, MA: NBER.

Meyer, Bruce D., and Dan T. Rosenbaum. 2001. "Welfare, the Earned Income Tax Credit, and the Labor Supply of Single Mothers." *Quarterly Journal of Economics*, 116:1063–1114.

Meyer, Bruce D., and James X. Sullivan. 2006. "Consumption, Income and Material Well-Being After Welfare Reform." National Bureau of Economic Research Working Paper 11976. Cambridge, MA: NBER.

Miller, Amalia R., and Lei Zhang. 2007. "The Effects of Welfare Reform on the Academic on the Academic Performance of Children in Low-Income Households." Unpublished paper.

Moffitt, Robert A. 2003. "The Temporary Assistance for Needy Families Program," in *Means-Tested Transfer Programs in the United States*. Robert A. Moffitt, ed. Chicago: University of Chicago Press, 291–364.

Osborne, Cynthia, and Jean Knab. 2007. "Work, Welfare, and Young Children's Health and Behavior in the Fragile Families and Child Wellbeing Study." *Children and Youth Services Review*, 29:762–781.

Pavetti, LaDonna A., Michelle K. Derr, and Heather Hesketh. 2003. "Review of Sanction Policies and Research Studies." Report submitted to the Department of Health and Human Services, Office of the Assistant Secretary for Planning and Evaluation. Washington, DC: Mathematica Policy Research.

Pavetti, LaDonna A., and Jacqueline Kauff. 2006. "When Five Years Is Not Enough: Identifying and Addressing the Needs of Families Nearing the TANF Time Limit in Ramsey County, Minnesota." Lessons from the Field series. Princeton, NJ: Mathematica Policy Research.

Schmidt, Lucie, and Purvi Sevak. 2004. "AFDC, SSI, and Welfare Reform Aggressiveness: Caseload Reductions vs. Caseload Shifting." *Journal of Human Resources*, 39:792–812.

Seefeldt, Kristin S., and Sean M. Orzol. 2005. "Watching the Clock Tick: Factors Associated with TANF Accumulation." *Social Work Research*, 29:215–229.

Slack, Kristen Shook, Jane L. Holl, Joan Yoo, Laura B. Amsden, Emily Collins, and Kerry Bolger. 2007. "Welfare, Work, and Health Care Access Predictors of Low-Income Children's Physical Health Outcomes." *Children and Youth Service Review*, 29: 782–801.

Slack, Kristen Shook, Katherine Magnuson, Lawrence Berger, Joan Yoo, Rebekah Levine Coley, Rachel Dunifon, Amy Dworsky, Ariel Kalil, Jean Knab, Brenda J. Lohman, and Cynthia Osborne. 2007. "Family Economic Well-Being Following the 1996 Welfare Reform: Trend Data from Five Non-Experimental Panel Studies." *Children and Youth Services Review*, 29:698–720.

Smolensky, Eugene, and Jennifer Appleton Grootman, eds. 2003. Chapter 7. *Working Families and Growing Kids: Caring for Children and Adolescents*. Washington, DC: National Academies Press.

Sullivan, James X. 2006. "Welfare Reform, Saving, and Vehicle Ownership: Do Asset Limits and Vehicle Exemptions Matter?" *Journal of Human Resources*, 41:72–105.

Tekin, Erdal. 2005. "Child Care Subsidy Receipt, Employment, and Child Care Choices of Single Mothers." *Economic Letters*, 89: 1–6.

Turner, Lesley J., Sheldon Danziger, and Kristin S. Seefeldt. 2006 "Failing the Transition from Welfare to Work: Women Chronically Disconnected from Employment and Cash Welfare." *Social Science Quarterly*, 87:227–249.

Waldfogel, Jane. 2007. "Welfare Reforms and Child Well-Being in the US and the UK." *Swedish Economic Policy Review*, 14:137–168.

Witte, Ann Dryden, and Magaly Queralt. 2003. "Impacts of Eligibility Expansions and Provider Reimbursement Rate Increases on Child Care Subsidy Take-up Rates, Welfare Use and Work." National Bureau of Economic Research Working Paper 9693. Cambridge, MA: NBER.

Wu, Chi-Fang, Maria Cancian, Daniel R. Meyer, and Geoffrey L. Wallace. 2006. "How Do Welfare Sanctions Work?" *Social Work Research*, 30:33–50.

TWO

Welfare Reform and the Level and Composition of Income

Christopher Bollinger, Luis Gonzalez, and James P. Ziliak

I. Introduction

The Personal Responsibility and Work Opportunity Reconciliation Act (PRWORA) of 1996 had many goals, not least of which was ending dependence on government benefits through promotion of work. The new welfare program was expected to work in conjunction with the Earned Income Tax Credit (EITC), whose expanded generosity in the early 1990s increased the incentive for low-income families to enter the labor force. A significant body of research was spawned in the wake of welfare reform and EITC expansions, but most of the analyses have relied on data and outcomes prior to 2000 (Grogger and Karoly 2005; Hotz and Scholz 2003), and research on interactions between the macroeconomy and social policy reforms on income levels, as well as on the distribution of income, is scarce (Meyer and Sullivan 2006; Mills, Alwang, and Hazarika 2001; Schoeni and Blank 2000). In this chapter we estimate how welfare reform, the macroeconomy, and the EITC affected the level and composition of income across the distribution of single-mother families.

The target of welfare reform was low-income single mothers, as this demographic group historically comprised over 90 percent of the caseload. Although the typical (noncensored) spell on Aid to Families with Dependent Children (AFDC) for single mothers was only about eight months (Blank and Ruggles 1996), the public perception of long-term dependence and intergenerational transmission was widespread and not altogether false from a lifetime perspective (Blank 1997). This perception spurred policymakers, first

We thank Peter Gottschalk and seminar participants at the University of Kentucky Center for Poverty Research conference "Ten Years After: Evaluating the Long-Term Effects of Welfare Reform on Children, Families, Welfare, and Work" and at the Upjohn Institute for helpful comments on an earlier draft.

at the state level with waivers and then at the federal level with PRWORA, to construct a new program that not only discourages long-term use via the five-year federal lifetime limit on benefit receipt but also discourages entry into the program altogether via diversion payments and work requirements (Grogger, Haider, and Klerman 2003). The Temporary Assistance for Needy Families (TANF) program, unlike AFDC, focuses less on providing cash benefits than on providing in-kind assistance. Indeed, nearly 70 percent of TANF funds are spent on in-kind transfers and 30 percent on cash, the direct opposite of the former AFDC program (Chapter Ten, this volume). As a consequence of the policy lens on single mothers, most welfare reform research has been directed at understanding the consequences of the legislation for single mothers.

In a widely publicized study, Primus et al. (1999) examined changes in the earnings and income of female-headed households in the periods 1993–1995 and 1995–1997 and found that disposable income in the lowest quintile rose from 1993 to 1995 during a period of rapid economic growth (and state experiments with welfare waivers) but then fell an average of $580 after passage of PRWORA. While the authors attribute more than three-fourths of the income decline to declines in cash-assistance and food stamp income, it is not possible to conclude that welfare reform per se is the reason for the income declines because the authors fail to control for other factors that might have affected earnings for this subpopulation, such as the macroeconomy. Moffitt (1999) provides a more rigorous analysis of the effect of welfare reform on the earnings of female-headed families and concludes that in the period leading up to PRWORA (1977–1995), the state-specific welfare waivers led to an average increase in earnings of $274, although there was no significant increase in the earnings of women with less than a high school degree.

Schoeni and Blank (2000) update and extend the analysis of Moffitt (1999) both to 1998 and to other outcomes such as poverty status and family structure. Unlike Moffitt, they find a significant welfare-reform-induced increase in personal and family earnings for women with less than a high school education in the pre-PRWORA period; however, there is no additional increase after the passage of PRWORA. They do find strong evidence that welfare reform both in the waiver period and in the TANF period reduced the incidence of poverty for the subpopulation of less-skilled women, which is broadly corroborated in Gundersen and Ziliak (2004). These results also appear to be broadly consistent with several welfare "leaver" studies such as Danziger et al. (1999) and Cancian et al. (2000), although the latter emphasize acute postwelfare income declines among women with substantial barriers to employment such as mental health problems and drug dependency.

Grogger (2003) used data from the 1979–1999 waves of the Current Population Survey (CPS) to estimate whether and to what extent time limits affected the outcomes of female-headed families. He exploited the fact that families with young children are more likely to be affected by short time limits because of a longer eligibility horizon, and found that time limits reduced welfare use and raised employment but had no discernible impact on earnings or income. In a break from most papers in the literature, Meyer and Rosenbaum (2001) adopt a quasi-structural approach to model the effect of the tax and transfer system on the employment of single mothers between 1984 and 1995. Although they do find some evidence that waivers encouraged employment, the striking conclusion of their analysis is that expansions in the EITC dominated all other policy reforms in the 1990s and accounted for about 60 percent of the rise in labor force participation of single mothers in the mid-1990s.

In this chapter, we use data from the 1980–2005 waves (1979–2004 calendar years) of the March Annual Social and Economic Study of the CPS to update the previous literature on single-mother families by incorporating data through the first decade of welfare reform and to extend the literature in two important directions. First, many in the research community believed that the strong macroeconomy of the late 1990s not only had a direct positive effect on employment and earnings of low-skilled workers, it also had the secondary effect of fostering the transition from welfare to work. That is, state and federal efforts to implement welfare reform were aided by the fact that jobs that historically were absent for this demographic group existed in abundance in the late 1990s. The literature has been hindered from identifying this effect because the strong growth of the 1990s was shared by all states, thus limiting the cross-state variation in economic conditions needed to identify the interaction between the economy and policy. With the onset of the 2001 recession and the subsequent recovery, it is now possible to exploit cross-state over-time variation in the business cycle to aid in identifying the effect of interactions between the economy and welfare reform on income and earnings.[1]

The second extension we consider is estimating heterogeneous effects of welfare reform, the macroeconomy, and EITC expansions on income and earnings at various points of the income and earnings distributions. Bitler,

---

[1] A recent paper by Herbst (2008) examines interactions between welfare reform and the economy on employment, confirming the widespread conjecture that a strong economy accommodates welfare reform. Our project differs from Herbst's by our focus on income and earnings and by the fact that we examine heterogeneous effects of welfare reform, the macroeconomy, and the EITC across the income distribution.

Gelbach, and Hoynes (2006) stress the importance of heterogeneous treatment effects in the evaluation of welfare reform because heterogeneous effects are predicted by the canonical model of labor supply and due to interest in the distributional consequences of major social policy reforms. Virtually all research on welfare reform and the EITC has focused on average impacts, and while this frequently is of first-order interest to program evaluation, it limits our understanding of program effects at other points of the distribution.[2] Bitler et al. use data from a random assignment experiment in Connecticut to examine heterogeneous treatment effects because of concerns that TANF was implemented both in a relatively short time period (about 18 months) and in a period of strong macroeconomic growth. As argued previously, with the added business cycle variation induced by the 2001 recession, it is possible to identify heterogeneous effects of welfare reform in nationally representative samples by interacting policy changes with the macroeconomy. This allows us to examine whether the results of Bitler et al. are generalizable, and to our knowledge it also provides a first test of heterogeneous effects of the EITC on income and earnings distributions.

Our results show that TANF raised disposable incomes an average of 8 percent among higher-skilled mothers, and raised earnings among low-skilled mothers in the lower half of the distribution by as much as 20 percent, but also resulted in a significant equal-sized loss of after-tax total income among the low-skilled. Strong local economies in the mid-1990s that fostered income and earnings gains among the less skilled accommodated welfare waivers. The EITC expansions of the 1990s boosted before-tax earnings across the earnings distribution, especially for the low-skilled in the bottom half of the distribution, but also resulted in significant losses of total income for the low-skilled. The earnings gains among the low-skilled a decade after the implementation of TANF and expansions of the EITC have been more than offset by losses in transfer income and have left the most vulnerable single mothers either running in place or falling behind.

---

[2]   Mills et al. (2001) use nonparametric density reweighting techniques to compare the single-mother family income distribution in 1993 to that in 1999, and their counterfactual experiments suggests that most of the income gains in that six-year period were from strong economic conditions and not welfare reform. Schoeni and Blank (2000) compare the effects of waivers and TANF across education groups at the 20th and 50th percentiles of family income and find that waivers did not alter the distribution of income but that TANF raised incomes at the 50th percentile while leaving those at the 20th percentile unchanged. Our distributional analysis expands on theirs by including seven more years of data, interactions between welfare reform and the economy, the EITC, and more points of the distribution.

II. Data

The data come from the 1980–2005 waves of the March Annual Social and Economic Study of the CPS. The unit of observation is single-female family heads between the ages of 16 and 54 with dependent children present under the age of 18.[3] Single heads include never-married women as well as those divorced, separated, or widowed. The mothers are allocated to 13 different five-year date-of-birth cohorts (starting in 1919 and ending in 1983) and, within each birth cohort, to three separate education groups—less than high school, high school graduate, and more than high school—yielding 39 separate birth-education cohorts. The five birth cohorts from 1949 to 1963 provide complete information over the entire sample period, but the earlier and later cohorts only provide partial information for identification much like the information one would find in a standard unbalanced panel of families. Because the consistency of the grouping estimator to be described is based in part on the number of observations per cell being large, we follow Blundell, Duncan, and Meghir (1998) and drop cohort-education cells with fewer than 50 observations.

Our analysis focuses primarily on disposable family income and its components, especially labor-market earnings. Disposable income is gross income less net tax payments, where gross income is the sum of family income and the value of public food assistance programs. Family income is the same as that used in official Census Bureau calculations of poverty and inequality and includes earnings, Social Security (retirement, disability, and survivors benefits), Supplemental Security Income (SSI), Unemployment Insurance, workers' compensation, AFDC/TANF and other forms of public cash welfare, veterans' payments, pension income, rent/interest/dividend income, royalties, income from estates, trusts, educational assistance, alimony, child support, assistance from outside the household, and other income sources. We define earnings as total family earnings from wage and salary income, nonfarm self-employment, and farm self-employment. Because the Census Bureau defines a family as two or more persons related by birth, marriage, or adoption, family earnings contains the earnings of the mother as well as those of dependent children and other related adults such as a resident grandparent. It does not contain the earnings of cohabiting

---

[3]   Moffitt (1999) and Schoeni and Blank (2000) include the entire population of women because marital choices induced by welfare reform may endogenously affect the demographic composition of single mothers, while Grogger (2003) only admits single mothers. Although there is some evidence that marriage responds to welfare policies, it is limited in magnitude and scope (Edin and Kefalas 2006; Ellwood 2000; Fitzgerald and Ribar 2004).

partners or other nonfamily members in the household. We append to family income the (Census Bureau's) imputed dollar value of public food assistance programs, which include the Food Stamp Program and the National School Lunch and Breakfast Programs.

To construct after-tax total income, we subtract tax payments from gross income and add back refundable EITC income. Tax payments are the sum of federal, state, and payroll taxes that are estimated for each family in each year using the National Bureau of Economic Research (NBER) *TAXSIM* program. The *TAXSIM* module calculates federal, state, and payroll marginal tax rates and tax payments using basic information on labor income, taxable nonlabor income, dependents, and certain deductions such as property tax payments and child care expenses.[4] The federal and state taxes include the respective EITC code for each tax year and state, thus allowing for the possibility of negative tax payments. We assume that the family bears only the employee's share of the payroll tax rate.

In addition to total disposable income, we examine independently the trends in the components of income. Included in this are family earnings, EITC income, AFDC/TANF income, SSI income, Social Security Disability Insurance (SSDI) income, food stamp and school lunch income, and other nontransfer nonlabor income. The *TAXSIM* program provides only the EITC bundled within the federal and state tax functions and does not provide separate estimates. Thus, we rely on the Census Bureau's simulated EITC credit for our analysis of trends in EITC income. Other nonlabor income includes all other government and private transfers and nonlabor income as specified in the preceding definition of gross income.

If the respondent refuses to supply earnings or transfer information, then the Census Bureau uses a "hotdeck" imputation method to allocate income to those with missing data. Bollinger and Hirsch (2006) argue that including allocated data generally leads to an attenuation bias on estimated regression coefficients based on allocated data. Hence, we follow their recommendation and drop those mothers with allocated earnings or transfer income. In addition, 0.6 percent of the remaining sample has negative or zero values for total income, and we drop these observations. All income sources are deflated by the personal consumption expenditure deflator with the 2005 base year. The total number of observations is 94,939 single-female-headed families.

---

[4] The CPS does not have information on certain inputs to the *TAXSIM* program such as annual rental payments, child care expenses, or other itemized deductions. We set these values to zero when calculating the tax liability.

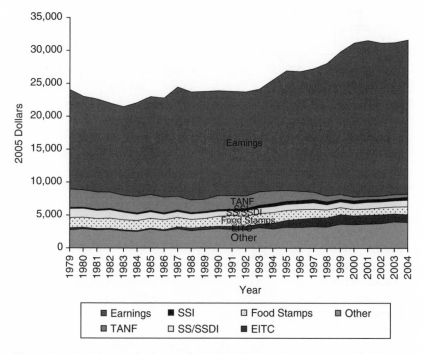

Figure 2.1. Mean Income by Source for Single Mothers, Ages 16 to 54, All Education Levels

III. Trends in the Level and Composition of Income, 1979–2004

We begin with a depiction of trends in income levels and composition. Part of the observed trends to be described is a mechanical artifact of the structure of transfer programs. That is, the programs are income conditioned and tax away benefits as other income sources increase. This means that as earnings rise, benefits from TANF, food stamps, and SSI necessarily fall (EITC benefits first rise but then fall with earnings). The other part of the observed trends is a behavioral response to changes in economic conditions, social policies, and possible preferences concerning work and welfare. In this section we do not make any claims about causal factors underlying the observed changes; we simply document facts.

In Figure 2.1 and Table 2.1 we show average income levels for all single mothers pooled together. The figure shows pretax income by source plus food stamps and the EITC, while the table shows the same data plus after-tax total income inclusive of food stamps. Through the 1980s and into the mid-1990s, average real disposable income of single mothers was

Table 2.1. *Average income levels of single mothers ages 16–54, by source and year*

Variable name	1980	1985	1990	1995	2000	2004
Disposable Income	$20,159	$19,741	$20,928	$23,310	$26,818	$28,083
Earnings	14,214	14,873	15,909	18,160	23,363	23,418
Earned Income Tax Credit (EITC)	231	155	380	1,041	1,346	1,156
Temporary Assistance for Needy Families (TANF)	2,643	2,436	2,147	1,652	591	448
Supplemental Security Income (SSI)	159	181	226	453	406	443
Social Security/ Disability Income (SSDI)	1,355	994	779	929	890	1,001
Food Stamp Program and School Lunch (FSP)	1,530	1,490	1,510	1,518	956	1,210
Other Nonlabor Income	2,921	2,884	2,961	3,189	3,603	3,955
Number of Observations	3,239	3,217	3,667	3,190	5,033	4,930

Note: All income sources are expressed in real 2005 dollars with the personal consumption expenditure deflator.

fairly constant at about $20,000, but beginning in the mid-1990s there was a sizable increase in average real income, reaching a peak of $32,000 before taxes in 2004 (and just over $28,000 after payroll, state, and federal tax payments, as shown in Table 2.1). The composition of income, however, shifted dramatically during this period. Labor market earnings at the mean grew substantially, and with the rise in employment and earnings and increased EITC program generosity, income from the EITC increased as well. During this period income from SSI also expanded, which could be due in part to both the *Zebley* decision—the 1990 Supreme Court ruling that liberalized child eligibility for SSI—and substitution from AFDC into SSI (Kubik 1999; Schmidt and Sevak 2004). Mean income from TANF fell 85 percent between 1979 and 2004, and income from food stamps fell 40 percent between the peak participation year of 1994 and the trough participation year of 2001.

Figure 2.2 reveals that much of the change in the level and composition of income in Figure 2.1 is driven by changes at the extensive margin of work and

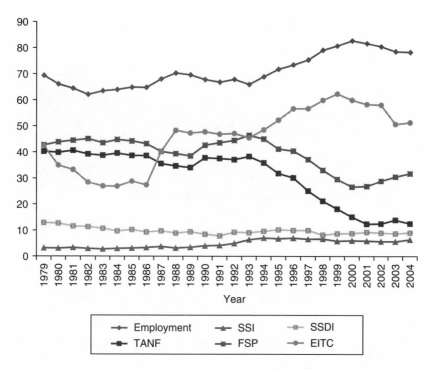

Figure 2.2. Participation Rates in Work and Welfare of Single Mothers, Ages 16 to 54

transfer program participation. The growth in earnings in the late 1980s and again in the late 1990s occurred in part because of strong growth in employment, which in turn led to substantial increases in participation in the EITC. In the late 1990s, the decline in TANF and food stamp income shown in Figure 2.1 was largely due to the massive declines in program participation. Although Food Stamp Program participation has rebounded in the 2000s, TANF participation remains fixed at its post–welfare reform low. Programs such as food stamps and SSI have benefit levels indexed to inflation, which means that changes in income from these sources undoubtedly come from changes in participation. As TANF benefits are largely fixed in nominal terms, except for periodic adjustments in some states, the decline in TANF income reflects both declines in real benefit generosity and program participation, though the latter is the key factor given the relatively low levels of inflation in recent years.

In Figures 2.3–2.5 we depict average pretax income sources plus the EITC by three broad groups of education attainment—less than high school, high school graduate with no college, and more than high school. Mean income among mothers with less than a high school education rose 24 percent in real

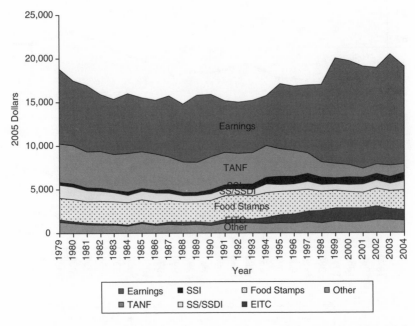

Figure 2.3. Mean Income by Source for Single Mothers, Ages 16 to 54, Less Than High School Education

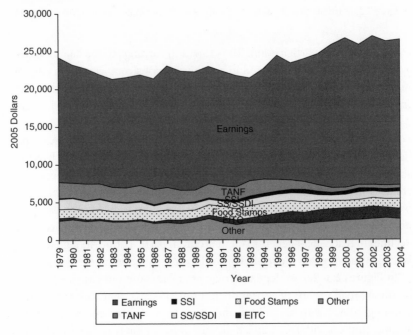

Figure 2.4. Mean Income by Source for Single Mothers, Ages 16 to 54, High School Education

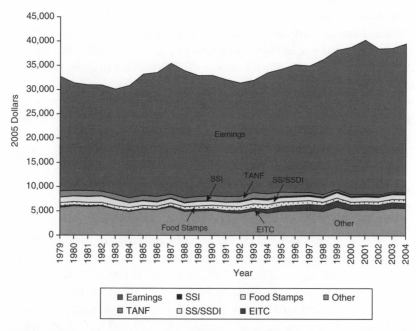

Figure 2.5. Mean Income by Source for Single Mothers, Ages 16 to 54, More Than High School Education

terms between 1993 and 2004, but this gain simply returned the average low-skilled mother to an income level comparable to that at the start of the period in 1979. Underlying these trends were large shifts away from TANF and food stamps and towards earnings and the EITC, along with some rise in average SSI income. Indeed, Figure 2.3 highlights the possible interaction of the business cycle and policy reforms for this demographic group, as earnings are pro-cyclical and transfers are countercyclical. However, social policy reforms can induce a trend shift in these basic relationships, a point that we will attempt to identify more precisely in the regression models to be presented.

It is clear from Figures 2.4 and 2.5 that as one moves up the education distribution the role of transfers falls substantially, even at the means, and is nearly nonexistent at the median (not depicted). An important exception, especially among single mothers with a high school education but no college, is the EITC (to a lesser extent, food stamps is an exception as well). Unlike mothers with less than high school, the high school and more than high school groups had real income growth of 9 and 20 percent at the means, respectively. This differential growth is consistent with the inequality literature that emphasizes divergence across education and labor-market experience groups (Lemieux 2006).

Because of evidence that deep poverty in the United States rose in the late 1990s and into the early 2000s (Ziliak 2006), in Figures 2.6–2.8 we take a closer look at changes in the level and composition of income at different points of the single-mother income distribution, with a particular emphasis on the bottom half of the distribution at the 10th, 25th, and 50th percentiles. As seen in Figure 2.6, changes in average income for mothers in the 10th percentile of the income distribution were quite substantial. Income at the 10th percentile ranged from about $6,800 to $8,200 between 1979 and 2004. For purposes of comparison, the poverty threshold for a family with one adult and two related children in real 2005 dollars is $15,735, so that the 10th percentile falls at about one-half of the poverty line for a three-person family. At the 10th percentile mothers rely quite heavily on transfers on average, but after welfare reform, fewer than half of mothers even at this low level of income are receiving any cash support from TANF, SSI, Social Security, and SSDI, or earnings except for a few years. It is important to highlight that some of these mothers may be receiving in-kind assistance from TANF, such as child care subsidies or transportation assistance, that is not recorded in the CPS. Indeed, because about 70 percent of TANF funds are now delivered as in-kind assistance, it is likely that the figures overstate the loss of support of TANF and may in fact reflect the change in delivery of welfare. That said, the figures underscore important changes in financial liquidity among the very poor.

Figures 2.7 and 2.8 depict changes in the mean level and composition of income at the first quartile and median of the income distribution. Real income grew by about one-third at the mean since the mid-1990s for mothers at the first quartile, and unlike the income of the broad group of mothers with less than a high school education, real income grew about 12 percent overall from 1979 to 2004 at the first quartile. This growth was driven by strong increases in earnings and the EITC. Trends in mean earnings and income at the 50th percentile in Figure 2.8 are nearly coincident with those of mothers with a high school degree, as seen in Figure 2.4, although there is some evidence of stronger earnings growth at the median in Figure 2.8. In general, though, the typical single mother with a high school degree falls at about the median of the single-mother income distribution.

IV. Interactions between Social Policy, Education, and the Business Cycle on the Level and Distribution of Income and Earnings

The figures show clearly that rising average real incomes beginning in the mid-1990s among single-mother families were driven by sizable gains in labor-market earnings, at least at the 25th percentile and higher. During

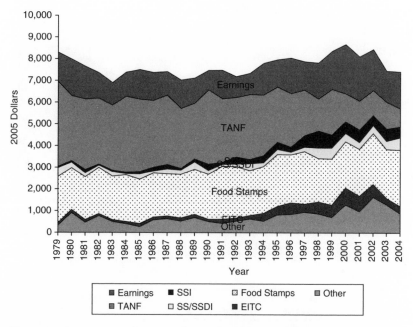

Figure 2.6. Mean Income by Source for Single Mothers, Ages 16–54, 10th Percentile of the Income Distribution

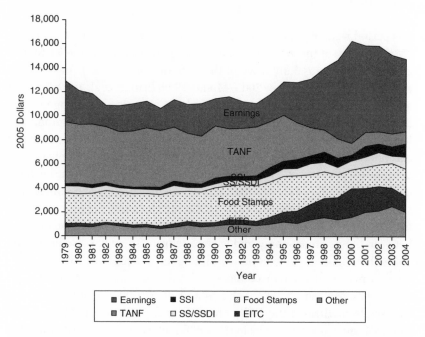

Figure 2.7. Mean Income by Source for Single Mothers, Ages 16 to 54, 25th Percentile of the Income Distribution

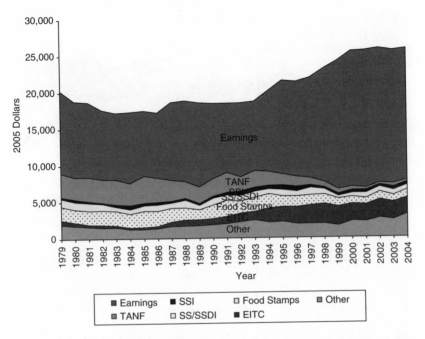

Figure 2.8. Mean Income by Source for Single Mothers, Ages 16 to 54, Median of the Income Distribution

this period welfare was reformed, the EITC was expanded, and the macro-economy grew at the fastest pace since the late 1960s. The evidence to date concerning the causal influence of these factors on disposable income and earnings is mixed (Grogger 2003; Moffitt 1999; Primus et al. 1999; Schoeni and Blank 2000), and little attention has been given to identifying interactions between welfare reform and the economy in general and among different skill groups. Moffitt (1999) and Schoeni and Blank (2000) are notable exceptions in that they examined interactions between welfare policies and educational attainment. Moffitt also discusses interactions with the business cycle, although he addresses the issue by simply splitting the sample into subperiods of the 1980s and early 1990s and does not exploit cross-state over-time variation in business cycle conditions with direct interactions between the macroeconomy and welfare reform. There has also been little research in national samples on identifying the heterogeneity of social policy reforms and the macroeconomy across the income distribution (Bitler et al. 2006; Mills et al. 2001; Schoeni and Blank 2000). Figure 2.6 shows that single-mothers at the 10th percentile of the income distribution had minimal gains in total income in the 1990s and have actually lost ground in the 2000s, suggesting that the economy and policies likely had differential effects on the economic status of single mothers, depending on the mothers' positions in the income distribution. We extend the literature both by estimating interactions between social policy, education, and the business cycle and by estimating the effects of policy interactions on income and earnings levels as well as their distributions.

The reduced-form models of income and earnings we estimate are given as

$$
\ln(y_{ijst}) = x_{it}\beta + z_{st}\gamma + (w_{st} * I(e < 12))\varphi + (w_{st} * c_{st})\eta \\
+ (w_{st} * I(e < 12) * c_{st})\chi + \varepsilon_{ijst}
$$
(1)

where $\ln(y_{ijst})$ is the natural log of real disposable income (or before-tax earnings) for person i, in cohort j, residing in state s, in time period t; x_{it} is a vector of observable characteristics of the single mother and her family; z_{st} is a vector of time-varying state-level variables including welfare policies w_{st} and business-cycle indicators c_{st}; $I(e < 12)$ is an indicator variable equal to 1 if the mother has fewer than 12 years of schooling, and thus $w_{st} * I(e < 12)$ is an interaction between welfare policies and education level; $w_{st} * c_{st}$ is an interaction between welfare policy and the business cycle; $w_{st} * I(e < 12) * c_{st}$ is a triple interaction among welfare reform, low education, and the business cycle; and ε_{ijst} is a five-way error component to capture multiple sources of unobserved heterogeneity. Prior to interacting the welfare indicators with the business cycle, we demean the business cycle measure, which implies that the coefficient on the direct effect of the cycle yields the average impact and the interactions yield deviations from the mean cycle.

The key policy coefficients of interest are γ, ϕ η, χ, which capture the effects on after-tax real income and before-tax earnings of welfare reform, the EITC, and the business cycle and interactions among the variables. We parameterize welfare reform policies in one of two ways. In the first case, we use one binary indicator for the waiver period that takes a value of 1 in the year the state implements any waiver from its AFDC program during the 1992–1996 period and a value of 0 before and after the 1992–1996 period. Our second binary indicator takes a value of 1 in the year that the state implemented its TANF program and 0 in the years leading up to TANF. This specification permits nonlinearity in the effects of waivers and TANF and has been a common approach in much of the welfare reform literature (Blank 2002). A downside of the latter, however, is the fact that states implemented their TANF programs within about 20 months of each other, which may inhibit identification. To this end, the interactions with skill level and business cycle conditions, each of which varies across states and time, will enhance identification of welfare reform. In terms of hypothesized directions of effects, we do not have strong priors on the direct effect of waivers and TANF on disposable income, but we do with regard to earnings. That is, we predict a positive effect of waivers and TANF on earnings because of the explicit work requirements as part of welfare reform, but the net effect on total income could go in either direction because it is possible that earnings gains could be more than offset by transfer losses such that total income falls. We do hypothesize that welfare reform has a stronger and more positive effect on earnings and income in states with more robust economic growth, as these states are more able to accommodate transitions from welfare to work.

The second approach to modeling welfare reform that we adopt is to use detailed characteristics of states' reform packages. Here we include indicators for whether or not the state has a time limit less than the federal level, exemptions from work requirements, sanctions on benefits for failing to adhere to program rules, expanded earnings disregards, family caps on benefit amounts, and work requirements. We also include an interaction between the time limit and whether there is a child under age six in the family. Grogger (2003) hypothesizes that mothers with young children are more likely to bank benefits for a "rainy day." If this is true, we should see that time limits have a more immediate positive effect on their earnings and income. A concern with the disaggregated waiver approach is that there is too much collinearity to identify individual policies; for this reason, we do not allow a nonlinearity pre- and post-TANF. That is, these policies are set equal to 1 in the year in which TANF was adopted, whether in the waiver period or in the TANF period, and remain equal to 1 for the rest of the sample period. We also do not interact these policies with education or the business cycle because of the unwieldy number of coefficients; this specification is best viewed as a check on the base case of no interactions.

The other major policy variable of interest is the EITC. The EITC is a federal policy, and in the absence of any variation aside from time series, it is not separately identifiable from general macroeconomic effects. Hotz, Mullin, and Scholz (2005), using California administrative data, exploit the fact that after passage of the Omnibus Budget Reconciliation Act (OBRA) in 1990, the size of the EITC credit varied by family size, depending on whether the filing unit had zero, one, or two or more qualifying children in the family. They note that using the across-family size over-time variation permits identification of the EITC on welfare use and employment.[5] We adopt a

---

[5] One could also use the fact that some states have supplemental EITC programs, but this source of variation has not been too successful (Gundersen and Ziliak 2004; Neumark and Wascher 2001).

similar strategy using data from the CPS where we assign to each family, depending on the number of qualifying children, the phase-in rate for the federal credit. The phase-in rate provides a first-dollar subsidy to low-wage workers, and thus we also interact the EITC subsidy rate with the indicator variable for less than high school education to allow for differential effects of the credit across skill levels. We expect the EITC to have a positive effect on earnings based on the positive employment effects identified in Meyer and Rosenbaum (2001) and Hotz et al. (2005), and we expect this effect to be enhanced among the low-skilled. The effect on income is less clear for the same reasons as welfare reform, namely, earnings gains induced in part by the expanded generosity of the EITC may result in lower disposable income if other income sources fall more than earnings and the EITC rise.

Our measures of business cycle activity include the state unemployment rate and the log of the state employment-to-population ratio. Although use of the unemployment rate is common in labor and macroeconomics, the unemployment rate is a convolution of factors affecting the supply side and the demand side of the labor market. Thus, employment per capita may serve as a better indicator of demand conditions, especially for low-income workers at the margins of being in and out of the labor force (Bartik and Eberts 1999; Hoynes 2000). Indeed, the NBER's Business Cycle Dating Committee uses the employment-to-population ratio as one of its metrics in favor of the unemployment rate. For comparison purposes, we conduct our analyses using both measures of the cycle.

Our specification of equation (1) also controls for observed and unobserved heterogeneity. The observed heterogeneity in x_{it} includes variables that are standard in human capital models, such as a quartic in age, the race of the mother, the number of dependent children under age 18, and an indicator variable that equals 1 if there are children under age six in the family. For the unobserved heterogeneity we specify a five-way error component as

$$\varepsilon_{ijst} = \alpha_j + \delta_s + \nu_{st} + \lambda_t + \xi_{it} \tag{2}$$

where α_j is a cohort-specific fixed effect, δ_s is a state-specific fixed effect, ν_{st} is a state-specific trend, λ_t is a year fixed effect, and ξ_{it} is a person-specific random error.

The cohort effects are modeled as indicator variables for whether the mother is in one of 39 five-year birth by education (less than high school, high school, more than high school) cohorts. The idea is that demand-side shocks such as skill-biased technological change may have differentially affected members of different birth cohorts and skill levels (Blundell et al. 1998), and including the birth-education cohort indicators controls for such heterogeneous influences on earnings and income. The baseline effect of education on income and earnings thus comes from the cohort fixed effects. The controls for state fixed effects and trends is fairly standard in the literature—the fixed effects to control for time-invariant (or at least very slow to change) differences across states such as weather, geography, preferences for welfare, education systems, and so on, and the trends to control for trending differences across states. There is some debate in the literature on whether state trends are appropriate because of the additional demands for identification placed on variables such as welfare policies—the policy reforms must affect outcomes over and above state fixed and trending effects—and thus we include specifications with and without state trends (Blank 2002). Finally, year effects control for common macroeconomic forces that affect all single mothers the same amount in a given year. With controls for the number of children and year effects, any estimated effect of the EITC, which varies by year and family size, should be due to the policy itself.

For estimation of the models of income levels we use ordinary least squares (OLS), and for the earnings models we use two-step sample selection methods (Heckman 1979). There is ample evidence that selection into the labor force among single mothers is not random, even after controlling for multiple forms of unobserved heterogeneity, thus rendering least squares estimation inconsistent for the earnings models. The two-step estimators allow for nonrandom sample selection, and this model is more robust than the Tobit model because of the proportionality constraint imposed by the Tobit model on the extensive and intensive margins.[6] To assist in identifying the participation margin for the two-step estimator, we include in the participation equations but not in the earnings equations family nonlabor income (total income less labor market earnings); the generosity of AFDC/TANF benefits, which vary by state, time, and family size; the generosity of food stamp benefits, which vary by time and family size; and the presence of young children. To identify the effects of the social policies on the distribution of income and

---

[6] An alternative to the Tobit model that breaks the proportionality link is the hurdle model. This model allows variables to have different effects on the extensive and intensive margins, but conditional on having earnings, it is assumed that log earnings are normally distributed. The two-step model assumes that log earnings are truncated normal. The difference between the two approaches is that the hurdle model assumes that the correlation between the extensive and intensive margins is zero, i.e., there is no selection on unobservables problem. We estimated the hurdle model, and the results are broadly consistent with the two-step estimates presented. We also attempted to use a less parametric estimator, namely, the censored least absolute deviations estimator, but we were unsuccessful in obtaining convergence, most likely due to the large number of parameters to be estimated and the fact that median earnings are zero in many years of the 1980s and early 1990s for large subpopulations of single mothers, especially the less skilled.

earnings among single mothers, we use the quantile regression estimator and estimate the models at the 20th, 30th, 40th, 50th, 60th, and 75th percentiles. We report asymptotic standard errors for the quantile regressions.[7]

A. Results on the Levels of Income and Earnings

In Table 2.2 we present the OLS estimates with robust standard errors for each of our disposable income specifications, where the first four columns include state-specific trends and the second four columns omit state trends. We focus the bulk of our discussion on results inclusive of state trends, except to highlight when important differences emerge. Indeed, the key difference in Table 2.2 between the models with state trends and those without such trends is the effect of the business cycle on disposable income. With state trends the disposable income of single mothers is unresponsive to changes in the unemployment rate but is strongly procyclical with respect to the log employment-population ratio. Just the opposite result obtains for models without state trends. It is surprising that the effect of the business cycle is so sensitive to the inclusion or absence of state trends, and in the case of the unemployment rate, it is suggestive that it offers no identifying variation for total income beyond a linear trend. Because the dependent variable is in logarithmic form, the coefficient on log employment per capita is an elasticity and implies that a 1 percent increase in the employment-population ratio leads to a 0.6 percent increase in disposable income. Note that the average growth rate in employment per capita across states and over the two-decade period from 1979 to 1999 was about 0.5 percent, so that within the sample this translates into about a 0.3 percent increase in real after-tax income.

In the base case of specification (1), with no interactions between welfare policies and the business cycle, the pre-TANF waivers increased mothers' incomes by about 2.2 percent relative to the incomes of mothers in states without waivers, and post-TANF disposable income was about 6 percent higher. Neither effect, however, is statistically significant at the usual levels. Likewise, expansions in the EITC do not significantly increase after-tax income on average and actually result in lower incomes among the less skilled. A 1 percentage point increase in the EITC subsidy rate lowers

---

[7]   We experimented with bootstrapped standard errors as well, but the combination of sample size and number of parameters made convergence unstable. In cases where we could compare asymptotic to bootstrapped standard errors, the asymptotic errors on the state policy variables were smaller, but in no case did the coefficient change from being significant with asymptotic errors to insignificant with bootstrap errors. The similarity is likely due in part to the logarithmic transformation of the dependent variable, which reduces the influence of heteroskedasticity.

Table 2.2. *The effect of welfare reform, the macroeconomy, and the EITC on log disposable income*

	With state-specific trends				Without state-specific trends			
Coefficient	(1)	(2)	(3)	(4)	(1)	(2)	(3)	(4)
Age	0.588***	0.596***	0.596***	0.587***	0.593***	0.601***	0.599***	0.593***
	(0.075)	(0.075)	(0.075)	(0.075)	(0.075)	(0.075)	(0.075)	(0.075)
Age Squared/100	−2.300***	−2.332***	−2.332***	−2.295***	−2.321***	−2.352***	−2.345***	−2.318***
	(0.327)	(0.326)	(0.327)	(0.326)	(0.327)	(0.326)	(0.327)	(0.326)
Age Cubed/1,000	0.414***	0.419***	0.419***	0.412***	0.418***	0.423***	0.422***	0.417***
	(0.062)	(0.062)	(0.062)	(0.062)	(0.062)	(0.062)	(0.062)	(0.062)
Age Quartic/10,000	−0.028***	−0.028***	−0.028***	−0.028***	−0.028***	−0.029***	−0.029***	−0.028***
	(0.004)	(0.004)	(0.004)	(0.004)	(0.004)	(0.004)	(0.004)	(0.004)
Race=White	0.105***	0.105***	0.105***	0.105***	0.106***	0.106***	0.106***	0.106***
	(0.006)	(0.006)	(0.006)	(0.006)	(0.006)	(0.006)	(0.006)	(0.006)
Have Child < 6 Yrs	−0.149***	−0.149***	−0.149***	−0.146***	−0.149***	−0.149***	−0.149***	−0.146***
	(0.007)	(0.007)	(0.007)	(0.007)	(0.007)	(0.007)	(0.007)	(0.007)
Number of Children	0.043***	0.043***	0.043***	0.043***	0.043***	0.043***	0.043***	0.043***
	(0.003)	(0.003)	(0.003)	(0.003)	(0.003)	(0.003)	(0.003)	(0.003)
Governor Is Democrat	−0.003	−0.004	−0.004	−0.005	0.002	0.001	−0.000	0.000
	(0.006)	(0.006)	(0.006)	(0.006)	(0.006)	(0.006)	(0.006)	(0.006)

	(1)	(2)	(3)	(4)	(5)	(6)	(7)	(8)
Unemployment Rate	−0.003	−0.002	−0.003	−0.003	−0.007**	−0.006**	−0.010***	−0.007**
	(0.004)	(0.004)	(0.004)	(0.004)	(0.003)	(0.003)	(0.003)	(0.003)
Log (Emp/Pop)	0.566***	0.533***	0.536***	0.570***	0.081	0.005	−0.085	0.083
	(0.174)	(0.176)	(0.181)	(0.180)	(0.127)	(0.131)	(0.136)	(0.132)
Pre–TANF Waiver	0.022	0.022	0.023		0.024	0.024	0.022	
	(0.015)	(0.017)	(0.017)		(0.015)	(0.016)	(0.017)	
TANF	0.059	0.087**	0.082**		0.069*	0.086**	0.078**	
	(0.039)	(0.041)	(0.040)		(0.039)	(0.040)	(0.039)	
EITC Subsidy Rate	0.127	0.097	0.094	0.142	0.135	0.108	0.108	0.149
	(0.156)	(0.156)	(0.156)	(0.157)	(0.156)	(0.155)	(0.155)	(0.157)
EITC × Educ <12	−0.604***	−0.407***	−0.380***	−0.605***	−0.609***	−0.414***	−0.389***	−0.610***
	(0.065)	(0.100)	(0.099)	(0.065)	(0.064)	(0.099)	(0.099)	(0.064)
Waiver × Educ <12		0.033	0.012			0.034	0.014	
		(0.032)	(0.032)			(0.032)	(0.032)	
TANF × Educ <12		−0.077**	−0.086***			−0.075**	−0.083***	
		(0.031)	(0.028)			(0.031)	(0.028)	
Waiver × UR		−0.001				−0.008		
		(0.009)				(0.009)		
TANF × UR		−0.002				−0.010		
		(0.009)				(0.006)		

(continued)

Table 2.2 *Continued*

Coefficient	With state-specific trends				Without state-specific trends			
	(1)	(2)	(3)	(4)	(1)	(2)	(3)	(4)
Waiver × UR × Educ <12		−0.053***				−0.053***		
		(0.016)				(0.016)		
TANF × UR × Educ <12		0.001				0.001		
		(0.013)				(0.013)		
Waiver × Log (Emp/Pop)			−0.074				0.182	
			(0.241)				(0.225)	
TANF × Log (Emp/Pop)			0.008				0.280**	
			(0.171)				(0.105)	
Waiver × Log (Emp/Pop) × Educ <12			1.454***				1.487***	
			(0.461)				(0.461)	
TANF × Log (Emp/Pop) × Educ <12			0.134				0.159	
			(0.235)				(0.234)	
Time Limit				0.011				0.004
				(0.029)				(0.022)
Time Limit × Child <6 Yrs				−0.010				−0.010
				(0.014)				(0.014)
Exemption				−0.037				−0.021
				(0.036)				(0.035)

80

	(1)	(2)	(3)	(4)	(5)	(6)	(7)	(8)
Sanctions	0.043				0.047			
	(0.034)				(0.033)			
Earnings Disregard		0.002				−0.004		
		(0.022)				(0.021)		
Family Cap			0.018				0.011	
			(0.019)				(0.011)	
Work Requirement				0.002				0.002
				(0.025)				(0.025)
Constant	4.371***	4.332***	4.349***	4.371***	4.021***	3.964***	3.959***	4.022***
	(0.634)	(0.634)	(0.634)	(0.634)	(0.627)	(0.626)	(0.626)	(0.627)
Observations	94,939	94,939	94,939	94,939	94,939	94,939	94,939	94,939
R-squared	0.20	0.20	0.20	0.20	0.20	0.20	0.20	0.20

Notes: Robust standard errors in parentheses. All models control for cohort fixed effects, year fixed effects, and state fixed effects.
***$p < 0.01$, **$p < 0.05$, *$p < 0.1$.

after-tax income among mothers with less than a high school education by about 0.5 percent (0.127–0.604 percent), suggesting that transitions into work induced by the expanded generosity of the EITC result in lower total income among the less skilled. This finding, which is most likely due to lower transfer payments, is robust across all specifications in Table 2.2 and is explored further in the distributional analysis presented later.

Specifications (2) and (3) admit interactions between the business cycle and welfare reform, as well as with education. With the added controls for heterogeneity, we identify an economically and statistically significant increase in disposable income of over 8 percent after passage of PRWORA. Shown by the equal-sized negative coefficient on the interaction between the TANF and less than high school variables, this effect is concentrated among mothers with 12 or more years of schooling. This result differs from that of Schoeni and Blank (2000, table 2.2), who find evidence of a positive waiver effect on family income among low-educated women but no effect of TANF on average income. There are several possible reasons for the discrepancy of our results, including our use of six additional years of data (Schoeni and Blank only have data up to one to two years after the implementation of TANF), our inclusion of interactions between the business cycle and welfare policies, our restriction to single mothers (they include all women), and our broader definition of income (they use before-tax income and exclude food stamps and school lunch). Schoeni and Blank do find that TANF raised incomes at the mean of the distribution and higher, so it is possible that with the passing of more years after PRWORA, we are able to identify a more significant mean impact (positive for the high-skilled and negative for the low-skilled).

The only evidence of interactions between welfare reform and the business cycle is during the waiver period, and this is concentrated among the low-skilled. During the waiver period, a low-skilled single mother living in a state with an unemployment rate 1 percentage point below the mean unemployment rate had after-tax income that was 5.3 percent higher. Likewise, that same mother, if residing in a state with log employment per capita 1 percentage point above the mean, had income that was 1.5 percent higher. Both estimates provide evidence that strong economic growth accommodated state experiments with welfare programs in the mid-1990s. There is no such corresponding evidence in the TANF era. Finally, we find no evidence that the mean impacts in specification (1) were masking important heterogeneity among types of welfare policies, as we find no statistically significant effects of time limits, exemptions, and the like in specification (4).

In Table 2.3 we present parallel estimates to the income models for before-tax earnings based on two-step selection estimators. The two-step

Table 2.3. *Two-step estimates of the effect of welfare reform, the macroeconomy, and the EITC on labor-market earnings*

Coefficient	With state-specific trends				Without state-specific trends			
	(1)	(2)	(3)	(4)	(1)	(2)	(3)	(4)
Age	0.864***	0.862***	0.864***	0.864***	0.874***	0.871***	0.869***	0.875***
	(0.122)	(0.123)	(0.123)	(0.122)	(0.123)	(0.123)	(0.123)	(0.123)
Age Squared	−3.061***	−3.051***	−3.062***	−3.061***	−3.104***	−3.091***	−3.083***	−3.106***
	(0.538)	(0.538)	(0.538)	(0.538)	(0.538)	(0.539)	(0.539)	(0.538)
Age Cubed	0.492***	0.490***	0.492***	0.491***	0.500***	0.497***	0.496***	0.500***
	(0.102)	(0.102)	(0.102)	(0.102)	(0.102)	(0.102)	(0.102)	(0.102)
Age Quartic	−0.030***	−0.030***	−0.030***	−0.030***	−0.031***	−0.030***	−0.030***	−0.030***
	(0.007)	(0.007)	(0.007)	(0.007)	(0.007)	(0.007)	(0.007)	(0.007)
Race = White	0.072***	0.072***	0.072***	0.072***	0.073***	0.073***	0.073***	0.073***
	(0.011)	(0.011)	(0.011)	(0.011)	(0.011)	(0.011)	(0.011)	(0.011)
Number of Children	−0.123***	−0.123***	−0.123***	−0.123***	−0.123***	−0.122***	−0.123***	−0.123***
	(0.007)	(0.007)	(0.007)	(0.007)	(0.007)	(0.007)	(0.007)	(0.007)
Governor Is Democrat	−0.011	−0.011	−0.010	−0.012	−0.000	0.001	−0.001	−0.004
	(0.011)	(0.012)	(0.012)	(0.012)	(0.010)	(0.010)	(0.010)	(0.010)
Unemployment Rate	−0.004	−0.001	−0.003	−0.004	−0.004	−0.004	−0.009	−0.002
	(0.007)	(0.007)	(0.007)	(0.007)	(0.006)	(0.006)	(0.006)	(0.006)

(continued)

Table 2.3. *Continued*

Coefficient	With state-specific trends				Without state-specific trends			
	(1)	(2)	(3)	(4)	(1)	(2)	(3)	(4)
Log (Emp/Pop)	1.039***	1.054***	1.165***	1.143***	0.713***	0.617**	0.539**	0.913***
	(0.329)	(0.334)	(0.346)	(0.341)	(0.235)	(0.240)	(0.250)	(0.244)
Pre-TANF Waiver	0.033	0.027	0.038		0.044	0.038	0.041	
	(0.029)	(0.032)	(0.032)		(0.029)	(0.032)	(0.032)	
TANF	−0.004	−0.036	0.006		0.009	−0.021	−0.008	
	(0.067)	(0.070)	(0.068)		(0.066)	(0.069)	(0.067)	
EITC Subsidy Rate	0.130	0.140	0.132	0.158	0.147	0.153	0.150	0.171
	(0.267)	(0.268)	(0.268)	(0.268)	(0.267)	(0.269)	(0.269)	(0.269)
EITC × Educ <12	−0.398***	−0.458**	−0.410**	−0.396***	−0.414***	−0.486**	−0.457**	−0.415***
	(0.125)	(0.205)	(0.204)	(0.125)	(0.125)	(0.205)	(0.204)	(0.125)
Waiver × Educ <12		0.043	0.015			0.045	0.022	
		(0.068)	(0.066)			(0.068)	(0.067)	
TANF × Educ <12		0.027	−0.001			0.036	0.011	
		(0.054)	(0.051)			(0.054)	(0.051)	
Waiver × UR		−0.003				−0.006		
		(0.017)				(0.016)		
TANF × UR		−0.027*				−0.023**		
		(0.014)				(0.010)		

84

Waiver × UR × Educ <12	−0.035	−0.036
	(0.033)	(0.033)
TANF × UR × Educ <12	0.013	0.016
	(0.017)	(0.017)
Waiver × Log(Emp/Pop)	−0.581	−0.159
	(0.475)	(0.450)
TANF × Log (Emp/Pop)	−0.244	0.408**
	(0.311)	(0.182)
Waiver × Log (Emp/Pop) × Educ <12	0.407	0.442
	(1.005)	(1.006)
TANF × Log (Emp/Pop) × Educ <12	0.016	0.056
	(0.363)	(0.362)
Time Limit	−0.111**	−0.061
	(0.053)	(0.040)
Time Limit × Child <6 Yrs	−0.009	−0.008
	(0.018)	(0.018)
Exemptions	−0.006	−0.011
	(0.069)	(0.068)
Sanctions	0.014	−0.006
	(0.066)	(0.065)

(continued)

Table 2.3. *Continued*

Coefficient	With state-specific trends				Without state-specific trends			
	(1)	(2)	(3)	(4)	(1)	(2)	(3)	(4)
Earnings Disregard				0.026				0.028
				(0.042)				(0.041)
Family Cap				0.037				0.068***
				(0.035)				(0.019)
Work Requirement				0.036				0.032
				(0.048)				(0.048)
Constant	2.269**	2.232**	2.330**	2.312**	1.842*	1.809*	1.820*	1.933*
	(1.020)	(1.021)	(1.021)	(1.021)	(1.013)	(1.014)	(1.014)	(1.014)
Observations	94,939	94,939	94,939	94,939	94,939	94,939	94,939	94,939
R-squared	.	.	.	.	.	.	.	.

Notes: Standard errors in parentheses. All models control for cohort fixed effects, year fixed effects, and state fixed effects.

*** $p < 0.01$, ** $p < 0.05$, * $p < 0.1$.

earnings estimates are similar to the income results in Table 2.2. The only business cycle indicator that affects earnings, conditional on being in the labor force, is the employment-population ratio. The mean impact of the EITC is zero and, perhaps surprisingly, is economically and statistically negative among the less skilled. In addition, welfare reform has little discernible effect on the intensive margin of earnings (although qualitatively, the effect of waivers on the less skilled is about 6 to 7 percent).[8] The welfare reform results are broadly consistent whether one examines the aggregated policy variables or the disaggregated variables, as in specification (4). The EITC effect is not inconsistent with labor supply theory in the presence of nonlinear budget constraints, although the results do suggest a fairly strong behavioral response among the less skilled. The distributional results to be discussed help clarify these mean effects.[9]

B. Results on the Distribution of Income and Earnings

The levels models, while admitting some observed and unobserved heterogeneity based on the skill level of the mother and on business cycle conditions, nonetheless provide estimates only at the means of the income and earnings distributions. Although there is not much guidance from the welfare reform and EITC literatures on how or whether the signs of the coefficients may change once we move away from the means of these distributions, we believe that the effects of the policies are likely to be heterogeneous across the distributions, as welfare dependence has historically been most concentrated in the lower tails. Moreover, the more highly educated may be better equipped to negotiate the various administrative challenges of applying for and maintaining benefit eligibility.[10] In Tables 2.4 and 2.5 we present at six different quantiles of the disposable income distribution results from our preferred specifications of Table 2.2, that is, specifications (3) and (4).

The results in Table 2.4 show that TANF had an economically and statistically significant effect on after-tax incomes of single mothers across

---

[8] In results not tabulated, we estimated the Lee (1984) sample selection model that admits deviations from linearity imposed by the Heckman method. The only result that changes is the statistical significance of the interaction between the EITC and less than a high school education.

[9] Schoeni and Blank (2000) estimate their models with and without zero earnings and likewise find no statistical evidence of waiver effects when zeros are omitted. They do not treat the zeros as possibly missing nonrandomly, as we do here.

[10] Ribar and Edelhoch (2008) show that over a third of participants in the Food Stamp Program in South Carolina lose benefits even though they remain eligible simply by failing to fill out the paperwork.

Table 2.4. *The effects of welfare reform, the macroeconomy, and the EITC across the distribution of log income*

Coefficient	Quantile					
	20th	30th	40th	50th	60th	75th
Age	0.812***	0.537***	0.522***	0.473***	0.378***	0.341***
	(0.083)	(0.064)	(0.053)	(0.053)	(0.051)	(0.055)
Age Squared	−3.242***	−2.089***	−2.006***	−1.765***	−1.345***	−1.197***
	(0.360)	(0.280)	(0.230)	(0.230)	(0.230)	(0.240)
Age Cubed	0.582***	0.375***	0.360***	0.311***	0.230***	0.206***
	(0.069)	(0.054)	(0.045)	(0.045)	(0.043)	(0.046)
Age Quartic	−0.039***	−0.026***	−0.025***	−0.021***	−0.015***	−0.014***
	(0.005)	(0.004)	(0.003)	(0.003)	(0.003)	(0.003)
Race = White	0.117***	0.123***	0.119***	0.120***	0.118***	0.114***
	(0.007)	(0.006)	(0.005)	(0.005)	(0.005)	(0.005)
Have Child < 6 Yrs	−0.172***	−0.152***	−0.126***	−0.106***	−0.087***	−0.065***
	(0.008)	(0.007)	(0.0053)	(0.005)	(0.005)	(0.005)
Number of Children	0.081***	0.060***	0.044***	0.032***	0.023***	0.014***
	(0.004)	(0.003)	(0.003)	(0.003)	(0.003)	(0.003)
Governor Is Democrat	−0.008	−0.011*	−0.008	−0.004	−0.008	0.004
	(0.008)	(0.006)	(0.005)	(0.005)	(0.005)	(0.005)
Unemployment Rate	−0.004	−0.009**	−0.004	−0.004	−0.002	−0.007**
	(0.005)	(0.004)	(0.003)	(0.003)	(0.003)	(0.003)
Log (Emp/Pop)	0.392	0.233	0.472***	0.613***	0.669***	0.458***
	(0.240)	(0.190)	(0.160)	(0.160)	(0.150)	(0.160)

	(1)	(2)	(3)	(4)	(5)	(6)
Pre–TANF Waiver	0.016	0.012	0.024	0.011	0.024	0.022
	(0.023)	(0.018)	(0.015)	(0.015)	(0.014)	(0.015)
TANF	0.069	0.076**	0.083***	0.068**	0.058*	0.053*
	(0.048)	(0.038)	(0.031)	(0.031)	(0.030)	(0.032)
EITC Subsidy Rate	-0.543***	-0.136	0.074	0.265**	0.460***	0.501***
	(0.190)	(0.150)	(0.120)	(0.120)	(0.120)	(0.120)
EITC × Educ <12	-0.486***	-0.585***	-0.657***	-0.659***	-0.563***	-0.448***
	(0.130)	(0.099)	(0.082)	(0.083)	(0.080)	(0.086)
Waiver × Educ <12	0.041	0.031	0.008	0.036	0.018	0.033
	(0.042)	(0.033)	(0.027)	(0.027)	(0.026)	(0.028)
TANF × Educ <12	-0.190***	-0.111***	-0.052**	-0.005	0.016	0.034
	(0.032)	(0.025)	(0.021)	(0.021)	(0.020)	(0.022)
Waiver × Log (Emp/Pop)	-0.174	-0.368	-0.427*	-0.396*	-0.173	-0.144
	(0.340)	(0.260)	(0.220)	(0.220)	(0.220)	(0.230)
TANF × Log (Emp/Pop)	-0.110	-0.092	-0.162	-0.210	-0.104	-0.014
	(0.220)	(0.170)	(0.140)	(0.140)	(0.140)	(0.150)
Waiver × Log (Emp/Pop) × Educ <12	1.072*	0.690	0.947**	0.967**	0.972**	1.318***
	(0.620)	(0.490)	(0.420)	(0.430)	(0.420)	(0.450)
TANF × Log (Emp/Pop) × Educ <12	0.125	0.404**	0.467***	0.402**	0.356**	0.509***
	(0.240)	(0.190)	(0.160)	(0.160)	(0.150)	(0.160)
Constant	1.653**	4.171***	4.456***	5.279***	6.139***	7.010***
	(0.680)	(0.530)	(0.440)	(0.440)	(0.430)	(0.450)
Observations	94,939	94,939	94,939	94,939	94,939	94,939

Notes: Standard errors in parentheses. All models control for cohort fixed effects, year fixed effects, and state fixed effects and trends.

*** $p < 0.01$, ** $p < 0.05$, * $p < 0.1$.

Table 2.5. *The effects of disaggregated welfare policies across the distribution of log income*

Coefficient	Quantile					
	20th	30th	40th	50th	60th	75th
Age	0.749***	0.528***	0.522***	0.469***	0.380***	0.339***
	(0.080)	(0.071)	(0.058)	(0.049)	(0.049)	(0.054)
Age Squared	−2.947***	−2.051***	−2.016***	−1.756***	−1.361***	−1.195***
	(0.350)	(0.310)	(0.250)	(0.220)	(0.220)	(0.240)
Age Cubed	0.523***	0.368***	0.363***	0.310***	0.235***	0.206***
	(0.067)	(0.060)	(0.049)	(0.042)	(0.041)	(0.046)
Age Quartic	−0.035***	−0.025***	−0.025***	−0.021***	−0.016***	−0.014***
	(0.005)	(0.004)	(0.003)	(0.003)	(0.003)	(0.003)
Race = White	0.117***	0.122***	0.119***	0.120***	0.117***	0.114***
	(0.007)	(0.006)	(0.005)	(0.004)	(0.004)	(0.005)
Have Child <6 Yrs	−0.162***	−0.153***	−0.132***	−0.116***	−0.0972***	−0.0792***
	(0.010)	(0.009)	(0.007)	(0.006)	(0.006)	(0.007)
Number of Children	0.081***	0.061***	0.045***	0.032***	0.024***	0.014***
	(0.004)	(0.003)	(0.003)	(0.002)	(0.002)	(0.003)
Governor Is Democrat	−0.011	−0.013*	−0.007	−0.006	−0.007	0.005
	(0.008)	(0.007)	(0.006)	(0.005)	(0.005)	(0.005)
Unemployment Rate	−0.004	−0.009**	−0.005	−0.005*	−0.003	−0.007**
	(0.008)	(0.004)	(0.003)	(0.003)	(0.003)	(0.003)
Log (Emp/Pop)	0.380	0.177	0.409**	0.593***	0.647***	0.497***
	(0.230)	(0.210)	(0.170)	(0.150)	(0.140)	(0.160)

	(1)	(2)	(3)	(4)	(5)	(6)
EITC Subsidy Rate	-0.362**	-0.149	0.066	0.218*	0.367***	0.466***
	(0.180)	(0.160)	(0.130)	(0.110)	(0.110)	(0.120)
EITC × Educ <12	-0.951***	-0.799***	-0.757***	-0.649***	-0.496***	-0.320***
	(0.077)	(0.068)	(0.056)	(0.048)	(0.047)	(0.052)
Time Limit	0.091**	0.063*	0.036	0.024	-0.001	-0.021
	(0.037)	(0.033)	(0.027)	(0.023)	(0.022)	(0.025)
Time Limit × Child <6 Yrs	-0.044***	0.004	0.017	0.031***	0.031***	0.038***
	(0.016)	(0.014)	(0.011)	(0.0096)	(0.0095)	(0.011)
Exemption	-0.105**	-0.081*	-0.04	-0.072**	-0.055*	-0.043
	(0.047)	(0.042)	(0.034)	(0.030)	(0.029)	(0.033)
Sanctions	0.036	0.034	0.022	0.040	0.057**	0.057*
	(0.046)	(0.041)	(0.034)	(0.029)	(0.029)	(0.032)
Earnings Disregard	0.022	0.020	0.017	0.013	-0.005	0.009
	(0.028)	(0.025)	(0.021)	(0.018)	(0.017)	(0.019)
Family Cap	0.018	0.009	-0.002	0.014	0.005	0.005
	(0.024)	(0.021)	(0.017)	(0.015)	(0.015)	(0.016)
Work Requirement	-0.020	-0.012	-0.001	0.006	0.021	0.003
	(0.032)	(0.029)	(0.024)	(0.020)	(0.020)	(0.022)
Constant	2.014***	4.118***	4.389***	5.321***	6.139***	7.091***
	(0.660)	(0.590)	(0.480)	(0.410)	(0.400)	(0.450)
Observations	94,939	94,939	94,939	94,939	94,939	94,939

Notes: Standard errors in parentheses. All models control for cohort fixed effects, year fixed effects, and state fixed effects and trends.

*** p < 0.01, **p < 0.05, *p < 0.1.

the distribution, yielding a direct, positive 5 to 8 percent gain among mothers with at least a high school diploma but a sizable income loss at the 20th and 30th percentiles (12 and 3.4 percent, respectively) among mothers with less than a high school education. Above the 20th percentile there is robust evidence that strong employment growth enhanced the positive income effects of TANF for the less skilled, although not enough to offset the negative effects of the reform at the 20th and 30th percentiles. There is qualitative evidence of a positive effect of waivers on income at all six points of the distribution, even among the less skilled, but the effects are not statistically different from zero. Likewise with the EITC, the evidence shows consistently that the less skilled suffer income losses relative to the more skilled, and it is not until the 75th percentile that the less skilled have income gains from an expanded EITC. Indeed, at the 20th percentile, single mothers at all skill levels suffer losses of after-tax income from the higher EITC, and it is not until the median of the distribution that skilled mothers (those with 12 or more years of schooling) obtain significant gains in after-tax income from the EITC. Although the EITC is designed to enhance the self-reliance of single mothers, it appears that many are "running in place" because of offsetting income losses from other sources.

In Table 2.5 we focus attention on the disaggregated welfare policy results. At the 20th and 30th percentiles stringent time limits led to higher income levels, perhaps because mothers in these states sought alternative income support (but not because of their own earnings, as shown later), but the effect of time limits fades quickly after the 30th percentile. The exception is if a child under age six is present where there is evidence of higher incomes at the median of the distribution and above. Note that Grogger's (2003) hypothesis that single mothers with young children are more likely to bank benefits in the presence of time limits is ambiguous with respect to total income because it is not known if the loss of transfers will be equaled or exceeded by gains from earnings and other income sources. The results in Table 2.5 suggest that the gains from possible benefit banking in the upper half of the distribution outweighed the losses. There is also evidence that exemptions and sanctions policies led to lower and higher incomes, respectively, at many points of the distribution. Some of these effects are not obvious from theory. Thus, we turn next to earnings models to examine whether the results are theory consistent with labor market earnings or whether the disaggregated policies are largely picking up noise.

In Tables 2.6 and 2.7 we report the quantile estimates of specifications (3) and (4) for the positive log earnings distribution. These models are best viewed as the distributional analogs to the two-step estimates in Table 2.3,

Table 2.6. *The effects of welfare reform, the macroeconomy, and the EITC across the distribution of log earnings*

	Quantile					
Coefficient	20th	30th	40th	50th	60th	75th
Age	1.144***	1.170***	1.129***	1.160***	1.158***	0.758***
	(0.210)	(0.140)	(0.110)	(0.0970)	(0.086)	(0.071)
Age Squared	−3.728***	−3.897***	−3.893***	−4.180***	−4.310***	−2.786***
	(0.910)	(0.630)	(0.500)	(0.430)	(0.380)	(0.310)
Age Cubed	0.548***	0.584***	0.609***	0.682***	0.725***	0.472***
	(0.170)	(0.120)	(0.094)	(0.081)	(0.071)	(0.060)
Age Quartic	−0.032***	−0.034***	−0.037***	−0.042***	−0.046***	−0.031***
	(0.012)	(0.008)	(0.007)	(0.006)	(0.005)	(0.004)
Race = White	0.191***	0.148***	0.115***	0.103***	0.097***	0.085***
	(0.018)	(0.012)	(0.010)	(0.008)	(0.007)	(0.006)
Have Child <6 Yrs	−0.162***	−0.100***	−0.063***	−0.044***	−0.022***	−0.008
	(0.020)	(0.014)	(0.011)	(0.009)	(0.008)	(0.007)
Number of Children	−0.312***	−0.255***	−0.212***	−0.176***	−0.142***	−0.108***
	(0.010)	(0.007)	(0.006)	(0.005)	(0.004)	(0.004)
Governor Is Democrat	−0.012	−0.017	−0.006	−0.001	0.003	0.005
	(0.019)	(0.013)	(0.011)	(0.009)	(0.008)	(0.007)

(continued)

Table 2.6. *Continued*

Coefficient	Quantile					
	20th	30th	40th	50th	60th	75th
Unemployment Rate	-0.027**	-0.008	-0.004	-0.003	-0.006	-0.006
	(0.012)	(0.008)	(0.006)	(0.005)	(0.005)	(0.004)
Log (Emp/Pop)	1.755***	1.460***	1.303***	1.094***	0.924***	0.744***
	(0.580)	(0.400)	(0.320)	(0.270)	(0.240)	(0.200)
Pre–TANF Waiver	0.061	0.058	0.056*	0.055**	0.050**	0.041**
	(0.055)	(0.037)	(0.029)	(0.025)	(0.022)	(0.018)
TANF	0.137	0.096	0.076	0.029	0.072	0.020
	(0.120)	(0.079)	(0.062)	(0.053)	(0.047)	(0.039)
EITC Subsidy Rate	2.477***	1.881***	1.616***	1.252***	0.927***	0.527***
	(0.450)	(0.310)	(0.240)	(0.210)	(0.180)	(0.150)
EITC × Educ <12	-0.153	0.0304	-0.143	-0.460***	-0.590***	-0.719***
	(0.360)	(0.250)	(0.190)	(0.160)	(0.150)	(0.120)
Waiver × Educ <12	0.179	0.090	0.121*	0.006	0.027	-0.054
	(0.120)	(0.080)	(0.063)	(0.053)	(0.047)	(0.039)
TANF × Educ <12	0.210**	0.233***	0.211***	0.138***	0.095***	0.090***
	(0.090)	(0.061)	(0.048)	(0.041)	(0.036)	(0.030)
Waiver × Log (Emp/Pop)	-1.540*	-1.182**	-0.924**	-0.836**	-0.183	-0.154
	(0.790)	(0.550)	(0.430)	(0.370)	(0.320)	(0.270)

TANF × Log (Emp/Pop)	−0.757	−0.168	−0.282	−0.134	0.0689	0.265
	(0.520)	(0.360)	(0.280)	(0.240)	(0.210)	(0.180)
Waiver × Log (Emp/Pop) × Educ <12	0.640	0.255	1.425	1.384*	1.629**	0.984*
	(1.670)	(1.190)	(0.940)	(0.800)	(0.710)	(0.580)
TANF × Log (Emp/Pop) × Educ <12	−0.411	−0.078	0.214	0.205	0.658***	0.519**
	(0.620)	(0.420)	(0.340)	(0.290)	(0.250)	(0.210)
Constant	−2.341	−2.424**	−1.673*	−0.900	−0.131	3.906***
	(1.730)	(1.200)	(0.940)	(0.810)	(0.710)	(0.590)
Observations	73,447	73,447	73,447	73,447	73,447	73,447

Notes: Standard errors in parentheses. All models control for cohort fixed effects, year fixed effects, and state fixed effects and trends.

*** $p < 0.01$, ** $p < 0.05$, * $p < 0.1$.

Table 2.7. *The effects of disaggregated welfare policies across the distribution of log earnings*

	Quantile					
Coefficient	20th	30th	40th	50th	60th	75th
Age	1.180***	1.239***	1.144***	1.150***	1.141***	0.745***
	(0.230)	(0.140)	(0.120)	(0.094)	(0.087)	(0.076)
Age Squared	-3.908***	-4.238***	-3.969***	-4.141***	-4.257***	-2.732***
	(1.000)	(0.600)	(0.520)	(0.410)	(0.380)	(0.340)
Age Cubed	0.585***	0.654***	0.624***	0.676***	0.719***	0.462***
	(0.190)	(0.110)	(0.098)	(0.078)	(0.072)	(0.064)
Age Quartic	-0.034***	-0.039***	-0.038***	-0.042***	-0.046***	-0.030***
	(0.013)	(0.008)	(0.007)	(0.005)	(0.005)	(0.004)
Race = White	0.189***	0.144***	0.114***	0.104***	0.096***	0.085***
	(0.020)	(0.012)	(0.010)	(0.008)	(0.007)	(0.007)
Have Child <6 Yrs	-0.214***	-0.130***	-0.081***	-0.058***	-0.035***	-0.016*
	(0.027)	(0.016)	(0.014)	(0.011)	(0.010)	(0.009)
Number of Children	-0.312***	-0.251***	-0.212***	-0.175***	-0.144***	-0.109***
	(0.011)	(0.007)	(0.006)	(0.005)	(0.004)	(0.004)
Governor Is Democrat	-0.014	-0.021	-0.011	-0.003	-0.001	0.003
	(0.022)	(0.013)	(0.011)	(0.009)	(0.008)	(0.007)

	(1)	(2)	(3)	(4)	(5)	(6)
Unemployment Rate	-0.028**	-0.010	-0.006	-0.004	-0.004	-0.006
	(0.013)	(0.008)	(0.007)	(0.005)	(0.005)	(0.004)
Log (Emp/Pop)	1.509**	1.331***	1.191***	1.060***	0.998***	0.921***
	(0.630)	(0.380)	(0.320)	(0.260)	(0.240)	(0.210)
EITC Subsidy Rate	2.261***	1.642***	1.499***	1.134***	0.894***	0.487***
	(0.490)	(0.300)	(0.250)	(0.200)	(0.190)	(0.160)
EITC × Educ <12	0.483**	0.844***	0.534***	-0.0235	-0.202**	-0.432***
	(0.230)	(0.140)	(0.120)	(0.096)	(0.088)	(0.078)
Time Limit	-0.087	-0.067	-0.063	-0.051	-0.019	-0.042
	(0.098)	(0.059)	(0.050)	(0.040)	(0.037)	(0.033)
Time Limit × Child <6 Yrs	0.118***	0.078***	0.043**	0.033*	0.032**	0.023*
	(0.042)	(0.025)	(0.021)	(0.017)	(0.016)	(0.014)
Exemption	-0.175	-0.163**	-0.047	-0.066	-0.005	0.009
	(0.130)	(0.075)	(0.064)	(0.051)	(0.048)	(0.042)
Sanctions	0.110	0.118	0.055	0.038	0.024	-0.016
	(0.120)	(0.072)	(0.062)	(0.050)	(0.046)	(0.041)
Earnings Disregard	0.046	0.030	0.010	0.045	0.031	0.032
	(0.078)	(0.047)	(0.040)	(0.032)	(0.030)	(0.026)
Family Cap	0.018	0.036	0.038	0.017	0.033	0.044**
	(0.064)	(0.039)	(0.033)	(0.026)	(0.024)	(0.021)

(continued)

Table 2.7. *Continued*

Coefficient	Quantile					
	20th	30th	40th	50th	60th	75th
Work Requirement	0.132	0.059	0.054	0.019	0.033	-0.004
	(0.089)	(0.054)	(0.046)	(0.036)	(0.034)	(0.029)
Constant	-2.575	-2.887**	-1.700*	-0.728	0.142	4.156***
	(1.890)	(1.150)	(0.980)	(0.780)	(0.720)	(0.630)
Observations	73,447	73,447	73,447	73,447	73,447	73,447

Notes: Standard errors in parentheses. All models control for cohort fixed effects, year fixed effects, and state fixed effects and trends.

***$p < 0.01$, **$p < 0.05$, *$p < 0.1$.

although, due to convergence problems with the censored least-absolute deviations (CLAD) estimator, we do not correct for the fact that the distribution is censored at zero.[11] The estimates in Table 2.6 reveal that pre-TANF waivers increased earnings in the 40th percentile and higher for mothers at all skill levels, but the positive earnings effects of TANF were most pronounced among the low skilled at the low end of the earnings distribution—about 20 percent at the 20th percentile compared to 9 percent at the 75th percentile. The lack of effect with the two-step estimates of Table 2.3 suggests that mean impacts do miss a lot of the welfare reform story, and the results here generalize to national samples the heterogeneity found in Bitler et al. (2006). With the business cycle interactions of Table 2.6 a somewhat complicated picture emerges between the waiver and TANF eras, which help us to understand the lack of business-cycle effects in Table 2.3. In the waiver period strong local economies, relative to the mean, actually inhibited earnings gains among the high-skilled in the bottom half of the distribution but fostered earnings gains among the low-skilled, especially at higher points of the distribution. However, in the TANF era, there is some qualitative evidence similar to the waiver results for the high-skilled in the low end of the distribution, but it is not statistically significant. As in the waiver period, the low-skilled at higher points of the earnings distribution experienced higher earnings gains if they lived in states with above-average employment per capita growth.

Tables 2.6 and 2.7 both reveal the strong, positive behavioral response of an expanding EITC on the earnings of single mothers, especially in the bottom half of the earnings distribution. There a 1 percentage point increase in the subsidy rate increases before-tax earnings of mothers with at least 12 years of schooling by about 2.5 percent at the 20th percentile and by just over 1 percent at the median. For low-skilled mothers, the negative effects of the EITC on mean earnings found in Table 2.3 appear to be driven by those in the top half of the earnings distribution. What these results suggest is that a more generous subsidy rate mechanically increases the fraction of mothers eligible for the EITC, and those higher up in the earnings distribution then face the phase-out rate of 21.06 percent. Holding before-tax hourly wages constant, then, the low-skilled respond behaviorally by reducing their work effort and, thus, their earnings in response to the more generous credit.

---

[11] In the spirit of the sample selection framework, ideally we would employ a quantile regression estimator with random censoring as described by Honore, Khan, and Powell (2002). Although such an estimator is beyond the scope of the current project, we doubt that convergence would be attained given the large number of parameters to be estimated.

In terms of disaggregated waiver effects, Table 2.7 shows that there is robust evidence in favor of the Grogger (2003) hypothesis of benefit banking resulting in higher earnings, especially at the low end of the distribution. Although Grogger found no evidence in favor of his hypothesis for mean earnings (nor did we in Table 2.3), Table 2.7 highlights the importance of examining the distributional consequences of welfare reform and related social policies such as the EITC.

V. Conclusion

We documented dramatic changes in the level and composition of income across the distribution during the welfare reform era. At the 10th percentile, single mothers still rely quite heavily on transfers, on average, but after welfare reform, fewer than half of mothers even at this low level of income receive any cash support from TANF, SSI, Social Security and SSDI, or earnings. At the same time, average real income at the 25th percentile grew by about 32 percent between 1993 and 2004 and by about 12 percent overall from 1979 to 2004. This growth was driven by strong increases in earnings and the EITC.

We attempted to identify causal effects of welfare reform, expansions in the EITC, and macroeconomic growth across the distributions of disposable income and before-tax earnings. Our regression results showed that TANF raised disposable incomes among higher-skilled single mothers an average of 8 percent, raised earnings among low-skilled single mothers in the lower half of the distribution by as much as 20 percent, but it also led to a significant equal-sized losses of after-tax total income among the low-skilled. Strong local economies in the mid-1990s accommodated welfare waivers that fostered income and earnings gains among the less skilled, which lends additional credence to the notion that "a rising tide lifts all boats." The EITC expansions of the 1990s boosted before-tax earnings across the earnings distribution, especially for the low-skilled in the bottom half of the distribution, but also resulted in significant losses of total income for the low-skilled.

Our estimates showed that the earnings gains among the low-skilled from the implementation of TANF and expansions of the EITC have been more than offset by losses in transfer income and have left the most vulnerable single mothers either running in place or falling behind. This poses a dilemma for policymakers because, on the one hand, low-skilled single mothers have acquired more labor-market experience than they would have in the absence of welfare reform and the expanded EITC, and returns to experience accumulate over the life course, so that earnings gains are likely to beget more earnings gains provided that the mothers remain in the labor force. On the other hand, after-tax income including the cash value of food stamps, which is a common barometer for economic well-being, has fallen in the wake of the social policy reforms and thus has potentially jeopardized the well-being of the children in these families. A possible policy response to this outcome of rising earnings but falling total income is to provide more generous work supports through the EITC and Food Stamp Program. This outcome could also reflect the "work first" strategies adopted by most states in the wake of welfare reform. Recent evidence from Hotz, Imbens, and Klerman (2006) indicates that welfare programs focusing on human capital developments have a better payoff in the long run, suggesting that the longer-term policy response is to couple work supports with skill upgrading.

References

Bartik, Timothy, and Randall Eberts. 1999. "Examining the Effect of Industry Trends and Structure on Welfare Caseloads," in *Economic Conditions and Welfare Reform*. Sheldon Danziger, ed. Kalamazoo, MI: Upjohn Institute, 119–157.

Bitler, Marianne, Jonah Gelbach, and Hilary Hoynes. 2006. "What Mean Impacts Miss: Distributional Effects of Welfare Reform Experiments." *American Economic Review,* 96(4): 988–1012.

Blank, Rebecca. 1997. *It Takes a Nation: A New Agenda for Fighting Poverty*. Princeton, NJ: Princeton University Press.

Blank, Rebecca M. 2002. "Evaluating Welfare Reform in the United States." *Journal of Economic Literature,* 40: 1105–1166.

Blank, Rebecca, and Patricia Ruggles. 1996. "When Do Women Use Aid to Families with Dependent Children and Food Stamps? The Dynamics of Eligibility versus Participation." *Journal of Human Resources,* 31(1): 57–89.

Blundell, Richard, Alan Duncan, and Costas Meghir. 1998. "Estimating Labor Supply Responses Using Tax Reforms." *Econometrica,* 66(4): 827–861.

Blundell, Richard, Luigi Pistaferri, and Ian Preston. 2006. "Consumption Inequality and Partial Insurance." Mimeo. London: University College London.

Bollinger, Christopher, and Barry Hirsch. 2006. "Match Bias from Earnings Imputation in the Current Population Survey: The Case of Imperfect Matching." *Journal of Labor Economics,* 24(3): 483–520.

Cancian, Maria, Robert Haveman, Daniel Meyer, and Barbara Wolfe. 2000. "Before and After TANF: The Economic Well-Being of Women Leaving Welfare." Institute for Research on Poverty Special Report No. 77, Madison: University of Wisconsin.

Danziger, Sandra K., Mary E. Corcoran, Sheldon Danziger, and Colleen M. Heflin. 2000. "Work, Income, and Material Hardship after Welfare Reform." *Journal of Consumer Affairs,* 34(1): 6–30.

Edin, Kathryn, and Maria Kefalas. 2006. *Promises I Can Keep: Why Poor Women Put Motherhood Before Marriage*. Berkeley: University of California Press.

Ellwood, David. 2000. "The Impact of the Earned Income Tax Credit and Social Policy Reforms on Work, Marriage, and Living Arrangements." *National Tax Journal*, 53(4:2): 1063–1105.

Fitzgerald, John M., and David C. Ribar. 2004. "Transitions in Welfare Participation and Female Headship." *Demography*, 41(2): 189–212.

Grogger, Jeffrey. 2003. "The Effects of Time Limits, the EITC, and Other Policy Changes on Welfare Use, Work, and Income Among Female-Headed Families." *Review of Economics and Statistics*, 85(2): 394–408.

Grogger, Jeffrey, Steven J. Haider, and Jacob Klerman. 2003. "Why Did the Welfare Rolls Fall during the 1990s?" *American Economic Review Papers and Proceedings*, 93(2): 288–292.

Grogger, Jeffrey, and Lynn A. Karoly. 2005. *Welfare Reform: Effects of a Decade of Change*. Cambridge, MA: Harvard University Press.

Gundersen, Craig, and James P. Ziliak. 2004. "Poverty and Macroeconomic Performance across Space, Race, and Family Structure." *Demography*, 41(1): 61–86.

Heckman, James. 1979. "Sample Selection Bias as Specification Error." *Econometrica*, 47:1, 153–161.

Herbst, Chris. 2008. "Do Social Policy Reforms Have Different Impacts on Employment and Welfare Use As Economic Conditions Change?" *Journal of Policy Analysis and Management*, 27(4): 867–894.

Honore, Bo, Shakeeb Khan, and James Powell. 2002. "Quantile Regression Under Random Censoring." *Journal of Econometrics*, 109(1): 67–105.

Hotz, V. Joseph, Guido Imbens, and Jacob Klerman. 2006. "Evaluating the Differential Effects of Alternative Welfare-to-Work Training Components: A Reanalysis of the California GAIN Program." *Journal of Labor Economics*, 24(3): 521–566.

Hotz, V. Joseph, Charles Mullin, and John Karl Scholz. 2005. "Examining the Effect of the Earned Income Tax Credit on the Labor Market Participation of Families on Welfare." Unpublished manuscript, Madison: University of Wisconsin.

Hoynes, Hilary W. 2000. "Local Labor Markets and Welfare Spells: Do Demand Conditions Matter?" *Review of Economics and Statistics*, 82(3): 351–368.

Kubik, Jeffrey. 1999. "Incentives for the Identification and Treatment of Children with Disabilities: The Supplemental Security Income Program." *Journal of Public Economics*, 73(2): 187–215.

Lee, Lung-Fei. 1984. "Tests for the Bivariate Normal Distribution in Econometric Models with Selectivity." *Econometrica*, 52(4): 843–863.

Meyer, Bruce, and Dan Rosenbaum. 2001. "Welfare, the Earned Income Tax Credit, and the Labor Supply of Single Mothers." *Quarterly Journal of Economics*, 116(3): 1063–1114.

Meyer, Bruce, and James Sullivan. 2006. "Consumption, Income, and Material Well-Being After Welfare Reform." National Bureau of Economic Research Working Paper 11976. Cambridge, MA: NBER.

Mills, Bradford, Jeffrey Alwang, and Gautum Hazarika. 2001. "Welfare Reform and the Well-Being of Single Female Headed Families: A Semi-Parametric Analysis." *Review of Income and Wealth*, 47(1): 81–104.

Moffitt, Robert. 1999. "The Effect of Pre-PRWORA Waivers on AFDC Caseloads and Female Earnings, Income, and Labor Force Behavior," in *Economic Conditions and Welfare Reform*. Sheldon Danziger, ed., Kalamazoo, MI: Upjohn Institute, 91–118.

Neumark, David, and William Wascher. 2001. "Using the EITC to Help Poor Families: New Evidence and a Comparison with the Minimum Wage." *National Tax Journal,* 54(2): 281–317.

Primus, Wendell, L. Rawlings, K. Larin, and Kathryn Porter. 1999. "The Initial Impacts of Welfare Reform on the Incomes of Single-Mother Families." Washington, DC: Center on Budget and Policy Priorities.

Ribar, David, and Marilyn Edelhoch. 2008. "Earnings Volatility and the Reasons for Leaving the Food Stamp Program," in *Income Volatility and Food Assistance in the United States.* Dean Jolliffe and James P. Ziliak, eds. Kalamazoo, MI: Upjohn Institute, 63–102,

Schmidt, Lucie, and Purvi Sevak. 2004. "AFDC, SSI, and Welfare Reform Aggressiveness: Caseload Reductions versus Caseload Shifting." *Journal of Human Resources,* 39(3): 792–812.

Schoeni, Robert, and Rebecca Blank. 2000. "What Has Welfare Reform Accomplished? Impacts on Welfare Participation, Employment, Income, Poverty, and Family Structure." National Bureau of Economic Research Working Paper 7627. Cambridge, MA: NBER.

Ziliak, James P. 2006. "Understanding Poverty Rates and Gaps: Concepts, Trends, and Challenges." *Foundations and Trends in Microeconomics,* 1(3): 127–199.

THREE

How Have Expansions in the Earned Income Tax Credit Affected Family Expenditures?

Qin Gao, Neeraj Kaushal, and Jane Waldfogel

I. Introduction

Since the passage of the 1996 Personal Responsibility and Work Opportunity Reconciliation Act (PRWORA), millions of welfare recipients have left welfare and entered the workforce. For many the transition from welfare to work has not reduced economic hardship, partly because a significant proportion of the income gain from work is offset by the loss in cash benefits, as indicated in Chapter Two of this volume. Many struggle to make ends meet based on earnings from low-paid jobs. Even families whose incomes are modestly above the official poverty line often face significant material difficulties (Blank 2002, 2006; Grogger and Karoly 2005; Grogger, Karoly, and Klerman 2002; Lichter and Jayakody 2002). Our prior research on the effects of welfare reform on family expenditures suggests that families affected by the reforms have increased expenditures on work-related expenses such as transportation, adult clothing, and food away from home (Kaushal, Gao, and Waldfogel 2007).

One very prominent element of welfare reform was the increased generosity of the Earned Income Tax Credit (EITC). In an effort to make work pay, the federal government dramatically increased nonwelfare support for

This is a revised version of a paper presented at the University of Kentucky Center for Poverty Research (UKCPR) Conference "Ten Years After: Evaluating the Long-Term Effects of Welfare Reform on Children, Families, Welfare, and Work," April 12–13, 2007. This project was supported by a grant from the UKCPR through the U.S. Department of Health and Human Services, Office of the Assistant Secretary for Planning and Evaluation, grant number 5 UO1 PE000002-05. The opinions and conclusions expressed herein are solely those of the authors and should not be construed as representing the opinions or policy of the UKCPR or any agency of the federal government. We are grateful to Becky Blank, Tim Smeeding, Jim Sullivan, and Jim Ziliak for helpful comments. We also thank the UKCPR for providing data for our EITC measure.

low-income working families, in particular the EITC.[1] Viewed by policymakers as an integral part of welfare reform, the EITC is widely considered—in the words of former New Jersey Senator Bill Bradley—"an effective, practical tool that provides working Americans the chance to climb the economic ladder to the middle class and build better opportunities for their families" (Bradley in "Proposes to Restore Funds for Earned Income Tax Credit" on October 24, 1995, as cited in Williams 1997; see also Ellwood 2000). Now larger than any federal cash-transfer program for low-income families in the United States, the EITC in 2003 provided a total credit of $39 billion to 22 million households. In 2006, the maximum federal EITC refund was $2,747 for taxpayers with one qualifying child and $4,536 for taxpayers with two or more qualifying children.[2] In addition, several states have implemented state-level EITC programs, which supplement the value of the benefit received through the federal EITC. In 2006, 15 states provided refundable state-level EITCs, which varied from 5 to 43 percent of the federal EITC (Furman 2006; Okwuje and Johnson 2006).

In this chapter, we extend our prior work on the effects of welfare reform on family expenditures by examining specifically how the EITC expansions since the early 1990s have affected expenditures in single-mother families. We focus on single mothers since they were the main target of welfare reform and by far the biggest beneficiary of EITC.[3,4] We examine the following questions: What is the effect of EITC expansions on total expenditures in single-mother families? How do EITC expansions affect debt? Is a more generous EITC associated with more spending on work-related items such as food away from home and adult clothing? And are EITC payments being used to acquire big-ticket items after the receipt of the tax refund (e.g., to buy a car or major appliance) or do families use the refund to smooth out consumption over the course of the year?

[1] Other such efforts include expansions in child care subsidies, Medicaid and health insurance coverage for children in low-income families, and increases in the minimum wage (Blank 2006).

[2] A qualifying child must be under 19 (or 24 for full-time students) or permanently disabled and must have lived with the parent for more than half of the year.

[3] Theoretically, both welfare reform and EITC expansions may change incentives to marry. However, previous research suggests that neither welfare reform nor EITC expansions have large effects on marriage (Blank 2002; Dickert-Conlin and Houser 2002; Ellwood 2000; Grogger et al. 2002). Welfare reform and EITC expansions may also change incentives for single mothers to cohabit. We include single mothers in our analysis regardless of whether they cohabit. The data we use do not contain information about their cohabitation status.

[4] In 2003, approximately 75 percent of tax relief or direct spending from the federal EITC accrued to taxpayers who filed as single heads of households (U.S. House of Representatives, Committee on Ways and Means, 2004 *Green Book*).

To answer these questions, we use the Consumer Expenditure Survey (CE) data for 1994–2004 and study the associations between state and federal EITC expansions and household expenditures, debt, patterns of expenditures, and purchase of consumer durables for families headed by single mothers. To isolate the effects of the EITC, we examine three distinct groups of single-mother families, selected on the basis of their economic vulnerability and likelihood of receiving EITC, as indicated by mothers' education: low-educated (mother's education < high school), medium-educated (mother's education = high-school or some college), and high-educated (mothers with a college degree or higher education). As has been well documented in the literature, these three groups were also differentially affected by PRWORA. The least educated, who were most likely to become dependent on cash welfare, were clearly the most affected by its denial, and the most educated, who were least likely to receive cash welfare, were largely unaffected by its denial.

EITC eligibility and benefit amounts are conditional on employment status and family earnings. While single mothers without a high school degree are most likely to have earnings below the EITC threshold, they also have a relatively low employment rate compared to the more educated groups of single mothers.[5] Single mothers with at least a BA degree have the highest employment rate of the three, but a large proportion of them are also likely to have earnings above the EITC earnings threshold.[6] Thus, based on annual earnings and employment status, our crude estimates suggest that the medium-educated group is likely to have benefited the most from the EITC expansions. Our analysis thus examines how EITC expansions affected expenditures in families most and least affected by the EITC expansions that accompanied PRWORA.[7]

---

[5] Using data from the 2004 March Current Population Survey (CPS), we estimated that among single mothers aged 18 to 54 without a high school degree, only 51 percent were employed in the week prior to the survey. The corresponding numbers were 73 percent for single mothers with a high school degree or some college and 88 percent for single mothers with at least a BA degree.

[6] For working single mothers aged 18 to 54 with at least a BA degree, using the 2004 March CPS data, we estimated that only 45 percent had annual earnings of $35,000 or less. The corresponding numbers were 92 percent for working single mothers without a high school degree and 80 percent for working single mothers with a high school degree or some college.

[7] These will not necessarily be the same families that are most affected by other aspects of welfare reform. As we discuss elsewhere, employment increases were steepest for the least-educated single mothers, although from a very low base. We control for other aspects of welfare reform in our models and thus allow the EITC and other aspects of welfare reform to have distinct effects.

II. Policy Background and Previous Research

The EITC operates as a refundable tax credit to subsidize workers in low-income families. The refundable aspect is important, since it means that a taxpayer with no tax liability receives a refund from the government for the full amount of the credit (and that a taxpayer with liability less than the value of the credit receives the difference between the two). Eligibility for EITC depends on earned income (or adjusted gross income) and the number of qualifying children in the family. The EITC schedule has three sections. In the first section, applied to families with very low incomes, the credit generally equals a specified percentage of earned income up to a maximum amount. The 2006 phase-in credit rate is 34 percent for families with one qualifying child and 40 percent for families with two or more qualifying children.[8] In the second section, families within a certain income range receive the maximum amount of credit. In 2006, the maximum credit amount was $2,747 for a family with one qualifying child and $4,536 for a family with two qualifying children. Finally, for families within a specified phase-out income range, the tax credit is gradually decreased to zero. In 2006, the EITC income threshold was $32,001 for a taxpayer with one qualifying child and $36,348 for a taxpayer with two qualifying children. Because the EITC is administered through the tax system, and not as a separate program, it is generally believed to target working poor families extremely well (Blank 2002, 2006; Hotz, Mullin, and Scholz 2006).

Since its inception in 1975, the EITC has experienced several major expansions. The 1986 Tax Reform Act (TRA) increased the credit rate from 10 to 14 percent of family earnings and indexed the maximum credit rate to inflation. The Omnibus Budget Reconciliation Act (OBRA) of 1990 further revised the policy to make more generous EITC benefits available to families with two or more children compared to those with only one eligible child. The largest expansion in EITC came with the 1993 OBRA, resulting from the Clinton administration's effort to fulfill its campaign promise to "make work pay" (Blank 2006). The expansions implemented during 1994–1996 doubled the phase-in credit rate from 19.5 percent of earnings to 40 percent, and increased the maximum credit from $1,511 to $3,556 and the phase-out credit rate from 14 to 21 percent for families with two qualifying children.[9]

---

[8] Since 1994, a small EITC has also been available for low-income workers without children.

[9] For families with one qualifying child, the phase-in rate was increased from 18.5 percent in 1993 to 34 percent in 1996, the maximum refundable credit from $1,434 to $2,152, and

The success of the federal EITC has led a number of states to enact state EITCs to supplement the federal credit. However, not all state EITCs are refundable, as the federal credit is. Vermont enacted the first refundable state EITC in 1988, followed by Wisconsin in 1989, Minnesota in 1991, and New York in 1994. Fourteen states had refundable state EITCs by 2004 (the latest year of data we analyze here).[10] Appendix Table 3.1 summarizes the progress of enacting refundable state EITCs by state and year and also provides information on their generosity as a percentage of the federal EITC. These state-level tax instruments supplement the federal EITC, adding to both the impact and the total outlays for the EITC (Greenstein and Shapiro 1998).

Figure 3.1 summarizes the trends of the combined state and federal EITC generosity (in dollars) for families with two or more children by state and year (up to 2004). Our analysis focuses on the period 1993–2004, when social policies toward single mothers changed dramatically. On the one hand, state and federal welfare reform restricted cash welfare to a lifetime maximum of five years under strict work requirements; on the other hand, the EITC was expanded generously by the federal government, supplemented by the initiation or expansion of refundable state EITCs. In 1993, the maximum federal EITC credit available to a family with two or more children (in 2004 dollars) was $1,975; by 1996 it had more than doubled to $4,281. Although the federal maximum refundable EITC (in real terms) has remained relatively unchanged since 1996, increases in state refundable EITCs have raised the overall available credit in several states by about $800.

These expansions resulted in both increased numbers of recipients and higher refunds. During 1975–1994, the first two decades of the EITC's existence, the number of families receiving EITC almost tripled; this number has plateaued at around 19 million families since 1994 (Figure 3.2). The amount of credit, however, has continued to rise. Overall, the total federal EITC credit increased 12 times during 1975–1993. The real total credit amount further increased from $26.9 billion in 1994 to $35.3 billion in 2003 (in 2004 dollars). Overall, the average credit per family increased from $1,415 in 1994 to $1,832 in 2003, an increase of $35 per month.

The EITC is now not only the nation's largest cash assistance program targeting low-income working families, but is also considered a highly effective antipoverty policy. Research using data from the Census Bureau suggests that the EITC has been instrumental in lifting more than 4 million

---

the phase-out rate from 13 percent to 16 percent.

[10] Five states provide nonrefundable credits, with one (Michigan) offering a new refundable credit starting in 2008 (Nagle and Johnson 2006).

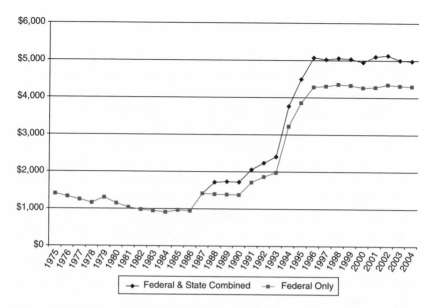

Figure 3.1. Maximum Refundable EITC Available to a Family with Two or More Children (in 2004 dollars)
Sources: U.S. House of Representatives, Committee on Ways and Means, 2004 Green Book Table 13-12, and Center for Budget and Policy Priorities, March 8, 2006 report "A Hand Up: How State Earned Income Tax Credits Help Working Families Escape Poverty In 2006" (available at http://www.cbpp.org/3-8-06sfp.pdf).

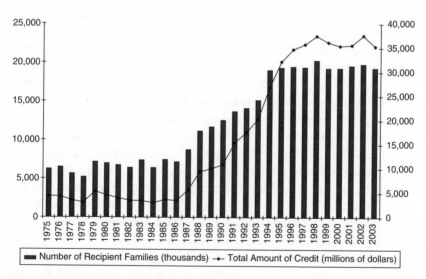

Figure 3.2. Federal Earned Income Tax Credit: Number of Recipients and Amount of credit, 1975–2003 (credit in 2004 dollars)
Note: Figures for 2002 and 2003 are preliminary.
Source: U.S. House of Representatives, Committee on Ways and Means, 2004 Green Book Table 13-14.

people out of poverty each year, including more than 2 million children (Blumenthal, Erard, and Ho 2005). The poverty rate among children would have been nearly one-fourth higher without the EITC (Greenstein 2005). Greenstein (2005) concludes that the EITC lifts more children out of poverty than any other single program or category of programs.

Using macro-level retail data from 1982–2001, Edwards (2004) finds that the EITC is much more effective in stimulating the economy than broad-based tax refunds since a majority of EITC recipients spend the refund money rather than saving it. A growing number of studies find that the EITC has been effective in increasing labor force participation among single parents, particularly single mothers (Eissa and Liebman 1996; Eissa and Nichols 2005; Grogger 2003; Hotz and Scholz 2003; Meyer and Rosenbaum 2000, 2001a, 2001b; Neumark and Wascher 2007), but has reduced the total family labor supply of married couples (Dickert, Houser, and Scholz 1995; Eissa and Hoynes 2004; Ellwood 2000).

However, one important outcome—family expenditures—has been much less studied. Many analysts have argued for studying expenditures given the well-recognized deficits in using income and poverty as measures of economic well-being (e.g., not being able to take into account work-related expenses and cross-household transfers) (Blank 2006; Meyer and Sullivan 2003; Rector 2004; see also the discussion in Haskins 2001). Studying expenditures is also important if we are to determine whether the EITC is promoting spending on items that benefit children.

Two small-scale studies provide some suggestive evidence that the EITC increases low-income families' spending, especially on durable goods. Smeeding and colleagues (2000) analyze data from a survey of 823 low-income families in the Chicago area that filed tax returns in the spring of 1998 and were eligible to receive EITC. The authors asked families how they planned to use the EITC money. They found that almost 70 percent of recipients had in mind an "economic or social mobility"—related use of EITC including saving, expenses (purchases, repairs, or insurances) for a car, paying tuition, or moving. Another 13 percent planned on purchasing other durable goods, while almost half planned to use their refund to pay for utilities, rent, food, or clothing.[11] Follow-up interviews confirmed that actual spending was largely consistent with these plans.

An ethnographic study of 42 extremely low-income families in Wisconsin examines how these families used their tax refunds (Romich and Weisner

---

[11] Percentages total more than 100% because families could report more than one planned use of their refund.

2000). This study finds that these families tended to use their lump-sum tax refunds to purchase durable goods, and in particular, to make large purchases such as furniture or a car. In the short term, families also put EITC money into savings. Two-thirds of the parents in the ethnographic sample who received EITC or a substantial tax refund reported expenditures on children as a priority use of the check. They tended to spend money on children's clothing (the most common response), private school tuition (three instances), and establishing saving accounts in a child's name (two instances). Despite its very insightful findings, this study clearly is limited by its small sample size.

To our knowledge, there is only one other study that has used a micro-level national dataset to examine the links between EITC and family expenditures.[12] Using the CE 1982–1996 data, Barrow and McGranahan (2000) compare the expenditures of EITC-eligible and EITC-ineligible families based on simulated EITC eligibility. Focusing on the seasonality of expenditures, they find that EITC-eligible families spent less per month, on average, on durable and nondurable goods than the ineligible families but that EITC-eligible families spent more on durable goods in February, the modal month of EITC refunds, than the ineligible families.

In this chapter, we use CE data to study the associations between EITC expansions and total family expenditures, total family debt, expenditure patterns, and purchase of durables for all single-mother families and for single-mother families distinguished by the level of the mother's education. In doing so, we build on the Barrow and McGranahan (2000) study; however, our study differs from theirs in its inclusion of family debt and detailed patterns of expenditures and in its analyses of separate education groups. We also build on a series of recent studies (Kaushal et al. 2007; Meyer and Sullivan 2003, 2004, 2006) that have provided evidence on how welfare reform affected the patterns of expenditure and ownership of durable goods among single-mother families. The present study differs, however, in focusing on the effects of the EITC rather than on the effects of welfare reform more generally.

---

[12] Several researchers have studied the link between tax and transfer systems and consumption patterns. For example, Agarwal, Liu, and Souleles (2007) examined consumers' spending and debt reactions to tax rebates; Kniesner and Ziliak (2002) studied how the progressive income tax provides consumption insurance; Stephens (2003) examined how Social Security recipients smooth out consumption between checks; Shapiro and Slemrod (1995) investigated changes in tax withholding schedules on personal consumption behaviors; Shapiro and Slemrod (2003) examined how consumers respond to tax rebates; Parker (2003) investigated the effect on household consumption of predictable changes in Social Security taxes; and Gruber (2000) studied whether cash welfare smoothed the consumption of women who transition to single motherhood through divorce.

III. Data

The CE is conducted by the Bureau of Labor Statistics (BLS), U.S. Department of Labor, collecting extensive information on the expenditure patterns of American families. It consists of two different components: a quarterly Interview Survey (IS) and a weekly Diary Survey (DS). Our analysis is based on the IS for the years 1994–2004 , which provides detailed information on expenditures incurred by a sample of consumer units, where a consumer unit is defined as all members of a housing unit related by blood, marriage, adoption, or some other legal arrangement; or two or more persons living together who use their incomes to make joint expenditures; or a single person who is living with others but is financially independent (BLS 2005).[13] The IS sample is a rotated panel in which approximately 7,500 units are interviewed every three months for five consecutive quarters, after which these households are replaced by new units.[14] Thus, by design, 20 percent of the sample is replaced every year. The first quarter is a contact interview, while in the second to fifth quarters, households are asked about their expenditures over the previous three months. Since the IS's are based on recall data on expenditures in the past three months, they suffer from response recall errors (Battistin 2003).[15]

We restrict the analysis to single-mother families with children, where the mother is not married and is aged 18–54 years. The CE provides detailed demographic information on each consumer unit including the respondent's age, education level, marital status, race and ethnicity, state and region of residence, family size, number of children, and number of elderly persons (aged 65 or above) in the family. As detailed later, we conduct some analyses of all single-mother families and then separate analyses of families headed by mothers with low, medium, and high levels of education.

In this chapter, we use the monthly expenditure data of the IS. We first classify monthly expenditures into 10 major categories—housing and utilities; food; alcohol and tobacco; clothing and footwear; transportation; health; leisure; personal care; education (including reading); and miscellaneous—and

---

[13] Ideally, we would like to investigate 1990–1993 as well; however, the CE data do not contain state codes for 1990–1992 and the data for 1993 are formatted in a very different and more complex manner, and therefore we did not include them.

[14] The sample size was increased in 1999. During 1990–1998, in any single quarter the IS consisted of about 5,000 units.

[15] One potential concern is that time constraints may result in working mothers dropping out of CE or answering questions with less care. There is no way we can check whether respondents took less care in answering the survey after welfare reform. According to CE documentation, during 1990–2004 there is a steady decline in response rate, a trend similar to that found in response rates in all national surveys during this period (Caban et al. 2005).

study whether state and federal EITCs affect expenditures on these major categories. The CE also provides data on expenditures on more narrowly defined items, such as work-related expenses or purchase of durable goods. More specifically, we use CE data to define expenditure categories that may be associated with increased work effort (e.g., expenditures on food away from home; adult's clothing, footwear, and accessories). For comparison, we also study changes in expenditures on food at home and children's clothing, footwear, and accessories. We also examine whether the EITC expansions enable families to purchase durable goods such as vehicles or major household appliances. In addition, the CE asks families about the amount of debt owed.[16] Details on the measures of each expenditure category are presented in Appendix Tables 3.2 (major categories) and 3.3 (detailed items).

To take account of differences in household size and composition, following Kaushal et al. (2007), we adjust expenditures in the 10 major categories for each household using an equivalence scale, which assigns a weight of 0.67 to the first adult, 0.33 to all other persons in the household over age 17, and 0.2 to children ages 17 or less. More specific items (such as adult clothing, footwear and accessories; children's clothing, footwear and accessories) are deflated by the number of adults or children in the family who are likely to use these goods and services. Expenditures are expressed in 2004 dollars using the Personal Consumption Expenditure deflator of the Bureau of Economic Analysis.

Our measure of EITC generosity is constructed as the combined maximum state and federal EITC benefits for families with one or more children in effect in the prior calendar year, compiled by the University of Kentucky Center for Poverty Research (UKCPR).[17] We use the tax schedule from the prior year because this is what determines the value of the credit that a family receives when they file their taxes the following spring. This measure is matched to the CE microdata by state, year, and number of children present in the household.[18,19]

---

[16] The questions about debt were only asked twice for each family, i.e., in their second and fifth interviews.

[17] The file is entitled "State-Level Data of Economic, Political, and Transfer-Program Information for 1980–2007" and is available at http://www.ukcpr.org/AvailableData.aspx.

[18] Some previous studies have also used other aspects of EITCs that vary by state, such as subsidy rates by income level, but they largely agree that the results using these specifications are generally similar to those using the maximum total state and federal refundable credit measure (Grogger 2003; Hotz and Scholz 2003; Meyer and Rosenbaum 2001b).

[19] Wisconsin's state EITC rate varies by number of children. It is currently 4 percent of the federal EITC if the family has one child, 14 percent if there are two children, and 43 percent if there are three or more children. Minnesota's credit for families with children is not expressly structured as a percentage of the federal credit. Depending on the income level, the credit for families with children may range from 25 percent to 45 percent of the federal

To determine whether a household lived in a state that had a state refundable EITC (in addition to the federal EITC), we must identify the state in which the household resided. For nondisclosure reasons, codes for smaller states are either suppressed or recoded in the CE. For the period 1994–2004, CE data provide state codes for all or some consumer units for 35 (during 1994–1995) to 36 states (1996–2004), among which 11 states had enacted refundable state EITCs by 2004.[20] The cases with state codes account for about 80 percent of the CE sample. We do not use the other 20 percent of the CE sample for which the state of residence is not identified.

State of residence indicators are used to merge the following information with the CE data: state monthly unemployment rate; real combined maximum food stamps and Aid to Families with Dependent Children/ Temporary Assistance for Needy Families (AFDC/TANF) benefit for a family of four; whether a state had an AFDC waiver; and whether a state had implemented TANF.[21] We follow the earlier literature on the effects of welfare reform and use dummy variables for whether a state had implemented an AFDC waiver or TANF. We lag these variables by one month on the assumption that they will not affect expenditures in the month in which they come into effect.

IV. Methods

To examine the association between expansions in state and federal EITCs and family expenditures, we begin with the following regression model:

$$Y_{ist} = \gamma_s + \gamma_t + \gamma_m + \beta_e E_{st} + \beta_p P_{st} + \beta_x X_{ist} + \varepsilon_{ist} \tag{1}$$

where Y_{ist} represents the monthly equivalized expenditure of family i from state s in year t; E_{st} is EITC generosity (the combined real value of the federal and state maximum refundable credits, by number of children in the family, according to the prior year's tax schedule) in state s in year t; P_{st}

---

credit; taxpayers without children may receive a 25 percent credit. We use the average rate, currently 33 percent, in our measure.

[20] State codes were available for all consumer units in 17 to 19 states and for most consumer units in another 16 to 18 states.

[21] The data on welfare policies are drawn from the Assistant Secretary for Planning and Evaluation of the Department of Health and Human Services, as well as from the Urban Institute (http://www.urban.org/content/Research/NewFederalism/Data/StateDatabase/ StateDatabase.htm) and the State Documentation Project of the Center on Budget and Policy Priorities (http://www.cbpp.org). Data on monthly unemployment rates are obtained from the BLS.

indicates time-varying state policy and contextual variables, namely, maximum state cash welfare and food stamps benefit for a family of four in year t; whether a state had an AFDC waiver and whether it implemented TANF in month $m - 1$ of year t, and monthly state unemployment rate; X_{ist} represents a vector of demographic and socioeconomic characteristics, namely, mother's age (six categories: 18–23, 24–29, 30–35, 36–41, 42–47, and 48–54), race/ethnicity (non-Hispanic white, non-Hispanic black, Hispanic, and other), whether she lives in an urban area, number of children, family size, and number of persons age 65 or above; and γ_s, γ_t, and γ_m are state, year, and month fixed effects, respectively. When estimating models for all single mothers, we also include controls for the mother's educational level (less than high school, high school or some college, or BA degree or higher education).

A majority of families receive tax refunds in February. In 2006, for instance, 58 percent of the EITC refunds were made in February and 19 percent in March, followed by approximately 8 percent each in January and April (U.S. Department of the Treasury 2006). Given the lumpy nature of EITC refunds, the EITC may influence the seasonality of expenditures, resulting in higher expenditures during these four months and in February in particular. Or, since for some families EITC refunds constitute a significant proportion of their annual income, they may smooth out expenditures in the course of the year. To examine whether EITC has influenced the seasonality of family expenditures, we estimate the following two regression models:

$$Y_{ist} = \tilde{\gamma}_s + \tilde{\gamma}_t + \tilde{\gamma}_m + \beta * E_{st} + \beta_j(Jan * E_{st}) + \beta_f(Feb * E_{st})$$
$$+ \beta_m(Mar * E_{st}) + \tilde{\beta}_a(Apr * E_{st}) + \tilde{\beta}_x X_{ist} + \varepsilon_{ist} \qquad (2)$$

$$Y_{ist} = \tilde{\gamma}_s + \tilde{\gamma}_t + \tilde{\gamma}_m + \beta * E_{st} + \beta_f(Feb * E_{st}) + \beta_x \tilde{X}_{ist} + \tilde{\varepsilon}_{ist} \qquad (3)$$

The symbol ~ is used to distinguish coefficients from equation (1). Equation (2) has four additional terms compared to equation (1): these are, respectively, interaction terms between dichotomous indicators for January, February, March, or April and the EITC generosity measure. These interaction terms capture the additional effects—if any—of the EITC in those months, over and above any increase in average monthly expenditure associated with the EITC.

Because the majority of families receive their EITC benefits in February, we also estimate a more parsimonious model, as shown in equation (3).

This model has just one additional term compared to equation (1): an interaction term between a dichotomous indicator for February and the EITC. This interaction term captures the additional effect—if any—of the EITC in February, over and above any increase in average monthly expenditure associated with the EITC.

If the EITC influenced seasonal spending, we should see increased expenditures during the January to April period, when families receive the EITC refund. Further, this effect should be most prominent in February, when a major proportion of the EITC refund is received. On the other hand, if a majority of families smooth out expenditures, there would be no significant difference in seasonal spending. Families may use the EITC credit to retire debt. To see if that is the case, we estimate equations (1)–(3) with total family debt as the dependent variable.

In addition to carrying out analyses for all single-mother families, we examine three distinct groups of single mothers, using the mother's education as a way to define the groups most and least likely to have been affected by the EITC expansions. The low-educated group (education < high school) has very low earnings, making its members ideal candidates for EITC.[22] However, they also have a relatively low employment rate, which may restrict their EITC eligibility. We separate out this group because its members are highly vulnerable to social policy changes and were most affected by welfare reform. Whether and how EITC expansions have influenced the expenditure patterns of this group is critical to assess the efficacy of this policy. The medium-educated group (those with a high school degree or some college) is also of interest and indeed might be most influenced by EITC expansions. They are more likely to be employed than the low-educated but still have earnings low enough to make a large proportion of this group eligible for EITC.[23] In comparison, the high-educated group (those with a BA degree or higher education) has much higher family earnings and therefore would be least affected by EITC expansions and other aspects of welfare reform. Thus, the high-educated group serves as a comparison group.

As a robustness check on the results, we reestimate all of our models, separating households where an adult was employed in the past year and

[22] According to our analyses of the March CPS, in 2003 the average personal income of single mothers without a high school degree was approximately $9,100 per year and their family earnings were about $11,000. The distribution of their earnings in 2003 suggests that 98 percent had annual personal earnings less than the then federal EITC income ceiling of about $35,000, and 95 percent had family earnings less than the EITC ceiling.

[23] In 2003 (our estimates from March CPS), 89 percent of single mothers with a high school degree or some college had personal earnings lower than the then federal EITC income ceiling, and 84 percent had family earnings lower than the ceiling.

households where no adult was employed in the past year. Clearly, since the EITC creates employment incentives, whether a household has a working member is likely to be endogenous. Nevertheless, examining households separately by work status is useful as a specification check. Since the EITC is limited to employed households, any results we find for the EITC should be confined to those households. Conversely, if we find effects of the EITC for nonemployed households, this would be an indication that such effects might be spurious.

V. Results

A. Descriptive Analysis

Partly as a result of changes in welfare reform and EITC expansions and partly on account of the 1990s economic boom, the labor force participation of single mothers increased sharply in the late 1990s. We can see this in the employment data for the single mothers in our CE sample (Figure 3.3). On average, during 1994–1996, approximately 74 percent of the single mothers in our sample had worked in the previous 12 months. This proportion increased to 85 percent by 2000, followed by a marginal decline during 2001–2004. This trend is almost entirely reflective of the trend in employment experienced by the low- and medium-educated groups, with the high-educated group exhibiting no long-term trend in employment. During 1994–1996, about 51 percent of single mothers with less than a high school degree had worked in the previous 12 months; that proportion increased to 70 percent by 2000, followed by a decline in the 2001 recession. During 2001–2004, the average employment rate of this group was approximately 65 percent. The medium-educated group (with high school or some college education) also increased its labor force participation—from an average of about 78 percent employed during the prior year during 1994–1996 to about 86 percent during 2001–2004.

How did changes in welfare policies and EITC expansions influence expenditures in single-mother families? To provide some preliminary evidence on this issue, we first study trends in total monthly expenditures in single-mother families stratified by the mother's education. Figure 3.4 presents these trends. For all single mothers, there appears to be a modest upward trend in real monthly expenditures since 1996. Expenditures in families headed by low-educated single mothers remained more or less stagnant at around $1,250 during 2001–2004. Notice that this is the group that experienced the largest change in lifestyle by moving from welfare

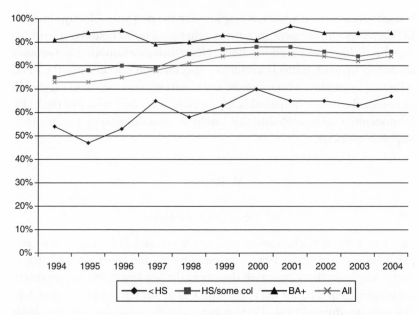

Figure 3.3. Annual Trends in the Share of Single Mothers Employed During the Past 12 Month by Education
Source: Authors' calculations using the CE data

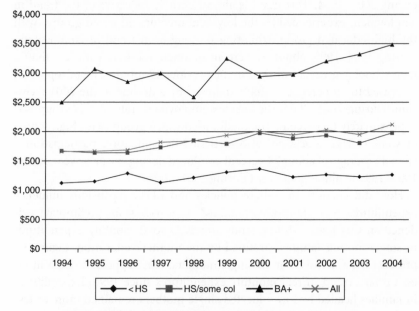

Figure 3.4. Annual Trends in Total Monthly Equivalized Expenditures among Single-Mother-Headed Families by Mother's Education (in 2004 dollars)
Source: Authors' calculations using the CE data

to work in large numbers. However, their overall average material well-being, as measured by total monthly expenditures, remained more or less unchanged. Clearly, those who moved from welfare to work benefited from the EITC expansions as well as from increases in earned income, but these gains were offset by losses in welfare income; for those who were not able to get secure jobs, EITC expansions were not much help.

There is also little evidence of any major change in expenditures in families headed by single mothers with a high school degree or some college, although their expenditure levels are somewhat higher in the 2000–2004 period than they were in the early 1990s. Average monthly expenditures in families headed by single mothers with at least a BA degree registered sharp fluctuations during 1994–2000 and have been steadily rising since then. This suggests that there were factors other than welfare reform and EITC expansions that affected trends in expenditures and that caution needs to be exercised in interpreting these trends. Figure 3.4 is based on expenditure data unadjusted for changes in demographics and economic factors. Next, we apply multivariate regression models, discussed in detail in Section IV, to examine the associations between EITC expansions as well as welfare reforms and family expenditures.

B. Multivariate Analysis

We begin this analysis by examining the associations between EITC expansions, welfare reform, and total family expenditures. Table 3.1 presents the results of this analysis. The top panel of the table presents estimates using equation (1), the middle panel using equation (2), and the bottom panel using equation (3). Each column in a panel is based on a separate regression estimated on a sample of single-mother families described in the column heading. In addition to the variables listed in the rows of each panel, each regression controls for a rich set of demographic variables, namely, mothers' age, race/ethnicity, whether she lives in an urban area, family size, number of children under age 18 and number of persons in the family aged 65 or above, state, year, and month fixed effects, and state unemployment rate. Mothers' education is also controlled for in regressions run on all single mothers.

Column 1 presents the regression results for all single mothers. In the model with main effects only (top panel), the EITC has a negligible effect on total expenditures. However, in the model with January–April interaction terms (middle panel), we observe a statistically significant increase in expenditures associated with the EITC in February (along with a marginally significant

Table 3.1. *Effects of EITC generosity on total monthly equivalized expenditures among single-mother Families, by mothers' education*

	All	< HS	HS/some college	BA+
Main Effects Only				
EITC	−0.006	−0.043	0.012	0.080
	(0.022)	(0.029)	(0.026)	(0.088)
Max TANF/FS	−0.051	0.586	0.160	−1.026
	(0.485)	(0.502)	(0.575)	(2.049)
AFDC Waiver	−54.365	−73.647	−40.678	−211.087
	(60.456)	(74.290)	(75.704)	(289.349)
TANF Implemented	118.564	−16.377	111.375	447.788
	(74.508)	(79.610)	(91.136)	(286.044)
Main Effects and EITC ∗ Jan–April Interactions				
EITC	−0.022	−0.048	−0.002	0.051
	(0.023)	(0.030)	(0.027)	(0.099)
EITC ∗ Jan	0.065+	−0.056	0.078+	0.075
	(0.036)	(0.065)	(0.046)	(0.116)
EITC ∗ Feb	0.097*	0.002	0.132**	0.000
	(0.039)	(0.048)	(0.045)	(0.161)
EITC ∗ March	0.042	0.067	0.028	0.039
	(0.038)	(0.043)	(0.045)	(0.154)
EITC ∗ April	−0.021	0.050	−0.092*	0.217
	(0.040)	(0.038)	(0.046)	(0.172)
Max TANF/FS	−0.042	0.568	0.157	−1.003
	(0.484)	(0.504)	(0.575)	(2.053)
AFDC Waiver	−58.271	−72.719	−44.308	−224.669
	(60.519)	(74.691)	(75.848)	(288.628)
TANF Implemented	119.353	−18.469	111.333	447.348
	(74.563)	(79.889)	(91.195)	(286.856)
Main Effects and EITC ∗ Feb Interactions				
EITC	−0.014	−0.043	0.001	0.083
	(0.022)	(0.029)	(0.026)	(0.091)
EITC ∗ Feb	0.088*	−0.004	0.130**	−0.032
	(0.037)	(0.046)	(0.043)	(0.154)

Table 3.1. *Continued*

	All	< HS	HS/some college	BA+
Max TANF/FS	−0.053	0.586	0.150	−1.029
	(0.485)	(0.502)	(0.575)	(2.051)
AFDC Waiver	−55.755	−73.619	−42.735	−209.648
	(60.447)	(74.268)	(75.731)	(288.186)
TANF Implemented	118.691	−16.412	111.129	447.871
	(74.512)	(79.599)	(91.171)	(286.147)
N	13,562	2,629	8,927	2,006

Notes: In each column, each panel is from a separate regression. The models also include controls for the mother's age, race/ethnicity, whether she lives in an urban area, family size, number of children under age 18, number of persons in the family age 65 or above, state, year, and month effects, and state monthly unemployment rate. Models for all single mothers also control for the mother's education level (< HS, HS/some college, or BA+). Expenditures are expressed in December 2004 dollars using the Personal Consumption Expenditure index of the Bureau of Economic Analysis. Heteroskodasticity-adjusted standard errors clustered at the consumer unit are in parentheses. $+p < 10\%$; $*p < 5\%$; $**p < 1\%$.

increase in January). In this model, a one dollar increase in maximum EITC credit is associated with a nearly 10 cent increase in total expenditure in February. The results are similar in a model that includes only a February interaction term (bottom panel). Here a one dollar increase in maximum EITC credit is associated with a nearly 9 cent increase in total expenditure in February. Welfare reform, captured by two dummy variables—whether a state had an AFDC waiver and whether a state implemented TANF in month $m - 1$ of year t—has no significant effects on total family expenditures.

When the sample is disaggregated by mothers' education (columns 2–4), we find significant effects of the EITC only for the medium-educated group (column 3). For this group, there are no main effects of EITC on total expenditures but there are strong seasonal effects. Models estimated using equations (2) and (3) (middle panel and bottom panel, respectively) indicate that a one dollar increase in maximum EITC credit is associated with a 13 cent increase in total expenditures in February among the medium-educated group. Results from equation (2) also point to a marginally significant increase in expenditures for this group in January, as well as a significant decline in April. The effects of the welfare reform variables continue to be insignificant across all three education groups. This is consistent with our earlier finding that welfare reform is not associated with any statistically significant change in total expenditures among low-educated single-mother families (Kaushal et al. 2007).[24]

As a robustness check, we repeat these models but separate the sample by whether any adult in the household was employed in the past year. The results (not shown but available on request) confirm that, as we would expect, the positive effects of EITC on expenditures were confined to employed households, with no significant effects seen for nonemployed households.

We next examine whether EITC expansions were associated with any change in total family debt. Results in Table 3.2 suggest that EITC expansions lowered family debt. A one dollar increase in EITC lowered debt by about 4 cents for all single-mother families. This reduction in debt is seen as an average effect rather than a seasonal effect. The association between welfare reform variables and debt is statistically insignificant in models for all single-mother families. When the sample is restricted to low-educated single mothers, a one dollar increase in the EITC lowered debt by about 2 cents; and waivers and TANF have opposite effects, with waivers raising debt by close to $60 and TANF lowering debt by just over $130. In the analysis for the medium-educated group (single mothers with a high school degree or some college, column 3), one dollar in EITC lowers debt by a marginally significant 4 cents in a model with only main effects (this effect is no longer significant when interaction terms are added), but welfare reform has no statistically significant association with debt for this group. Finally, when the sample is restricted to the high-educated group (column 4), neither the EITC nor the welfare reform variables have an effect on debt.

Again as a specification check, we stratify our samples by whether any adult in the household was employed in the previous year. Since those who did not work were unlikely to benefit from EITC, we should find the estimated effect of EITC to be negligible for this group. And indeed, this is the case: The only groups for which we find any significant effects of EITC on debt are those employed in the past year (results not shown but available on request).

To sum up, the analysis presented in Tables 3.1 and 3.2 suggests that EITC expansions are associated with an increase in expenditures in February, the month in which the EITC refund peaks, in families headed by medium-educated single mothers—those with a high school or some college education. The EITC is also associated with a reduction in total family debt for this group, although this association is only marginally significant (model

---

[24] Also see Chapter Two in this volume.

Table 3.2. *Effects of EITC generosity on total debt among single-mother families, by mothers' education*

	All	< HS	HS/some college	BA+
Main Effects Only				
EITC	−0.043*	−0.021+	−0.041+	−0.022
	(0.018)	(0.011)	(0.024)	(0.041)
Max TANF/FS	−0.447	0.134	−0.100	−2.777**
	(0.280)	(0.239)	(0.412)	(0.945)
AFDC Waiver	−0.913	58.494*	11.939	−201.525
	(34.720)	(24.442)	(50.747)	(191.782)
TANF Implemented	−46.245	−131.357*	−63.607	96.642
	(45.600)	(55.452)	(59.189)	(167.628)
Main Effects and EITC * Jan–April Interactions				
EITC	−0.044+	−0.021+	−0.044	−0.013
	(0.023)	(0.011)	(0.032)	(0.045)
EITC * Jan	0.021	0.013	0.016	0.020
	(0.024)	(0.021)	(0.027)	(0.089)
EITC * Feb	−0.051	−0.017	−0.059	−0.064
	(0.043)	(0.020)	(0.061)	(0.073)
EITC * March	0.037+	−0.019	0.051+	0.032
	(0.022)	(0.030)	(0.030)	(0.066)
EITC * April	0.006	0.028	0.024	−0.097
	(0.024)	(0.023)	(0.029)	(0.080)
Max TANF/FS	−0.441	0.137	−0.094	−2.778**
	(0.279)	(0.239)	(0.411)	(0.945)
AFDC Waiver	−1.429	58.058*	11.358	−197.581
	(33.892)	(24.245)	(49.290)	(192.461)
TANF Implemented	−46.327	−131.501*	−63.815	97.180
	(45.554)	(55.491)	(59.284)	(167.368)
Main Effects and EITC * Feb Interactions				
EITC	−0.038*	−0.019+	−0.035	−0.017
	(0.019)	(0.012)	(0.025)	(0.041)
EITC * Feb	−0.058	−0.019	−0.068	−0.061
	(0.041)	(0.020)	(0.059)	(0.071)

(continued)

Table 3.2. *Continued*

	All	< HS	HS/some college	BA+
Max TANF/FS	−0.445	0.134	−0.095	−2.784**
	(0.280)	(0.239)	(0.413)	(0.943)
AFDC Waiver	0.001	58.642*	13.021	−198.835
	(34.594)	(24.484)	(50.508)	(191.977)
TANF Implemented	−46.329	−131.546*	−63.478	96.798
	(45.560)	(55.520)	(59.208)	(167.479)

Notes: In each column, each panel is from a separate regression, with controls for the full set of welfare policy variables, monthly unemployment rate, demographic characteristics, state, year, and month effects, as detailed in the notes for Table 3.1. Heteroskodasticity-adjusted standard errors clustered at the consumer unit are in parentheses. $+p < 10\%$; $*p < 5\%$; $**p < 1\%$. Sample sizes are the same as those presented in Table 3.1.

based on equation (1)) or insignificant. We find no significant association between EITC expansions and expenditures in families headed by single mothers without a high school degree or those with at least a BA degree. However, for the low-educated group, we do find evidence that EITC expansions result in slightly lower total family debt.

Next, we study the association between EITC expansions and patterns of expenditures on major categories of spending. Although we present results for all groups, we are mainly interested in finding whether EITC expansions influenced expenditure patterns for the medium-educated group since our analysis thus far has suggested that EITC expansions increased total expenditures for this group. We are also interested in whether there are any effects for the low-educated group for whom we found reductions in debt associated with the EITC. The results for patterns of expenditures are presented in Table 3.3. All regressions are based on equation (3), and we present the estimated coefficient for EITC and the interaction between EITC and the dichotomous variable indicating whether the expenditure is for the month of February. The dependent variables—the 10 major expenditure categories—are listed in the row headings.

Estimates presented in Table 3.3 suggest that EITC expansions are associated with significantly increased expenditures by medium-educated single-mother families on food, clothing, transportation, and education and with marginally significant increased expenditures on housing, and alcohol and tobacco. The food, clothing, and alcohol and tobacco effects are main effects,

Table 3.3. *Summary of effects of EITC generosity on monthly equivalized spending on major categories of expenditure among single-mother families, by mothers' education*

	All	<HS	HS/some college	BA+
Housing				
EITC	−0.020*	−0.033*	−0.012	−0.021
	(0.009)	(0.013)	(0.010)	(0.038)
EITC * Feb	0.019+	−0.005	0.024+	−0.001
	(0.011)	(0.018)	(0.014)	(0.040)
Food				
EITC	0.016**	0.009	0.013**	0.037**
	(0.003)	(0.006)	(0.004)	(0.012)
EITC * Feb	0.003	−0.010	0.007	0.001
	(0.004)	(0.007)	(0.005)	(0.014)
Alcohol and Tobacco				
EITC	0.001+	0.002	0.002+	−0.001
	(0.001)	(0.002)	(0.001)	(0.002)
EITC * Feb	−0.001	−0.004*	0.000	−0.005
	(0.001)	(0.002)	(0.001)	(0.003)
Clothing				
EITC	0.009**	−0.000	0.008**	0.026**
	(0.002)	(0.003)	(0.003)	(0.009)
EITC * Feb	0.002	−0.000	0.006	−0.022*
	(0.003)	(0.005)	(0.004)	(0.010)
Transportation				
EITC	−0.009	−0.009	0.001	−0.011
	(0.014)	(0.020)	(0.018)	(0.050)
EITC * Feb	0.055+	0.004	0.073*	0.038
	(0.029)	(0.033)	(0.035)	(0.115)
Health				
EITC	0.000	−0.004	0.000	0.017*
	(0.002)	(0.004)	(0.002)	(0.008)
EITC * Feb	0.003	0.001	0.005	−0.001
	(0.003)	(0.004)	(0.004)	(0.012)

(continued)

Table 3.3. *Continued*

	All	< HS	HS/some college	BA+
Leisure				
EITC	0.003	−0.000	−0.003	0.036**
	(0.003)	(0.002)	(0.003)	(0.010)
EITC * Feb	0.006	0.001	0.008	−0.002
	(0.005)	(0.004)	(0.007)	(0.021)
Personal care				
EITC	−0.000	−0.000	0.000	0.000
	(0.000)	(0.001)	(0.000)	(0.001)
EITC * Feb	0.000	0.000	0.000	−0.001
	(0.000)	(0.001)	(0.000)	(0.001)
Education				
EITC	−0.002	−0.001	−0.003	0.018
	(0.003)	(0.001)	(0.002)	(0.021)
EITC * Feb	0.006*	−0.003+	0.007*	0.007
	(0.003)	(0.002)	(0.003)	(0.014)
Miscellaneous				
EITC	−0.009+	−0.004	−0.003	−0.017
	(0.005)	(0.004)	(0.003)	(0.025)
EITC * Feb	−0.007	0.013	−0.001	−0.047
	(0.011)	(0.012)	(0.004)	(0.061)

Notes: In each column, each panel is from a separate regression, with controls for the full set of welfare policy variables, monthly unemployment rate, demographic characteristics, state, year, and month effects, as detailed in the notes for Table 3.1. Heteroskodasticity-adjusted standard errors clustered at the consumer unit are in parentheses. $+p < 10\%$; $*p < 5\%$; $**p < 1\%$. Sample sizes are the same as those presented in Table 3.1.

with a one dollar increase in EITC associated with a $0.013 increase in average monthly expenditures on food, a $0.008 increase in average monthly spending on clothing, and a $0.002 increase in average monthly spending on alcohol and tobacco (marginally significant). In contrast, the transportation and education effects are interaction effects, indicating that more generous EITCs are associated with increased expenditures on those items in the month of February. Specifically, we find that a one dollar increase in

EITC is associated with increased February spending of about 2 cents on housing (marginally significant), 7 cents on transportation, and 0.7 cents on education. We find no evidence that more generous EITCs increase spending in any of the 10 categories among the low-educated group, but we do find some positive associations between more generous EITCs and spending for the high-educated group; the point estimates are larger than the corresponding estimates for the medium-educated group. Since we think that the high-educated group is relatively less likely than the medium-educated group to receive EITCs,[25] it may be that these effects for the high-educated group reflect other tax policies for which we are not controlling.

Results (not shown but available on request) that stratify samples based on whether any adult in the household worked last year or not suggest that all the statistically significant results presented in Table 3.3 were driven by trends in expenditure for the medium-educated single mothers who had at least one working family member last year, providing some validity that the results in Table 3.3 were associated with EITC.

The results in Table 3.3 suggest that the EITC is associated with an increase in average monthly expenditure on food and clothing and footwear. In our previous research, we found that welfare reform was associated with increased spending on food away from home (rather than food at home) and adult clothing and footwear (rather than children's clothing and footwear). To get some insight into the EITC and expenditures on these categories, we further examine the association between EITC and expenditure on food at home and food away from home, and on expenditure on adult clothing and footwear and children's clothing and footwear; the results are presented in Table 3.4.

Again focusing on the results for the medium-educated group, we find that a one dollar increase in the maximum available EITC refund is associated with a \$0.010 increase in average monthly spending on food at home and a \$0.003 increase in average monthly spending on food away from home; there is also a marginally significant further increase in spending on food away from home during the month of February. The estimated average monthly effect on children's clothing is negative, but with a positive interaction term indicating a slight increase in expenditures in the month of February. For adult clothing, the average monthly effect of the

---

[25] Assuming that all single mothers who worked and earned less than \$35,000 were eligible for EITC in 2004, we estimate, using the March CPS data, that 58 percent of single mothers with a high school degree or some college were eligible for EITC compared to 40 percent of single mothers with a BA or higher degree and 50 percent of single mothers without a high school degree.

Table 3.4. *Summary of effects of EITC generosity on monthly equivalized spending on specific food and clothing expenditure items among single-mother families, by mothers' education*

	All	< HS	HS/some college	BA+
Food at Home				
EITC	0.013**	0.011+	0.010**	0.022**
	(0.003)	(0.006)	(0.003)	(0.008)
EITC * Feb	0.001	−0.011+	0.004	0.004
	(0.003)	(0.006)	(0.004)	(0.009)
Food Away from Home				
EITC	0.003*	−0.002	0.003*	0.015*
	(0.001)	(0.002)	(0.001)	(0.007)
EITC * Feb	0.002	0.001	0.003+	−0.003
	(0.002)	(0.003)	(0.002)	(0.009)
Children's Clothing and Footwear				
EITC	−0.001	−0.001	−0.002*	0.005*
	(0.001)	(0.001)	(0.001)	(0.002)
EITC * Feb	0.002+	−0.001	0.002*	−0.002
	(0.001)	(0.002)	(0.001)	(0.003)
Adults' Clothing and Footwear				
EITC	0.003*	−0.002	0.002	0.011*
	(0.001)	(0.002)	(0.001)	(0.005)
EITC * Feb	0.002	0.001	0.005+	−0.013*
	(0.002)	(0.003)	(0.003)	(0.006)

Notes: In each column, each panel is from a separate regression, adjusted for the welfare policy variables, monthly unemployment rate, demographic characteristics, state, year, and month effects, as detailed in the notes for Table 3.1. Heteroskodasticity-adjusted standard errors clustered at the consumer unit are in parentheses. $+p < 10\%$; $*p < 5\%$; $**p < 1\%$. Sample sizes are the same as those presented in Table 3.1.

EITC is insignificant, with a marginally significant positive effect of $0.005 in February.

As a specification check, we repeat the analysis in Table 3.4 by stratifying samples on the basis of whether the family had an employed member last year. As in our previous analysis, we find (results not shown but available on request) that the estimates in Table 3.4 were driven by the changes in expenditures in the sample of medium-educated single mothers with a working member last year, with the estimated effects for medium-educated single mothers without a working member last year modest and statistically insignificant.

Table 3.5. *Summary of effects of EITC generosity on monthly equivalized expenditures on vehicles and major appliances among single-mother families, by mothers' education*

	All	< HS	HS/some college	BA+
Total Expenditure on Vehicles				
EITC	−0.009	−0.005	0.001	−0.019
	(0.014)	(0.020)	(0.018)	(0.049)
EITC * Feb	0.057*	0.004	0.073*	0.047
	(0.028)	(0.033)	(0.035)	(0.115)
Purchase of New Cars and Trucks				
EITC	0.001	−0.004	0.001	−0.012
	(0.009)	(0.007)	(0.012)	(0.039)
EITC * Feb	0.033	0.006	0.036+	0.058
	(0.020)	(0.004)	(0.021)	(0.108)
Purchase of Used Cars and Trucks				
EITC	0.001	0.004	0.006	0.015
	(0.009)	(0.017)	(0.012)	(0.028)
EITC * Feb	0.022	0.008	0.029	0.011
	(0.019)	(0.023)	(0.026)	(0.036)
Purchase of Major Appliances				
EITC	−0.000	−0.001	−0.001	0.006
	(0.001)	(0.001)	(0.001)	(0.004)
EITC * Feb	0.003+	0.000	0.005*	−0.004
	(0.002)	(0.002)	(0.002)	(0.005)

Notes: In each column, each panel is from a separate regression, with controls for the welfare policy variables, monthly unemployment rate, demographic characteristics, state, year, and month effects, as detailed in the notes for Table 3.1. Heteroskodasticity-adjusted standard errors clustered at the consumer unit are in parentheses. $+p < 10\%$; $*p < 5\%$; $**p < 1\%$. Sample sizes are the same as those presented in Table 3.1.

The final objective of our study is to examine whether EITC expansions are associated with any change in ownership of consumer durables. We focus on total expenditures on cars and trucks; the purchase of new cars and trucks; purchase of used cars and trucks; and purchase of major appliances. Again, we present results for all three education groups, but we expect to find effects only for single mothers with a high school degree or some college since this is the group for which we found an increase in expenditures associated with EITC expansions.

Estimates in Table 3.5 suggest that EITC expansions are associated with an increase in expenditure on vehicles in February by medium-educated single mothers. A one dollar increase in EITC is associated with an increased expenditure in February (over the monthly average) on vehicles of 7.3 cents. We also find some evidence of purchases of new cars (marginally significant) and major appliances in February associated with EITC expansions in families headed by single mothers with a high school or some college education. We find no statistically significant association between EITC and expenditure on vehicles, or purchase of cars or major appliances, in families headed by low- or high-educated single mothers.

When the data are stratified by mother's employment (results not shown but available on request), we find some evidence of an increase in average monthly expenditure on vehicles and ownership of used cars associated with EITC expansions in families headed by medium-educated mothers without any working members last year. Since unemployed households did not benefit from EITC expansions, this suggests that there may be unobserved factors (e.g., economic trends, trends in prices of major appliances and used vehicles) correlated with EITC expansions that may have affected the outcomes for this group. These factors may have also affected the purchases by families with at least one employed member headed by medium-educated mothers, and therefore we need to be careful in interpreting our results. Interestingly, we find the seasonality effect of EITC (increased expenditure in February) to be present only for the single-mother medium-educated group with at least one working household member, providing some validity to our finding that families spend some of their EITC refunds on buying vehicles and major appliances.

VI. Conclusion

In this chapter, we provide new evidence on a question that has received relatively little attention to date, namely, how EITC expansions have affected the expenditures of the single-mother families who were their primary target. Dividing single mothers by their education level, we find the most consistent evidence of EITC effects on expenditures for the medium-educated group—the group with a high school degree or some college. This is a group that has a high probability of being employed but typically has earnings low enough to be eligible for the EITC, so finding effects for this group is not surprising. Note that we estimate the intention to treat (ITT) effect, which is different from the effect of treatment (policy) on the treated (TOT). Since a different proportion of each group actually receives the EITC benefit and the average amount of benefit differs across groups, the actual effect of the treatment on the treated (the effect of EITC expansions on families that receive EITC) is likely to be different from our estimates of the ITT effects.

We find that the EITC has had some effects on average monthly spending for the medium-educated group of single mothers. These average monthly effects include increases in spending on food (both at home and away from home), alcohol and tobacco, and clothing. The results also suggest that more generous EITCs may be associated with lower levels of total family debt for this group.

We also find that more generous EITCs are associated with increased total expenditures for this group in February and with increased expenditures that month on several major categories, including housing, transportation, and education, as well as several more detailed items, including food away from home, children's clothing and footwear, and adult clothing and footwear, as well as total expenditures on vehicles, purchase of new cars and trucks, and purchase of major appliances.

Thus, for the medium-educated group, we find evidence that more generous EITCs are associated with higher spending month in and month out on a few categories of items (and possibly less debt) but more strongly with increases in spending on a wider set of items in February, when a majority of families receive the credits.

We also find evidence that the low-educated group—the women with less than a high school education—used their EITC refunds to retire debt instead of increasing expenditure. This result echoes the finding from the earlier study by Smeeding et al. (2000), in which they asked EITC recipients about their preferred use of EITC refunds and half of those interviewed said that their top priority would be to pay off bills. We also find large effects of both welfare waivers and TANF on debt for the low-educated group; these effects should certainly be explored further in future work.

There are several limitations to this study and several directions for future work. A continuing challenge is to isolate those groups most likely to be affected by the EITC expansions and to compare them to a similar group that is less likely to be affected. In our work, we have compared single mothers of different education levels and, as a specification check, further subdivided them by both employment and education. However, as we have discussed earlier, dividing single mothers on the basis of their employment is problematic, as we know that EITC expansions have affected single mothers' employment decisions. A related challenge is to control for other factors that may be confounded with the EITC expansions. Our models control for an extensive set of individual, family, and state-level variables

Appendix Table 3.1. *The progress of refundable state EITCs and their generosity*

State	Year enacted	Percent of federal EITC
Vermont	1988	25% before 2000 and 32% since 2000
Wisconsin	1989	4% if one child, 14% if two children, 43% if three or more children
Minnesota[a]	1991, restructured in 1998	Set as a percentage of the federal EITC before 1998: 10% in 1991–1992; 15% in 1993–1997. The 1998 restructuring made the state EITC a percentage of earned income. It averaged 25% of the federal EITC during 1998–2000 and 33% since 2001
New York	1994	7.5% in 1994; 10% in 1995; 20% during 1996–1999; 22.5% in 2000; 25% in 2001; 27.5% in 2002; 30% since 2003
Massachusetts	1997	10% in 1997–1998; 15% since 1999
Kansas	1998	10% before 2002; 15% since 2002
Maryland[b]	1998	10% in 1998–1999; 15% in 2000; 16% in 2001–2002; 20% since 2003
Colorado	1999	8.5% in 1999; 10% in 2000–2001; suspended since 2002
District of Columbia	2000	10% in 2000; 25% in 2001–2004; 35% since 2005
New Jersey	2000	10% in 2000; 15% in 2001; 17.5% in 2002; 20% in 2003 and after if income below $20,000
Oklahoma	2002	5%
Illinois	2003	5%
Indiana[c]	2003	6%

Rhode Island	2003	The state EITC is set at 25%; 10% of the state credit refundable in 2003–2005 and increased to 15% in 2006
Nebraska	2006	8%
Oregon	2006	5%; increased to 6% in 2008
Michigan	Legislation passed in 2006	10% in 2008; 20% in 2009 and after

[a] Minnesota has a Working Family Credit, which is not expressly structured as a percentage of the federal EITC but rather as a percentage of earned income, although the eligibility is the same. It is structured to avoid the problem of total family resources decreasing as work increases.

[b] A Maryland taxpayer may claim either the refundable credit or the larger nonrefundable credit (set at 50% of the federal EITC), but not both credits.

[c] Indiana enacted a state EITC in 1999 that was not based on the federal EITC. It was available only to families with income below $12,000. Moreover, unlike the federal credit, the amount of the Indiana credit declined rather than increased as a parent entered the workforce and increased his or her earnings. It switched to being based on the federal EITC in 2003.

Sources: Center on Budget and Policy Priorities (http://www.cbpp.org) and State EITC Online Resource Center (http://www.stateeitc.com), and various state sources such as the Colorado Fiscal Policy Institute (http://www.cclponline.org/ccs/about_CFPI.html), Washington, DC, Office of Tax and Revenue (http://otr.cfo.dc.gov/), Maryland Budget and Tax Policy Institute (http://www.marylandpolicy.org/), New Jersey Policy Perspective (http://www.njpp.org), New York State Department of Taxation and Finance (http://www.tax.state.ny.us/), and Vermont Legislative Joint Fiscal Office (http://www.leg.state.vt.us/jfo/).

Appendix Table 3.2. *Major expenditure categories*

Category	Description
Housing and utilities	Housing expenditures include the following four categories:
	1. Shelter cost, including owned dwelling (mortgage interest, property taxes, and maintenance, repairs, insurance, and other expenses), rent, and other lodging costs
	2. Utility cost, including natural gas, electricity, fuel oil and other fuels, telephone services, water and other public services
	3. Household operations, including domestic services (babysitting and child day care included) and other household expenses
	4. House furnishings and equipment, including household textiles, furniture, floor coverings, major appliances (such as a built-in dishwasher, garbage disposal, purchase and installation of a refrigerator or home freezer, clothes washer or dryer, cooking stove, range or oven, microwave oven, portable dishwasher, window air conditioner, electric floor cleaning equipment, and sewing machines), small appliances (such as dinnerware, flatware, glassware, nonelectric cookware, small electrical kitchen appliances, portable heating and cooling equipment), and other miscellaneous household equipment
Food	Food at home and away from home
Alcohol and tobacco	Alcoholic beverages and tobacco and smoking supplies
Clothing	Clothing and footwear for men, women, boys and girls, and other apparel products and services
Transportation	Cars and trucks (new and used), other vehicles, gasoline and motor oil, vehicle finance charges, maintenance and repairs, vehicle insurance, rental, leases, licenses, and other charges, and public transportations, both local and on trips
Health	Health insurance, medical services, prescription drugs, and medical supplies

Leisure	Fees and admissions to entertainment activities, televisions, radios, and sound equipments, pets, toys, and playground equipments, and other entertainment
Personal care	Wigs, hairpieces, or toupees, electric personal care appliances, and personal care services for males and females, including haircuts
Education (including reading)	Tuition, school books, supplies, and equipment for college, elementary and high school, day care center, nursery school and other schools, rentals of books and equipment, and other school-related expenses; newspapers and magazines (subscriptions and nonsubscriptions), books (through and not through book clubs), and encyclopedias and other sets of reference books
Miscellaneous	Including miscellaneous expenditures (membership fees for credit card memberships and shopping clubs, lotteries and pari-mutuel losses), legal fees (excluding real estate closing costs), funeral, burial, or cremation expenses, including limousine and flowers, safe deposit boxes, charges for checking accounts and other banking services, purchase and upkeep of cemetery lots or vaults, accounting fees, interest on line of credit home equity loan (properties other than owned homes and occupational expenses), and cash contributions (alimony and child support expenditures, support for college students, gifts to nonfamily members of stocks, bonds, mutual funds, and cash contributions to charities, churches or religious organizations, educational institutions, political organizations and other organizations, and other cash gifts), life and other personal insurance, and retirement, pensions, and Social Security contributions
Total	Total of above

Appendix Table 3.3. *Debt, specific expenditure items, and expenditures on vehicles and major appliances*

Category	Description
Debt	Total amount owed to creditors at the second or fifth interview
Food at home	Food purchased for preparation and consumption at home
Food away from home	Food purchased for consumption away from home (including restaurant meals, take-out meals, and fast food)
Children's clothing	Children's clothing, footwear, and accessories
Adult's clothing	Adult's clothing, footwear, and accessories
Total expenditure on vehicles	Purchase of new or used cars, trucks, and other vehicles (net outlay); gasoline and motor oil; vehicle finance charges, maintenance and repairs, insurance, rental, leases, licenses, and other charges
Major appliances	Built-in dishwasher, garbage disposal, or range hood for jobs considered replacement or maintenance/repair; purchase and installation of refrigerator or home freezer, clothes washer and dryer, cooking stove, range or oven, microwave oven, portable dishwasher, window air conditioner, electric floor cleaning equipment, sewing machines

including controls for the major elements of welfare reform, as well as state, year, and month fixed effects, but there may be unobserved factors correlated with EITC expansions that may confound our findings.

In spite of these limitations, these results have some implications for the future direction of the EITC as well as welfare reform more broadly. First and most notably, as discussed earlier, the EITC seems to have the strongest impact on medium-educated single mothers, namely, those with a high school degree or some college education, even though low-educated single mothers were the main target of welfare reform in general. Noting this difference is important for improving the effectiveness of both the EITC and welfare reform in future. Secondly, the EITC may enable medium-educated single-mother families to increase both their stability (by spending more on housing and the purchase of major appliances) and mobility (by spending more on transportation, education, vehicles, and purchases of new cars and trucks), especially in February, the typical month of receiving the EITC refund. These expenditures could help families to manage both work and family life more effectively, and thus reinforce the positive anti-poverty impact of the EITC and help achieve the overall goal of welfare reform. Thirdly, findings from this study suggest that the EITC may be able to help low- and medium-educated single-mother families to pay off debt. Policymakers should take these lessons into consideration when formulating future directions of the EITC and welfare reform.

References

Agarwal, Sumit, Chunlin Liu, and Nicholas S. Souleles. 2007. "The Reaction of Consumer Spending and Debt to Tax Rebates: Evidence from Consumer Credit Data." *The Journal of Political Economy*, 115(6): 986–1019.

Barrow, Lisa, and Leslie McGranahan. 2000. "The Effects of the Earned Income Credit on the Seasonality of Household Expenditures." *National Tax Journal*, 53(4), Part 2, "Special Issue: The Earned Income Tax Credit," 1211–1243.

Battistin, Erich. 2003. "Errors in Survey Reports of Consumer Expenditures." *IFS Working Paper* 03/07, London: Institute for Fiscal Studies.

Blank, Rebecca M. 2002. "Evaluating Welfare Reform in the United States." *Journal of Economic Literature*, 40: 1105–1166.

2006. "What Did the 1990s Welfare Reforms Accomplish?" in *Public Policy and the Income Distribution*. Alan J. Auerbach, David Card, and John M. Quigley (eds.), New York: Russell Sage, 33–79.

Blumenthal, Marsha, Brian Erard, and Chih-Chin Ho. 2005. "Participation and Compliance with the Earned Income Tax Credit." *National Tax Journal*, 58(2): 189–213.

Bureau of Labor Statistics. 2005. "2003 Consumer Expenditure Interview Survey Public Use Microdata Documentation." http://www.bls.gov/cex/csxintvw.pdf.

Caban, A. J., D. J. Lee, L. E. Fleming, O. Gómez-Marín, W. LeBlanc, and T. Pitman. 2005. "Obesity in U.S. workers: The National Health Interview Survey, 1986 to 2002." *American Journal of Public Health*, 95:1614–1622.

Center for Budget and Policy Priorities. 2006. "A Hand Up: How State Earned Income Tax Credits Help Working Families Escape Poverty in 2006." http://www.cbpp.org/3-8-06sfp.pdf.

Dickert, Stacy, Scott Houser, and John Karl Scholz. 1995. "The Earned Income Tax Credit and Transfer Programs: A Study of Labor Market and Program Participation," in *Tax Policy and the Economy*, Vol. 9. James Poterba, ed. Cambridge, MA: MIT Press, 1–50.

Dickert-Conlin, Stacy, and Scott Houser. 2002. "EITC and Marriage." *National Tax Journal*, 55(1): 25–40.

Edwards, Ryan D. 2004. "Macroeconomic Implications of the Earned Income Tax Credit." *National Tax Journal*, 57(1): 45–65.

Eissa, Nada, and Hilary W. Hoynes. 2004. "Taxes and the Labor Market Participation of Married Couples: The Earned Income Tax Credit." *Journal of Public Economics*, 88(9–10): 1931–1958.

Eissa, Nada, and Jeffrey B. Liebman. 1996. "Labor Supply Response to the Earned Income Tax Credit." *The Quarterly Journal of Economics*, 111(2): 605–637.

Eissa, Nada, and Austin Nichols. 2005. "Tax-Transfer Policy and Labor-Market Outcomes." *The American Economic Review*, 95(2): 88–93.

Ellwood, David T. 2000. "The Impact of the Earned Income Tax Credit and Social Policy Reforms on Work, Marriage, and Living Arrangements." *National Tax Journal*, 53(4), Part 2: 1065–1106.

Furman, Jason. 2006. "Tax Reform and Poverty." Washington, DC: Center on Budget and Policy Priorities (April 10). Available at http://www.cbpp.org/4-10-06tax.pdf.

Greenstein, Robert. 2005. "The Earned Income Tax Credit: Boosting Employment and Aiding the Poor." Washington, DC: Center on Budget and Policy Priorities (August 17). Available at http://www.cbpp.org/7-19-05eic.htm.

Greenstein, Robert and Issac Shapiro. 1998. "New Research Findings on the Effects of the Earned Income Tax Credit." Washington, DC: Center on Budget and Policy Priorities (March 11). Available at http://www.cbpp.org/311eitc.htm.

Grogger, Jeffrey. 2003. "The Effects of Time Limits, the EITC, and Other Policy Changes on Welfare Use, Work, and Income among Female-Head Families." *Review of Economics and Statistics*, 85(2): 394–408.

Grogger, Jeffrey, and Lynn A. Karoly. 2005. *Welfare Reform: Effects of a Decade of Change.* Cambridge, MA: Harvard University Press.

Grogger, Jeffrey, Lynn A. Karoly, and Jacob Alex Klerman. 2002. "Consequences of Welfare Reform: A Research Synthesis." RAND Working Paper DRU-2676-DHHS. Available at http://www.acf.hhs.gov/programs/opre/welfare_Employ/res_systhesis/reports/consequences_of_wr/rand_report.pdf.

Gruber, Jonathan. 2000. "Cash Welfare as a Consumption Smoothing Mechanism for Divorced Mothers." *Journal of Public Economics*, 75(2): 157–182.

Haskins, Ron. 2001. "Effects of Welfare Reform on Family Income and Poverty," in *The New World of Welfare*. Rebecca Blank and Ron Haskins, eds. Washington, DC: Brookings Institution Press, 103–136.

Hotz, V. Joseph, Charles H. Mullin, and John Karl Scholz. 2006. "Examining the Effect of the Earned Income Tax Credit on the Labor Market Participation of Families on Welfare." *National Bureau of Economic Research Working Paper 11968*. Cambridge, MA: NBER.

Hotz, V. Joseph, and John Karl Scholz. 2003. "The Earned Income Tax Credit," in *Means-Tested Transfer Programs in the United States*. Robert A. Moffitt (ed.), Chicago: University of Chicago Press, 141–198.

Kaushal, Neeraj, Qin Gao, and Jane Waldfogel. 2007. "Welfare Reform and Family Expenditures: How Are Single Mothers Adapting to the New Welfare and Work Regime?" *Social Service Review*, 81(3): 369–396.

Kniesner, Thomas J., and James P. Ziliak. 2002. "Tax Reform and Automatic Stabilization." *The American Economic Review*, 92(3): 590–612.

Lichter, Daniel T., and Jayakody, Rukamalie. 2002. "Welfare Reform: How Do We Measure Success?" *Annual Review of Sociology*, 28: 117–141.

Meyer, Bruce D., and Dan T. Rosenbaum. 2000. "Making Single Mothers Work: Recent Tax and Welfare Policy and Its Effects." *National Tax Journal*, 53(4), Part 2, "Special Issue: The Earned Income Tax Credit, December": 1027–1062.

2001a. "Making Single Mothers Work: Recent Tax and Welfare Policy and its Effects," in *Making Work Pay: The Earned Income Tax Credit and Its Impact on America's Families*. Bruce D. Meyer and Douglas Holtz-Eakin (eds.) New York: Russell Sage, 69–115.

2001b. "Welfare, the Earned Income Tax Credit, and the Labor Supply of Single Mothers." *Quarterly Journal of Economics*, 116(3): 1063–2014.

Meyer, Bruce, and James X. Sullivan. 2003. "Measuring the Well-Being of the Poor Using Income and Consumption." *Journal of Human Resources*, 38(S): 1180–1220.

Meyer, Bruce. 2004. "The Effects of Welfare and Tax Reform: The Material Well-Being of Single Mothers in the 1980s and 1990s." *Journal of Public Economics*, 88: 1387–1420.

Meyer, Bruce. 2006. "Consumption, Income and Material Well-being after Welfare Reform." NBER Working paper 11976.

Nagle, Ami, and Nicholas Johnson. 2006. "A Hand Up: How State Earned Income Tax Credits Help Working Families Escape Poverty in 2006." Washington, DC: Center on Budget and Public Priorities (March 8). Available at http://www.cbpp.org/3-8-06sfp.pdf.

Neumark, David, and William Wascher. 2007. "Minimum Wages, the Earned Income Tax Credit, and Employment: Evidence from the Post-Welfare Reform Era." *National Bureau of Economic Research Working Paper No. 12915.* Cambridge, MA: NBER.

Okwuje, Ifie, and Nicholas Johnson. 2006. "A Rising Number of State Earned Income Tax Credits Are Helping Working Families Escape Poverty." Washington, DC: Center on Budget and Public Priorities (October 20). Available at http://www.cbpp.org/10-12-06sfp.htm.

Parker, Jonathan A. 2003. "Consumption Risk and Expected Stock Returns." *The American Economic Review*, 93(2), Papers and Proceedings of the One Hundred Fifteenth Annual Meeting of the American Economic Association.

Rector, Robert. 2004. "Understanding Poverty and Economic Inequality in the United States." *Backgrounder No. 1756.* Washington, DC: The Heritage Foundation.

Romich, Jennifer L., and Thomas Weisner. 2000. "How Families View and Use the EITC: Advance Payment versus Lump Sum Delivery." *National Tax Journal*, 53(4), Part 2, "Special Issue: The Earned Income Tax Credit," 1245–1265.

Shapiro, Matthew D., and Joel Slemrod. 1995. "Consumer Response to the Timing of Income: Evidence from a Change in Tax Withholding." *The American Economic Review*, 85(1): 274–283.

2003. "Consumer Response to Tax Rebates." *The American Economic Review*, 93(1): 381–396.

Smeeding, T. M., K. R. Phillips, and M. O'Connor. 2000. "The EITC: Expectation, Knowledge, Use, and Economic and Social Mobility." *National Tax Journal*, 53(4), Part 2, "Special Issue: The Earned Income Tax Credit," 1187–1209.

Stephens, Melvin. 2003. "3rd of the Month": Do Social Security Recipients Smooth Consumption between Checks?" *The American Economic Review*, 93(1): 406–422.

U. S. Department of the Treasury. 2006. "Monthly Treasury Statement." Available at http://fms.treas.gov/mts/backissues.html.

U. S. House of Representatives, Committee on Ways and Means. 2004 *Green Book.* Washington, DC: U.S. Government Printing Office.

Williams, James. 1997. "The Earned Income Tax Credit and Welfare Reform." *The Richmond Journal of Law and the Public Interest*, 1(2), Available at http://law.richmond.edu/rjolpi/Issues_Archived/1997_Spring_Welfare_Reform/JWILLIAMS_FIN.htm.

FOUR

How Families Are Doing Nine Years after
Welfare Reform

2005 Evidence from the Three-City Study

Bianca Frogner, Robert Moffitt, and David C. Ribar

I. Introduction

Much of what we understand about economic outcomes associated with welfare reform comes from studies of families who were initially on welfare and who left after welfare reform ("leaver" studies), from studies of low-income families in the first few years after reform, and from randomized trial evaluations conducted at around the time of the reform. Blank (2002) reviewed numerous studies that indicated that employment and labor supply for disadvantaged families increased in the immediate aftermath of welfare reform. She also reported that the evidence regarding impacts on incomes and well-being was generally positive, although the leaver studies showed smaller gains. More recently, Grogger and Karoly (2005) and Blank (Chapter One, this volume) summarized evidence from experimental and observational studies that indicated that specific types of reforms, especially mandatory work activities, and welfare reform as a whole contributed to higher levels of employment, larger incomes, and less poverty among welfare households. However, as Moffitt (2002) has pointed out, the rise in incomes in the experimental studies was largely confined to studies without time limits; in the experiments with such limits, which most closely reflect actual welfare reform in the states, the rise in income was insignificant (Bloom and Michalopoulos 2001).

Further, the income gains shown in observational cross-sectional data-sets like the Current Population Survey (CPS) or the National Survey of America's Families were almost all a result of increases in income among families not on welfare; incomes for leavers per se rose very little (see the reviews by Blank and by Grogger and Karoly on this point as well). This finding is consistent with other work showing that much of the effect of welfare reform on the caseload arose from a decline in entry rates rather than a rise in exit rates (Grogger, Haider, and Klerman 2003). Similarly, analyses by Bollinger, Gonzalez, and Ziliak (Chapter Two, this volume) show that income gains were concentrated among single mothers at the top of the income distribution; single mothers at the bottom of the distribution saw earnings gains but experienced benefit cuts, leading to either no change or, in some cases, to actual declines in their average disposable incomes. Tabulations from the Survey of Income and Program Participation (SIPP), which also followed families over time as they left welfare, show very modest increases in income after leaving as well (Bavier 2001a, 2001b; see also Cancian et al. 2002).

A further issue of some importance is the source of the income gains that have been observed for leavers from the Temporary Assistance for Needy Families (TANF) program, however modest. Both Bavier (2001a, 2001b) and Danziger et al. (2002, table 1) found that a large fraction of the gains in income came from increased earnings by members of the family other than the welfare recipient herself. For the recipient herself, earnings gains after leaving welfare were largely canceled out by benefit losses.

In this chapter, we survey and summarize the evidence on these issues that is available from the Three-City Study. The Three-City Study is a longitudinal survey, which began in 1999 with 2,400 low-income families with children living in Boston, Chicago, and San Antonio. Although the families were economically vulnerable, the survey purposely included welfare participants and nonparticipants. Follow-up interviews, with high rates of participation, were conducted in 2000–2001 and 2005.

The Three-City Study occupies a particular niche in the data sources on welfare reform. While a chief disadvantage is that the study took place only in three cities, and hence policy variation is limited, it is one of the longest ongoing panel surveys of low-income families (1999 to 2005, or seven years) in the United States and has some of the most recent data (2005) available. Thus, the survey provides the first detailed postrecession information on how this population is doing. In addition, the survey is rich in information and detail on respondent well-being and behavior at each of the three interview waves, having collected a comprehensive set of household income components for all household members. Unlike the administrative data used by Mueser, Stevens, and Troske (Chapter Five, this volume), the sampling frame of the Three-City Study includes nonwelfare families, so that welfare entry decisions as well as welfare exit decisions can be studied.

We use these data to investigate three main issues. First, we examine how patterns of welfare use among families in the Three-City Study changed up to the time of the most recent survey in 2005. We document the incidence of welfare receipt at each interview but also examine exit and entry behavior (transition patterns) in the data. Second, we investigate the economic, demographic, social, and health correlates of different types of transition outcomes. We are especially interested in how incomes, employment, and the composition of incomes changed with welfare status. Third, we examine the role that work plays in helping families become economically self-reliant after leaving welfare. Without a careful look at the data, the answer is less than clear. On the one hand, increased earnings can be offset by losses of means-tested assistance income. On the other hand, transitional assistance and the Earned Income Tax Credit (EITC) act to subsidize work. Thus, it is an open question whether work really "pays" for disadvantaged families. Along the way, in examining these issues, we will also see how incomes have changed for leavers, nonleavers, and those never on welfare and whether the additional income from other household members is important for income levels after welfare.

II. The Three-City Study

The first interviews in the Three-City Study were conducted in 1999 among low-income families (families with incomes below 200 percent of the poverty line) with children between the ages of 0–4 and 10–14 years living in low- and moderate-income neighborhoods. Approximately 2,400 interviews were conducted, and included welfare and nonwelfare families. The response rate in the first wave of interviews was 74 percent. Follow-up interviews were conducted in 2000–2001 and 2005 with the original children from the sample, their initial caregivers, and any new caregivers if the children's living arrangements had changed. Retention in the second and third waves was very high, with 90 percent of the households (2,205) from the first wave being reinterviewed in the second wave and 84 percent of the households (2,038) being reinterviewed in the third wave. In each wave, caregivers (usually the mothers) provided current and retrospective information about their public assistance experiences and employment. The caregivers also provided information about their incomes, demographic characteristics, backgrounds, health status, and other circumstances. We analyze information from all three waves of the survey.

For our study, we select caregivers who participated in all three waves, including some caregivers who eventually lived apart from the focal child. Because we wish to examine employment behavior among potential welfare recipients, we restrict the sample to caregivers who were 62 years old or younger (working age) and who were living with at least one child under the age of 18. We also exclude observations for a few caregivers who did not answer the questions relevant to our analysis, including the program use, income, and employment questions. With these restrictions, our final analysis sample includes observations for 1,555 caregivers, about two-thirds of the original sample. All of our statistical analyses use weights that adjust for differential sampling and response rates in the original interviews and for selection due to attrition and the exclusion criteria in our specific data set. The sample lost to follow-up exhibits few differences in Wave 1 demographic characteristics, and separate analyses of attrition bias arising from unobservables suggests that a few demographic variables were affected, but these are controlled for in our analyses (Moffitt, 2004).

A. The Cities

The three cities for the study were originally selected because they were representative of large urban areas in the United States and because they were in states with markedly different welfare policies. In 1999, Massachusetts was a high-benefit state with short time limits, a family-cap policy, and moderate sanctions but many types of exemptions. Illinois was a medium-benefit state with a standard five-year time limit and a family-cap provision. Illinois allowed families to receive benefits for some time before requiring work, but it also imposed tougher sanctions than the other states. Texas was a low-benefit work-first state with short time limits, no family cap, and weak sanctions; it also emphasized diversion. All three states offered transitional Medicaid and child care to families that left welfare for employment.

For the most part, these descriptions still characterized the programs in 2005. Massachusetts continued to have the highest benefits, with a maximum monthly payment of $618 for a family of three with no other income, while Texas had the lowest benefits, with a maximum monthly payment of $223 for a family of three. Time limit policies were also similar across years, with Massachusetts and Texas continuing to opt for short time limits and Illinois keeping the five-year federal limit. The states also continued to offer transitional assistance. Among the changes in policies, Illinois dropped its family-cap provision in 2004. Illinois also adopted a diversion program.

Over the period covered by our study, welfare caseloads in all three states fell substantially. The steepest drop occurred in Illinois, where the average monthly TANF caseload fell by more than two-thirds from 123,000 families in 1999 to 38,000 families in 2005. In Texas the average monthly TANF caseload fell by just under a quarter, while in Massachusetts the caseload fell by one-tenth. Nationally, the average number of families on TANF each month fell by slightly more than a quarter over the same period.

Employment conditions also varied within and across areas. Boston (Suffolk County) and San Antonio (Bexar County) had the most favorable labor market conditions, with unemployment rates of 3.5 and 3.3 percent in 1999, peak unemployment rates of 6.6 and 6.2 percent in 2003, and more favorable rates of 5.4 and 5.0 percent by 2005. The rates in 1999 were below the corresponding national average, while the rates in later years were generally at or above the national averages. Unemployment was higher in Chicago (Cook County), where the rates were 5.0 percent in 1999, 7.4 percent in 2003, and 6.5 percent in 2005. In terms of poverty rates, the ordering was very different, with Boston, San Antonio, and Chicago experiencing poverty rates of 21, 17, and 15 percent, respectively, in 2005.

There were also differences in the population characteristics of the cities. San Antonio had the smallest proportion of black residents (7 percent) and the highest proportion of Hispanic residents (56 percent) of the three cities. The proportions of black and Hispanic residents in Chicago were 26 and 22 percent, respectively, while the proportions in Boston were 25 and 17 percent, respectively. San Antonio and Chicago had lower proportions of single-mother families than did Boston. About one-quarter of family households with own children under age 18 were headed by unmarried women in San Antonio and Chicago, while 40 percent of such families were headed by unmarried women in Boston.

B. Demographic, Health, and Social Characteristics of the Analysis Sample

Sample averages for selected characteristics of our sample of caregivers measured at the times of their interviews are listed in Table 4.1. From the statistics for the first wave, the Three-City Study's initial restriction to economically disadvantaged families is plainly evident. On average, the caregivers had low levels of schooling—42 percent did not finish high school, and a further 37 percent completed no more than high school.[1] One-quarter of the caregivers were 25 years of age or younger in 1999, and two-thirds were age 35 or younger. Two-thirds of the caregivers were unmarried, and two-thirds reported experiencing domestic violence. Substantial proportions reported physical and mental health problems, with 14 percent indicating

---

[1] Some caregivers reported inconsistent school completion information; for our analyses, we constructed a single education variable that used information from all three survey waves to resolve these inconsistencies.

Table 4.1. *Caregiver demographic and income characteristics of the sample at Waves 1, 2, and 3*

Fixed characteristics			
Race-Ethnicity[a]			
Hispanic	52.4		
Non-Hispanic, Black	40.7		
Non-Hispanic, White	5.3		
Education			
No Degree	41.9		
HS/GED	36.9		
Above HS/GED	21.2		

Time-varying characteristics	Wave 1 (1999)	Wave 2 (2000–2001)	Wave 3 (2005)
Age			
25 or Younger	24.5	19.7	6.6
26–35	42.2	42.7	33.7
36 or More	33.3	37.7	59.7
Living Arrangements and HH Composition			
Married	31.6	31.8	32.3
Cohabiting	7.2	10.4	10.3
Number in Household	4.9	4.9	4.8
Children Under Three in Household	54.0	46.3	27.2
Physical and Mental Health			
Health Is Excellent/Very Good/Good	76.3	77.2	70.4
Health Is Fair/Poor	23.7	22.8	29.6
Has Functional Disability	13.8	16.1	22.3
Depression Score > "Caseness" Cutoff	7.5	6.6	6.6
Ever Experienced Domestic Violence	65.0	60.7	—[NA]
Network Support Above Median for Sample	42.9	41.5	50.5
Program Participation			
TANF Participation	31.6	23.0	11.7
Food Stamp Participation	49.4	43.3	47.7
Medicaid Participation	70.5	67.1	67.4
SSI Participation	13.2	15.3	16.2
Employed	50.0	58.9	57.8

Note: Means of characteristics for caregivers from the Three-City Study who completed all three waves of data collection and who had children at all three waves. Estimates use sample weights.

NA: Equivalent Wave 3 variable not available.

[a] Frequency of "other" race-ethnicity category not displayed.

functional disabilities in 1999, 24 percent reporting that they were in fair or poor health, and 8 percent indicating high levels of depression symptoms.[2] Just over half of the sample was Hispanic; 41 percent were non-Hispanic blacks, and the remaining 5 percent were non-Hispanic whites (henceforth, we refer to this group simply as "whites"). While the study interviewed substantial proportions of black and Hispanic caregivers in all three cities, it only interviewed white caregivers in Boston and Chicago. The reason for the smaller fraction of white caregivers is that they were less concentrated in poor neighborhoods in the cities.

The caregivers in our sample experienced changes in their demographic and health circumstances over the course of the study. In some cases, these changes reduced their disadvantages; in other cases, the changes may have increased them. One trend was the rise in the number of caregivers living with a spouse or romantic partner. Marriage rates increased by less than 1 percent, from just under 32 percent of the sample to just over 32 percent, while cohabitation rates increased from 7 to 10 percent. Couple households tend to have more money and time resources than single-adult households, so this trend might have contributed to better economic outcomes. At the same time, the number of caregivers with very young children (under three years of age) fell by half, from 54 percent of the sample in 1999 to 27 percent in 2005. Given the time demands of young children, this trend too might have contributed to better economic outcomes.

Employment also increased over the sample period. In the first wave of the study, half of the caregivers were working. In the second wave, the employment rate increased to 59 percent, and in the third wave, the employment rate was 58 percent.

A negative trend was the worsening health status of the caregivers. The number of caregivers reporting that they were in fair or poor health increased from 24 percent in 1999 to 30 percent in 2005. Also, the number of caregivers reporting functional disabilities rose from 14 to 22 percent over the three waves of the study. Several of these trends—both positive and negative—are consistent with the aging of our sample cohort.

III. Welfare Participation and Transitions

The figures at the bottom of Table 4.1 indicate that TANF participation among the Three-City caregivers fell by nearly two-thirds, from 32 percent

---

[2] Symptoms are measured using the Behavioral Symptoms Inventory, with high levels defined as T-scores ≥ 63.

in 1999 to 12 percent in 2005.[3] This drop was much greater than the average leaving rates recorded for our states. The larger drop in our sample may be attributable to natural life cycle changes in our sample. As the caregivers aged and their youngest children reached school age, their assistance needs may have diminished. This seems, however, to be an incomplete explanation, as participation in other types of assistance, including the Food Stamps Program, held fairly steady over the period. In addition, regressions of our main outcome variables on the mother's age, the children's ages, and wave dummies generate coefficients on the latter that still decline over time at a rate only slightly smaller than that implied by the raw means.

Another explanation for the large drop in welfare use, at least initially, is "regression to the mean." Our sample was initially selected on the basis of its income characteristics and therefore included some households whose incomes were permanently low and others whose incomes were only temporarily low. Over time, we would expect that households with temporarily low incomes would return to their long-term trends. In a general longitudinal sample, households with temporarily high and low incomes balance out; however, our initial sample excluded high-income households. As a consequence, the reversions to long-term trends overwhelmingly involved increases in income. We see evidence for this explanation in some of our other figures, where incomes increase and poverty rates fall much faster between the first and second waves than between the second and third waves.

Participation rates for the other assistance programs did not change nearly as much over time as they did for welfare. Food stamp use fell from 49 percent in 1999 to 43 percent in 2000–2001 before rebounding to 48 percent in 2005. Medicaid receipt fell from just over 70 percent in 1999 to 67 percent in 2000–2001 and 2005. Participation in the Supplemental Security Income (SSI) program increased modestly over the period, rising from 13 percent in 1999 to 16 percent in 2005. The moderately high participation rates in these other programs indicate that many families remained disadvantaged and in need, even if they were not receiving TANF assistance.

The estimates from Table 4.1 document that welfare use fell, but they do not indicate how the changes were distributed. For example, they do not show whether the TANF recipients in Wave 3 were drawn primarily from previous recipients or new entrants. To examine this, we report all of the

---

[3]   In these and subsequent analyses, we characterize caregivers as welfare participants if either they or their dependents reported receiving any income from welfare during the preceding month. We do not characterize caregivers as welfare dependents if other household members received benefits.

Table 4.2. *TANF participation and transitions across the three waves*

		Weighted percent
Transition patterns		
On W1, On W2, On W3	(Continuous recipients)	4.4
On W1, On W2, Off W3	(Late leavers)	12.7
On W1, Off W2, Off W3	(Early leavers)	12.5
On W1, Off W2, On W3	(Reentrants)	2.1
Off W1, On W2, On W3		1.5
Off W1, On W2, Off W3	(Entrants)	4.4
Off W1, Off W2, On W3		3.8
Off W1, Off W2, Off W3	(Continuous nonrecipients)	58.7
Transition Rates		
Exit Rate at W2[a]		46.1
Exit Rate at W3[b]		74.3
Exit Rate, W1–W3[c]		79.5
Entry Rate at W2[d]		8.6
Entry Rate at W3[e]		6.7
Entry Rate, W1–W3[f]		7.7
Reentry Rate at W3[g]		14.4

Note: Means of characteristics for caregivers from the Three-City Study who completed all three waves of data collection and who had children at all three waves. Estimates use sample weights.
[a] Ratio of caregivers on TANF at Wave 1 but off at Wave 2 to all those on TANF at Wave 1.
[b] Ratio of caregivers on TANF at Wave 2 but off at Wave 3 to all those on TANF at Wave 2.
[c] Ratio of caregivers on TANF at Wave 1 but off at Wave 3 to all those on TANF at Wave 1.
[d] Ratio of caregivers off TANF at Wave 1 but on at Wave 2 to all those off TANF at Wave 1.
[e] Ratio of caregivers off TANF at Wave 2 but on at Wave 3 to all those off TANF at Wave 2.
[f] Ratio of caregivers off TANF at Wave 1 but on at Wave 3 to all those off TANF at Wave 1.
[g] Ratio of caregivers on TANF at Wave 1, off at Wave 2, and back on at Wave 3 to all those on at Wave 1 and off at Wave 2.

welfare transitions across the three waves in Table 4.2. The estimates reveal that welfare use was highly concentrated (even in a low-income sample such as ours), with only 41 percent of the caregivers ever reporting receipt at one of the three interview dates. When we look at specific transition patterns, we see that just over 4 percent of the caregivers were observed receiving welfare at all three interviews. Another 13 percent were on welfare at the first two interviews but left by the third interview; a nearly equal number were on welfare only for the first interview. Only 14 percent of the caregivers who were not initially on welfare ever reported receipt in a subsequent interview, and only 4 percent of the caregivers who were off welfare during both of the first two interviews reported receipt in the third interview. Of the 12 percent of caregivers who reported receiving welfare in Wave 3, two-thirds had reported receiving welfare in a previous interview.

As we would expect from these patterns, the welfare recipients in our sample experienced very high rates of exit, while the nonrecipients had low rates of entry. Among the caregivers who were receiving TANF at the first interview, 46 percent were off welfare in the second interview, and among those receiving TANF at the second interview, 74 percent were off welfare at the third interview. In terms of entry, only 9 percent of the nonrecipients from Wave 1 were recipients at Wave 2, and only 7 percent of the nonrecipients from Wave 2 were recipients at Wave 3. Many of the TANF entrants at Wave 3 (36 percent) were caregivers who had previously received benefits at Wave 1. The probability of entry into welfare at Wave 3 was more than twice as high among previous recipients (14 percent) as among those without prior TANF receipt (6 percent).

IV. Correlates of Different Welfare Transition Paths

In addition to documenting the various transitions in TANF receipt, we examine the characteristics of caregivers and their households that are associated with those transitions. Table 4.3 lists the average demographic, social, and health characteristics of caregivers conditional on their welfare histories. Specifically, we distinguish between five types of caregivers who

1. received TANF in all three waves (continuous recipients);
2. received TANF in the first two waves but were off TANF in the last wave (late leavers);
3. received TANF in the first wave but were off TANF in the second and third waves (early leavers);
4. did not receive TANF in the first wave but received TANF in either the second or third wave (entrants); and
5. never received TANF (continuous nonrecipients).

The transition patterns are categorized this way to simplify the interpretation of the results but also partly because of the small number of observations in some of the categories involving entry. The small number of observations also prevents us from examining the reentrants (caregivers

Table 4.3. *Means of selected variables for TANF transition groups at Waves 1, 2, and 3*

	On/on/on			On/on/off			On/off/off			Off/on W2 or on W3			Off/off/off		
	W1	W2	W3	W1	W2	W3	W1	W2	W3	W1	W2	W3	W1	W2	W3
Fixed Characteristics															
Race-Ethnicity[a]															
Hispanic		33.0			37.5			36.7			49.7			61.7	
Non-Hispanic, Black		60.6			58.7			61.3			36.8			30.7	
Non-Hispanic, White		5.9			2.9			1.5			10.0			5.8	
Education															
No Degree		45.9			61.0			49.0			48.1			34.1	
HS/GED		35.7			30.9			36.6			32.9			39.1	
Above HS/GED		18.3			8.1			14.4			19.0			26.8	
Time-Varying Characteristics	W1	W2	W3	W1	W2	W3	W1	W2	W3	W1	W2	W3	W1	W2	W3
Age															
25 or Younger	31.7	29.7	2.4	31.2	25.6	9.3	31.7	26.8	8.4	19.3	14.5	13.8	32.4	25.8	4.5
26–35	33.3	30.0	37.7	44.0	45.4	42.8	43.0	44.6	46.7	42.6	42.0	33.2	42.3	48.5	28.6
36 or More	35.0	40.2	59.9	24.8	29.0	48.0	25.3	28.6	44.9	38.1	43.5	53.0	25.3	25.8	66.9
Living Arrangements															
Married	8.2	6.2	6.5	17.8	11.9	20.6	19.9	16.4	22.4	34.1	33.7	17.7	39.3	41.9	42.1
Cohabiting	2.1	4.2	10.3	4.7	10.0	15.6	5.7	7.6	7.4	4.9	10.0	12.7	8.8	11.6	9.2

Number in HH	5.0	4.8	4.5	5.3	5.4	5.4	5.2	5.1	4.7	4.8	4.9	4.6	4.7	4.8	4.7
Child Under Three in HH	62.6	53.2	21.2	69.2	60.5	30.8	64.4	56.4	31.7	60.5	56.7	25.6	46.6	38.7	26.2
Health															
Health Good to Excellent	62.4	59.9	53.4	69.9	62.7	57.7	82.0	80.9	71.7	75.3	72.2	73.5	78.4	81.7	74.0
Health Fair to Poor	37.6	40.1	46.6	30.1	37.3	42.3	18.0	19.1	28.4	24.7	27.8	26.5	21.7	18.3	26.0
Functional Disability	42.2	50.0	64.7	26.1	31.7	40.3	18.6	10.9	25.4	7.4	18.8	24.4	8.6	10.3	13.8
Depressed	19.4	20.0	18.6	12.2	9.3	13.7	3.9	4.7	11.4	14.1	15.0	8.4	5.0	3.7	2.5
Ever Experienced Domestic Violence	61.8	63.1	—[NA]	71.1	67.4	—[NA]	78.7	74.3	—[NA]	57.0	57.0	—[NA]	62.9	56.4	—[NA]
Network Support Above Median for Sample	64.3	59.1	62.3	53.1	50.8	62.5	39.9	40.1	57.4	44.6	50.4	63.7	39.7	36.9	43.4
Program Participation															
Food Stamp Participation	100.0	100.0	100.0	100.0	100.0	72.5	100.0	51.6	61.7	53.8	69.3	84.9	21.4	21.0	27.5
Medicaid Participation	97.6	100.0	100.0	98.6	99.0	89.0	93.8	84.8	75.3	81.1	88.5	85.7	54.6	49.9	54.6
SSI Participation	43.4	51.1	69.2	18.1	26.2	34.0	11.8	13.7	10.0	16.1	12.4	23.2	9.7	11.1	8.1
Employed	21.8	34.3	16.6	27.1	33.5	42.2	38.3	69.7	56.2	52.7	44.0	43.0	60.0	67.1	68.0

Note: Means of characteristics for caregivers from the Three-City Study who completed all three waves of data collection and who had children at all three waves. Estimates use sample weights.

NA: Equivalent Wave 3 variable not available.

[a] Frequency of "other" race-ethnicity category not displayed.

151

who were on TANF in Wave 1, off in Wave 2, and back on in Wave 3). The columns in Table 4.3 are organized by these categories from left to right; within each category, average characteristics from the first, second, and third waves of the study are tabulated.

The estimates in Table 4.3 indicate that black caregivers were more likely than other caregivers to have received TANF at Wave 1; as such, they constituted a disproportionately large share of the continuous TANF recipients and the early and late leavers. Hispanic caregivers were more likely to remain independent of TANF across the three waves, possibly because of the number of noncitizens among this group. This contrasts with figures based on national averages (Loveless and Tin 2006), which indicate that Hispanics are more likely to participate in TANF and other assistance programs than non-Hispanics; the restriction to low-income families in the Three-City Study may account for the differences. White caregivers were more likely to appear among the TANF entrants and less likely to appear among the leavers.

Younger caregivers were more likely to be continuous nonrecipients, while older caregivers were more likely to be entrants. Among the caregivers who were initially receiving TANF, those who were older than 35 years of age were more likely than those who were younger to remain on the program.

Single caregivers were much more likely to participate and remain on TANF than married or cohabiting caregivers. Although two of the three states (Illinois and Massachusetts) relaxed the special eligibility rules for two-adult households, it was still difficult for most two-adult households to qualify under the standard income eligibility rules. Changes in marital status also appear to be associated with transitions on and off TANF. When we examine leavers and entrants, we see that average marriage rates for leavers increased across the three waves, while average marriage rates for entrants decreased. We note, however, that cohabitation rates rose very strongly even for continuous recipients. Despite their higher rates of marriage and cohabitation, caregivers who were continuous nonrecipients tended to have slightly smaller households overall than other caregivers. Thus, continuous nonrecipients may have been doubly advantaged in terms of having access to more resources from adults while living in households with fewer children and thus fewer needs.

Caregivers who initially had young children were more likely to be receiving TANF in Wave 1 and more likely to enter the program than other caregivers. Interestingly, however, caregivers who had a young child in Wave 3 (and most likely gave birth during the study) were more likely to be represented in one of the leaver groups and less likely to have been continuous participants.

Health and disability status were other strong correlates of participation. Caregivers in poor health or with functional disabilities were more likely to be continuous TANF recipients and also were more likely to be late leavers. Among the caregivers who were continuous participants, nearly half reported being in poor health by the third wave of the study and about two-thirds reported a functional disability. Rates of depression were also higher among the continuous participants, late leavers, and entrants than among the other groups. We also see that the health declines noted earlier for the whole sample appear to have been concentrated among the continuous recipients and the leavers, although functional disability also increased among entrants. The results indicate that many of the caregivers who remained on welfare throughout the study period may have been acutely disadvantaged in terms of their ability to sustain themselves independently.

The last row in Table 4.3 lists employment rates for the different transition groups. Continuous recipients had the lowest rates of employment of the five groups, and continuous nonrecipients had the highest rates. The differences in work behavior were stark. By the third wave of the survey, only one-sixth of the continuous recipients were working, while just over two-thirds of the continuous nonrecipients were working. Caregivers who left TANF or entered TANF tended to fall in between these two extremes. When we examine the changes within groups, we find that caregivers who left TANF had much higher rates of employment in their first interviews off the program than in the previous interviews. Caregivers who entered TANF had lower rates of employment in later interviews than in earlier interviews. Thus, work appears to be strongly associated with TANF receipt both cross-sectionally and longitudinally.

The descriptive analyses of welfare use and other outcomes do not account for indirect associations that may arise through other observed variables. For example, the differences across recipient groups in employment might be partly attributable to differences in health status or the presence of small children. To examine the direct associations, we estimate multivariate conditional logit (fixed effects) models of changes in welfare from Wave 2 to Wave 3. Besides accounting for different observed variables, the conditional logit specifications also control for unmeasured time-invariant characteristics of caregivers, such as underlying attitudes and abilities that might be associated with welfare use and the other observed measures. Estimated marginal effects from alternative specifications of the conditional logit models are reported in Table 4.4.

Table 4.4. *Logit estimates of changes in welfare status from Wave 2 to Wave 3*

	All caregivers		Wave 1 TANF recipients		Wave 1 TANF nonrecipients	
	(a)	(b)	(a)	(b)	(a)	(b)
Changes from Wave 2 to 3 in:						
Employed	−0.112**	−0.152**	−0.050	−0.056	−0.263**	−0.349**
	(0.050)	(0.061)	(0.047)	(0.048)	(0.122)	(0.140)
Married	−0.142**	−0.142*	−0.061	−0.028	−0.011	0.067
	(0.070)	(0.083)	(0.064)	(0.064)	(0.160)	(0.182)
Cohabiting	−0.151**	−0.147	−0.063	−0.079	−0.319**	−0.299
	(0.073)	(0.106)	(0.069)	(0.086)	(0.144)	(0.217)
Number in Household	0.029	0.010	0.035	0.037	0.073	−0.011
	(0.026)	(0.031)	(0.025)	(0.022)	(0.053)	(0.077)
Children Under Three	0.066	0.061	0.012	−0.002	0.211	0.257**
	(0.053)	(0.057)	(0.048)	(0.044)	(0.133)	(0.131)
Poor or Fair Health	0.102	0.028	0.035	−0.029	0.183	0.071
	(0.076)	(0.070)	(0.062)	(0.050)	(0.144)	(0.161)
Functionally Disabled	0.059	0.029	−0.071	−0.098*	0.606***	0.668***
	(0.072)	(0.087)	(0.054)	(0.056)	(0.169)	(0.233)
Depressed	−0.098	−0.027	0.007	0.080	−0.162	0.063
	(0.092)	(0.099)	(0.083)	(0.089)	(0.155)	(0.201)
Changes from Wave 1 to 2 in:						
Employed		−0.070		0.001		−0.132
		(0.066)		(0.050)		(0.146)
Married		0.005		0.135		0.047
		(0.121)		(0.082)		(0.243)
Cohabiting		−0.067		−0.083		−0.086
		(0.132)		(0.097)		(0.306)
Number in Household		−0.017		−0.008		−0.202*
		(0.024)		(0.016)		(0.107)
Children Under Three		−0.001		−0.028		0.218
		(0.077)		(0.074)		(0.204)
Poor or Fair Health		−0.177**		−0.124**		−0.240
		(0.075)		(0.056)		(0.167)

Table 4.4. *Continued*

	All caregivers		Wave 1 TANF recipients		Wave 1 TANF nonrecipients	
	(a)	(b)	(a)	(b)	(a)	(b)
Functionally		0.015		−0.040		0.014
Disabled		(0.072)		(0.055)		(0.195)
Depressed		0.026		0.078		0.037
		(0.085)		(0.097)		(0.213)

Note: Estimated marginal effects from conditional logit models. Models estimated using weighted data from the Three-City Study. Estimated standard errors appear in parentheses.
* Significant at the .10 level; **significant at the .05 level; ***significant at the .01 level.

The first column in Table 4.4 lists results from a model in which changes in welfare receipt from Waves 2 to 3 for all the caregivers in the sample depend on changes in their employment, marriage, cohabitation status, household size, the presence of children under age three, health status, disability, and depression status over the same period. The estimation results indicate that contemporaneous changes in employment, marriage, and cohabitation were all strongly negatively associated with transitions to welfare.

In the second column of Table 4.4, we report results from an extended model that adds earlier (Wave 1 to 2) changes in the explanatory variables to the set of contemporaneous changes. Thus, the model accounts more fully for a caregiver's employment, household, and health history. In the extended model, contemporaneous changes in employment and marriage continue to have significant negative associations with changes in welfare use. The coefficient on cohabitation is unchanged but is less precisely estimated and loses its significance. From these first two models, the contemporaneous changes in employment status and living arrangements appear to be the strongest correlates of welfare transitions.

We reestimate the models conditioning on TANF receipt in the first wave of the study. The estimates indicate that welfare use among the caregivers who were initially receiving TANF was not especially sensitive to changes in any of the characteristics, except for disability status. Instead, most of the associations that we measured in the first two columns appear to have come from entry behavior among caregivers who were not initially receiving TANF. For this group, changes in Wave 2 to 3 employment and cohabitation status were especially strong negative correlates of welfare use, while changes in disability were strong positive correlates.

V. Components of Income

Income is a key outcome that is associated with welfare participation and an important indicator of well-being. Table 4.5 shows the average total incomes of caregivers with different welfare histories. It also lists the components of income, including earnings of the caregiver and other household members, benefits from different public assistance programs, and tax subsidies from the EITC.[4] All of the income amounts in this table and in our subsequent analyses are adjusted for inflation using the Consumer Price Index for Urban Consumers (CPI-U) and expressed in 2005 values.

In Table 4.5, there are clear differences between the average incomes and poverty rates of caregivers who received TANF at one or more of the interviews and the averages among those who did not receive TANF at any interview. The TANF recipients had substantially lower household incomes and higher rates of poverty than the nonrecipients. More intriguing are the differences across different types of recipient groups. First, there appears to be little difference in income among the continuous recipients and the two leaver groups initially at Wave 1, although the association goes in the direction one should expect (stayers have the lowest incomes, followed by late leavers followed by early leavers). More surprising, by Wave 3 the continuous recipients had incomes that were higher than those of the late leavers and almost as high as those of the early leavers. However, this is mostly a result of large increases in SSI and Social Security Disability Insurance (SSDI) payments for the continuous recipients; from Wave 1 to Wave 3, these payments rose from $339 per month to $622 per month, possibly a reflection of worsening health but also possibly a result of a policy-related push to move families from state-funded TANF to federally funded SSI and SSDI. Without this increase, continuous recipient incomes would have risen much less and, by Wave 3, their household incomes would have been $1,213 as compared to $1,365 for late leavers and $1,805 for early leavers (likewise excluding SSI and SSDI income).

The two leaver groups are of particular interest given the past research discussed in the Introduction. The most striking result is the importance

---

[4] The EITC amounts are calculated using the TAXSIM program, available at http//www. nber.org/taxsim (Feenberg and Coutts 1993). Our calculations assume that all eligible families participate and claim the maximum benefits possible based on an annualization of their monthly incomes and circumstances.

Table 4.5. *Income at Waves 1, 2, and 3, by welfare transition group*

	On/on/on			On/on/off			On/off/off			Off/on W2 or on W3			Off/off/off		
	W1	W2	W3	W1	W2	W3	W1	W2	W3	W1	W2	W3	W1	W2	W3
HH Monthly Income with EITC	1,376	1,491	1,835	1,414	1,540	1,684	1,593	1,872	1,906	1,577	1,775	1,713	1,784	2,391	2,415
Poverty Rate w/ EITC	80%	79%	59%	78%	72%	68%	66%	59%	49%	56%	58%	60%	50%	36%	36%
Monthly Earnings															
Individual	145	172	175	215	300	419	313	849	754	637	453	448	717	932	1,008
Others in HH	79	94	215	132	209	346	234	408	494	296	429	345	600	959	888
TANF															
Individual	375	349	344	385	339	0	412	0	0	0	224	239	0	0	0
Others in HH	15	12	17	15	14	16	30	1	0[a]	8	3	11	1	1	0[a]
Food Stamps															
Individual	285	275	283	355	336	314	293	187	238	164	209	276	76	73	100
Others in HH	20	6	76	23	27	53	21	4	14	8	4	24	5	5	7
SSI															
Individual	250	307	428	122	147	184	73	86	73	108	72	134	66	71	52
Others in HH	47	40	58	10	6	39	18	21	9	42	11	28	7	21	27

(continued)

Table 4.5. *Continued*

	On/on/on			On/on/off			On/off/off			Off/on W2 or on W3			Off/off/off		
	W1	W2	W3	W1	W2	W3	W1	W2	W3	W1	W2	W3	W1	W2	W3
SSDI															
Individual	9	73	99	23	18	34	13	15	7	7	25	17	11	8	11
Others in HH	33	9	37	22	19	62	20	15	12	29	46	61	27	20	29
Social Security															
Individual	5	0	0	0	0[a]	3	0[a]	0	0[a]	0[a]	0[a]	0	3	1	7
Others in HH	1	3	26	2	3	8	13	8	16	0[a]	5	6	18	23	19
Other Income	54	42	29	26	24	83	42	81	81	46	139	52	77	85	64
EITC Amount (Potent.)	50	53	13	73	90	98	104	155	112	169	101	65	143	115	92

Note: Means of characteristics for caregivers from the Three-City Study who completed all three waves of data collection and who had children at all three waves. Estimates use sample weights. Income amounts adjusted by the CPI-U and expressed as constant (December 2005) dollars. Other income includes child support and help from friends and relatives.

[a] Amount is nonzero but less than $1.

of increased earnings of other household members after leaving welfare. In the absence of this change, the increases in own earnings are almost completely canceled out by declines in TANF and Food Stamp benefits. But with an almost 200 percent increase in other household earnings for late leavers and 60 percent increase for early leavers upon leaving, total household income was able to rise. On the other hand, it should also be noted that this source of income rose for the continuous recipients and those never on welfare as well. Nevertheless, this raises the question of whether "work pays" for women who leave welfare. In terms of their own earnings, it certainly does not; their earnings are not enough to counter the loss in benefit income. Similar findings have been reported by Bavier (2001a, 2001b) and Cancian et al. (2002) in their analysis of welfare leavers and by Bollinger et al. (Chapter Two, this volume) for a national sample of single mothers in the CPS.

Table 4.6 examines the source of the increase in other household earnings in more detail. There it can be seen that the largest increases in this income for leavers come from spouses and partners (though, for continuous recipients, it mostly comes from earnings of natural child as children age and begin earning income). As we saw earlier, there were significant increases in marriage and cohabitation rates for these leavers; Table 4.6 again shows increases in the percentage of households that include such individuals, but it also shows that the percentage of spouses and partners who have earnings increases after leaving welfare. These increases are considerably larger than those for continuous recipients or never-recipients.

The top panel of Table 4.7 lists results from regression models in which the dependent variables are the changes in caregivers' total household incomes from Waves 2 to 3 and the independent variables are changes in their employment, TANF receipt, marital status, cohabitation status, household size, the presence of small children, health status, disability status, and symptoms of depression. As with our earlier multivariate analyses, the object of these regression analyses is to provide measures of direct associations rather than to generate any causal estimates. For brevity, only the coefficients on employment, TANF receipt, marriage, and cohabitation are shown. The estimates indicate that contemporaneous changes in employment and TANF receipt were positively conditionally associated with income changes, as were contemporaneous changes in marital status and cohabitation status. These same associations appeared in models (second column) that accounted for Wave 1 to 2 changes in the explanatory variables.

Table 4.6. *Other household member earnings at Waves 1, 2, and 3 by welfare transition group*

	On/on/on			On/on/off			On/off/off			Off/on on W2 or on W3			Off/off/off		
	W1	W2	W3	W1	W2	W3	W1	W2	W3	W1	W2	W3	W1	W2	W3
Monthly Earnings															
Others in HH[a]	79	94	215	132	209	346	234	408	494	296	429	345	600	959	888
Spouse/Partner	21	11	83	60	140	328	188	208	385	240	333	237	431	735	700
Natural Children	1	14	138	88	35	51	29	119	71	64	49	150	144	116	180
Other	78	102	14	76	46	16	136	177	122	75	145	9	137	187	118
Percent of HHs with Different Types of HH Members															
Spouse/Partner	5.3	5.4	15.8	21.2	21.7	35.7	24.8	23.3	29.1	38.9	36.9	26.2	47.3	52.5	49.8
Natural Children	93.9	96.3	89.7	99.5	99.0	94.3	99.6	99.3	95.9	98.6	97.9	93.3	98.0	97.7	96.5
Other	57.9	26.6	25.0	44.0	38.8	36.4	50.1	44.0	34.0	42.4	31.5	30.2	38.2	35.5	34.8
Percent of HH Members of Each Type Who Have Earnings															
Spouse/Partner	3.6	1.7	6.9	5.4	15.5	21.9	16.5	15.1	24.5	23.0	25.5	13.5	28.0	41.3	38.1
Natural Children	0.2	3.4	15.7	8.0	6.7	7.2	4.0	13.2	10.9	5.3	9.7	18.2	9.8	10.4	18.6
Other	6.8	4.8	2.3	5.1	4.6	1.2	7.4	7.0	7.8	5.2	7.9	0.7	6.7	9.3	7.7

Note: Means of characteristics for caregivers from the Three-City Study who completed all three waves of data collection and who had children at all three waves. Estimates use sample weights. Monthly earnings include zeros for households that do not have any of the types of family members and zeros for households that have a type of family member but did not have earnings.

Income amounts adjusted by the CPI-U and expressed as constant (December 2005) dollars.

[a] Other household members earnings is not equal to the sum of the parts due to imputation methods.

Table 4.7. *Regression estimates of changes in total household income from Wave 2 to Wave 3*

	All caregivers		Wave 1 TANF recipients		Wave 1 TANF nonrecipients	
	(a)	(b)	(a)	(b)	(a)	(b)
Models with Employment						
Δ_{23} Employed	848***	849***	925***	1,019***	799***	744***
	(97)	(102)	(113)	(120)	(128)	(131)
Δ_{23} Received TANF	216**	173	226**	414***	323*	338*
	(104)	(112)	(95)	(143)	(190)	(204)
Δ_{23} Married	544***	490***	468**	498**	559***	499***
	(135)	(139)	(223)	(238)	(164)	(164)
Δ_{23} Cohabiting	730***	788***	717***	797***	735***	779***
	(173)	(188)	(174)	(203)	(233)	(261)
Δ_{12} Employed		79		194		−13
		(112)		(136)		(153)
Δ_{12} Received TANF		−16		346*		224
		(107)		(209)		(294)
Models with Earnings						
Δ_{23} Earnings (/$000)	836***	851***	1,016***	954***	784***	817***
	(66)	(82)	(81)	(71)	(80)	(96)
Δ_{23} Received TANF	284***	245**	241***	328***	506***	639***
	(102)	(110)	(82)	(114)	(188)	(183)
Δ_{23} Married	464***	416***	496**	457**	452***	408***
	(125)	(133)	(201)	(207)	(151)	(154)
Δ_{23} Cohabiting	724***	793***	666***	719***	742***	800***
	(164)	(169)	(153)	(173)	(220)	(229)
Δ_{12} Earnings (/$000)		75		−190**		142
		(156)		(93)		(179)
Δ_{12} Received TANF		−32		132		394*
		(113)		(151)		(221)

Note: Models also include controls for number in household, children under age three, health status, disability status, and depression. Models estimated using weighted data from the Three-City Study. Estimated standard errors appear in parentheses.

* Significant at the .10 level; **significant at the .05 level; ***significant at the .01 level.

The bottom panel of Table 4.7 repeats this analysis substituting caregivers' earnings for employment in the list of explanatory variables. The coefficients on earnings help to show whether a dollar increase in earnings contributes to a larger or smaller increase in caregivers' total incomes. The association would be less than dollar-for-dollar if caregivers lose a lot of benefits as their earnings increase but might be more than dollar-for-dollar if they gain substantially from the EITC or other transitional assistance. On average, a one dollar increase in earnings was associated with an 84 to 85 cent increase in total incomes, indicating that caregivers got to keep most of what they earned and lost only a modest amount of income through reduced benefits.

The next two columns of Table 4.7 list results for income change models estimated for the caregivers who received TANF in Wave 1, while the final two columns list results for models estimated for the other caregivers who were initially off TANF. The object of these analyses is to see whether the potential contributions of work, welfare receipt, and other factors to income were higher among caregivers who were or were not initially TANF recipients. We might suspect, for instance, that the TANF recipients would have faced a higher implicit tax rate on their earnings. In general, changes in employment and earnings were more strongly associated with income gains for the Wave 1 TANF recipients than for the nonrecipients. As with the full sample of caregivers, welfare receipt, marriage, and cohabitation were also conditionally associated with higher income for both subgroups.

VI. Working and Nonworking Welfare Leavers

Welfare leavers are a heterogeneous group that includes caregivers who have worked their way off welfare (see, e.g., Danziger et al. 2002; Harris 1993; Moffitt and Winder 2003), those who have experienced a change in their marital or couple status (Cherlin and Fomby 2004), and those who have been sanctioned off TANF or otherwise failed to comply with program rules (Moffitt 2003). As a policy matter, we are especially interested in how the economic outcomes for working and nonworking leavers compare. Such a comparison can help to tell us whether work pays for disadvantaged families in the sense that it allows them to enjoy a better standard of living than they could attain if they simply received welfare. As Harris (1993) and Edin and Lein (1997) have pointed out, work and welfare are not mutually exclusive—many single mothers combine these activities. Also, Edin and Lein (1997) and Venkatesh (2006) have further shown that unreported ("shady") work and barter contribute resources to low-income households.

Nevertheless, a goal of welfare reform was to promote economic independence and a higher standard of living through work and other responsible behavior.

In Table 4.8, we first pool the observations for the caregivers who left TANF in either Wave 2 or Wave 3 (combine the data for our early and late leavers) to create a general subset of TANF leavers. Averages of the total incomes, poverty rates, earnings, and other components of income for this group in each wave of the study are listed in the first three columns of Table 4.8. Next, we distinguish between leavers who were and were not employed at the time of the Wave 3 interview. Averages of the economic variables for the employed leavers appear in the middle three columns of the table, and averages for the nonemployed leavers appear in the final three columns.

In Wave 1, the caregivers who would go on to become employed leavers had incomes that were very similar to the incomes of those who would go on to become nonemployed leavers. Wave 1 earnings were higher for the employed group by $171, while disability assistance was higher for the nonemployed group. Aside from these differences, the composition of Wave 1 incomes was similar across the groups. By Wave 3, differences in income between the employed and nonemployed leavers were much greater, as one would expect. Employed leavers in Wave 3 had $2,253 in total income and $1,190 in own earnings, on average, while nonemployed leavers had household incomes of $1,350. For the employed leavers, the increase in own earnings from Wave 1 to Wave 3 was far larger than the loss in TANF and Food Stamp benefits, thus making it clear that work pays for this group. The employed leavers were also helped by a more than 200 percent increase in earnings from others in the household as well. For the nonemployed leavers, however, there was also a large increase in this source of income. While somewhat less in magnitude (an increase of $213 compared to $262 for employed leavers), earnings from others in the household nevertheless were an important source of income to offset the loss of TANF benefits. Tabulations similar to those of Table 4.6 show that the source of this increase was, again, increases in the presence of spouses and partners in the household and an increase in the percentage of such individuals who had earnings. Further, the nonemployed leavers almost doubled their receipt of SSI and SSDI benefits, again possibly because of declines in health or pressures to move families from TANF to these programs. Together, these two sources of additional income prevented nonemployed leavers' monthly household income from falling more than it did; there was only a $129 reduction in monthly income for this group despite the loss of own earnings and welfare

Table 4.8. *Income at Waves 1, 2, and 3 for welfare leavers employed and not employed in Wave 3*

	On /on/off and On/ off/off			Employed in W3			Not Employed in W3		
	W1	W2	W3	W1	W2	W3	W1	W2	W3
HH monthly Inc. w/ EITC	1,503	1,704	1,794	1,527	1,845	2,253	1,479	1,568	1,350
Poverty Rate with EITC	73%	66%	59%	68%	59%	35%	76%	72%	81%
Monthly Earnings									
Individual	263	571	585	350	764	1,190	179	385	0
Others in HH	183	307	420	188	342	450	177	274	390
Pos. Earn. from Others in HH	21%	30%	34%	23%	33%	40%	20%	28%	29%
TANF									
Individual	398	171	0	392	130	0	404	211	0
Others in HH	22	8	8	19	2	1	26	13	14
Food Stamps									
Individual	324	263	277	320	257	237	328	269	315
Others in HH	22	16	33	13	4	10	30	27	56
SSI									
Individual	98	117	129	56	62	39	138	170	217
Others in HH	14	14	24	25	19	18	3	8	30
SSDI									
Individual	18	16	21	13	4	3	23	28	38
Others in HH	21	17	37	18	14	9	24	20	64
Social Security									
Individual	0[a]	0[a]	2	0[a]	0	0	0[a]	0[a]	3
Others in HH	7	5	12	0[a]	1	9	14	9	14
Other Income	34	52	82	27	55	77	41	50	87
EITC Income (Potential)	88	122	105	102	167	186	74	78	27

Note: Means of characteristics for caregivers from the Three-City Study who completed all three waves of data collection and who had children at all three waves. Estimates use sample weights. Income amounts adjusted by the CPI-U and expressed as constant (December 2005) dollars. Other income includes child support and help from friends and relatives.

[a] Amount is nonzero but less than $1.

benefits. Thus, we find again the importance of other household income and disability benefits.

An alternative way to compare outcomes among welfare leavers is by their work "readiness" rather than their actual employment behavior. Welfare recipients differ in their skills, physical abilities, family responsibilities, and other characteristics that affect their ability to find and sustain employment. The goal of welfare reform of moving caregivers from welfare to work is more likely to have been successful for those with characteristics that lead them to greater potential for employment.

To measure work readiness, we estimated longitudinal reduced-form binary choice models of employment with family structure, age, education, health and disability status, depression status, race/ethnicity, city, and receipt of child or other support as the explanatory variables (results available upon request). We used the estimates from these models to predict probabilities of employment in each wave. Welfare leavers in our caregiver sample with predicted work probabilities above 50 percent in Wave 1 (186) were classified as "initially work ready." Welfare leavers with predicted work probabilities below 50 percent in Wave 1 and below 50 percent in either Wave 2 or Wave 3 (185) were classified as "never work ready," and caregivers with predicted work probabilities below 50 percent in Wave 1 and above 50 percent in both Waves 2 and 3 (65) were classified as "becoming work ready." Means of the total income and income component variables for the leavers in each work-readiness category are reported in Table 4.9.

Leavers who were initially work ready had total monthly incomes in Wave 1 that were more than $100 above the incomes of the leavers who were never work ready but more than $100 below the incomes of those who subsequently became work ready. The differences in Wave 1 arose mainly from the work-ready leavers having higher employment and earnings than the other two groups but fewer earnings from other household members than the leavers who would become work ready.

Employment and earnings grew for all three groups of leavers from Wave 1 to Wave 2, though the initially work-ready group continued to have the highest earnings. Others' earnings also grew for the initially work-ready and never work-ready leavers but not for the leavers who became work ready. Overall, total incomes in Wave 2 were highest for the initially work-ready group.

Substantial divergences appeared by Wave 3. The initially work-ready group continued to see increases in own and, to a lesser extent, others' earnings, leading to higher incomes generally. In contrast, employment and earnings among the never work-ready group fell. Despite some increases

Table 4.9. *Income at Waves 1, 2, and 3 for welfare leavers with different histories of work-readiness*

	Initially work ready			Never work ready			Became work ready		
	W1	W2	W3	W1	W2	W3	W1	W2	W3
HH Monthly Inc. w/ EITC	1,537	1,805	1,925	1,415	1,662	1,518	1,663	1,609	2,212
Poverty Rate with EITC	70%	56%	55%	83%	74%	71%	50%	65%	36%
Monthly Earnings									
Individual	396	688	866	220	480	211	81	548	863
Others in HH	114	315	371	131	283	365	482	349	680
Positive Earnings									
Individual	44%	61%	73%	29%	44%	21%	18%	49%	64%
Others in HH	14%	30%	33%	20%	32%	29%	42%	27%	49%
TANF									
Individual	417	136	0	386	203	0	385	171	0
Others in HH	11	2	4	27	16	13	38	0[a]	4
Food Stamps									
Individual	348	272	261	315	274	303	288	213	247
Others in HH	9	4	13	29	31	36	33	2	77
SSI									
Individual	72	89	68	132	159	213	57	73	64
Others in HH	1	18	19	5	4	31	65	20	13
SSDI									
Individual	0[a]	13	12	27	22	38	36	11	0
Others in HH	12	18	24	24	10	63	32	34	3
Social Security									
Individual	0[a]	0	0	0	0[a]	4	0[a]	0	0[a]
Others in HH	0[a]	6	9	17	10	15	0[a]	0	15
Other Income	36	62	128	29	54	65	44	30	23
EITC Income (Potential)	113	169	140	54	84	58	119	116	142

Note: Means of characteristics for caregivers from the Three-City Study who completed all three waves of data collection and who had children at all three waves. Estimates use sample weights. Income amounts adjusted by the CPI-U and expressed as constant (December 2005) dollars. Other income includes child support and help from friends and relatives.

[a] Amount is nonzero but less than $1.

in disability income, total incomes for the never-ready group also declined from Waves 2 to 3. The leavers who became work ready changed positions with the initially work-ready group to achieve the highest incomes in Wave 3. The gains came in nearly equal parts from own earnings and other household members' earnings. While own earnings for the initially and becoming work-ready groups were nearly identical in Wave 3, other household members' earnings were nearly $300 for the latter group.

Table 4.10 lists results of regression models of the correlates of income changes for the samples of TANF leavers (first two columns), continuous recipients (second two columns), and continuous nonrecipients (final two columns). For each group, changes in employment are strongly positively associated with changes in income, with the associations being larger for TANF leavers and continuous recipients than for continuous nonrecipients. This confirms the positive associations from the descriptive analysis. Marrying and entering a cohabiting relationship are also positively associated with changes in income for TANF leavers and for continuous nonrecipients but not necessarily for continuous recipients.

VII. Conclusions

This chapter analyzes 1999–2005 data from the Three-City Study on low-income caregivers with children. The chapter considers the caregivers' welfare use and then investigates characteristics and outcomes that are correlated with welfare use. The Three-City Study is advantageous in this regard because it is a general low-income sample and is not limited to welfare recipients or welfare leavers. The Three-City Study also has some of the most up-to-date information on low-income families.

Our analyses reveal that welfare use declined among the Three-City caregivers. In 1999, just under one-third of caregivers were receiving TANF; by 2005, the number had fallen to about one-ninth. The drop in participation is consistent with national trends but also may reflect the aging of the sample cohort. Longitudinal analyses indicate that exit rates from TANF were very high, while entry rates were low. Over the period of our study, the group of caregivers who continued to receive TANF became much more select. The caregivers who remained on TANF for all of the waves of the study worked less, had lower rates of marriage, and reported worse health and higher rates of disability than other caregivers. On or off welfare, many caregivers in our sample remained needy. By the third wave of the study, two-thirds were receiving Medicaid and just under half were receiving food stamps.

Table 4.10. *Regression estimates of changes in total household income from Wave 2 to Wave 3 for TANF leavers, continuous recipients, and continuous nonrecipients*

	TANF leavers		Continuous TANF recipients		Continuous TANF nonrecipients	
	(a)	(b)	(a)	(b)	(a)	(b)
Models with Employment						
Δ_{23} Employed	911***	1,053***	896***	1,372***	658***	705***
	(120)	(128)	(273)	(377)	(129)	(155)
Δ_{23} Married	541**	582**	284	35	582***	459***
	(238)	(260)	(349)	(326)	(181)	(184)
Δ_{23} Cohabiting	901***	1,079***	−353	−574*	804***	713***
	(220)	(244)	(285)	(308)	(228)	(295)
Δ_{12} Employed		230		489		73
		(149)		(343)		(170)
Models with Earnings						
Δ_{23} Earnings (/\$000)	963***	922***	1,102***	1,366***	760***	839***
	(82)	(73)	(257)	(262)	(85)	(99)
Δ_{23} Married	550***	515**	277	448	473***	342**
	(214)	(235)	(304)	(330)	(161)	(164)
Δ_{23} Cohabiting	788***	876***	−154	−330	810***	740***
	(196)	(210)	(309)	(307)	(209)	(245)
Δ_{12} Earnings (/\$000)		−178**		415*		197
		(86)		(226)		(196)

Note: Models also include controls for number in household, children under age three, health status, disability status, and depression. Models estimated using weighted data from the Three-City Study. Estimated standard errors appear in parentheses.
* Significant at the .10 level; **significant at the .05 level; ***significant at the .01 level.

On average, caregivers who remained off TANF for all three waves had the highest incomes and the best economic circumstances. There were only modest differences in income, however, among the other caregivers who stayed on TANF, left TANF, or entered TANF. For the group that remained on TANF over the course of the study, higher disability payments appear to have contributed to their income gains.

Our findings also reveal striking evidence of changes in income among the different recipient groups. Leavers saw increases in their household incomes after leaving welfare that were largely due to increases in the earnings of spouses and partners; the trend arose partly because marriage and cohabitation rates rose and partly because more spouses and partners with earnings were in the household after leaving welfare. Continuous recipients (stayers) also experienced rising incomes but, in their case, this arose primarily because of increases in SSI and SSDI payments; two possible reasons for the increase are declining health and a policy-related push to move families from state-funded TANF to federally funded SSI and SSDI. Such disability payments also rose for leavers who were non-employed after leaving; their incomes fell slightly but much less than they would have without an increase in this source of income. Nonemployed leavers also benefited from more spouses and partners in the household, and more with earnings. Even with this, however, nonemployed leavers' incomes were below their incomes while previously on welfare; thus, they were worse off.

On the critical issue of whether work pays, which we define as having occurred when the increase in a leaver's own earnings after leaving welfare exceeds the loss of benefits, we find that it does so for employed leavers. However, it does not do so overall; when leavers as a whole are considered, employed and nonemployed combined, increases in average own earnings are completely offset by declines in TANF and Food Stamp benefits. Incomes for leavers rise, on average, but this is because of increases in other household members' earnings and increases in disability payments. But, on average, going off welfare does not result in sufficient work to compensate for the loss of benefits.

The picture that our data paint nine years after the enactment of welfare reform is a positive one for most families. On average, the caregivers in our sample were enjoying higher incomes and lower rates of poverty in 2005 than they did in 1999, with the economic gains coming primarily from increased earnings. The picture, however, was not positive for all families or for every measure. Although average incomes grew and TANF utilization fell, many families remained dependent on other types of assistance, and nearly half of the families remained poor. Outcomes were especially bad for the substantial fraction of families that were off TANF but without a working caregiver. As Blank (Chapter One, this volume) and others have pointed out, disconnected leavers remain a significant policy challenge.

As we consider policies in the next decade, it appears important that the United States maintain its system of in-kind supports. Although work and earnings among disadvantaged families have grown, many have remained poor. These in-kind supports need to better accommodate working poor families.

The welfare system also must come to terms with the significant number of families with adults who appear unable to work. States need to reexamine their policies for caregivers with physical or mental health problems, including their exemption criteria for work activities and time limits. Policymakers should also consider follow-on programs, such as employment-support programs, for leavers who have experienced long spells of joblessness. In keeping with the original goals of welfare reform, the objective of these programs should be to encourage and support employment among those who can work while maintaining a safety net for those who cannot work.

An earlier version of this chapter was presented at the annual meetings of the Association for Public Policy Analysis and Management November 2006 in Madison, Wisconsin. The authors thank Rich DePolt for research assistance and Andrew Cherlin, Robert LaLonde, Jim Quane, Daniel Schroeder, and Jim Ziliak for helpful comments. The financial assistance of the National Institute of Child Health and Human Development and other government organizations and foundations is also gratefully appreciated. The views expressed in this chapter are those of the authors and do not necessarily reflect those of the funding agencies and organizations. For more information about the Three-City Study, including online copies of all publications, please visit the study Web site at http://www.jhu.edu/threecitystudy.

References

Bavier, Richard. 2001a. "Welfare Reform in Wave Files from the 1996 Panel of the Survey of Income and Program Participation." *Monthly Labor Review*, 124:13–24.

Bavier, Richard. 2001b. "Welfare Reform in Wave Files from the 1996 Panel of the Survey of Income and Program Participation." ACF Conference, Washington, DC, May.

Blank, Rebecca. 2002. "Evaluating Welfare Reform in the United States." *Journal of Economic Literature*, 40:1105–1166.

Bloom, Dan, and Charles Michalopoulos. 2001. *How Welfare and Work Policies Affect Employment and Income: A Synthesis of Research*. New York: MDRC.

Cancian, Maria, Robert Haveman, Daniel Meyer, and Barbara Wolfe. 2002. "Before and After TANF: The Economic Well-Being of Women Leaving Welfare." *Social Service Review*, 76:603–641.

Cherlin, Andrew, and Paula Fomby. 2004. "Welfare, Work, and Changes in Mothers' Living Arrangements in Low-Income Families." *Population Research and Policy Review*, 23:543–565.

Danziger, Sheldon, Colleen Heflin, Mary Corcoran, Elizabeth Oltmans, and Hui-Chen Wang. 2002. "Does It Pay to Move from Welfare to Work?" *Journal of Policy Analysis and Management*, 21:671–692.

Edin, Kathryn, and Laura Lein. 1997. *Making Ends Meet: How Single Mothers Survive Welfare and Low-Wage Work.* New York: Russell Sage.

Feenberg, Daniel, and Elisabeth Coutts. 1993. "An Introduction to the TAXSIM Model." *Journal of Policy Analysis and Management,* 12:189–194.

Grogger, Jeffrey, Steven Haider, and Jacob Klerman. 2003. "Why Did the Welfare Rolls Fall in the 1990s?" *American Economic Review,* 93:288–292.

Grogger, Jeffrey, and Lynn Karoly. 2005. *Welfare Reform: Effects of a Decade of Change.* Cambridge, MA: Harvard University Press.

Harris, Kathleen. 1993. "Work and Welfare Among Single Mothers in Poverty." *American Journal of Sociology,* 99:317–352.

Loveless, Tracy, and Jan Tin. 2006. "Dynamics of Economic Well-Being: Participation in Government Programs, 2001 Through 2003. Who Gets Assistance?" *Current Population Report P70–108.* Washington, DC: U.S. Census Bureau.

Moffitt, Robert. 2002. "From Welfare to Work: What the Evidence Shows," in *Welfare Reform and Beyond: The Future of the Safety Net.* Isabel Sawhill, R. Kent Weaver, Ron Haskins, and Andrea Kane, eds. Washington, DC: Brookings Institution Press, 79–88.

——— 2003. "The Role of Nonfinancial Factors in Exit and Entry in the TANF Program." *Journal of Human Resources,* 38:1221–1254.

——— 2004. "The Three-City Study Incentive Experiment: Results from the First Two Waves." Unpublished manuscript. Johns Hopkins University. Available at http://www.jhu.edu/threecitystudy.

Moffitt, Robert, and Katie Winder. 2003. "The Correlates and Consequences of Welfare Exit and Entry: Evidence from the Three-City Study." Unpublished manuscript, Johns Hopkins University. Available at http://www.econ.jhu.edu/People/Moffitt/wp0103.pdf.

——— 2005. "Does It Pay to Move from Welfare to Work? A Comment on Danziger, Heflin, Corcoran, Oltmans, and Wang." *Journal of Policy Analysis and Management,* 24:399–410.

Venkatesh, Sudhir. 2006. *Off the Books: The Underground Economy of the Urban Poor.* Cambridge, MA: Harvard University Press.

FIVE

The Impact of Welfare Reform on Leaver Characteristics, Employment, and Recidivism

Peter R. Mueser, David W. Stevens, and Kenneth R. Troske

I. Introduction

Welfare reform legislation at both the state and national levels since the mid-1990s has transformed the U.S. cash assistance program for single parents and their children. Among the stated goals of the federal reform legislation was to "end the dependence of needy parents on government benefits by promoting job preparation, work, and marriage."[1] By 2000, caseloads had declined in every state from peaks in the mid-1990s, with the national caseload declining by more than one-half.[2] Yet, whether these declines represent improvements in the long-run well-being of current and former welfare recipients remains a contentious issue. Research has shown that postreform welfare leavers have low levels of job skills and are working in jobs with low wages, few benefits, and little security.

[1] Personal Responsibility and Work Opportunity Reconciliation Act of 1996, Public Law 104–193, August 22, 1996.
[2] Reviews of the literature on the impacts of welfare reform and the economy on caseloads are provided in Bell (2001), Blank (2002), and Grogger and Karoly (2005); a broader survey of the literature on the factors influencing welfare caseloads is provided in Mayer (2000). Meyer and Rosenbaum (2001) provide an analysis focusing on the role of the federal Earned Income Tax Credit. Perhaps the most influential single study is the Council of Economic Advisors (1999) report, although its findings that legislation played a central role in caseload declines have been questioned (see especially Ziliak et al. 2000). See Danziger (1999) for a good collection of early studies.

We would like to thank Tricia Gladden, Harry Holzer, Robert Hutchens, Lucie Schmidt, and James Ziliak, seminar participants at Clemson University, and conference participants at the University of Kentucky for helpful comments. Mueser and Troske would like to thank the Employment Policies Institute for financial support. June Cheng and Kyung-Seong Jeon provided excellent research assistance. All errors are our own.

Reforms to welfare have been associated with substantial increases in the levels of employment for recipients (Department of Health and Human Services 2000). We know that those who leave welfare are likely to be working but that their earnings are often very low and that many of them are suffering substantial hardship (Acs and Loprest 2004; Frogner, Moffitt, and Ribar, Chapter Four this volume; Parrott 1998; Tweedie, Reichert, and O'Connor 1999). In contrast to expectations, it does not appear that reforms have caused welfare caseloads to become more disadvantaged (Moffitt and Stevens 2001), although since the implementation of Temporary Assistance for Needy Families (TANF) the nonwhite proportion has increased substantially (Zedlewski and Anderson 2001).[3]

Although we know that employment has played an important role in welfare exit and return both prior to and following reform (e.g., Frogner et al., Chapter Four this volume; Lane and Stevens 1995, 2001), existing studies provide little basis for examining *changes* in the dynamics of welfare use and employment occurring with reform. This is because studies of welfare reform often focus on recipients after reform as opposed to comparing the behavior of recipients before and after reform. Two studies that do make this comparison are Loprest (2001) and Cancian et al. (2002). Loprest uses a national sample to compare individuals leaving welfare in 1995–1997 with those leaving in 1997–1999. She finds that the levels of employment and earnings are, if anything, higher in the more recent period. Unfortunately, this does not provide a clear picture of the impact of reforms since most states had already enacted major reforms to their welfare system prior to or during the 1995–1997 period. Cancian et al. use administrative data from Wisconsin and compare individuals leaving welfare in September 1995 with those leaving welfare in September 1997. Similar to Loprest, Cancian et al. find that the rate of employment is higher in the later cohort, but, in contrast to Loprest, they find that earnings are lower. However, Cancian et al. are also unable to make a clear comparison between leavers prior to welfare reform and after welfare reform because Wisconsin had substantially reformed its welfare system prior to 1995.

Based on the national Survey of Income and Program Participation, Bavier (2001) provides comparisons of employment rates between leavers at different points in time as far back as the 1980s. He argues that postreform employment rates for welfare leavers are not generally higher than during earlier periods of economic growth. He also does some limited comparisons

---

[3]   There is also evidence that the proportion of child-only cases has increased. Payees in child-only cases are not generally counted as TANF recipients, and we are not aware of any studies that consider their characteristics.

for years in the late 1990s that suggest that leavers may actually be worse off after reforms. Grogger and Karoly (2005) identify the effects of welfare reform based on a review of experimental studies, observational studies focused on particular reforms, and studies that consider reform "as a bundle." They find that reforms have increased employment for low-skilled individuals but that the effects on income and recipients' long-run well-being are less clear-cut. They suggest that there may be "tradeoffs among the goals of reducing dependency, promoting work, and alleviating need" (p. 153).

One of the main limitations of these previous studies is that they are handicapped by a short time frame, observing postreform recipients in the late 1990s, when economic growth was at near-unprecedented levels.[4] In contrast, this chapter explores the impact that welfare reform has had on the well-being of recipients by examining the dynamics of welfare participation and employment in Maryland and Missouri from 1991 to 2004. Federal welfare reform replaced Aid to Families with Dependent Children (AFDC) with TANF in late 1996 in both states. But, like most other states, Maryland and Missouri had instituted substantial reforms by that time, with the most important state reforms implemented in 1995. While the structure of welfare reforms differed substantially across states,[5] those in Maryland and Missouri are representative of the general move toward more severe constraints on recipients and greater emphasis on employment. Missouri's welfare caseload displays a pattern very similar to that for the United States as a whole, reaching a peak in 1994, followed by a decline to approximately half of the peak level by the end of the decade. In Maryland the decline from the peak in the early 1990s was even greater, with the caseload in 2000 less than one-third of its level in the earlier period.

We first examine changes in the demographic and family characteristics of welfare recipients and those moving onto and off welfare over the period 1991–2005, the period of active welfare reform. Aside from providing an initial indication of the impacts of welfare reforms, these analyses suggest the degree to which results may be influenced by changes in the characteristics of welfare recipients due to reform (Hoynes 2001). We also examine changes in the welfare and employment history of recipients moving onto and off welfare over this period.

---

[4] An earlier analysis of welfare reform in Missouri, extending through 1999, is provided in Carrington, Mueser, and Troske (2002). King and Mueser (2005) look at the employment experiences of welfare recipients in six cities over the period of welfare reform, but their analysis extends only through 1999.

[5] The difficulties in classifying states' reforms are illustrated by McKernan, Bernstein, and Fender (2005).

We then consider the experiences of three cohorts of welfare leavers: those leaving welfare in fiscal year 1993 (July 1992–June 1993), those leaving welfare in fiscal year 1997 (July 1996–June 1997), and those leaving in fiscal year 2002 (July 2001–June 2002). The first period identifies welfare leavers prior to welfare reform. At that point, the caseload was near its peak in both states and the regulations governing welfare were essentially those of the standard AFDC program, which had changed relatively little since the early 1980s. The second period occurs after substantial policy change. Our ability to compare recipients prior to reform with recipients after reform is one of the main strengths of our analysis. Using these data, we examine the dynamics of employment and welfare recidivism for welfare leavers as well as changes in the characteristics of welfare leavers' employers. This latter analysis is important because previous research has shown that employer characteristics, such as employment size-class, industry, and total payroll are correlated with an employee's wages, benefits, wage growth, and employment stability (Brown, Hamilton, and Medoff 1990; Davis and Haltiwanger 1992; Krueger and Summers 1988; Troske 1999). The third period is well after the implementation of the primary reforms and covers a period when the economy had stopped growing and had moved into a modest recession. A comparison of the detailed patterns for these cohorts allows us to directly consider changes occurring over the period of welfare reform as well as to identify the relative importance of the economy.

The contribution by Frogner et al. (Chapter Four) to this volume focuses on a panel study of individuals over the period 1999–2005, allowing inferences of how employment and program participation evolved over a six-year period for a sample of low-income households in the post–welfare reform regime. Given that our study follows individuals for only two years following departure from welfare, we are not able to provide this level of detail. In contrast, our study allows inferences of how program participant experiences have changed over the period of welfare reform. By considering three cohorts of participants, our analysis is able to distinguish the patterns of welfare participation and employment that are stable over our entire period from those that represent important breaks.

II. Welfare Reform and the Maryland and Missouri Economies in Context

In both Maryland and Missouri, important welfare reform initiatives were implemented in 1995. In Maryland, the Family Investment Program was implemented county by county beginning in 1995, requiring up-front job search and including various child support provisions. In August 1996, statewide waivers were granted specifying work requirements; TANF was formally implemented in October.

Late in 1994, Missouri began implementation of major welfare legislation. The new legislation required recipients to agree to a plan for obtaining self-supporting employment within two years, raised allowable asset levels, increased efforts to establish paternity, required minor parents to live with their parents, established a wage supplementation program, and imposed sanctions on recipients who failed to meet program requirements. Despite the apparently broad scope of the legislation, in part it codified changes already underway; in the short run, it provided only moderate changes in the rules faced by a typical recipient. In April 1995, a federal waiver specifying work requirements was approved. Federal welfare reform replaced AFDC with TANF at the end of 1996 but associated policy changes in Missouri were relatively small, since state reform had already occurred, and no state legislation was passed at that time.

In both states, between 1993 and 1998, recipients faced increased restraints and growing pressure to participate in training and employment programs. The changes are reflected in the likelihood that a recipient would face sanctions for violations of the rules. Prior to 1994, in keeping with federal AFDC regulations, very few sanctions were applied in any state. By 1998, the proportion of the caseload facing sanctions was about 11 percent in both Maryland and Missouri, higher than that in the median state, with a rate of 5 percent, but still below about a third of the states (U.S. General Accounting Office 2000, p. 52). In addition to the program changes enacted, there were important changes in the way caseworkers were trained and rewarded during the 1990s. Until the early 1990s, caseworkers were evaluated for accuracy in processing applicants and ensuring that they were placed on the welfare rolls promptly. The legislative activity of the 1990s appears to have placed particular emphasis on the potentially temporary nature of welfare payments, and caseworkers were told to emphasize this to recipients.

Although there are numerous differences across states, neither Maryland nor Missouri is an outlier in terms of the policies adopted. In particular, welfare recipients in both states faced increased financial incentives to work and a welfare bureaucracy that was motivated to move recipients toward self-sufficiency. Thus, an examination of welfare recipients in these states before and after welfare reform can tell us much about the broader impact of reform.

Beyond welfare reform, perhaps the most important policy change increasing work incentives over the period of our study was the dramatic increases in the federal Earned Income Tax Credit (EITC), occurring over the period 1994–1996 (Chapter Three, this volume). Maryland has had a state EITC since 1987, which was made refundable in 1998. As in most states with an EITC, the Maryland program provides a benefit that is calculated as a proportion of the federal program payment. Missouri does not have a state EITC.

Extrapolating from the experiences in Maryland and Missouri requires some understanding of how the economic environment faced by welfare recipients in these states compares with that of welfare recipients in other states. Table 5.1 presents summary data on the economies of Maryland, Missouri, and the United States as a whole for 1991, before welfare reform began; for 1999, after important reforms had been in place for several years; and for 2004, following the 2001 national recession. These statistics are based on the annual Outgoing Rotation Group (ORG) files from the Current Population Survey (CPS). The table shows that the fraction of employment accounted for by broad industries in 1991 was quite similar for Missouri and the United States as a whole. Both Missouri and the United States shifted from manufacturing to services and construction. Maryland has a somewhat different industrial structure, with a manufacturing employment percentage just over one-half of the Missouri and U.S. percentages and a higher concentration in professional services and government.

Table 5.1 also compares racial compositions. Whereas Missouri has a close to average share of African Americans, other minorities are underrepresented. In 1999, Asians account for only about 1 percent of the Missouri population, compared with 4 percent for the country as a whole, and Hispanics account for less than 2 percent of the Missouri population, compared with over 11 percent for the country as a whole. In contrast, Maryland has a much larger African American population than Missouri or the country as a whole, whereas the proportion Asian corresponds closely to the average for the United States. Like Missouri, Maryland has a smaller Hispanic population than the United States as a whole.

The remainder of Table 5.1 compares the income and earnings of our two states with those of the U.S. population as a whole. The panels indicate that average personal and household income in Missouri is generally slightly below that of the United States as a whole, whereas the averages for Maryland are substantially higher. These same patterns are observed in the data for average weekly earnings and average hourly wages.

In terms of the rural–urban division, Missouri is quite typical of the United States, with two large metropolitan areas, Kansas City and St. Louis. Based on the 2000 decennial census, the proportion metropolitan

Table 5.1. *Summary data for Maryland, Missouri, and the United States*

	1991			1999			2004		
	Maryland	Missouri	USA	Maryland	Missouri	USA	Maryland	Missouri	USA
Employment by Industry (in percent)									
Mining	0.00	0.23	0.59	0.00	0.12	0.42	0.00	0.21	0.37
Construction	7.53	4.88	6.32	6.91	7.65	6.73	8.18	7.87	7.82
Manufacturing	9.49	17.23	17.29	7.75	13.78	14.85	5.90	10.58	11.72
Transportation and Public Utilities	6.68	8.01	6.58	7.14	7.70	6.94	4.16	5.58	4.87
Trade	19.40	23.66	21.83	18.22	21.21	21.27	13.68	16.93	15.21
Finance, Insurance, Real Estate	6.66	5.68	6.26	6.88	6.28	6.36	6.39	7.11	6.95
Services	36.86	33.66	33.45	41.48	35.82	36.46	51.02	45.85	47.00
Government	11.88	3.26	4.65	10.49	4.87	4.35	10.22	4.07	4.42
Race (in percent)									
White	71.95	89.54	84.72	68.35	89.47	83.31	66.86	87.06	81.77
Black	25.30	9.25	11.42	27.25	9.11	11.96	27.06	9.93	11.67
American Indian, Eskimo, Aleut	0.03	0.40	0.61	0.33	0.38	0.82	0.29	0.36	0.75

Asian, Pacific Islander	2.28	0.60	2.93	4.08	1.04	3.90	4.61	1.50	4.48
Hispanic Origin (in percent)	2.85	0.56	8.60	3.89	1.22	10.42	6.77	2.65	12.58
Income/Earnings (1999 Quarter 2 Dollars)									
Average Weekly Earnings[a]	622.93	483.76	539.81	681.91	551.72	585.54	710.17	572.76	608.04
Average Hourly Wage	15.64	12.17	13.61	16.85	13.50	14.51	17.34	14.35	15.17
Median Hourly Wage	13.19	9.90	11.33	14.17	11.46	11.92	14.47	12.26	12.26

[a] Top coded at $1,923 (1991), $2,885 (1999), $2,885 (2004). All dollars are inflation adjusted to the quarter.

Source: Annual Outgoing Rotation Group File of the Current Population Survey in the United States (1991, 1999, 2004). Employment is calculated for the noninstitutional, civilian population age 16 or over.

in Missouri is 68 percent, while the proportion in the United States as a whole is 80 percent. In contrast, 93 percent of Maryland's population was defined as metropolitan in the 2000 decennial census. In sum, although Missouri is a fairly representative state from most demographic and economic perspectives, Maryland is clearly richer, more racially diverse, and more urban than Missouri or the United States as a whole.[6]

In sum, the evidence presented here suggests that the economies of Maryland, Missouri, and the rest of the United States both started and ended the 1990s in a similar position, although workers in Maryland have higher wages throughout the period, and that the labor markets evolved in a similar fashion over this period. This suggests that the people affected by Maryland and Missouri welfare reform in the 1990s were operating in an economic environment that was fairly representative of general economic conditions in the United States over this period.

III. Data

Our data on AFDC/TANF recipients come from administrative records maintained by the states of Maryland and Missouri. Our analyses focus on female payees in the AFDC-Basic program or its TANF successor who are at least 18 and at most 56 years of age.[7] Child-only cases are omitted, since the payee in such cases receives a grant on behalf of children but is exempt from the work or training requirements that parents face. Welfare recipients with only in-kind payments are also excluded.[8]

---

[6] We have also examined the evolution of the labor market in these two states and the United States as a whole over this period using data from the 1991–2004 CPS. This analysis shows that the labor market dynamics are similar for Maryland, Missouri, and the United States. These results are available in Mueser, Stevens, and Troske (2007).

[7] We limit the analysis to individuals who are at most 56 years old because we are focusing on subsequent employment and older workers may not have the same incentives to work. As a practical matter, given that most recipients are fairly young, this restriction has very little effect on our results.

[8] The decision to focus on cash recipients reflects both substantive considerations and data availability. We do not have data on several of the larger in-kind programs (housing and child care subsidies), so we are not able to look at any comprehensive indicator of in-kind payments. In addition, we believe that cash payments are useful in identifying a meaningful class of program participants. Historically, cash payments have distinguished AFDC from a variety of means-tested subsidies, many of them operating under local rules and often with waiting lists. Under TANF, this distinction continues to have significance because states retained many salient features (e.g., grant levels) of the prior program, even as the number of cash recipients and therefore the overall importance of cash payments declined.

Since two-parent families receiving payments under the AFDC-UP program are omitted, the unit of our analysis is a single mother with children who receives cash welfare payments or, equivalently, a welfare case headed by such an individual. We have aggregated data into quarters, so that recipients are those who receive payments and met our other selection criteria in any month during a quarter. A recipient in a given quarter is defined as a welfare *arrival* or *entry* if she was not a recipient in the prior quarter; and she is defined as an *exit* or *leaver* if she is not a recipient in the subsequent quarter. Since our information on program participation is limited to Maryland and Missouri, an individual who had received welfare payments outside the state would be considered a new arrival, and welfare in the previous state would not be measured.[9]

Employment and earnings information for each state derives from "wage record" data maintained by the state agency in support of its Unemployment Insurance program.[10] For every individual employed in a covered job, the files indicate total quarterly earnings, along with selected employer information. While the vast majority of the employment for state residents is included in these files, self-employment, illegal or informal employment, and certain employment exempt from reporting requirements, as well as employment outside the state, are not included.[11] We match recipient records from the welfare data to the wage record data using the Social Security number. If we do not find a record for an individual in a given quarter in the wage record data, we consider the individual to be not employed.

Other work using welfare data from Maryland and Missouri suggests that the basic demographic structure of welfare caseloads, levels of employment for welfare recipients, and changes in these patterns over the 1990s

[9] Payees under 18 years of age are not included in our analysis, so such cases are coded as a welfare entry on reaching 18. Since special rules apply to payees under 18, we believe it is most useful to view them as entering a new program at that point.

[10] See Hotz and Scholz (2002) for a discussion of the advantages and limitations of these data for studying the employment patterns of welfare recipients. As Edin and Lein (1997) show, prior to welfare reform, a large share of AFDC recipients received payments from undocumented employment. Since reforms increased incentives to hold formal, documented jobs, increases in reported employment for recipients may partly reflect substitution of formal for informal employment. As our focus is on welfare leavers, this bias is expected to be less important.

[11] In the case of Missouri, we have wage record data for Kansas as well as Missouri. Approximately 15 percent of the jobs held by welfare recipients in Jackson County, Missouri (the central county of Kansas City), are in Kansas. In contrast, very few residents of St. Louis, Missouri, have jobs in Illinois. In the case of Maryland, a substantial concentration of population is on the border with the District of Columbia and Virginia, but welfare recipients are concentrated in Baltimore City and Baltimore County, so we expect that few commute to jobs outside the state.

are similar to those of other states. Mueser and King (2001) compare welfare patterns for Kansas City, Missouri, and Baltimore, Maryland, throughout the 1990s with those in four other major metropolitan areas in the Midwest and South and find broadly similar patterns across the six metropolitan areas. Dyke et al. (2006) evaluate job training programs for welfare recipients in Missouri and North Carolina, finding marked similarities in the structure of such programs and their impacts. Appendix Table A-5.1 contains summary statistics for each cohort of leavers used in the ensuing analysis.

IV. Caseload and Employment Dynamics

In this section, we examine changes in the caseload over the period of our study, movements onto and off welfare, and the characteristics of the caseload and of those beginning and ending welfare spells.

A. Patterns of Welfare Entry and Exit

Figure 5.1 provides the basic information on the dynamics of the caseload and its change in our two states. Since there is appreciable seasonal variation in arrivals and departures, as well variation due to small numbers, statistics are presented for a four-quarter moving average.[12] In Maryland (Panel A), the caseload grew in the early 1990s to a peak of just over 62,000 recipients in the third quarter of 1992, remaining close to that peak through the end of 1994.[13] However, in the following two years, the caseload declined by about a quarter and continued a steep decline until about 2000, when it stood at less than 20,000. Finally, since 2000, the caseload has continued to decline, although the decline is much more modest. Looking at the number of departures and arrivals, we see that the decline was a function both of declining arrivals and of increased departures.

In Missouri (Panel B), the caseload grew steadily in the early 1990s and reached a peak of just over 74,500 in the third quarter of 1994. In 1995, as in Maryland, it began a steady and sharp decline. Again, paralleling Maryland,

---

[12] The quarter indicated in the figures is the fourth quarter of the year to which the average applies. The appendices in Carrington et al. (2002) show the extent of seasonal and other quarter-to-quarter variation in such data.

[13] Maryland replaced its data management software during the period 1995:1–1996:3. The unusual pattern of arrivals shown in the figure for the moving average over 1996:4–1997:3 reflects a single outlier in 1996:4, which undoubtedly reflects data inconsistencies, not actual variation in flows.

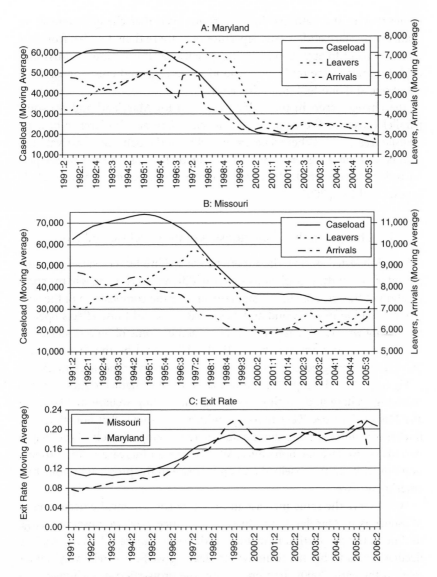

Figure 5.1. Caseload Dynamics
Note: All measures calculated as four-quarter moving average.

the caseload has continued to decline since 2000, but at a much slower rate. The caseload decline reflects both an increase in departures and a decline in arrivals.

The similarity in the patterns for the two states is striking. Panel C of Figure 5.1 presents the departure rates in the two states, showing the similarities in the patterns. It is clear, however, that changes were more dramatic in Maryland, where departure rates more than doubled from less than 8 percent to approximately 20 percent over this period. In Missouri, departure rates were initially at around 11 percent, and these increased to about one and one-half times that level.

The changes seen in the welfare caseload for Maryland and Missouri parallel those for the country as a whole (National Conference of State Legislatures 2005). Where data are available on the patterns of arrivals and leavers for other local areas or for the United States as a whole, we see patterns that are very similar to these (Gittleman 2001; King and Mueser 2005; Mueser and King 2001).

B. Changes in the Characteristics of the Caseload and Flows

We are interested in how the experience of welfare leavers varies over the period of our study. One obvious source of differences is changes in the composition of this group. Did welfare reform alter the composition of the welfare population in Maryland and Missouri? If so, did those effects operate by altering who is attracted to or leaves welfare? Some observers suggested that under welfare reform the relatively able would be the first to move off welfare, leaving behind those least prepared to enter the labor market.

Figures 5.2 and 5.3 provide information on the characteristics of those receiving welfare and on those entering and exiting welfare in Maryland and Missouri, respectively. In Maryland, Panel A shows that nonwhites are underrepresented among those entering and exiting, a result of the longer periods on welfare for nonwhites. We observe an increase in the proportion nonwhite in the caseload and an increase in the proportion nonwhite entering welfare.

We observe the same increase in the proportion nonwhite occurring in Missouri as in Maryland, but, in contrast, since 2000 we observe a large decline in the proportion nonwhite in Missouri (Figure 5.3, Panel A). The decline seems to be due to nonwhites leaving welfare at relatively higher rates in the early 2000s than previously. The proportion nonwhite among recipients declines to below 45 percent, lower than in the early 1990s at the beginning of our series.[14]

---

[14] In order to examine the reasons behind the increase in the proportion nonwhite in more detail, we have plotted the number of arrivals and departures separately for whites and nonwhites in Maryland and Missouri, respectively. In both states, the number of whites arriving on welfare had declined by more than the number of nonwhites. Increases in departure rates occurred for both whites and nonwhites in both states, although their

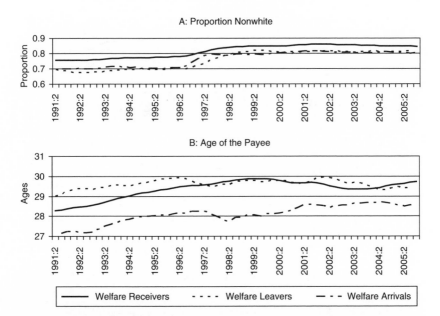

A: Proportion Nonwhite

B: Age of the Payee

Welfare Receivers · · · · Welfare Leavers — · · Welfare Arrivals

Figure 5.2. Characteristics of Recipients, Arrivals, and Leavers: Maryland
Note: All measures calculated as four-quarter moving average. Missing race treated as white.

In Figures 5.2 and 5.3 (Panel B) we observe a small increase in age of payee through the mid-1990s and then a moderate decline. Average age for both arrivals and departures is increasing. The change over time is modest relative to the range in ages from 20 to 40 that we observe in both samples (the standard deviation exceeds 7). Those exiting are about two years older than those entering, with the difference declining over time as individuals spend shorter periods receiving welfare.

The average educational level of recipients in Missouri changed very little prior to 2000 (Figure 5.3, Panel C) but had increased by almost 0.2 years by the end of our series. Both arrivals and leavers have more schooling than the caseload as a whole, reflecting the shorter spells of educated recipients. The marked decline in the average educational level of leavers in the second half of 2002 reflects a single quarter (2002:3), and it corresponds with the

relative importance differed by state. Notwithstanding the differences between whites and nonwhites, perhaps the most important observation is that in both states, although the overall decline in the white caseload is greater, for both whites and nonwhites changes in flows onto and off welfare are substantial and play an important role in observed caseload declines. Results are available in Mueser et al. (2007).

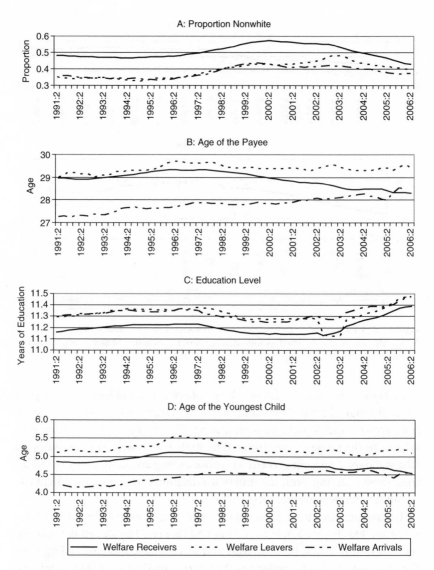

Figure 5.3. Characteristics of Recipients, Arrivals, and Leavers: Missouri
Note: All measures calculated as four-quarter moving average.

first set of recipients who were removed from the rolls because of the impo-
sition of the 60-month lifetime limit. Individuals terminated at this point
were likely to have received welfare for extended periods prior to impo-
sition of the time limit. The age of an average recipient's youngest child
declined by almost half a year over the period since 1995 (Panel D), consistent with regulations that make it harder to continue to receive welfare over

longer periods. It is clear that recipients are leaving when their children are younger.[15]

Looking at the two sets of figures together, there is some evidence that the implementation of TANF in late 1996 had an influence on the dynamics, given that several graphs show marked changes in trend at around that time. However, it is the stability rather than the change that is most notable. The relative stability in mean education for the caseload (in Missouri) up to 2002 suggests that reform did not differentially affect more able recipients. More generally, the stability suggests that the selection effects of welfare reform are not so strong as to vitiate comparisons over time in the experiences of welfare recipients.

Figures 5.4 and 5.5 provide information on the prior welfare and employment experience for the welfare population.[16] Panel A in both figures suggests a substantial decline in the extent to which recipients have prior welfare experience. In the two prior years, the average recipient had received payments during approximately 70 percent of the time, which decreases gradually to just over 50 percent in both states. The decline was less marked for those exiting welfare, who became more like the average recipient. Many of the initiatives associated with welfare reform—most notably time limits—place emphasis on removing long-term recipients from welfare, and these statistics show the impact of such policies.

Panel B shows welfare payments as a proportion of the sum of such payments and earnings, where earnings are based on wage record data. We see that over the period, welfare payments gradually became less important as a source of income, corroborating national trends reported in Chapter Two of this volume. In Maryland the contribution declined from nearly 80 percent to less than 60 percent, and in Missouri from nearly 70 percent to about 46 percent. There was a more modest decline among those leaving welfare, whose proportions are initially about 10 percentage points below the caseload average but are very similar by the end of the period. The prior reliance on welfare of those entering welfare declined slightly in both states.

Perhaps most striking is the increase in the extent of prior earnings for welfare recipients (Panel C). The proportion of the prior eight quarters with positive earnings was initially about 20 percent in Maryland and a bit under 30 percent in Missouri, and it increased by a full 20 percentage points in both states, peaking at around 2002. From 2002 to 2005, we

---

[15] Data on education and age of the recipient's youngest child are not available in our longitudinal extract of Maryland administrative records.

[16] In Maryland, we have no information on the amount of the welfare grant for 1996:4–2003:4, which reduces the time series available for Panel B.

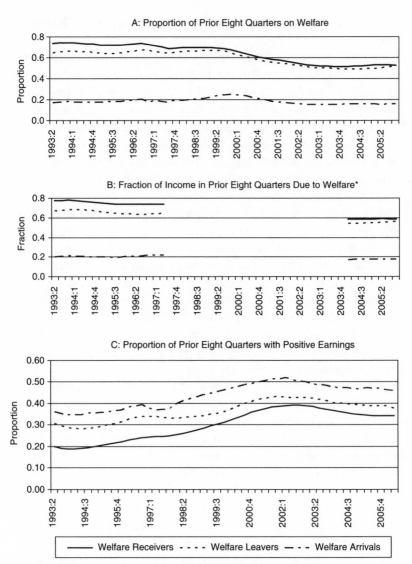

*AFDC/TANF grant amounts for 1996:4–2003:4 are missing in Maryland data.

Figure 5.4. Welfare and Employment History: Maryland
Note: All measures calculated as four-quarter moving averages.

observe a modest decline of 5–10 percentage points. For those leaving welfare and those entering, the trends in prior work are very similar. We also see that the leavers become more similar to the overall caseload during the 1990s.

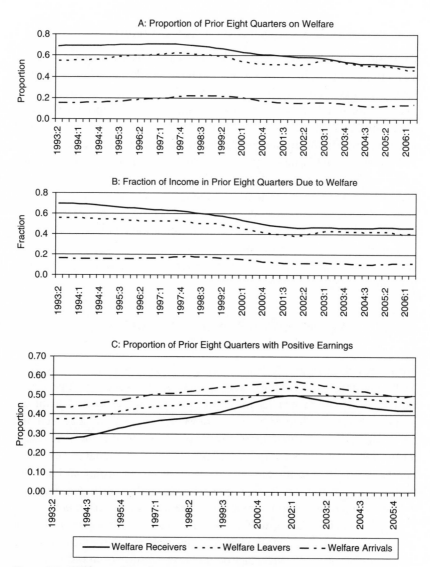

Figure 5.5. Welfare and Employment History: Missouri
Note: All measures calculated as four-quarter moving averages.

The results in Figures 5.4 and 5.5 provide remarkably similar patterns for each of the three measures of welfare and employment history. Welfare reform is associated with both a large increase in the percentage of welfare recipients who had worked in prior quarters and a fairly substantial decline in the fraction of a welfare recipient's prior income coming from welfare. There is a slight erosion in these employment measures since 2002.

V. Comparing Three Leaver Cohorts

To consider how the experiences of welfare leavers have changed over time, we focus here on three cohorts leaving welfare: in July 1992–June 1993, July 1996–June 1997, and July 2001–June 2002. The first period predates major welfare reform in both states, and with relatively few exceptions, the rules correspond to those of the AFDC system that had been largely unchanged since the early 1980s. In neither state were there signs of caseload decline. The second period is nearly two years after implementation of the states' major welfare reforms, which occurred in both states at around 1995; formal implementation of the federal TANF program began in late 1996 in both states. During this period, the economy is growing and caseloads are declining, with levels at least 10 percent below their peaks. In the third period, the state economies pass through a modest recession. Caseloads have declined appreciably since their peak, but the rate of decline in caseloads has slowed significantly.

A. The Impact of Reforms on Welfare Leavers: Employment and Recidivism

The top panels in Figures 5.6 and 5.7 show the proportion of leavers who are back on welfare in each of the next eight quarters. The solid line indicates the earliest period, the dashed line the middle period, and the dotted line the last period.[17] A leaver is defined by receipt of welfare in a particular quarter and no welfare in the following quarter, so by construction, this measure is zero for the first quarter after the quarter of exit. The lines show that in the second quarter, about 10 percent of leavers are again receiving welfare and that this proportion increases for all of the cohorts through the fourth quarter.

The difference between the first two cohorts is substantial in both states. Four quarters after leaving welfare, approximately 21–23 percent of former recipients in the first cohort are again receiving welfare. For the second cohort, the proportion is up to 8 percentage points lower. The decline in welfare receipt

---

[17] The statistics in these figures aggregate the experiences of individuals leaving welfare in any of the specified quarters. For example, those who leave welfare in 1992:3 are followed for 1992:4–1994:3, while those who leave welfare in 1992:4 are followed for 1993:1–1994:4. This means that an individual who left welfare, returned, and then left again within 1992:3–1993:2 would be counted as a leaver twice in this analysis. (The number of such cases is small.) We were concerned about possible differences in the experiences of individuals leaving welfare in different quarters within each period, so we calculated statistics in both panels of these figures separately for each exit quarter. Although small differences exist, these are dwarfed by the differences between the cohorts.

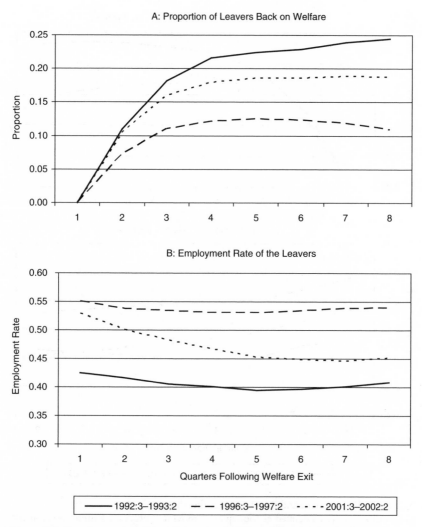

A: Proportion of Leavers Back on Welfare

B: Employment Rate of the Leavers

Quarters Following Welfare Exit

———— 1992:3–1993:2   — — 1996:3–1997:2   · · · · 2001:3–2002:2

Figure 5.6. Employment and Recidivism for the Three Cohorts: Maryland
Note: All measures calculated as four-quarter moving averages.

for this cohort in quarters 5–8 reflects the fact that some of those who return to welfare leave again, outnumbering the flow of those returning. In the final cohort, return probabilities are intermediate between the earlier two cohorts.

Panel B of Figures 5.6 and 5.7 provides employment rates for the welfare leavers in the three cohorts in the eight quarters after leaving. Although employment rates are about 10 percentage points lower in Maryland than in Missouri, the patterns are strikingly similar. In the late 1990s, welfare leavers are much more likely to be working than prior to welfare reform.

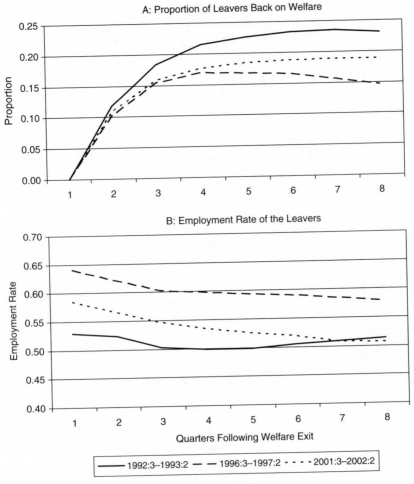

Figure 5.7. Employment and Recidivism for the Three Cohorts: Missouri
Note: All measures calculated as four-quarter moving averages. Earnings are adjusted for inflation to 1999:2

On the other hand, since 2000, with the slowing of the economy, the likelihood of employment has declined appreciably in both states, but in general it remains above the employment rate for the early 1990s.

If this increase in employment for more recent cohorts is primarily the result of the reformed programs' stringent work requirements, we might expect that the increased employment rate would be accompanied by a decline in earnings.[18] To examine this possibility, Figures 5.8 and 5.9

---

[18] Given that our earnings measure is total earnings in a quarter, there are three ways earnings could change: a change in a worker's hourly wage, a change in the number of hours

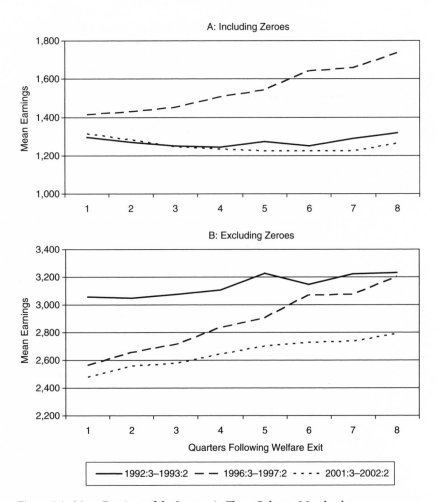

Figure 5.8. Mean Earnings of the Leavers in Three Cohorts: Maryland
Note: All measures calculated as four-quarter moving averages. Earnings are adjusted for inflation to 1999:2

compare earnings over time for our three cohorts of welfare leavers.[19] The top panel presents the average earnings for all leavers, including those with no earnings. In both states, Panel A shows that earnings are appreciably higher for the second cohort, in the late 1990s after welfare reform, than in the first. However, looking at the post-2000 cohort, we see that earnings have declined. In Maryland, they have returned to their level of the early

worked per day, or a change in the number of days worked in a quarter. Unfortunately, we are unable to determine what portion of the overall change is accounted for by each factor.

[19] Earnings are measured in 1999:2 dollars.

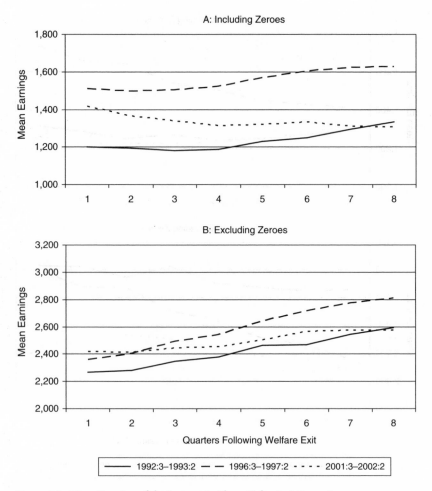

Figure 5.9. Mean Earning of the Leavers in Three Cohorts: Missouri
Note: All measures calculated as four-quarter moving averages. Earnings are adjusted for inflation to 1999:2

1990s, although in Missouri earnings remain somewhat higher until the end of the follow-up period. These results suggest that the strong economy plays an important role in causing the higher earnings observed following welfare reform.

Panel B graphs average earnings for those with jobs.[20] We see here that Maryland and Missouri show somewhat different patterns. In Maryland, in the first (prereform) cohort, earnings of those with jobs are appreciably

---

[20] Earnings vary substantially from quarter to quarter, in large part due to seasonal effects. Since the cohorts graphed in these figures combine leavers in four quarters, they smooth these effects.

higher than comparable earnings of the other cohorts (Figure 5.8). This would suggest that the reforms may be forcing individuals into lower-paying jobs. Average earnings for those employed are even lower in the third period, perhaps reflecting the economic downturn. In contrast, Panel B for Missouri (Figure 5.9) shows relatively small differences in average earnings, with earnings slightly higher for both cohorts following welfare reform. It does not appear that Missouri's welfare reform has pushed more challenged individuals into the labor market.

Tables 5.2 and 5.3 provide information on the welfare recipients' industry affiliations when they leave welfare and on whether these affiliations changed over the following two years. For each cohort, job characteristics are provided for the first quarter after leaving welfare (columns 1, 3, and 5) and for the eighth quarter after leaving welfare (columns 2, 4, and 6). By definition, none of those identified in the first quarter after leaving welfare are welfare recipients at that time, but the measures based on the eighth quarter after leaving welfare include individuals who returned to welfare. All statistics in the table focus on the characteristics of employers of welfare recipients, so individuals who are not employed are omitted.[21]

Panel A shows that welfare leavers are very likely to have jobs in retail trade and service firms, and that this proportion grew modestly between our cohorts.[22] Looking at the industry detail, we see that 9 to 14 percent of leavers are working in eating and drinking establishments in the quarter after leaving welfare in both Maryland and Missouri, with little trend over time. At over 13 percent, the initial proportion in manufacturing is nearly twice as high in Missouri as in Maryland, but the proportion declines by about half in both states over the period of our study. A dramatic increase occurred during the 1990s in help supply services ("temporary help").[23]

If we compare the first quarter after leaving welfare with the eighth quarter, we see that the progression is quite similar for the three cohorts across

---

[21] In Tables 5.2 and 5.3, for workers with more than one job in a quarter, we provide information on the employer paying the greatest earnings during the reference quarter.

[22] For the final cohort in Maryland, the distribution of industry would appear to differ dramatically from that in the earlier cohorts, but this is due to coding difficulties. For the recent cohort in Maryland, industry was coded using the North America Industry Classification System rather than the Standard Industrial Classification system, used for prior cohorts, and we were not able to make these comparable for all the categories presented here.

[23] This growth in the employment of welfare leavers in the temporary help industry reflects both the overall growth in employment in this industry (Autor 2003) and an increase in the relative reliance on such jobs for welfare recipients (Heinrich, Mueser, and Troske 2005).

Table 5.2.   Characteristics of welfare leavers one and eight quarters after leaving welfare: Maryland

	1992:3–1993:2		1996:3–1997:2		2001:3–2002:2	
	First quarter after leaving welfare	Eighth quarter after leaving welfare	First quarter after leaving welfare	Eighth quarter after leaving welfare	First quarter after leaving welfare	Eighth quarter after leaving welfare
	(1)	(2)	(3)	(4)	(5)	(6)
Percent Employed	42.1	40.3	53.6	53.2	52.4	44.9
Number Employed	9,348	8,941	16,536	16,413	7,420	6,335
A. Industry of Employment (in percent)						
Agric., Mining, Construction	1.2	1.3	1.3	1.6	1.0	1.1
Manufacturing	6.5	7.0	5.1	5.6	3.1	2.8
Trans., Com., etc.	2.1	2.4	2.4	3.1	8.0	8.5
Wholesale Trade	2.2	2.3	2.2	2.0	8.3	8.0
Retail Trade	29.0	26.6	33.8	28.1	19.3	18.1
5311 Dept. Stores	2.8	2.4	4.3	3.5	2.5	1.7
5411 Grocery Stores	4.6	4.3	5.8	4.7	1.7	1.3
5812 Eating & Drinking Places	11.4	10.2	13.4	10.3	9.4	9.1
Finance, Ins., Real Estate	3.5	4.0	3.1	4.1	3.4	4.3
Services	50.5	50.8	47.8	50.2	53.6	52.7
7011 Hotels, Motels	4.3	3.7	3.5	3.1	2.9	2.7

7363 Help Supply Services	6.3	5.1	8.1	7.8	9.0	7.1
8011 Office and Clinics of Doctors of Medicine	1.6	1.8	1.2	1.7	1.5	1.9
8051 Skilled Nursing Care	6.6	6.4	4.8	4.9	8.4	8.2
8062 Hospitals	4.5	4.8	2.7	3.3	4.3	5.1
8211 Elementary and Secondary School	3.0	4.1	2.9	3.3	3.1	3.2
8361 Residential Care	1.6	1.9	1.8	2.0	1.5	1.7
Public Administration	4.8	5.5	4.2	4.8	2.8	3.7
Industry Not Ascertained	0.1	0.0	0.2	0.3	0.6	0.8
B. Size of Firm (in percent)						
1–19	12.0	11.8	10.1	10.0	7.4	7.8
20–99	19.6	19.4	18.3	18.2	16.8	16.7
100–249	19.1	17.7	16.1	14.9	15.4	14.8
250–999	23.0	23.7	23.6	23.9	26.0	24.8
Over 1,000	26.4	27.4	31.8	33.0	34.4	35.9
C. Quarterly Earnings in Firm (in percent)						
Below $2,000	16.7	17.8	25.3	20.3	21.1	17.2
$2,000–3,999	34.6	32.1	37.9	33.5	34.4	32.7
$4,000–7,500	30.9	29.2	25.8	29.2	29.9	31.4
Over $7,500	17.8	22.0	11.0	16.9	14.7	18.5
Mean Quarterly Earnings	4,715	4,815	3,952	4,642	4,315	4,766

(continued)

Table 5.2 *Continued*

	1992:3–1993:2		1996:3–1997:2		2001:3–2002:2	
	First quarter after leaving welfare	Eighth quarter after leaving welfare	First quarter after leaving welfare	Eighth quarter after leaving welfare	First quarter after leaving welfare	Eighth quarter after leaving welfare
	(1)	(2)	(3)	(4)	(5)	(6)
D. Welfare Recipients in Firm (in percent)						
Less than 2%	74.6	75.4	77.8	78.4	82.7	82.7
2–10%	17.2	16.4	15.1	14.8	12.8	12.6
Over 10%	8.2	8.2	7.1	6.7	4.5	4.7

Note: All dollars are adjusted for inflation to quarter 2 of 1999.

Table 5.3. *Characteristics of welfare leavers one and eight quarters after leaving welfare: Missouri*

| | 1992:3–1993:2 | | 1996:3–1997:2 | | 2001:3–2002:2 | |
| | First quarter after leaving welfare | Eighth quarter after leaving welfare | First quarter after leaving welfare | Eighth quarter after leaving welfare | First quarter after leaving welfare | Eighth quarter after leaving welfare |
	(1)	(2)	(3)	(4)	(5)	(6)
Percent Employed	52.9	51.4	64.1	57.8	58.5	50.7
Number Employed	16,006	15,560	24,886	22,477	15,142	13,123
A. Industry of Employment (in Percent)						
Agric., Mining, Construction	1.3	1.4	1.3	1.4	1.4	1.2
Manufacturing	13.4	14.0	9.5	10.3	5.8	5.5
Trans., Com., etc.	3.1	3.5	3.0	3.8	3.3	3.1
Wholesale Trade	2.6	2.8	2.7	2.7	1.5	1.5
Retail Trade	27.5	25.2	28.4	25.7	29.7	26.9
5311 Dept. Stores	2.3	2.8	3.2	3.1	3.6	3.2
5411 Grocery Stores	3.4	3.2	3.5	3.4	3.3	3.3
5541 Gasoline Stations	2.9	2.5	3.2	2.8	3.6	3.1
5810 Eating & Drinking Places	13.8	11.6	13.2	11.1	13.4	11.7
Finance, Ins., Real Estate	2.7	3.3	3.3	4.3	3.2	3.6

(continued)

Table 5.3. *Continued*

	1992:3–1993:2		1996:3–1997:2		2001:3–2002:2	
	First quarter after leaving welfare	Eighth quarter after leaving welfare	First quarter after leaving welfare	Eighth quarter after leaving welfare	First quarter after leaving welfare	Eighth quarter after leaving welfare
	(1)	(2)	(3)	(4)	(5)	(6)
Services	47.3	47.1	49.9	49.2	53.6	50.1
7011 Hotels, Motels	*4.6*	*4.1*	*3.9*	*3.5*	*3.7*	*3.3*
7363 Help Supply Services	*5.2*	*6.2*	*8.2*	*6.9*	*7.1*	*5.4*
8051 Skilled Nursing Care	*9.4*	*7.7*	*8.6*	*7.7*	*9.5*	*8.9*
8052 Intermediate Care	*3.0*	*2.1*	*2.1*	*1.6*	*1.6*	*1.4*
8062 Hospitals	*3.2*	*3.7*	*3.1*	*3.7*	*3.2*	*3.1*
8322 Social Services	*1.3*	*1.6*	*2.2*	*2.5*	*2.8*	*3.0*
8361 Residential Care	*1.9*	*2.3*	*1.9*	*2.2*	*2.7*	*2.5*
Public Administration	1.5	2.0	1.6	2.4	1.4	1.3
Industry Not Ascertained	0.7	0.6	0.3	0.1	0.2	6.8
B. Size of Firm (in Percent)						
1–19	11.7	11.3	10.3	10.2	10.0	11.4
20–99	22.3	20.8	19.9	20.0	19.5	20.2
100–249	20.0	18.4	18.9	18.1	18.3	17.8

250–999	21.7	22.2	22.3	23.0	23.9	23.2
Over 1,000	24.2	27.2	28.6	28.7	28.2	27.4

C. Quarterly Earnings in Firm (in Percent)

Below $2,000	30.5	29.6	31.6	25.3	26.6	25.4
$2,000–3,999	41.6	37.6	39.7	38.1	41.3	40.5
$4,000–7,500	21.4	24.8	21.8	26.0	23.4	23.2
Over $,7500	6.3	8.1	6.9	10.6	8.6	11.0
Mean Quarterly Earnings	3,397	3,656	3,453	3,973	3,683	3,891

D. Welfare Recipients in Firm (in Percent)

Less Than 2%	74.8	76.7	78.2	78.4	79.2	77.1
2–10%	16.6	15.4	14.7	14.7	14.2	15.2
Over 10%	8.5	8.0	7.1	6.9	6.6	7.7

Note: All dollars are adjusted for inflation to quarter 2 of 1999.

both states. In general, over the two years following exit from welfare, there is a modest decline in employment in the least stable employment (e.g., retail trade, temporary help). As this pattern is largely unchanged for our later cohorts, we see no evidence in these tabulations suggesting that leavers in the recent period are more likely to remain in unstable or marginal jobs.

Panel B reports size statistics for firms hiring welfare leavers. Here we see that, among leavers in the two cohorts following welfare reform, appreciably more are working for the largest firms. Whereas in the earlier period workers tended to move to larger firms in the two years after leaving welfare, in the late 1990s and early 2000s there is little movement.

Turning to Panel C of Tables 5.2 and 5.3, we see that workers start in lower-paying firms and move to higher-paying ones. In the more recent periods, workers in Maryland are in somewhat lower-paying firms, whereas in Missouri, there is a slight move in the opposite direction. Finally, Panel D shows that welfare leavers are less likely than in the past to be working in a firm with a large share of welfare recipients. In the two years following welfare exit, there is little change in the distribution, although in the most recent period recipients do move to jobs where they are slightly more likely to be working with other recipients. Such shifts are small, however, compared to shifts between cohorts (especially in Maryland). We conclude that welfare reform does not appear to have pushed leavers into positions with employers who specialize in hiring welfare recipients.

In sum, we observe that welfare leavers following reform are at least as likely to be employed as leavers prior to reform. The characteristics of the firms they work for provide no indication that those with jobs have been forced into inferior employment.

B. The Determinants of Recidivism

As the conditions for departure from welfare shift, we might assume that welfare recidivism would have a different structure. To examine this possibility, we start by estimating the probability of returning to welfare within two years for our set of welfare leavers using a probit model controlling for demographic characteristics, past welfare and work experience, location, and the attributes of an individual's job in the quarter immediately after leaving welfare.[24] The analysis is performed separately for our three

---

[24] We also performed analyses predicting the chance of returning to welfare within one year, but the results were substantively indistinguishable from the two-year analysis.

cohorts of former welfare recipients in Maryland and Missouri.[25] We use the results from this estimation to predict the probability that an individual with various attributes returns to welfare within two years. The results from this exercise are presented in Tables 5.4 and 5.5. To obtain our baseline prediction, we use mean values of the control variables computed across all three cohorts.[26]

In specification (1) we include the standard demographic characteristics along with the time on welfare and the time working in the past two years when estimating the probability of returning to welfare. Time on welfare is measured as the proportion of quarters in the eight quarters prior to leaving that the individual was receiving welfare, and time working is measured in an analogous manner.

Specification (2) controls for the economic conditions of the local labor market by including the unemployment rate for the county where an individual lives and for whether she lives in an urban or suburban county within a large metropolitan area.[27] The urban counties consist of the counties containing the cities of Baltimore, St. Louis, and Kansas City, Missouri, as well as St. Louis County, Missouri. Suburban counties are those in the metropolitan areas around these major cities as well as the Maryland suburbs of Washington, D.C. We also control for the quarterly earnings received by former recipients in the initial quarter after leaving welfare. We include six dummy variables representing seven earnings categories. The excluded category contains individuals with no job—and therefore zero earnings—in the initial quarter off welfare. Finally, we include controls for the industry of a recipient's employer in the first quarter off welfare along with controls for the size of the employer.

In order to calculate the probabilities in row (1) of Tables 5.4 and 5.5, we use the estimated coefficients from the indicated cohort times the means of the control variables calculated over individuals in all three cohorts. The estimates in row (2) are obtained using the cohort-specific means for control variables, so that the difference between these rows indicates the importance of changes in recipient characteristics between cohorts.[28]

---

[25] Coefficient estimates for this model are available in Mueser et al. (2007).

[26] Control variable means are provided in Appendix Table A-5.1.

[27] The unemployment rate for an individual's county is measured as the county-level quarterly unemployment rate averaged over the eight quarters immediately after an individual leaves welfare. County-level quarterly unemployment comes from the Bureau of Labor Statistics Employment and Earnings data. Later, we report a test of alternative measures of labor market opportunity.

[28] Since the model is not linear, the averages reported for different specifications are not identical, and the average reported in row (2) does not correspond to the average recidivism

Table 5.4. *Probability of returning to welfare within two years for various attributes: Maryland*

Predicted probability for various groups	1992:3–1993:2 (1)	(2)	1996:3–1997:2 (1)	(2)	2001:3–2002:2 (1)	(2)
Average Individual in Sample	0.378	0.379	0.228	0.228	0.305	0.280
	(0.009)	(0.011)	(0.008)	(0.009)	(0.014)	(0.023)
Average Individual in Cohort	0.359	0.358	0.213	0.206	0.320	0.315
	(0.009)	(0.009)	(0.008)	(0.008)	(0.011)	(0.011)
White	0.327	0.315	0.168	0.171	0.235	0.214
	(0.017)	(0.019)	(0.017)	(0.019)	(0.030)	(0.036)
Nonwhite	0.396	0.402	0.253	0.250	0.333	0.306
	(0.011)	(0.012)	(0.010)	(0.010)	(0.014)	(0.023)
Unknown Race	0.604	0.600	0.131	0.123	0.138	0.132
	(0.039)	(0.040)	(0.022)	(0.022)	(0.078)	(0.082)
One Child Under 18	0.364	0.365	0.220	0.216	0.296	0.269
	(0.011)	(0.013)	(0.010)	(0.011)	(0.017)	(0.024)
Four Children Under 18	0.426	0.428	0.260	0.266	0.337	0.319
	(0.022)	(0.023)	(0.023)	(0.023)	(0.027)	(0.033)
4.0 Percent County Unemployment Rate		0.380		0.207		0.296
		(0.025)		(0.017)		(0.044)
7.5 Percent County Unemployment Rate		0.378		0.237		0.273
		(0.010)		(0.012)		(0.046)
Percent on Welfare Previous Eight Quarters = 0	0.328	0.332	0.199	0.200	0.205	0.208
	(0.020)	(0.021)	(0.019)	(0.019)	(0.024)	(0.030)
Percent on Welfare Previous Eight Quarters = 100	0.409	0.408	0.248	0.245	0.376	0.329
	(0.013)	(0.015)	(0.011)	(0.012)	(0.021)	(0.029)
Percent Working Previous Eight Quarters = 0	0.344	0.338	0.224	0.215	0.287	0.257
	(0.013)	(0.015)	(0.012)	(0.013)	(0.020)	(0.027)
Percent Working Previous Eight Quarters = 100	0.443	0.459	0.237	0.253	0.341	0.327
	(0.020)	(0.023)	(0.018)	(0.021)	(0.026)	(0.033)
No Job When Leaving		0.351		0.233		0.292
		(0.070)		(0.035)		(0.075)

Table 5.4. *Continued*

Predicted probability for various groups	1992:3–1993:2		1996:3–1997:2		2001:3–2002:2	
	(1)	(2)	(1)	(2)	(1)	(2)
Job with Quarterly Earnings $1–$500		0.479 (0.080)		0.327 (0.043)		0.362 (0.084)
Job with Quarterly Earnings $3,001–$4,000		0.344 (0.075)		0.164 (0.043)		0.220 (0.083)

Note: The probability is predicted using the mean value of attributes across all three cohorts. Standard errors are in parentheses.

The first notable result is that the patterns of effects are quite similar for the two states. Recidivism rates are between 35 and 38 percent for the first cohort; they decline to 29 percent or below in the second cohort and then increase—but not to the prior level—in the third cohort, with most estimates in the range 31–33 percent. Changes in characteristics are relatively unimportant, as the patterns in rows (1) and (2) are very similar. A partial exception is the most recent cohort in both states, where it appears that the recidivism rates would be 1–2 percentage points lower if individual characteristics had not changed.

These results mirror those seen in Panel A of Figures 5.6 and 5.7. Tables 5.4 and 5.5 show that we continue to see the decline in the recidivism rate following welfare reform even after controlling for demographic characteristics, local labor market conditions, and the characteristics of a leaver's employer. This finding shows that the fall in the probability of returning to welfare is not tied to changes in the characteristics of individuals leaving welfare, changes in the strength of the economy (as captured by our measures), or changes in the characteristics of welfare leavers' employers. Although the higher recidivism rates since 2000 suggest that unmeasured labor market differences[29] may well play a role, the economy is clearly not solely responsible for the decline occurring since the early 1990s.

When we compare the estimated impacts of individual characteristics and economic conditions across the cohorts, we see that during this period of dramatic change in the welfare laws, the basic structure of the

rate for the cohort (see Appendix Table A-5.1). Since differences are small, the basic patterns are not affected.

[29] Since unemployment rate in the county is controlled, any differences in the economy must be in addition to those reflected in unemployment.

Table 5.5. *Probability of returning to welfare within two years for various attributes: Missouri*

Predicted probability for various groups	1992:3–1993:2		1996:3–1997:2		2001:3–2002:2	
	(1)	(2)	(1)	(2)	(1)	(2)
Average Individual in Sample	0.366	0.349	0.292	0.290	0.318	0.321
	(0.008)	(0.009)	(0.007)	(0.008)	(0.009)	(0.009)
Average Individual in Cohort	0.357	0.354	0.292	0.289	0.331	0.330
	(0.008)	(0.008)	(0.007)	(0.007)	(0.008)	(0.008)
White	0.350	0.327	0.270	0.257	0.302	0.299
	(0.010)	(0.012)	(0.009)	(0.011)	(0.012)	(0.013)
Nonwhite	0.392	0.386	0.330	0.347	0.344	0.357
	(0.013)	(0.016)	(0.012)	(0.014)	(0.014)	(0.016)
One Child Under 18	0.354	0.337	0.282	0.281	0.328	0.331
	(0.010)	(0.011)	(0.009)	(0.010)	(0.012)	(0.012)
Four Children Under 18	0.395	0.378	0.315	0.310	0.295	0.298
	(0.018)	(0.018)	(0.016)	(0.016)	(0.018)	(0.019)
4.0 Percent County Unemployment Rate		0.340		0.284		0.313
		(0.011)		(0.008)		(0.016)
7.5 Percent County Unemployment Rate		0.360		0.296		0.330
		(0.009)		(0.013)		(0.013)
Years of Education = 9	0.418	0.391	0.357	0.344	0.358	0.355
	(0.014)	(0.015)	(0.013)	(0.013)	(0.015)	(0.015)
Years of Education = 12	0.352	0.338	0.275	0.275	0.307	0.311
	(0.008)	(0.009)	(0.008)	(0.008)	(0.010)	(0.010)
Percent on Welfare Previous Eight Quarters = 0	0.294	0.280	0.242	0.238	0.293	0.297
	(0.015)	(0.015)	(0.015)	(0.015)	(0.015)	(0.016)
Percent on Welfare Previous Eight Quarters = 100	0.424	0.405	0.333	0.332	0.337	0.339
	(0.013)	(0.013)	(0.010)	(0.011)	(0.015)	(0.015)
Percent Working Previous Eight Quarters = 0	0.311	0.296	0.252	0.250	0.258	0.261
	(0.012)	(0.013)	(0.012)	(0.013)	(0.016)	(0.017)
Percent Working Previous Eight Quarters = 100	0.439	0.420	0.346	0.343	0.399	0.401
	(0.016)	(0.017)	(0.013)	(0.015)	(0.014)	(0.015)
No Job When Leaving		0.331		0.279		0.315
		(0.026)		(0.023)		(0.028)

Table 5.5. *Continued*

Predicted probability for various groups	1992:3–1993:2		1996:3–1997:2		2001:3–2002:2	
	(1)	(2)	(1)	(2)	(1)	(2)
Job with Quarterly Earnings $1–$500		0.437 (0.032)		0.360 (0.028)		0.367 (0.033)
Job with Quarterly Earnings $3,001–$4,000		0.285 (0.037)		0.236 (0.027)		0.299 (0.032)

Note: The probability is predicted using the mean value of attributes across all three cohorts. Standard errors are in parentheses.

effects of these variables on the probability of returning to welfare is largely unchanged. Both the time on welfare and time working affect the probability that an individual returns to welfare. As one might expect, those with greater welfare experience are more likely to return to welfare.

Perhaps contrary to expectations, we also see that, in all three cohorts, people who worked more in the past are *more* likely to return to welfare in the future. Prior employment and welfare experience variables will be negatively correlated, so including welfare experience should influence the coefficient of time working. However, reestimating the model dropping the welfare experience variable has little effect on the coefficient of prior work experience. Comparing across cohorts, we find that these variables play a somewhat less important role in predicting return to welfare for the 1996–1997 cohort than for the others, with the difference particularly large for Maryland.

One possible explanation for the observed impact of work experience is that welfare leavers with more quarters of prior employment are likely to leave welfare with low-paying jobs and therefore are more likely to return to welfare. The estimates for specification (2) (see the bottom rows of Tables 5.4 and 5.5) show that those who leave welfare with low-paying jobs are more likely to return to welfare than those with relatively high-paying jobs *and are more likely to return to welfare than those with no job.* The coefficients on the earnings dummy variables (not shown) indicate that it is not until an individual has earnings of over $2,000–$4,000 in a quarter that she is less likely to return to welfare than an individual who has no job in the initial quarter after leaving welfare.

While it may seem odd that women with zero earnings are less likely to return to welfare than those with modest earnings, previous research has found that many welfare leavers with zero postwelfare earnings have changed their household circumstances (e.g., marriage) in ways that offer a more persistent means of support than do jobs with very low earnings (Blank and Ruggles 1994; Moffitt 1992). The higher probability of returning to welfare for those with no earnings may also be partly due to the higher rates of disability and Supplemental Security Income (SSI) use among these households, as Frogner et al. (Chapter Four, this volume) note. This pattern is related to the growth in recent years in the number of "disconnected women" who are neither working nor on welfare and with very low earnings (see Chapter One of this volume).

Although the basic observation that having a low-paying job is associated with return to welfare is confirmed, it is of interest that the relationship between the probability of returning to welfare and the *prior* work history is reduced only slightly when controls for type of job after departure from welfare are included in most specifications. Even after we control for industry and firm size, those with more quarters of employment are more likely to return to welfare. Controlling for current employment, an individual who has sought welfare despite consistent employment is less likely to obtain complete self-sufficiency than one with a more limited work history.

In order to investigate this issue further, we introduced controls for volatility of earnings in the eight quarters prior to the quarter to capture instability in a recipient's employment history. In many specifications, we found the expected positive effect, confirming the view that those recipients with prior income variability were more likely to return to welfare. However, even with such controls, individuals who obtained low-paying jobs after leaving welfare were more likely than those without jobs to return to welfare. We also considered specifications in which the impact of prior earnings volatility was permitted to vary according to the earnings on the job obtained following welfare exit. Although several of the estimated coefficients associated with these interactions were statistically significant (more than would be predicted by chance), the coefficient estimates did not correspond with any meaningful pattern.

One obvious question about the structure of recidivism for the 1996–1997 cohort is how much of the lower recidivism rate is due to the strong economy. The effect that differences in economic conditions have on the rate of welfare recidivism is partly captured by the average unemployment rate in an individual's county of residence during the two years following leaving. We observe differences between our states in the estimated impact of unemployment, however. In Missouri, cross-county differences in unemployment rates have a significant impact on the likelihood of returning to welfare, with a 1 percent increase in average unemployment causing a 1 to 1.5 percent increase in the chance of return. In contrast, in Maryland, we find very little evidence showing that changes in unemployment rates affect recidivism, as the estimated effect is not generally statistically significant. In neither state does including unemployment and other county-level controls in the regression have much impact on the other coefficients. Furthermore, average differences in unemployment between cohorts are small, so changes in unemployment play essentially no role in explaining the differences in recidivism across cohorts.[30]

We have tried a number of alternative specifications to capture the possible effects that economic conditions have on the probability of returning to welfare. As an alternative to the aggregate measure used previously—the average unemployment rate in the eight quarters after departure—we allowed each of the eight unemployment rates to enter separately, in essence controlling for potential lag or lead effects. Substantive conclusions were not affected. Similar to Hoynes (2000), we have tried using the employment-to-population ratio and the average earnings in a county to capture local labor market conditions. In none of these alternative specifications does it appear that changes in economic conditions account for a substantial portion of the observed changes in welfare recidivism.

Of course, these measures may not capture the true level of opportunities in the labor market for our recipients. As Black, McKinnish, and Sanders (2003) show, conventional measures of the local labor market may suffer endogeneity bias. Although we cannot apply instrumental variables methods as they do, our comparison of periods with dramatic differences in labor market opportunity provides an additional indicator of the robustness of our results.[31]

Although our efforts to account for economic differences during the period suggest that these do not play a decisive role, we have noted several cases where observed patterns for the first and third cohorts are more similar than the second. For example, in Maryland, the impact of prior work on recidivism is somewhat different in the middle cohort. Such differences may well reflect elements of the economic environment that we are unable to account for. Nonetheless, it is clear that however we treat differences in coefficients, recidivism is lower in the latter two periods than in the first.

[30] The mean for this variable varies between 6 and 7 percent in Maryland across the three cohorts and between 5 and 6 percent in Missouri. For both states, the standard deviation in each period is over 2 percentage points. Coefficient estimates on which this discussion is based are presented in Mueser et al. (2007).

[31] In other work, one of us has examined labor market indicators based on the Census Bureau Quarterly Workforce Indicator (QWI) system. These data provide detailed information on labor market experiences of individuals by age and gender, and so may allow a more targeted approach to gauging the labor market (see Herbst and Stevens 2007).

Overall, then, much of the decline in the probability of returning to welfare would appear to be attributable to welfare reform and other policy changes over this period.

VI. Conclusion

We have five main findings in this chapter. First, for the most part, there have been only modest changes in the characteristics of welfare recipients or the characteristics of those entering and leaving welfare between 1991 and 2004, despite dramatic declines in the overall caseload. This suggests that welfare reform has not significantly changed the type of person receiving welfare, and analyses focusing on welfare participants will not be seriously biased by selection.

Second, we find that there has been dramatic growth in the importance of employment for those in the welfare system. Not only are those leaving welfare more likely to be working than in the past, but so are welfare recipients and those entering welfare. We also show that this growth in employment has led to a decline among welfare recipients in the fraction of their income coming from welfare payments. In each case, although we see signs of reversal since 2000, there is no indication that the changes occurring in the 1990s have been undone.

Third, when we examine the earnings of welfare leavers who are working, we find little evidence that welfare reform has pushed less-skilled workers into the labor market. The average earnings of those leaving welfare after reform are at least as high as earnings prior to reform even during the recession occurring after 2000. On the other hand, we do observe, in Maryland but not Missouri, a decline in average earnings for those holding jobs after leaving welfare, suggesting that some kind of trade-off between employment and earnings may have occurred.

Fourth, we find that the type of firm employing welfare leavers has not changed much after welfare reform. It does not appear that, after welfare reform, recipients are any more likely to work for employers paying low wages or in industries with unstable employment, nor for that matter are they any more likely to have jobs offering upward mobility. Finally, we find that, since the early 1990s, there has been a significant decline in the probability that a welfare leaver returns to welfare. Although the modest increase in the rate of recidivism since 2000 suggests that the high rate of economic growth of the late 1990s played a role in the declines observed in recidivism immediately following reform legislation, the economy does not appear to be the primary factor.

Our results imply that welfare reform has not led to dramatic changes in the dynamics of welfare entry and exit. Although individuals leaving welfare following reform earn low wages and tend to work in less stable jobs, this was true of welfare leavers in the early 1990s as well. Moreover, even though the evidence is somewhat mixed across our two states, our data do not imply that welfare leavers after welfare reform are substantially worse off materially than welfare leavers prior to welfare reform. There is no question that former recipients are more likely to be working after leaving welfare, and they are much less likely to return to welfare than previously.

Although the dynamics of welfare have not changed with welfare reform, clearly the choices of welfare recipients have been influenced by changes in welfare along with the growth of a number of other benefits, most importantly the federal EITC, but also child care subsidies and subsidized medical care. While we have no direct measure of the overall impact of welfare reform on the disadvantaged population most likely to be affected by these changes, our results are consistent with those of others. Schoeni and Blank (2000), for example, show a generally positive impact on the well-being of those at the bottom of the distribution. Bollinger et al. (Chapter Two, this volume) present more nuanced findings, suggesting gains for some groups and losses for others, but with losses in transfers more than compensating for earnings gains overall.

In short, our results suggest that, in the face of these changes, welfare reform achieved the goals of increasing employment and reducing dependence on cash subsidies, and it did so without inducing the kinds of dramatic economic dislocation that some had feared. Still, in the light of other changes occurring in the economy, it does not appear that welfare reform has substantially improved the material conditions for recipients or others at the bottom of the income distribution, as the most ardent supporters of reform had predicted.

Appendix Table A-5.1. *Means of variables used in estimation*

	Maryland			Missouri		
	1992:3–1993:2 (1)	1996:3–1997:2 (2)	2001:3–2002:2 (3)	1992:3–1993:2 (1)	1996:3–1997:2 (2)	2001:3–2002:2 (3)
Return to Welfare Within Two Years	0.36	0.22	0.33	0.36	0.30	0.34
Nonwhite	0.68	0.74	0.82	0.34	0.37	0.45
Unknown Race	0.05	0.19	0.03			
Years of Education				11.32	11.38	11.27
Age	29.48	29.56	29.92	29.11	29.63	29.42
Number of Children Less Than 18	1.72	1.59	1.82	1.89	1.90	1.98
Dummy for Missing Number of Children Under 18		0.23	0.10			
Age of Youngest Child				5.13	5.50	5.16
Time on Welfare in Last Two Years	0.65	0.65	0.52	0.55	0.62	0.52
Time Working in Last Two Years	0.31	0.34	0.43	0.38	0.44	0.34
County Unemployment Rate	0.07	0.06	0.06	0.06	0.05	0.06
Suburban County (not Washington, D.C.)	0.22	0.22	0.20	0.11	0.11	0.09

Urban County (St. Louis, Kansas City)	0.19	0.22		0.40	0.41	0.46
Suburban County (Washington, D.C.)	0.40	0.36	0.15			
Urban County (Baltimore City)			0.54			
Earnings In Quarter After Leaving						
No Job	0.58	0.45	0.47	0.47	0.36	0.41
$1–$499	0.04	0.07	0.07	0.07	0.07	0.08
$500–$999	0.03	0.05	0.05	0.05	0.06	0.06
$1,000–$1,999	0.08	0.12	0.09	0.16	0.16	0.11
$2,000–$2,999	0.10	0.13	0.11	0.16	0.18	0.12
$3,000–$3,999	0.09	0.09	0.09	0.06	0.10	0.11
$4,000 or More	0.07	0.08	0.12	0.03	0.07	0.12
N	22,211	30,844	14,231	30,092	38,719	25,729

References

Acs, Gregory, and Pamela Loprest. 2004. *Leaving Welfare: Employment and Well-Being of Families That Left Welfare in the Post-Entitlement Era.* Kalamazoo, MI: Upjohn.

Autor, David H. 2003. "Outsourcing at Will: The Contribution of Unjust Dismissal Doctrine to the Growth of Employment Outsourcing." *Journal of Labor Economics,* 21(1): 1–42.

Bavier, Richard. 2001. "Welfare Reform Data from SIPP." *Monthly Labor Review,* 124(7): 13–24.

Black, Dan A., Terra G. McKinnish, and Seth G. Sanders. 2003. "Does the Availability of High-Wage Jobs for Low-Skilled Men Affect Welfare Expenditures? Evidence from Shocks to the Steel and Coal Industries." *Journal of Public Economics,* 87: 1921–1942.

Bell, Stephen H. 2001. "Why Are Caseloads Falling?" Urban Institute Discussion Paper 01–02, March.

Blank, Rebecca M. 1989. "Analyzing the Length of Welfare Spells." *Journal of Public Economics,* 39(3): 245–273.

———. 2002. "Evaluating Welfare Reform in the United States." *Journal of Economic Literature,* 40(4): 1105–1166.

Blank, Rebecca M., and Patricia Ruggles. 1994 "Short-Term Recidivism Among Public-Assistance Recipients." *American Economic Review,* May (*Papers and Proceedings of the American Economic Association*), 84(2): 49–53.

Brown, Charles, James Hamilton, and James Medoff. 1990. *Employers Large and Small.* Cambridge, MA: Harvard University Press.

Cancian, Maria, Robert Haveman, Daniel R. Meyer, and Barbara Wolfe. 2002. "Before and After TANF: The Economic Well-Being of Women Leaving Welfare." *Social Service Review,* 76(4): 603–641.

Carrington William J., Peter R. Mueser, and Kenneth R. Troske. 2002. "The Impact of Welfare Reform on Leaver Characteristics, Employment and Recidivism." University of Missouri Working Paper 02–05, June.

Council of Economic Advisors. 1999. *Technical Report: The Effects of Welfare Policy and the Economic Expansion on Welfare Caseloads: An Update.* Washington, DC: The White House.

Danziger, Sheldon H., ed. 1999. *Economic Conditions and Welfare Reform.* Kalamazoo, MI: Upjohn.

Davis, Steve J., and John Haltiwanger. 1992. "Gross Job Creation, Gross Job Destruction, and Employment Reallocation." *Quarterly Journal of Economics,* 107(3): 819–863.

Department of Health, and Human Services. 2000. "U.S. Temporary Assistance for Needy Families (TANF) Program: Third Annual Report to Congress." Available at http://www.acf.dhhs.gov/programs/opre/annual3.pdf.

Dyke, Andrew, Carolyn Heinrich, Peter R. Mueser, Kenneth T. Troske, and Kyung-Seong Jeon. 2006. "The Effects of Welfare-to-Work Program Activities on Labor Market Outcomes." *Journal of Labor Economics,* 24(3): 567–608.

Edin, Kathryn, and Laura Lein. 1997. *Making Ends Meet: How Single Mothers Survive Welfare and Low-Wage Work.* New York: Russell Sage.

Gittleman, Maury. 2001. "Declining Caseloads: What Do the Dynamics of Welfare Participation Reveal?" *Industrial Relations,* 40(4): 537–570.

Grogger, Jeffrey, and Lynn A. Karoly. 2005. *Welfare Reform: Effects of a Decade of Change.* Cambridge, MA: Harvard University Press.

Heinrich, Carolyn J., Peter R. Mueser, and Kenneth R. Troske. 2005. "Welfare to Temporary Work: Implications for Labor Market Outcomes." *Review of Economics and Statistics,* 87(1): 154–173.

Herbst, Chris, and David Stevens. 2007. "Did Welfare Reform Change Work Participation Dynamics? Evidence from Maryland." Paper presented at the Tenth Annual ACF/OPRE Welfare Research and Evaluation Conference, June.

Hotz, V. Joseph, and John Karl Scholz. 2002. "Measuring Employment and Income for Low-Income Populations with Administrative and Survey Data," in *Studies of Welfare Populations: Data Collection and Research Issues.* Washington, DC: National Academy Press, 275–315.

Hoynes, Hilary Williamson. 2000. "Local Labor Markets and Welfare Spells: Do Demand Conditions Matter?" *The Review of Economics and Statistics,* 82(3): 351–398.

2001. "How Are Families Who Left Welfare Doing Over Time? A Comparison of Two Cohorts of Welfare Leavers." *Economic Policy Review,* 7(2): 21–22.

King, Christopher, and Peter Mueser. 2005. *Welfare and Work: Experiences in Six Cities.* Kalamazoo, MI: Upjohn.

Krueger, Alan, and Lawrence Summers. 1988. "Efficiency Wages and the Inter-Industry Wage Structure." *Econometrica,* 56(2): 259–293.

Lane, Julia, and David Stevens. 1995. "Family, Work and Welfare History: Work and Welfare Outcomes." *American Economic Review,* May (*Papers and Proceedings of the American Economic Association*), 85(2): 266–270.

2001. "Welfare-to-Work Outcomes: The Role for the Employer." *Southern Economic Journal,* 67(4): 1010–1021.

Loprest, Pamela. 2001. "How Are Families Who Left Welfare Doing Over Time? A Comparison of Two Cohorts of Welfare Leavers." *Economic Policy Review,* 7(2): 9–19.

Mayer, Susan E. 2000. "Why Welfare Caseloads Fluctuate: A Review of Research on AFDC, SSI, and the Food Stamp Program." *New Zealand Treasury Working Paper* 00/7.

McKernan, Singe-Mary, Jen Bernstein, and Lynne Fender. 2005. "Taming the Beast: Categorizing Welfare Policies – A Typology of Welfare Policies Affecting Recipient Job Entry." *Journal of Policy Analysis and Management,* 24(2): 443–460.

Meyer, Bruce D., and Dan T. Rosenbaum. 2001. "Welfare, the Earned Income Tax Credit, and the Labor Supply of Single Mothers." *Quarterly Journal of Economics,* 16(3): 1063–1114.

Moffitt, Robert. 1992. "Incentive Effect of the U.S. Welfare System: A Review." *Journal of Economic Literature,* 30(1): 1–61.

Moffitt, Robert A., and David W. Stevens. 2001. "Changing Caseloads: Macro Influences and Micro Composition." *Economic Policy Review,* 7(2): 37–51.

Mueser, Peter R., and Christopher T. King. 2001. "Urban Welfare-to-Work Transitions in the 1990s." Paper presented at the meeting of the Association for Public Policy Analysis and Management, November.

Mueser, Peter R., David W. Stevens, and Kenneth R. Troske. 2007. "The Impact of Welfare Reform on Leaver Characteristics, Employment and Recidivism: An Analysis of Maryland and Missouri." IZA Discussion Paper 3131, Bonn, Germany, October.

National Conference of State Legislatures. 2005. "Welfare Caseload Watch." Available at http://www.ncsl.org/statefed/welfare/caseloadwatch.htm.

Parrott, Sharon. 1998. *Welfare Recipients Who Find Jobs: What Do We Know about Their Employment and Earnings?* Washington, DC: Center on Budget and Policy Priorities.

Schoeni, Robert F., and Rebecca M. Blank. 2000. "What Has Welfare Reform Accomplished? Impacts on Welfare Participation, Employment, Income, and Family Poverty." *National Bureau of Economic Research Working Paper no. 7627.* Cambridge MA: NBER.

Troske, Kenneth R. 1999. "Evidence on the Employer Size–Wage Premium from Worker-Establishment Matched Data." *The Review of Economics and Statistics*, 81: 15–26.

Tweedie, Jack, Dana Reichert, and Matthew O'Connor. 1999. "Tracking Recipients After They Leave Welfare: Summaries of New State Tracking Studies." National Conference of State Legislatures. Available at http://www.ncsl.org/statefed/welfare.

U.S. General Accounting Office. 2000. "Report to Congressional Requesters: State Sanction Policies and Number of Families Affected." March. Available at http://www.gao.gov/new.items/he00044.pdf.

Zedlewski, Sheila R., and Donald Anderson. 2001. "Do Families on Welfare in the Post-TANF Era Differ from Their Pre-TANF Counterparts?" Urban Institute Discussion Paper 01–03, February.

Ziliak, James P., David N. Figlio, Elizabeth E. Davis, and Laura S. Connoly. 2000. "Accounting for the Decline in AFDC Caseloads." *Journal of Human Resources*, 35: 570–586.

SIX

A Reexamination of the Impact of Welfare Reform on Health Insurance Among Less-Skilled Women

John C. Ham, Xianghong Li, and Lara Shore-Sheppard

I. Introduction

The enactment of the Personal Responsibility and Work Opportunity Reconciliation Act (PRWORA) in 1996 represented not only an "end to welfare as we know it" but the completion of a process begun in the late 1980s: the separation of Medicaid from cash assistance. Under the Aid to Families with Dependent Children (AFDC) program, receipt of Medicaid was automatic for welfare recipients, and to a large extent, leaving AFDC meant losing not only cash assistance but also Medicaid coverage. Recognizing the work disincentive inherent in this arrangement, the authors of PRWORA instructed states to set income standards for Medicaid that were related to AFDC standards in effect at the time of PRWORA's passage rather than to eligibility for the states' new Temporary Assistance for Needy Families (TANF) programs. Consequently, former welfare recipients would be permitted to keep their public health insurance even if they were not eligible for cash assistance. Despite this precaution, it is possible that welfare reform led to a loss of Medicaid coverage through a variety of channels. Indeed, case studies of 13 states done by researchers at the Urban Institute (Holahan, Wiener, and Wallin 1998) showed that declines in welfare caseloads were accompanied by declines in Medicaid enrollment.

We gratefully acknowledge the support of the National Science Foundation. We would like to thank Anna Aizer, Sarah Hamersma, and James Ziliak for providing data on parental Medicaid expansions and estimated welfare system parameters. Sarah Hamersma, James Ziliak, Lucie Schmidt, Tara Watson, and conference participants provided useful comments on an earlier draft of this chapter. We are grateful to Eileen Kopchik for her expert research assistance. Any opinions, findings, and conclusions or recommendations in this material are those of the authors and do not necessarily reflect the views of the National Science Foundation, the Federal Reserve Bank of San Francisco or the Federal Reserve System. We are responsible for any errors.

Women leaving welfare may have been unaware that they could keep their Medicaid coverage; potential applicants for welfare may have been deterred by the stricter welfare policies, missing Medicaid eligibility in the process; and in some states, the processes of applying for welfare and applying for Medicaid were sufficiently de-linked that a welfare applicant would need to go to a different office and provide different documentation in order to qualify for Medicaid. Moreover, restrictions on receipt of public programs by newly arrived immigrants may have led even eligible immigrants to avoid Medicaid (the so-called chilling hypothesis [Fix and Passel 1999]).[1] The possible effects of welfare reform on health insurance coverage were not limited to the effect on public coverage. The intent of welfare reform was for family heads to leave the welfare rolls and begin to work. Thus, welfare reform had implications for private coverage: As mothers began to work, they increased their chances of obtaining health insurance through an employer. To the extent that former or potential welfare recipients are unable to find jobs offering health insurance benefits, however, the impact on private coverage may be small. Similarly, if welfare reform affected the probability of marriage, the probability of receiving coverage through a spouse's employer may have increased, although evidence to date suggests that any effect of welfare reform on marriage probabilities is likely to be small (see Blank 2002 for a review).

While it is clear that welfare reform had the potential to affect health insurance coverage, evaluating the impact of welfare reform on health insurance coverage is complicated by several factors. As has been noted in the Introduction to this book, welfare reform did not take place in isolation, but rather occurred at a time of significant policy activity and macroeconomic change. Increases in the Earned Income Tax Credit (EITC) were increasing the return to working; expansions in Medicaid eligibility and the introduction of the State Children's Health Insurance Program (SCHIP) had extended some access to public insurance to welfare nonrecipients, specifically to children and pregnant women; and the economy was growing rapidly. These changes also had implications for health insurance coverage. Increases in the EITC, like welfare reform, increase the likelihood of labor force participation among potential welfare recipients and thus potentially the likelihood of private coverage, again with the caveat that low-wage jobs are much less likely to offer employer-sponsored coverage. Growth in the economy might also be expected to increase labor force attachment. Finally,

---

[1] For evidence on the chilling effect with respect to health outcomes, see Chapter Nine of this volume.

after a period of minimal growth in the early 1990s, health care spending trends had resumed their upward movement, leading to increases in the price of private health insurance (Strunk, Ginsburg, and Gabel 2002).

In this chapter, we use data from the 1990–2001 Surveys of Income and Program Participation (SIPP) to examine the impact of welfare reform and other policies on health insurance coverage among less-skilled women— the group of women most likely to be affected by welfare reform—where we define "less-skilled" variously as having a high school education or less or as having less than a high school education. While this issue has not gone unstudied in the substantial literature on the effects of welfare reform, our chapter makes several important contributions.

First, we consider the question of identification of the welfare reform effect in greater detail than has been done in previous studies. The results from studies conducted thus far have been conflicting, and thus the question of identification is an important one. The approach taken in most previous nonexperimental studies is to identify the effect of welfare reform using state-level variation in the existence and timing of welfare reforms or to modify this approach by introducing the possibility of an untreated comparison group. Studies using this latter approach (including Bitler, Gelbach, and Hoynes 2005; Cawley, Schroeder, and Simon 2005; Kaestner and Kaushal 2003) have typically chosen single mothers (or, in the case of Bitler et al., single women more generally) as the group affected by welfare reform (the treatment group) and have used married mothers (or married women more generally, in the case of Bitler et al.) or single women without children as a comparison group. For married mothers or single nonmothers to serve as comparison groups for the treatment group of single mothers, it must be the case that welfare reform did not affect either married mothers or single nonmothers, and that if welfare reform had not occurred, the trends in coverage would have been the same in the treatment and comparison groups. For example, this strategy rules out the possibility of spillovers to "untreated" individuals via the labor market (thus, increases in labor supply due to welfare reform cannot affect the labor market outcomes of women not directly affected by welfare reform) as well as ruling out the possibility that less-skilled women who have no children or are married might change their marriage, fertility, or labor market behavior in response to welfare reform. In the case of married mothers, this strategy assumes that married mothers who get their health insurance through their husbands have the same trends in coverage as single mothers. However, as we document later, there were substantial differences in trends in coverage across these groups even prior to welfare reform, casting doubt on the use of this strategy. We test whether this treatment group–comparison group strategy is supported by the data, and find that neither married mothers nor single women without children can be used as a comparison group for the treatment group of single women with children. We therefore estimate our models separately for four groups: single mothers, married mothers, single childless women, and married childless women.

Since we reject the untreated comparison group approach, we attempt to circumvent the problem of potential other factors affecting health insurance that change at the time of welfare reform by controlling for a richer set of covariates than has been done in previous studies. In particular, while various studies have controlled for Medicaid or SCHIP expansions or expansions in the EITC along with parameters of the state welfare program, the state minimum wage, and the state unemployment rate, they have not controlled for all of these factors simultaneously. We include not only these variables, but also two additional measures of the state's labor market: the 25th percentile of weekly wages and the male labor force participation rate. Moreover, we include a measure of health care costs at the state level to attempt to account for the potential role of rising health care costs in health insurance coverage probabilities. Despite our rich set of controls, unobservable changes across states occurring at the time of welfare reform that are correlated with welfare reform remain a possibility, so our results concerning the effects of welfare reform must be considered in light of this caveat.

Third, we focus on the effects of welfare reform among Hispanic women, a group that is of particular importance for evaluating welfare reform due to its overrepresentation among less-educated women and the fact that PRWORA targeted immigrants specifically. We estimate our models for the four groups defined by marital status and presence of children for all low-educated Hispanic women and then separately for immigrant and native Hispanics. Our results indicate that much of the observed effect of welfare reform on health insurance for single mothers is attributable to the effect on Hispanic immigrant women. Fourth, we consider the impact of persistence (or dynamics) in insurance coverage in addition to estimating cross-sectional relationships, primarily by including indicators for the lagged insurance state in our model. The problem with static models is that they assume that policy changes must have their full impact immediately. The specification including lagged insurance state allows the effects of policy changes through the natural dynamics of the model to grow over time as families become more familiar with them. We found that allowing for this type of dynamics was important in a related study (Ham and Shore-Sheppard 2005) of the effect of Medicaid expansions on children's coverage and find that persistence is also important here. Finally, we investigate whether take-up and participation are more likely once programs have been in place for some time; again, we found that this was an issue for children in our related study.

II. Trends in Insurance Coverage and Transition Rates

Despite all of the changes in policies and macroeconomic conditions occurring in the mid- to late 1990s, trends in the rate of health insurance coverage (overall and public and private) for less-skilled women show no obvious breaks. Figures 6.1–6.3 show estimates of coverage (public and private) or uninsured rates by month in the SIPP for the period 1986–2003 for four groups of less-skilled women (defined here as women with a high school degree or less) who were between 21 and 44 years old at the start of the respective SIPP panel: married women with children, married women without children, single women with children, and single women without children. Each point in the figure is the mean rate for a month from a particular panel, calculated using the weight for that year in the panel. Because the SIPP is composed of overlapping panels, most months have data from more than one panel. The data are sparse in early 1990, 1995, and 2000, however, as those years were only covered by at most one panel (the 1990, 1993, and 1996 panels, respectively). Another caveat is that since the SIPP, like all panel datasets, suffers from attrition, means from later in each panel are likely to be more noisy, as they are estimated from fewer observations. In addition to plotting the estimated rates, we plot the trend smoothed using a locally weighted regression smoothing method (lowess).

The trends in the fraction uninsured are broadly consistent for all four groups, remaining constant or falling slightly before 1990 but rising fairly steadily through the end of the period. The similarity in patterns of uninsurance masks fairly substantial differences in insurance trends by type of insurance, however. Single mothers experienced a marked decline in public (Medicaid) coverage beginning in late 1993, with their levels of private coverage remaining fairly constant, while single women without children experienced sharply declining levels of private coverage and little change in public coverage.[2] Married women (both mothers and nonmothers) also experienced steady declines in the level of private coverage over the entire

---

[2] Women who report a disability or who report receiving Supplemental Security Income are excluded from the sample. Including these women increases the reported rate of Medicaid coverage for single women without children substantially.

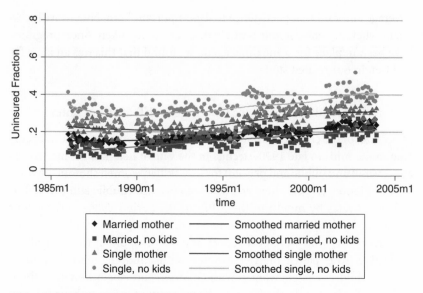

Figure 6.1. Fraction Uninsured (HS or less)

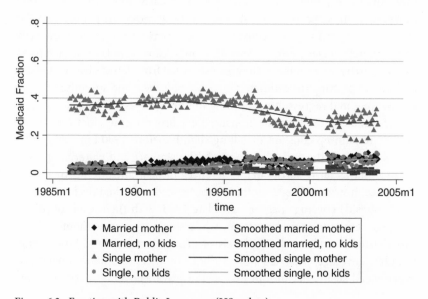

Figure 6.2. Fraction with Public Insurance (HS or less)

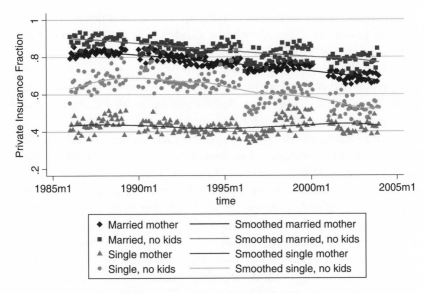

Figure 6.3. Fraction with Private Insurance (HS or less)

period observed in the data and little change in coverage by Medicaid. These national-level trends are broadly consistent with the hypothesis of a negative effect of welfare reform on Medicaid for single mothers and a limited positive effect on private insurance, although they are hardly definitive. In addition, the differences in the trends across groups even prior to welfare reform cast doubt on the use of either single childless women or married mothers as a comparison group. Given the differences in the trends before welfare reform, the assumption that the trends in coverage would have been the same across the groups in the absence of welfare reform seems unlikely to hold.[3]

Not surprisingly, the impact of welfare reform on health insurance has been examined by several groups of researchers; however, the results of these studies have been conflicting. As the general findings of the previous literature in this area are summarized in Chapter One of this volume, we focus here on the relationship between the existing literature and our contribution.

[3] In additional figures in the Supplemental Material for this chapter (available at http:// lanfiles.williams.edu/~lshore/), we examine trends in the empirical transition rates and find that the rates of both coverage loss and coverage gain increased after 1990 for all four groups, although the estimated rates are quite noisy. The fact that *both* insurance entry and exit rates increased suggests that the stability of insurance relationships declined over this period. This increase in insurance "churning" has also been observed for children (see Ham et al. 2008b), although for children the increased churning was not accompanied by significant overall coverage loss.

Our approach is closest in style to the approaches of Bitler et al. (2005), DeLeire, Levine, and Levy (2006), and Cawley et al. (2005). Two of these papers, Bitler et al. (2005) and Cawley et al. (2005), use a treatment-comparison methodology, using single mothers or single women as the treatment group and married mothers or married women as the comparison group. DeLeire et al. (2006) argue that the assumption that married women were unaffected by welfare reform is not plausible (although they do not test related assumptions, as we do). Consequently, they estimate models separately for various groups of women in the population, including single mothers, single childless women, and married mothers, as well as various racial subgroups. Relative to these papers, we make five main contributions. First, we test explicitly assumptions about whether women with different family structures can be used as comparison groups for the treatment group of interest: single women with children. Second, we estimate our models for more finely disaggregated groups, including native Hispanic and immigrant Hispanic single mothers.[4] Third, we include a richer set of covariates, particularly variables measuring the impact of the EITC and the extent of parental Medicaid expansions. Including these covariates increases the likelihood that the effect we are labeling "welfare reform" is indeed an effect of that policy. Fourth, we use the SIPP monthly data, which not only allows us to consider dynamic issues in insurance choice, but also has some advantages with respect to accuracy and timing of reported health insurance data. Finally, we estimate models where individuals react to policy changes with a lag.

III. Data

As noted previously, our primary data source is the SIPP, a series of longitudinal datasets collected for a random sample of the U.S. population by the Census Bureau. The SIPP has several advantages over other datasets that have been used to examine health insurance and welfare reform: Health insurance coverage is measured over a shorter recall period (four months instead of a year); there is rich information on family composition and demographics that directly corresponds to the reference period for

---

[4] Consequently, our chapter also contributes to the literature on the impact of welfare reform on immigrant health insurance. This literature includes Borjas (2003), Kaushal and Kaestner (2005), and Royer (2005), who find substantively different results, ranging from decreases in the proportion of immigrants uninsured due to increases in private insurance that more than compensated for the loss of public insurance (Borjas) to no statistically significant effect (Royer) to increases in the proportion of immigrant women uninsured (Kaushal and Kaestner).

the insurance information; and the source of coverage (public or private) is identified. Further, since SIPP is a panel dataset, it also allows us to examine persistence in insurance coverage. Like any dataset, the SIPP does have some flaws: The number of women in the dataset is smaller than in both of the other datasets commonly used (the March Current Population Survey [CPS] and the Behavioral Risk Factor Surveillance System), although each woman potentially contributes many months of data; there are a few months in the period we study that were not covered by any panel, and like all panel datasets, the SIPP suffers from attrition.[5]

The SIPP is collected in a series of panels, each one containing approximately 17,000 households, on average. For ease of interviewing, the entire sample is randomly split into four rotation groups, and one rotation group is interviewed each month. Each rotation group in a SIPP panel is interviewed once every four months about employment and program participation during the previous four months (termed a "wave"). We use the 1990, 1991, 1992, 1993, 1996, and 2001 panels, which cover the period from October 1989 to December 2003 (we use the 1986, 1987, and 1988 panels as well in our illustration of trends; the 1989 panel is not used because it was ended after only three waves). The length of each SIPP panel varies: 32 months for the 1990 and 1991 panels, 40 months for the 1992 panel, 36 months for the 1993 panel, 48 months for the 1996 panel, and 36 months for the 2001 panel. A new panel is introduced each year or every few years, which often yields more than one panel with data covering a particular point in time.

Our base analysis sample is composed of women with a high school degree or less, who are between 21 and 44 years of age the first month they are observed, and who live in states that are identified in the SIPP. (Throughout most of the panels, 41 states and the District of Columbia are identified, with that number increasing to 45 plus DC in the latest panel; the others are grouped for confidentiality.) Further, we only include women who do not report a disability or the receipt of Supplemental Security Income (SSI), since recipients of SSI are eligible for Medicaid and we want to avoid confounding the effects of changes in welfare policy with changes in SSI or the reported incidence of disability.[6] We chose high school or less education to

---

[5] We must assume that the attrition is random with respect to the estimated equations of interest—the incidence of public insurance, private insurance, and no insurance. This assumption can be relaxed in the fixed effects specification if the latent probability of attrition is person-specific and time-invariant.

[6] In fact, there is evidence that welfare reform may have affected SSI participation (see Schmidt and Sevak 2004).

capture women most likely to consider participating in welfare, although in many specifications we narrow our sample further to just women with less than a high school education. We further reduce the sample in this way because women with a high school education are a fairly heterogeneous group and include many women with very low probabilities of ever participating in welfare. Our age range is chosen to minimize the possibility that an individual would be affected by the Medicaid expansions for children (which in some states extended to individuals over age 18) and to capture women in their childbearing years (when they are most likely to participate in welfare). To address the possibility that our dynamic results may be biased by spurious transitions (for example, when a woman is erroneously coded as having public insurance in a given period although in fact she does not have public insurance in that period or in the preceding or following periods), we recode the data to eliminate any spells of one month's duration except for those occurring at the beginning or end of the sample period.

Another measurement issue in the SIPP is that of "seam bias." Census Bureau researchers have shown that there is a disproportionate number of transitions in the fourth month of a wave (see, e.g., Marquis and Moore 1990; Young 1989). The approach to this problem that has been used in the past is to use only the fourth month of data from each wave, discarding the other three months. However, this approach has several disadvantages (outlined in Ham, Li, and Shore-Sheppard 2008a). Instead, we use the data in monthly form and follow the suggestion of Ham et al. (2008a) to include a dummy variable for the fourth month in each equation, since they find that this procedure works reasonably well in that it mimics a much more complicated estimation scheme aimed at dealing with the seam bias.

Using the state of residence information available in the SIPP, we link information from other sources to our data, including welfare and welfare reform variables; the Medicaid eligibility limits applying to pregnant women, children, and parents (for states with these expansions); state-level Medicare expenditure data; the EITC maximum credit applying to each family; the monthly unemployment rate in the state; the 25th percentile of real weekly earnings in the state and the male labor force participation rate (both measured monthly); and the minimum wage in the state.[7]

---

[7] Means by marital status and the presence or absence of children for each of these variables are presented in Table A1 in the Supplemental Material available online. The Supplemental Material also includes a Data Appendix that provides information about the sources of these variables.

IV. Empirical Model

We begin our empirical work with a straightforward static linear probability model of the form that has become standard in the literature on welfare reform's effects on health insurance (see, e.g., Bitler et al. 2005, eq. 1):

$$I_{kist} = R_{st}\beta_k + L_{st}\alpha_k + X_{ist}\delta_k + \gamma_{ks} + v_{kt} + \varepsilon_{kist}, \quad k = p, m, n \tag{1}$$

In this equation, I_{kist} refers to a dummy variable equal to 1 if woman i living in state s had insurance type k in month t (k = private (p), Medicaid (m), or uninsured (n)). Thus, equation (1) is estimated separately for each type of insurance. R_{st} denotes dummy variables for the implementation of welfare reform, L_{st} is a vector of other characteristics of state policy and labor market, X_{ist} is a vector of characteristics of the woman and her family, γ_{ks} represents state fixed effects, v_{kt} represents year fixed effects, and ε_{kist} is an error term that has an unrestricted covariance across observations from state s (i.e., we cluster on state). The vector X_{ist} includes the woman's age, race, ethnicity, education, marital status, and the number of children in her family.

Again following the existing literature, we represent welfare reform with a dummy variable for the presence of a major statewide waiver and a dummy variable for the implementation of TANF. As our data are monthly, these dummy variables "turn on" in the month of implementation, rather than merely indicating the year of implementation. The waivers were implemented in various states over the period 1993–1996 and "turn off" once the state has implemented its TANF program (the earliest states implemented TANF in 1996, but most states' implementations occurred in 1997). The waivers and TANF are expected to be negatively associated with the probability of Medicaid participation but may be positively associated with the probability of having private coverage, so that the prediction for overall insurance coverage is ambiguous.

As discussed earlier, many changes were taking place over the time period we study in addition to welfare reform. These changes are captured in L_{st}. To measure the generosity of the welfare system in a state, we include the estimated guarantee for a family of three in a state and the estimated tax rate on earned income. These measures, which come from Ziliak (2007) following the methods of Fraker, Moffitt, and Wolf (1985) and McKinnish, Sanders, and Smith (1999), arguably portray more accurately the actual welfare circumstances facing the average recipient in a state than the statutory rates.[8] More generous welfare benefits would be expected to increase the probability of Medicaid participation (particularly pre-TANF) but would be expected to be negatively associated with private insurance since the likelihood of working is expected to be lower in high-benefit states. Along with welfare reform, the mid- to late 1990s saw a substantial increase in the EITC.[9] Expansions of the EITC have ambiguous effects on insurance coverage: They increase the return to work, which increases the probability of having private coverage, but reduce the incentive to be on welfare, which reduces the probability of public insurance. Of course, to the extent that the jobs obtained do not offer insurance as a benefit, there would be little effect on private insurance coverage except via an income effect: Conditional on working, family incomes will be higher, which should increase the demand for private insurance purchased in the nongroup market.

Prior to and following welfare reform, there were significant changes in eligibility for the Medicaid program and the introduction of SCHIP: Throughout the 1990s, pregnant women with incomes below 133 percent of the poverty level (or higher in some states) were eligible for Medicaid, while some states took advantage of the flexibility afforded by waivers and PRWORA to fund Medicaid coverage for parents with higher incomes than had previously been eligible. (See Aizer and Grogger 2003 for a review of the changes.) In addition, income limits for older teenagers were raised substantially, particularly after the introduction of SCHIP. To capture these changes in public insurance eligibility, we include three variables: the income eligibility limit for pregnant women in the state, the income eligibility limit under any parental expansion, and the income limit for 18-year-olds. Since increasing the limit for older children was an important part of SCHIP implementation in most states, we view this last variable as a way of measuring a state's commitment to SCHIP that is superior to the commonly used dummy variable for whether the state had an SCHIP plan since the latter variable exhibits very little variation across states or over time.

Along with changes in Medicaid eligibility, another significant feature of the health insurance landscape over the period we study is increasing health care costs. Since higher health care costs are likely to be reflected in higher prices for private health insurance, rising costs may spur losses in private coverage. As it is difficult to measure health care costs at the state

---

[8] We also tried using the statutory maximum benefit for a family of three and found similar results.

[9] See Chapter Three of this volume for a review of the changes to the EITC.

level explicitly, we use the average level of Medicare spending per enrollee in a state as our proxy for the cost of health care. Finally, L_{st} includes four characteristics of the labor market in the state: the minimum wage, the monthly unemployment rate, the 25th percentile of the weekly wage, and the male labor force participation rate (both measured monthly).

One potential drawback of the static model is that it implicitly assumes that a woman makes a new decision in each period about whether or not to obtain public or private insurance, and that this decision does not depend (in a structural sense) on the previous period's decision. However, insurance outcomes are closely related to job outcomes; families often gain access to private insurance when members find a job and can lose private insurance when they are laid off. Since there is substantial persistence in the labor market histories of disadvantaged women (see, e.g., Chay and Hyslop 1998; Eberwein, Ham, and LaLonde 1997; Ham et al. 2008a), we would expect this persistence to carry over into insurance determination. Also, the static model does not incorporate the notion of fixed costs: A woman on Medicaid has already paid the fixed costs of enrolling and is more likely to be on Medicaid next month.

A simple dynamic model is obtained by adding a lagged dependent variable to equation (1):

$$I_{kist} = \lambda_k I_{kist-1} + R_{st}\beta_k + L_{st}\alpha_k + X_{ist}\delta_k + \gamma_{ks} + \nu_{kt} + \varepsilon_{kist}, \quad k = p, m, n \tag{2}$$

where I_{kist-1} equals 1 if the individual had insurance type k last month and 0 otherwise, and the other variables are defined as previously.[10] As we note later, this model allows the short-run, medium-run, and long-run effects of variables affecting insurance status to differ. We expect the lagged dependent variable to be correlated with the error term and treat the lagged dependent variables as endogenous. To do this, we use lags of all time-varying variables in the equation as instruments. Note that unlike those using a standard time series dynamic model, we assume a short panel length T, and our asymptotic distributions for the parameters are obtained by letting the number of individuals $I \to \infty$ for fixed T. Thus, the standard concerns about stability do not apply here. Moreover, we feel that the short-run and intermediate-run policy effects are more relevant than a long-run policy effect calculated as

[10] In an earlier version of this chapter, we also estimated an equation including lags at $t - 2$ and $t - 3$; however, the coefficients on the further lags were statistically indistinguishable from zero. In addition, we estimated a specification including lagged values of an alternative insurance type (other than the current type). Again, the coefficient on the lag of the alternative type was zero. We have eliminated both models in the interest of saving space.

if $T \rightarrow \infty$ given how quickly policy has been changing over the past decade. The immediate impact of a change in one of the explanatory variables is given by its coefficient. However, permanent changes today in an independent variable will have additional effects in the future due to the presence of the lagged dependent variable.

In addition to dynamics at the individual level, we consider the possibility that it may take some time for individuals to respond to the welfare reforms. This may be because local implementation of policies may be delayed following state passage or because adjustments involving the labor market are rarely instantaneous. Women on welfare who are encouraged by the reform to find work may need time to find jobs, implying that they would continue on Medicaid after reform. On the other hand, to the extent that the policy's arrival was known ahead of time, women likely to be affected may have begun the adjustment process prior to the actual implementation of the law, reducing any delays. We examine this issue by replacing the simple reform implementation dummy variables in R_{st} with a set of dummy variables indicating the time since the reform was implemented.

In all of our models, we estimate each equation separately by group (married and single women with and without children), allowing each group to have its own set of coefficients. However, we begin by assessing the comparison group identification strategy used by several previous researchers. In terms of equation (1), this strategy involves pooling the comparison and treatment group data, including a dummy for treatment group, and then interacting this dummy with the welfare reform variables in R_{st}. The coefficient on this interaction is then interpreted as giving the marginal effect of welfare reform for the treatment group. We will discuss this approach before moving on to estimation of the models separately by group.

V. Assessing the Comparison Group Identification Strategy

As noted in the literature review, several papers (including Bitler et al. 2005; Cawley et al. 2005; Kaestner and Kaushal 2003) suggest both that the effect of welfare reform is felt solely by less-educated single mothers and that a comparison group (either less-educated married mothers or less-educated single childless women) can be used to eliminate the influence of omitted variables varying by state and year that are correlated with welfare reform and that affect health insurance coverage of less-educated women. In order for this approach to eliminate the influence of these omitted variables successfully, it must be the case that both the treatment group and the comparison group would have had the same state-level trends in insurance in the absence of the reform. This assumption is untestable. However, it is possible to test the assumptions that the state effects are the same for both groups and that the year effects are the same for both groups. If these assumptions are rejected, it casts doubt on the identifying assumption made in much of the literature that the state-by-year effects would be the same for both groups. In addition to providing indirect evidence about the identifying assumption, including interactions of state with treatment group status and year with treatment group status, provides direct evidence about whether the *specification* used in the previous research, which constrains the different groups to have the same time and state effects, is consistent with the data.

We show the results obtained by relaxing the constraints on time and state effects in Tables 6.1a and 6.1b. The top panel in each table gives the results for no insurance, the second panel gives the results for Medicaid, and the bottom panel gives estimates for private coverage. We use a different comparison group in each table. In Table 6.1a we show the results using all mothers, where the treatment group is single mothers and the comparison group is married mothers. The numbers presented are the coefficients on the welfare reform variables and their interactions, with the coefficients on the interactions between presence of welfare reform and the treatment group showing the treatment effects given the assumption being tested. (Other variables in the model include all of the demographic, policy, and labor market variables discussed previously.) For comparison, column 1 gives the fully pooled model, which is easily rejected. The model corresponding to the model used in the previous literature is in column 2 of each panel. According to this model, the implementation of TANF was associated with an increase in the likelihood that a single mother was uninsured, a reduction in the probability of having Medicaid, and an increase in private coverage, while the introduction of welfare waivers shows little effect.[11] However, this model is decisively rejected in the data in favor of models that allow single and married mothers to have different time effects, different state effects, or both. Including different time and state effects in the insurance status models typically reduces the magnitude of the welfare reform coefficients to such an extent that they are rarely statistically distinguishable from zero.

---

[11] The coefficients in the private and Medicaid regressions do not add up to 1 minus the coefficient in the uninsured regression because some women report having both types of insurance in a single month.

Table 6.1a. *Testing the restrictions implied by using married mothers as a control group for single mothers*

| | Uninsured | | | | |
| | (1) | (2) | (3) | (4) | (5) |
	Pooled	+Reform interactions	+Year interactions	+State interactions	Fully interacted
Major Waiver Implemented	0.005	0.004	0.008	−0.001	−0.0005
	(0.004)	(0.010)	(0.011)	(0.006)	(0.005)
TANF Implemented	−0.001	−0.015	0.002	−0.005	−0.005
	(0.008)	(0.009)+	(0.011)	(0.007)	(0.007)
Major Waiver * Single		0.003	−0.010	0.019	0.015
		(0.032)	(0.036)	(0.012)	(0.012)
TANF * Single		0.048	−0.010	0.015	0.014
		(0.017)**	(0.036)	(0.016)	(0.015)
Reject Single/Married Same?		yes	yes	yes	yes
Reject Year Interactions 0?			yes	yes	yes#
Reject State Interactions 0?				yes	yes

| | Medicaid | | | | |
| | (1) | (2) | (3) | (4) | (5) |
	Pooled	+Reform interactions	+Year interactions	+State interactions	Fully interacted
Major Waiver Implemented	−0.010	−0.012	−0.019	−0.003	0.0002
	(0.004)	(0.006)+	(0.007)**	(0.014)	(0.005)
TANF Implemented	−0.009	0.021	−0.016	−0.007	−0.007
	(0.004)	(0.008)**	(0.008)*	(0.006)	(0.007)
Major Waiver * Single		0.009	0.035	−0.017	−0.025
		(0.017)	(0.023)	(0.013)	(0.017)
TANF * Single		−0.097	0.027	−0.004	−0.003
		(0.013)**	(0.028)	(0.014)	(0.013)
Reject Single/Married Same?		yes	yes	yes	yes
Reject Year Interactions 0?			yes	yes	yes
Reject State Interactions 0?				yes	yes

Table 6.1a. *Continued*

	Private				
	(1)	(2)	(3)	(4)	(5)
	Pooled	+Reform interactions	+Year interactions	+State interactions	Fully interacted
Major Waiver					
Implemented	0.002	0.006	0.010	0.003	−0.002
	(0.006)	(0.006)	(0.007)	(0.006)	(0.006)
TANF Implemented	0.008	−0.007	0.012	0.010	0.010
	(0.009)	(0.010)	(0.009)	(0.009)	(0.009)
Major Waiver * Single		−0.016	−0.029	−0.008	0.004
		(0.019)	(0.023)	(0.014)	(0.015)
TANF * Single		0.048	−0.014	−0.009	−0.010
		(0.012)**	(0.020)	(0.020)	(0.021)
Reject Single/Married Same?		yes	yes	yes	yes
Reject Year Interactions 0?			yes	yes	yes
Reject State Interactions 0?				yes	yes

Notes: The entries in the table are the coefficients on the waiver and TANF variables and their interactions with treatment group status. The coefficients on the interactions give the implied treatment effect. In addition to the variables listed, other variables in the model include the demographic, policy, and labor market variables discussed in the text. Robust standard errors in parentheses, clustered at the state level. +significant at 10%; *significant at 5%; **significant at 1%. All F-test rejections at $p < 0.01$, with the exception of those marked # rejected at $p < 0.10$.

We repeat this exercise assuming that single childless women are the comparison group. (Single mothers are again the treatment group.) Here as well, the specifications restricting the two groups to have equal year and state effects are decisively rejected in favor of allowing these effects to differ.

Finally, since the presence of welfare reform itself might plausibly have led the year and state effects to differ across groups, we estimate similar models of health insurance for the four groups using only data prior to welfare reform (results not shown). We again find that the constraints of either equal year or state effects are decisively rejected in the data. Consequently, we conclude that at least in this context, models of health insurance should be estimated separately for the four groups of women in the data: married

Table 6.1b. *Testing the restrictions implied by using single women without children as a control group for single mothers*

		Uninsured			
	(1)	(2)	(3)	(4)	(5)
	Pooled	+Reform interactions	+Year interactions	+State interactions	Fully interacted
Major Waiver Implemented	0.012	0.036	0.031	0.001	0.010
	(0.009)	(0.020)+	(0.024)	(0.018)	(0.017)
TANF Implemented	−0.003	−0.002	0.002	−0.020	−0.010
	(0.012)	(0.015)	(0.018)	(0.017)	(0.017)
Major Waiver * Mother		−0.042	−0.032	0.019	0.004
		(0.029)	(0.037)	(0.022)	(0.020)
TANF * Mother		0.002	−0.009	0.031	0.019
		(0.018)	(0.035)	(0.023)	(0.023)
Reject Mothers/ Non-mothers Same?		no	yes	yes	yes
Reject Year Interactions 0?			yes	yes	no
Reject State Interactions 0?				yes	yes

		Medicaid			
	(1)	(2)	(3)	(4)	(5)
	Pooled	+Reform interactions	+Year interactions	+State interactions	Fully interacted
Major Waiver Implemented	−0.014	−0.038	−0.042	−0.004	−0.007
	(0.010)	(0.025)	(0.025)+	(0.008)	(0.008)
TANF Implemented	0.001	0.035	−0.011	0.015	0.003
	(0.009)	(0.018)+	(0.028)	(0.015)	(0.013)
Major Waiver * Mother		0.041	0.048	−0.020	−0.017
		(0.032)	(0.033)	(0.010)	(0.011)
TANF * Mother		−0.059	0.022	−0.025	−0.013
		(0.024)*	(0.044)	(0.022)	(0.020)

Table 6.1b. *Continued*

	Medicaid				
	(1)	(2)	(3)	(4)	(5)
	Pooled	+Reform interactions	+Year interactions	+State interactions	Fully interacted
Reject Mothers/ Non-mothers Same?		yes	yes	yes	yes
Reject Year Interactions 0?			yes	yes	yes
Reject State Interactions 0?				yes	yes

	Private				
	(1)	(2)	(3)	(4)	(5)
	Pooled	+Reform interactions	+Year interactions	+State interactions	Fully interacted
Major Waiver Implemented	−0.003	−0.001	0.007	−0.0007	−0.008
	(0.015)	(0.025)	(0.024)	(0.022)	(0.020)
TANF Implemented	0.0005	−0.032	0.006	0.003	0.004
	(0.016)	(0.023)	(0.024)	(0.024)	(0.022)
Major Waiver * Mother		0.003	−0.017	−0.003	0.011
		(0.023)	(0.025)	(0.018)	(0.017)
TANF * Mother		0.057	−0.010	−0.004	−0.003
		(0.019)**	(0.032)	(0.030)	(0.027)
Reject Mothers/ Non-mothers Same?		yes	yes	yes	yes
Reject Year Interactions 0?			yes	yes	yes
Reject State Interactions 0?				yes	yes

Notes: The entries in the table are the coefficients on the waiver and TANF variables and their interactions with treatment group status. The coefficients on the interactions give the implied treatment effect. In addition to the variables listed, other variables in the model include the demographic, policy, and labor market variables discussed in the text. Robust standard errors in parentheses, clustered at the state level. +significant at 10%; *significant at 5%; **significant at 1%. All F-test rejections at $p < 0.01$, with the exception of those marked # rejected at $p < 0.10$.

mothers, married nonmothers, single mothers, and single nonmothers.[12] Consequently, we take this approach throughout the remainder of the chapter.

VI. Results

Our results from estimation of equation (1) for the four groups of women are presented in Tables 6.2a–6.2d. We find that there is at best only weak evidence of an effect of welfare reform for women with a high school education or less. While none of the coefficients on waivers or TANF are statistically different from zero at conventional levels, we find a negative association between the implementation of welfare waivers and Medicaid participation for single mothers that has a p-value of 0.102. The point estimate implies that following the implementation of a major waiver, single mothers experienced a 2.4 percentage point reduction in Medicaid coverage, although again the standard error is sizable. Other policies show greater evidence of an impact, especially for married mothers. For these women, higher levels of the EITC are associated with a lower probability of Medicaid participation, a higher probability of private coverage, and a higher probability of coverage overall. A $1,000 higher EITC (roughly one standard deviation for married mothers) is associated with a 15 percentage point reduction in the probability that a married mother is uninsured. These estimates are consistent with the EITC encouraging greater attachment to the labor force, allowing women to gain private health insurance (on their own or from their spouses). Similarly, higher levels of parental Medicaid expansions are associated with a higher probability of Medicaid participation and a lower probability of being uninsured for married mothers.

Along with explicit policies, there is evidence that labor market conditions and health care costs play a role in coverage levels. In particular, better labor market conditions, as measured by lower unemployment rates or higher levels of the 25th percentile of weekly earnings, are associated with higher private insurance probabilities and lower Medicaid probabilities for several of the groups. For married mothers only, we find that higher

---

[12] Of course, it is possible that a less flexible specification—such as permitting each group to have its own state, year, and reform effects but restricting the coefficients on the other variables to be the same—would still yield consistent parameter estimates. We conducted extensive tests of these "partially pooled" models and found the implied constraints on the coefficients to be decisively rejected in virtually every case. Also, we could have considered married women without children as a comparison group for completeness, but omit it since this group is not used as a comparison group in the literature (for good reasons).

Table 6.2a. *Results for married mothers with high school or less education*

	(1)	(2)	(3)
	Uninsured	Medicaid	Private
Major AFDC Waiver Implemented	−0.0005	0.0002	−0.001
	(0.005)	(0.005)	(0.006)
TANF in Effect	−0.005	−0.007	0.010
	(0.007)	(0.007)	(0.009)
Estimated Welfare Benefit, Family of Three	−0.002	−0.106	0.088
	(0.120)	(0.049)*	(0.135)
Welfare Tax Rate on Earned Income	−0.0002	0.00003	0.0002
	(0.0002)	(0.0002)	(0.0003)
Maximum EITC	−0.015	−0.016	0.029
	(0.005)**	(0.002)**	(0.005)**
Minimum Wage	−0.003	0.003	−0.001
	(0.009)	(0.005)	(0.007)
Unemployment Rate	0.003	0.003	−0.005
	(0.002)	(0.003)	(0.003)+
25th Percentile of Earnings	−0.070	0.024	0.061
	(0.027)*	(0.021)	(0.032)+
Male Labor Force Participation Rate	−0.013	−0.009	0.028
	(0.018)	(0.015)	(0.018)
Medicare Spending per Enrollee	0.031	0.001	−0.036
	(0.012)*	(0.004)	(0.012)**
Medicaid Pregnancy Expansion Level	−0.005	0.003	0.004
	(0.009)	(0.008)	(0.012)
Parental Medicaid Expansion Level	−0.006	0.014	−0.006
	(0.003)*	(0.006)*	(0.005)
Medicaid/SCHIP Eligibility Limit for 18-Year-Olds	−0.007	0.001	0.007
	(0.004)+	(0.003)	(0.004)*
Number of Children in Family	0.023	0.032	−0.052
	(0.006)**	(0.004)**	(0.004)**
Age	−0.033	−0.034	0.062
	(0.004)**	(0.003)**	(0.005)**
Age Squared/100	0.040	0.044	−0.077
	(0.006)**	(0.004)**	(0.008)**

(*continued*)

Table 6.2a. *Continued*

	(1)	(2)	(3)
	Uninsured	Medicaid	Private
Black	−0.007	0.053	−0.035
	(0.014)	(0.011)**	(0.016)*
Hispanic Ethnicity	0.111	0.008	−0.118
	(0.014)**	(0.019)	(0.019)**
Highest Grade Completed	−0.038	−0.014	0.052
	(0.005)**	(0.003)**	(0.003)**
Fourth Month in Wave	−0.001	0.001	0.0004
	(0.0004)**	(0.0002)**	(0.0004)
Person-months	433,852	433,852	433,852
R-squared	0.11	0.08	0.18

Notes: Robust standard errors in parentheses, clustered at the state level. +significant at 10%; *significant at 5%; **significant at 1%.

Table 6.2b. *Results for married nonmothers with high school or less education*

	(1)	(2)	(3)
	Uninsured	Medicaid	Private
Major AFDC Waiver Implemented	0.002	−0.003	0.002
	(0.014)	(0.003)	(0.013)
TANF in Effect	−0.019	−0.004	0.023
	(0.018)	(0.006)	(0.016)
Estimated Welfare Benefit, Family of Three	−0.297	−0.007	0.307
	(0.157)+	(0.038)	(0.168)+
Welfare Tax Rate on Earned Income	0.0002	0.0002	−0.0003
	(0.0004)	(0.0001)	(0.0004)
Maximum EITC	0.075	0.012	−0.087
	(0.025)**	(0.017)	(0.032)**
Minimum Wage	0.005	0.010	−0.014
	(0.015)	(0.003)**	(0.016)

Table 6.2b. *Continued*

	(1)	(2)	(3)
	Uninsured	Medicaid	Private
Unemployment Rate	−0.005	−0.001	0.005
	(0.005)	(0.001)	(0.005)
25th Percentile of Earnings	−0.089	−0.009	0.098
	(0.066)	(0.012)	(0.065)
Male Labor Force Participation Rate	−0.027	−0.008	0.029
	(0.031)	(0.010)	(0.033)
Medicare Spending per Enrollee	0.019	−0.007	−0.013
	(0.018)	(0.005)	(0.019)
Medicaid Pregnancy Expansion Level	0.028	0.003	−0.024
	(0.021)	(0.007)	(0.021)
Parental Medicaid Expansion Level	−0.009	−0.004	0.014
	(0.008)	(0.003)	(0.008)+
Medicaid/SCHIP Eligibility Limit for 18-Year-Olds	−0.003	0.004	−0.001
	(0.007)	(0.002)*	(0.007)
Age	−0.003	−0.006	0.008
	(0.006)	(0.002)**	(0.006)
Age Squared/100	−0.002	0.007	−0.004
	(0.009)	(0.002)**	(0.009)
Black	0.034	0.019	−0.050
	(0.019)+	(0.005)**	(0.019)*
Hispanic Ethnicity	0.108	0.008	−0.115
	(0.035)**	(0.005)	(0.037)**
Highest Grade Completed	−0.053	−0.005	0.058
	(0.005)**	(0.001)**	(0.005)**
Fourth Month in Wave	−0.0004	0.00004	0.0004
	(0.001)	(0.0003)	(0.001)
Person-Months	106,330	106,330	106,330
R-squared	0.11	0.04	0.13

Notes: Robust standard errors in parentheses, clustered at the state level. +significant at 10%; *significant at 5%; **significant at 1%.

Table 6.2c. *Results for unmarried mothers with high school or less education*

| | (1) | (2) | (3) |
	Uninsured	Medicaid	Private
Major AFDC Waiver Implemented	0.014	−0.024	0.003
	(0.009)	(0.015)	(0.014)
TANF in Effect	0.009	−0.010	0.001
	(0.016)	(0.013)	(0.020)
Estimated Welfare Benefit, Family of Three	0.021	−0.258	0.264
	(0.179)	(0.211)	(0.145)+
Welfare Tax Rate on Earned Income	−0.0001	−0.0006	0.001
	(0.0005)	(0.0004)	(0.001)
Maximum EITC	−0.0003	−0.011	0.012
	(0.007)	(0.011)	(0.010)
Minimum Wage	−0.007	−0.004	0.012
	(0.011)	(0.008)	(0.010)
Unemployment Rate	−0.008	0.011	−0.004
	(0.005)	(0.004)*	(0.005)
25th Percentile of Earnings	−0.0002	−0.038	0.041
	(0.050)	(0.068)	(0.060)
Male Labor Force Participation Rate	−0.013	0.035	−0.010
	(0.034)	(0.045)	(0.034)
Medicare Spending per Enrollee	0.015	−0.028	0.011
	(0.017)	(0.021)	(0.023)
Medicaid Pregnancy Expansion Level	−0.052	0.004	0.044
	(0.020)*	(0.022)	(0.027)
Parental Medicaid Expansion Level	−0.021	0.001	0.021
	(0.009)*	(0.006)	(0.007)**
Medicaid/SCHIP Eligibility Limit for 18-Year-Olds	0.016	0.0001	−0.016
	(0.006)*	(0.011)	(0.008)+
Number of Children in Family	−0.025	0.095	−0.068
	(0.007)**	(0.008)**	(0.005)**
Age	0.011	−0.065	0.047
	(0.006)+	(0.005)**	(0.006)**
Age Squared/100	−0.018	0.072	−0.046
	(0.010)+	(0.008)**	(0.010)**

Table 6.2c. *Continued*

	(1)	(2)	(3)
	Uninsured	Medicaid	Private
Black	−0.061	0.159	−0.088
	(0.008)**	(0.013)**	(0.017)**
Hispanic Ethnicity	0.020	0.035	−0.055
	(0.023)	(0.043)	(0.032)+
Highest Grade Completed	−0.016	−0.039	0.054
	(0.002)**	(0.007)**	(0.006)**
Fourth Month in Wave	−0.003	0.005	−0.003
	(0.001)**	(0.001)**	(0.001)**
Person-Months	174,715	174,715	174,715
R-squared	0.06	0.20	0.15

Notes: Robust standard errors in parentheses, clustered at the state level. +significant at 10%; *significant at 5%; **significant at 1%.

Table 6.2d. *Results for unmarried nonmothers with high school or less education*

	(1)	(2)	(3)
	Uninsured	Medicaid	Private
Major AFDC Waiver Implemented	0.010	−0.007	−0.008
	(0.017)	(0.008)	(0.020)
TANF in Effect	−0.010	0.003	0.004
	(0.017)	(0.013)	(0.022)
Estimated Welfare Benefit, Family of Three	0.141	−0.040	−0.074
	(0.254)	(0.076)	(0.263)
Welfare Tax Rate on Earned Income	0.001	−0.00003	−0.001
	(0.0004)+	(0.0002)	(0.0004)*
Maximum EITC	0.022	0.005	−0.026
	(0.005)**	(0.005)	(0.004)**
Minimum Wage	−0.001	0.005	−0.004
	(0.012)	(0.005)	(0.011)
Unemployment Rate	−0.006	0.011	−0.003
	(0.008)	(0.003)**	(0.009)
25th Percentile of Earnings	−0.018	0.051	−0.026
	(0.051)	(0.031)	(0.052)

(*continued*)

Table 6.2d. *Continued*

	(1) Uninsured	(2) Medicaid	(3) Private
Male Labor Force Participation Rate	0.012	−0.003	−0.009
	(0.041)	(0.017)	(0.041)
Medicare Spending per Enrollee	0.024	−0.004	−0.017
	(0.019)	(0.010)	(0.019)
Medicaid Pregnancy Expansion Level	−0.050	−0.021	0.065
	(0.036)	(0.009)*	(0.033)+
Parental Medicaid Expansion Level	−0.002	0.028	−0.025
	(0.012)	(0.013)*	(0.007)**
Medicaid/SCHIP Eligibility Limit for 18-Year-Olds	0.011	−0.002	−0.007
	(0.008)	(0.004)	(0.008)
Age	0.003	−0.006	0.002
	(0.006)	(0.003)+	(0.006)
Age Squared/100	−0.014	0.007	0.007
	(0.010)	(0.005)	(0.010)
Black	0.080	0.054	−0.128
	(0.019)**	(0.009)**	(0.019)**
Hispanic Ethnicity	0.119	0.012	−0.134
	(0.023)**	(0.014)	(0.029)**
Highest Grade Completed	−0.046	−0.012	0.058
	(0.006)**	(0.004)**	(0.007)**
Fourth Month in Wave	−0.001	0.002	−0.001
	(0.001)	(0.0005)**	(0.001)
Person-months	134,695	134,695	134,695
R-squared	0.09	0.06	0.11

Notes: Robust standard errors in parentheses, clustered at the state level. +significant at 10%; *significant at 5%; **significant at 1%.

Medicare spending levels in the state are associated with lower probability of private coverage. Finally, the demographic variables are often highly significant. Across all four groups, age and education are positively associated with private insurance and negatively associated with public insurance, while having more children (when applicable), or being black or Hispanic, is negatively associated with private insurance and positively associated with public insurance.

Since there is a clear correlation between education and insurance outcomes, and since women with a high school education are fairly heterogeneous, we next examine whether the results change when we restrict our samples to women with less than a high school education.[13] The coefficients on the variables other than the main variables of interest change little, though fewer of them are statistically significant—not surprising given the fact that there are far fewer women with less than a high school degree. Thus, to save space, we report only the coefficients on the welfare reform variables (Table 6.3). The coefficients on these variables are larger (in absolute value) in several cases than they are when women with a high school degree are included. For the first time, we find some statistically significant evidence (albeit fairly imprecisely measured) that implementation of welfare reform is associated with changes in insurance coverage—in particular, reductions in Medicaid and increases in private coverage for single mothers. Our estimates suggest that the implementation of a major waiver is associated with a 5.9 percentage point reduction in Medicaid coverage, while the implementation of TANF is associated with a 5.2 percentage point increase in private coverage. The signs of the other two coefficients (major waiver in the private regression and TANF in the Medicaid regression) are similar, although the standard errors are substantial, so that the estimated effects are statistically indistinguishable from zero.

Interestingly, these results are broadly consistent with the findings of Bitler et al. (2005, table 6) and Cawley et al. (2005, table 2) despite our finding that their assumption of similar trends for married and single mothers in the absence of welfare reform is unlikely to hold in the data and despite some differences in specification and sample composition. Our results are not as consistent with the results of DeLeire et al. (2006). Notably, when our results in Table 6.3 are compared to the results in the first row of their table 5, the results for married mothers are similar but the results for unmarried women differ in several ways. While we find a statistically significant reduction in the probability of having Medicaid associated with the presence of a welfare waiver for single mothers, they find a positive and insignificant coefficient. Our results for TANF and for private insurance for single mothers are more similar, with substantially overlapping confidence

---

[13] The argument that high school–educated women should not necessarily be included in the definition of low-skilled women likely to be affected by welfare reform is made persuasively by DeLeire et al. (2006).

Table 6.3. *Results for women with less than high school education*

	Married mothers			Married nonmothers		
	Uninsured	Medicaid	Private	Uninsured	Medicaid	Private
Major AFDC Waiver						
Implemented	−0.004	−0.001	0.005	−0.046	−0.003	0.052
	(0.020)	(0.013)	(0.017)	(0.058)	(0.013)	(0.061)
TANF in Effect	−0.034	0.018	0.019	−0.102	0.021	0.091
	(0.018)+	(0.012)	(0.019)	(0.066)	(0.021)	(0.068)
Person-Months	98,170	98,170	98,170	17,412	17,412	17,412
R-squared	0.10	0.10	0.14	0.18	0.08	0.20

	Unmarried mothers			Unmarried nonmothers		
	Uninsured	Medicaid	Private	Uninsured	Medicaid	Private
Major AFDC Waiver						
Implemented	0.030	−0.059	0.028	−0.008	−0.021	0.033
	(0.019)	(0.033)+	(0.022)	(0.037)	(0.024)	(0.033)
TANF in Effect	−0.014	−0.036	0.052	0.001	0.003	0.011
	(0.032)	(0.030)	(0.023)*	(0.048)	(0.027)	(0.042)
Person-Months	51,099	51,099	51,099	23,801	23,801	23,801
R-squared	0.11	0.18	0.39	0.09	0.11	0.10

Notes: Robust standard errors in parentheses, clustered at the state level. +significant at 10%; *significant at 5%.

intervals. However, our results for unmarried nonmothers again differ, particularly for private insurance. DeLeire et al. find a positive and statistically significant coefficient on TANF, a result that essentially drives their overall conclusion of a positive effect of welfare reform on insurance coverage. We attempted to replicate this finding by changing our sample to match theirs more closely, without success. We were able to replicate their finding of a negative and statistically significant association between welfare waivers and Medicaid for single childless women by including women reporting disability in our sample, but even with that sample change and increasing the age range to match theirs (18–64), we were unable to find any evidence of a substantial positive association between TANF and private insurance for single childless women. One obvious possible explanation for the different results is our use of different datasets, in which the insurance variables are measured in different ways. Since SIPP is a monthly dataset, our insurance variable represents whether a woman reports having insurance in a given month. DeLeire et al. use the March supplement to the CPS, where the reference period for insurance coverage is much less clear. While a detailed comparison of the implications of the different datasets is beyond the scope of this chapter, we note that we did carry out such a comparison for children's health insurance in Ham and Shore-Sheppard (2005). There we concluded that it was possible to explain some, but not all, of the differences between results based on SIPP and results based on the CPS, and that CPS respondents seemed to be indicating whether they had insurance at the end of the previous calendar year.[14]

One striking difference between some of the results in the existing literature occurs for Hispanic women. While all of the authors who examine Hispanic women separately find large effects of welfare reform for Hispanic women, the nature of these effects differs. For example, Bitler et al. (2005) find evidence that waivers and TANF led to sizable losses in insurance coverage for Hispanic women, while DeLeire et al. (2006) find the opposite. In addition, the literature on the immigrant population has found similarly conflicting results. We estimate our model for all Hispanic women with less than a high school education, and then further divide this population into immigrant and native-born. These estimates are reported in Table 6.4. We find evidence that both the welfare waivers and TANF were associated with reductions in Medicaid coverage and increases in private coverage for all unmarried Hispanic mothers with less than a high school education, although the standard errors are large enough that the estimates are not always statistically significant at standard confidence levels. However, the statistically significant estimates suggest that the magnitude is sizable. Implementation of a major waiver is associated with a 15 percentage point reduction in Medicaid and consequently an 8.3 percentage point increase in the probability of being uninsured. Consistent with the literature on the impact of welfare reform for immigrant women, when we divide the sample of Hispanic women into immigrants and native-born, we find the effects to be largely concentrated among immigrant women. This evidence is consistent with a so-called chilling effect, with immigrants being dissuaded from

---

[14] Even if seam bias were to affect all individuals in the SIPP, the reported insurance period would still be more clearly defined and at the subannual level.

Table 6.4. *Results for Hispanic women with less than high school education, all and by immigrant status*

All Hispanic women

	Married mothers			Married nonmothers			Unmarried mothers			Unmarried nonmothers		
	(1)	(2)	(3)	(4)	(5)	(6)	(7)	(8)	(9)	(10)	(11)	(12)
	Uninsured	Medicaid	Private	Uninsured	Medicaid	Private	Uninsured	Medicaid	Private	Uninsured	Medicaid	Private
Major AFDC Waiver Implemented	-0.008	0.010	0.002	-0.048	-0.028	0.070	0.083	-0.150	0.064	-0.016	-0.058	0.073
	(0.025)	(0.020)	(0.026)	(0.079)	(0.037)	(0.075)	(0.027)**	(0.056)*	(0.052)	(0.050)	(0.030)+	(0.064)
TANF in Effect	0.012	0.027	-0.037	-0.079	0.027	0.063	0.019	-0.091	0.062	-0.013	-0.018	0.044
	(0.025)	(0.016)+	(0.028)	(0.066)	(0.043)	(0.050)	(0.046)	(0.059)	(0.047)	(0.065)	(0.040)	(0.064)
Person-Months	43,992	43,992	43,992	4,591	4,591	4,591	17,521	17,521	17,521	8211	8211	8211
R-squared	0.10	0.07	0.12	0.17	0.12	0.21	0.15	0.20	0.12	0.11	0.16	0.10

Immigrant Hispanic women

	Married mothers			Married nonmothers			Unmarried mothers			Unmarried nonmothers		
	(1)	(2)	(3)	(4)	(5)	(6)	(7)	(8)	(9)	(10)	(11)	(12)
	Uninsured	Medicaid	Private	Uninsured	Medicaid	Private	Uninsured	Medicaid	Private	Uninsured	Medicaid	Private
Major AFDC Waiver Implemented	-0.009	-0.0002	0.008	-0.036	-0.020	0.047	0.093	-0.149	0.067	-0.118	0.030	0.089
	(0.025)	(0.023)	(0.027)	(0.129)	(0.039)	(0.109)	(0.051)+	(0.065)*	(0.057)	(0.066)+	(0.034)	(0.075)

	Married Mothers			Married nonmothers			Unmarried mothers			Unmarried nonmothers		
	(1)	(2)	(3)	(4)	(5)	(6)	(7)	(8)	(9)	(10)	(11)	(12)
	Uninsured	Medicaid	Private	Uninsured	Medicaid	Private	Uninsured	Medicaid	Private	Uninsured	Medicaid	Private
TANF in Effect	0.029	0.020	−0.049	−0.019	0.018	−0.007	0.067	−0.153	0.093	−0.085	0.056	0.041
	(0.029)	(0.018)	(0.031)	(0.127)	(0.051)	(0.093)	(0.074)	(0.071)*	(0.054)+	(0.064)	(0.024)*	(0.066)
Person-Months	32,154	32,154	32,154	2820	2820	2820	9568	9568	9568	5115	5115	5115
R-squared	0.11	0.06	0.12	0.16	0.15	0.19	0.14	0.17	0.10	0.16	0.19	0.11

Native-born Hispanic women

	Married Mothers			Married nonmothers			Unmarried mothers			Unmarried nonmothers		
	(1)	(2)	(3)	(4)	(5)	(6)	(7)	(8)	(9)	(10)	(11)	(12)
	Uninsured	Medicaid	Private	Uninsured	Medicaid	Private	Uninsured	Medicaid	Private	Uninsured	Medicaid	Private
Major AFDC Waiver Implemented	−0.058	0.006	0.084	−0.170	−0.082	0.252	0.028	−0.073	0.039	0.216	−0.167	−0.052
	(0.041)	(0.039)	(0.054)	(0.191)	(0.044)+	(0.228)	(0.016)+	(0.077)	(0.078)	(0.128)	(0.053)**	(0.106)
TANF in Effect	−0.138	0.052	0.110	−0.103	−0.049	0.152	−0.060	0.014	0.032	0.004	−0.019	0.044
	(0.068)*	(0.050)	(0.084)	(0.078)	(0.023)*	(0.084)+	(0.051)	(0.072)	(0.067)	(0.151)	(0.081)	(0.094)
Person-Months	9724	9724	9724	1177	1177	1177	6699	6699	6699	2040	2040	2040
R-squared	0.17	0.17	0.21	0.43	0.28	0.48	0.20	0.31	0.24	0.25	0.33	0.29

Notes: Robust standard errors in parentheses, clustered at the state level. +significant at 10%; *significant at 5%; **significant at 1%.

participating in public programs even if they were eligible for the programs. However, it is striking that the effects on insurance coverage are similar for both the waivers and TANF, despite the fact that only TANF singled out immigrants for differential treatment. There are several possible explanations for the similarity between the waiver and TANF results. Immigrants may have been more responsive to welfare reform provisions in general (perhaps out of concern for being labeled a public charge), or conditions in low-skill immigrant labor markets may have been improving faster than conditions in labor markets dominated by low-skill natives over this time period, so that what we have identified is not solely an effect of welfare reform, but welfare reform combined with positive conditions in markets employing immigrant labor that are not captured by the three (state-specific, monthly) labor market variables we include in the model. Although we are unable to distinguish between the explanations using our data, our results highlight the importance of accounting for the presence of welfare waivers in examinations of TANF. Moreover, while the evidence for a reduction in Medicaid coverage and a (smaller) increase in private coverage among low-skill immigrant single mothers that is associated with welfare reform is fairly compelling, we are reluctant to attribute these changes solely to the exclusion of immigrants in PRWORA.

For comparison, we estimated our models for white (non-Hispanic) and black (non-Hispanic) women with less than a high school education (results available in the Supplemental Material online). We found little evidence of welfare reform effects for white women. For black women, we found evidence of Medicaid reductions and private coverage increases for several of the groups, although only the Medicaid results for married mothers and the private coverage results for married nonmothers and unmarried mothers are statistically distinguishable from zero. Thus, significant evidence of welfare reform impacts for the group theoretically most likely to have been affected—single mothers—is found primarily, if not exclusively, among less-educated Hispanic immigrant women.

A. Static Models with Individual Fixed Effects

Thus far, we have not included individual fixed effects in our model. While individual fixed effects have the advantage that they control for unobserved person-specific effects that may be correlated with the explanatory variables, such as a woman's taste for insurance or taste for work, including individual fixed effects makes the identification of the policy effect more challenging. In a fixed effects specification, identification of the effect of welfare reform comes from individuals who are observed both before and after welfare reform has occurred. Since we reject pooling married and single women and women with and without children, identification of fixed effect models comes from a relatively small number of women. As long as welfare reform is not correlated with unobserved individual-specific characteristics, controlling for state-specific characteristics, then omitting individual fixed effects will not lead to bias in our estimated coefficients. Nevertheless, as a robustness check, we estimate our model including individual fixed effects.

As noted previously, identification of an individual fixed effects model depends on women who are present both before and after welfare reform, the number of whom is quite small for detailed subgroups in the SIPP. As a result, we use the entire sample of women with less than a high school education rather than restricting our sample to Hispanic women. In order to restrict our attention to the effects of welfare reform, we removed from our sample women who changed their marital status or motherhood status or state of residence.[15] The results from the fixed effects models are reported in Table 6.5. It is immediately apparent that while most results are similar to the results from Table 6.3, this is not the case for the unmarried mothers. The statistically significant evidence of both a negative effect on Medicaid coverage and a positive effect on private coverage disappears. In fact, the only coefficient that is statistically different from zero is the estimated effect of welfare waivers on private coverage, but that estimate is unexpectedly negative. We see several possibilities to explain the differences in results between the ordinary least squares (OLS) and fixed effects models. Obviously, one possibility is that the fixed effect model is the true model; in that case, one would conclude that welfare reform had essentially no effect on health insurance for low-educated women. However, we are hesitant to draw that conclusion based on the evidence presented here. As identification in fixed effects models comes from women who are observed in both regimes, the identification here is based on relatively small samples of women; for example, only 376 single mothers experience a change in the presence of a waiver. Thus, it may be the case that the fixed effects estimation involves substantial small-sample bias. Another concern, given the small sample size, is that the women observed in both regimes are unrepresentative in some way, so that the models utilizing variation across women, as well as variation

---

[15] We checked whether our results differed if we did not make these exclusions and found they did not. In addition, estimating the cross-sectional model on this restricted sample yielded results that differed by 0.015 or less from the results in Table 6.3, and with similar levels of statistical significance.

Table 6.5. *Fixed effects results for women with less than high school education*

	Married mothers			Married nonmothers		
	Uninsured	Medicaid	Private	Uninsured	Medicaid	Private
Major AFDC Waiver Implemented	−0.006 (0.022)	−0.001 (0.011)	0.010 (0.013)	−0.076 (0.043)+	0.024 (0.007)**	0.051 (0.041)
TANF in Effect	−0.032 (0.019)	0.022 (0.012)+	0.018 (0.013)	−0.064 (0.036)+	0.016 (0.016)	0.055 (0.034)
Person-Months (Individuals)	82,949 (3,127)			11,309 (587)		
Individuals with Waiver Status Change	807			81		
Individuals with TANF Status Change	589			73		

	Unmarried mothers			Unmarried nonmothers		
	Uninsured	Medicaid	Private	Uninsured	Medicaid	Private
Major AFDC Waiver Implemented	0.017 (0.018)	0.010 (0.018)	−0.034 (0.015)*	0.026 (0.035)	−0.030 (0.025)	0.007 (0.036)
TANF in Effect	−0.010 (0.028)	−0.022 (0.027)	0.023 (0.022)	0.035 (0.050)	−0.025 (0.026)	−0.005 (0.044)
Person-Months (Individuals)	39,332 (1,803)			17,189 (1,050)		
Individuals with Waiver Status Change	373			167		
Individuals with TANF Status Change	306			136		

Notes: Robust standard errors in parentheses, clustered at the state level. + significant at 10%; *significant at 5%; **significant at 1%.

within a woman's history, better measure the true effect. Unfortunately, we are unable to answer this question with our data. Given the small sample size and oddly signed results in several of the fixed effects models, we find the OLS results more compelling, but we need to be cautious in drawing strong conclusions from them given the lack of agreement with the fixed effects results.

As discussed in Section IV, we also estimated a variety of models intended to capture dynamics, including both the model of equation (2) and a version of the static model that allows the effect of a policy change to depend on how long the change has been in place. In the interest of saving space, we do not discuss the results from these models here except to note that we find evidence of substantial persistence in insurance status but little statistically significant evidence of a welfare reform effect in these models. (Results from these models are available in the Supplemental Material online.)

VII. Conclusion

Since the goal of welfare reform was to move welfare (and hence Medicaid) recipients off welfare to employment, there has been substantial interest in whether reform affected the ability of women to obtain health insurance coverage. In this chapter, we examine two assumptions that have been made in most previous investigations of the effect of welfare reform's implementation on the insurance status of single mothers. Specifically, we ask whether either married mothers or single women without children can act as a valid comparison group for single mothers. We find that the answer to this question is a resounding no.

We then estimate our models on the four different groups of less-skilled women separately. Since there is no comparison group available, we include a rich specification of demographic, policy, and labor market variables along with state and year dummy variables. Nevertheless, we interpret our results cautiously, as the many changes occurring at the time of welfare reform complicate the identification of welfare reform substantially. Overall, our results provide some evidence that welfare reform was associated with a reduction in the probability of Medicaid coverage of nearly 6 percentage points and a somewhat, though not entirely, offsetting increase in private coverage among single mothers with less than a high school education. The evidence indicates that the effect was concentrated among minority women, particularly Hispanic immigrants, with a 15 percentage point reduction in Medicaid coverage and an 8 percentage point drop in overall coverage rates for these women.

Estimating a simple dynamic model indicates that insurance status is quite persistent, particularly in the case of private insurance coverage. These findings suggest that it would be worthwhile to consider a richer dynamic specification, such as a multi-spell, multi-state duration model of health insurance, as we considered for children's health insurance in Ham, Li, and Shore-Sheppard (2008b). However, we find no evidence that individuals respond to the implementation of different aspects of welfare reform with a lag.

Our evidence of a limited effect on Medicaid and private insurance for some groups is largely consistent with the findings of Bitler et al. (2005) and Cawley et al. (2005), although we show that the identifying assumptions used to obtain those findings do not hold in the SIPP data. Unlike DeLeire et al. (2006), who find little effect of welfare reform for single mothers but some effects elsewhere, we find the effect of welfare reform to be largely but not exclusively concentrated in the single-mother population and concentrated further among Hispanic immigrant single mothers. Consistent with DeLeire et al., however, we find stronger effects when we concentrate on the population with less than a high school education. Our results broadly align with the results from the literature on the effect of welfare reform on immigrants, although we do not find the greater than 100 percent "crowd-in" that Borjas (2003) finds when he compares all immigrants to all natives. Moreover, although the welfare waivers did not have an explicitly immigrant focus, we find that the effects of the waivers and TANF were similar for immigrant single mothers, suggesting that the greater responsiveness of immigrants to welfare reform can be attributed to other factors besides the immigrant provisions of PRWORA. Further research on immigrant health insurance is necessary to determine what those factors might be.

Overall, the evidence indicates that the effects of this work-oriented reform varied substantially across groups. For some groups, any loss in Medicaid coverage appears to have been largely offset by private coverage increases, while for others, particularly Hispanic immigrants, the reform resulted in a net loss of coverage. This heterogeneity in effects can make effective policy formation more difficult, as it indicates that any policy intended to ameliorate the effects of loss of access to Medicaid may be difficult to target accurately. One possible method that some states have used to provide coverage to low-income parents who do not have coverage through their employers is to extend coverage via SCHIP, while other states have attempted to provide incentives for low-wage or small employers to sponsor coverage. Perhaps the most closely watched attempt to ensure universal coverage under a largely employment-based system is Massachusetts's universal coverage mandate. In this system, very-low-income workers have access to subsidized insurance through the state, while somewhat higher-earning low-income workers are able to purchase affordable insurance through a state-sponsored market, even when the individual's employer does not sponsor a plan. It remains to be seen whether such an approach can help provide a smoother transition between welfare and work for all types of low-income women in the population.

References

Aizer, Anna, and Jeffrey Grogger. 2003. "Parental Medicaid Expansions and Health Insurance Coverage." National Bureau of Economic Research Working Paper 9907. Cambridge, MA: NBER.

Bitler, Marianne P., Jonah B. Gelbach, and Hilary W. Hoynes. 2005. "Welfare Reform and Health." *Journal of Human Resources,* 40(2): 309–334.

Blank, Rebecca M. 2002. "Evaluating Welfare Reform in the United States." *Journal of Economic Literature,* 40(4): 1105–1166.

Borjas, George. 2003. "Welfare Reform, Labor Supply, and Health Insurance in the Immigrant Population." *Journal of Health Economics,* 22(6): 933–958.

Cawley, John H., Mathis Schroeder, and Kosali I. Simon. 2005. "Welfare Reform and the Health Insurance Coverage of Women and Children." *Forum for Health Economics & Policy,* Forum: Frontiers in Health Policy Research, vol. 8, article 5. Available at http://www.bepress.com/fhep/8/5.

Chay, Kenneth Y., and Dean R. Hyslop. 1998. "Identification and Estimation of Dynamic Binary Response Panel Data Models: Empirical Evidence Using Alternative Approaches." Working Paper No. 5. Berkeley: Center for Labor Economics, University of California.

DeLeire, Thomas, Judith Levine, and Helen Levy. 2006. "Is Welfare Reform Responsible for Low-Skilled Women's Declining Health Insurance Coverage in the 1990s?" *Journal of Human Resources,* 41(3): 495–528.

Eberwein, Curtis, John Ham, and Robert LaLonde. 1997. "The Impact of Being Offered and Receiving Classroom Training on the Employment Histories of Disadvantaged Women: Evidence From Experimental Data." *The Review of Economic Studies,* 64(4): 655–682.

Fix, Michael, and Jeffrey S. Passel. 1999. "Trends in Noncitizens' and Citizens' Use of Public Benefits Following Welfare Reform: 1994–97." *Research report, March.* Washington, DC: Urban Institute. Available at http://www.urban.org/url.cfm?ID=408086.

Fraker, Thomas, Robert Moffitt, and Douglas Wolf. 1985. "Effective Tax Rates and Guarantees in the AFDC Program, 1967–1982." *Journal of Human Resources,* 20(2): 251–263.

Ham, John C., Xianghong Li, and Lara D. Shore-Sheppard. 2008a. "Correcting for Seam Bias When Estimating Discrete Variable Models, with an Application to Analyzing the Employment Dynamics of Disadvantaged Women in the SIPP." University of Maryland working paper.

    2008b. "The Dynamics of Children's Health Insurance, 1986–1999." Williams College working paper.

Ham, John C., and Lara D. Shore-Sheppard. 2005. "The Effect of Medicaid Expansions for Low-Income Children on Medicaid Participation and Private Insurance Coverage: Evidence from the SIPP." *Journal of Public Economics,* 89(1): 57–83.

Holahan, John, Joshua Wiener, and Susan Wallin. 1998. "Health Policy for the Low-Income Population: Major Findings from the Assessing the New Federalism Case

Studies."*Assessing the New Federalism Occasional Paper No. 18,* Urban Institute. Washington, DC: Urban Institute.

Kaestner, Robert, and Neeraj Kaushal. 2003. "Welfare Reform and Health Insurance Coverage of Low Income Families." *Journal of Health Economics,* 22(6): 959–981.

Kaushal, Neeraj, and Robert Kaestner. 2005. "Welfare Reform and Health Insurance of Immigrants." *Health Services Research,* 40(3): 697–722.

Marquis, Kent H., and Jeffrey C. Moore. 1990. "Measurement Errors in the Survey of Income and Program Participation (SIPP) Program Reports." *1990 Annual Research Conference Proceedings.* Washington, DC: U.S. Bureau of the Census.

McKinnish, Terra, Seth Sanders, and Jeffrey Smith. 1999. "Estimates of Effective Guarantees and Tax Rates in the AFDC Program for the Post-OBRA Period." *Journal of Human Resources,* 34(2): 312–345.

Royer, Heather. 2005. "The Response to a Loss in Medicaid Eligibility: Pregnant Immigrant Mothers in the Wake of Welfare Reform." University of Michigan working paper, Available at http://econ.ucsb.edu/~royer/prwora.pdf.

Schmidt, Lucie, and Purvi Sevak. 2004. "AFDC, SSI, and Welfare Reform Aggressiveness: Caseload Reductions versus Caseload Shifting." *Journal of Human Resources* 39(3): 792–812.

Strunk, Bradley C., Paul B. Ginsburg, and Jon R. Gabel. 2002."Tracking Health Care Costs: Growth Accelerates Again in 2001." *Health Affairs,* Web Exclusive, September 25. Available at http://content.healthaffairs.org/cgi/reprint/hlthaff.w2.299v1.

Young, Nathan. 1989. "Wave-Seam Effects in the SIPP." In *Proceedings of the Section on Survey Research Methods.* Alexandria, VA: American Statistical Association. Available at http://www.amstat.org/sections/SRMS/Proceedings/papers/1989_069. pdf.

Ziliak, James P. 2007. "Making Work Pay: Changes in Effective Tax Rates and Guarantees in U.S. Transfer Programs, 1983–2002." *Journal of Human Resources,* 42(3): 619–642.

SEVEN

How Welfare Policies Affect Child and Adolescent School Performance

Investigating Pathways of Influence with Experimental Data

Pamela Morris, Lisa A. Gennetian, Greg J. Duncan, and Aletha C. Huston

I. Introduction

Over the past 30 years, public programs for poor families have moved away from cash assistance to a focus on promoting parents' self-sufficiency through employment. Improving the well-being of children is an often expressed policy goal, but the bulk of the rhetoric and the evidence driving policy debates has centered on adult employment and reductions in the welfare rolls. Both experiments and welfare-leaver studies show that many families remain in poverty even when parents are employed full time. This has resulted in a shift in policy conversation from caseload reduction to concerns about reducing poverty and improving children's well-being in low-income families with working parents.

This chapter summarizes the results of research conducted as part of the Next Generation Project, a collaborative project involving researchers at MDRC and several universities, using evidence from a diverse set of experiments to understand some of the conditions under which policy-induced increases in employment among low-income single parents can help or hurt children.[1] Unique to this research is the synthesis of results

[1] For more information on the Next Generation Project, go to www.mdrc.org/NextGeneration.

This chapter was completed as part of the Next Generation Project, which examines the effects of welfare, antipoverty, and employment policies on children and families. This chapter was funded by the Next Generation Project funders: the David and Lucile Packard Foundation, the William T. Grant Foundation, the John D. and Catherine T. MacArthur Foundation, the Annie E. Casey Foundation, and grant no. R01HD045691 from the National Institute of Child Health and Human Development. The results reflect the views of the authors and not those of any of the funders. Contact author: Pamela Morris, Pamela.morris@mdrc.org, MDRC, 16 East 34th Street, New York, NY 10016. Phone: 212-340-8880, Fax: 212-684-0832.

from several random assignment experiments launched in the late 1980s and early 1990s to learn how policies designed to increase employment and reduce welfare receipt among low-income parents can affect the development of their children. This chapter goes beyond simply examining program impacts. We bring an interdisciplinary perspective to formulating and testing hypotheses about the ways in which changes in family functioning caused by the experimental programs facilitate or harm children's development. Specifically, we leverage the experimental nature of the data and the variety of policies tested to address the roles of income, employment, and child care in children's development. We limit this presentation to effects on achievement and school performance, because the evidence is clearest and because the measures are strongest. We note, however, that several of the studies also contain measures of social behavior and health.

We first review the overall patterns of program effects. Impacts on children's achievement and school performance vary by the age of the child at the time his or her parents entered the programs. For preschool children (from about two to five years old at study entry), programs with earnings supplements that boost both maternal employment and income improve children's achievement; programs that increase maternal employment without concomitant increases in income (e.g., through mandatory participation in employment-related services and time limit policies) generally have neither favorable nor unfavorable effects on children's achievement. Effects for children who were adolescents (ages 11 and older) when their parents entered the programs were very different, showing modest unfavorable impacts across a variety of program models. Inconsistent effects emerged for children in middle childhood (ages 6 to 10) at study entry.

Next, we describe the evidence from these studies that helps to uncover pathways by which programs have impacts on children and adolescents. For younger children, key hypothesized pathways include parent employment, family income, and child care. For adolescents, parents' employment, income, the allocation of household responsibilities, out-of-school activities, and parent supervision are possible pathways of influence. We strive to broaden the relevance of our findings by including a set of theoretically driven questions about policies that may improve the well-being of children living in poverty.

II. Background

Several theories provide hypotheses about how poverty and welfare policies might affect children and adolescents (see Duncan and Chase-Lansdale 2001; Huston, 2002; Zaslow et al. 2002). Nonexperimental research supports the hypothesis that policies designed to increase low-income parents' employment and income may affect children's development. In families headed by low-income single mothers, maternal employment is positively associated with children's cognitive and social development, but most of the association can be explained by selection; employed mothers have higher education, fewer children, and less prior welfare experience than do those who are not employed (Chase-Lansdale et al. 2003; Harvey 1999; Huston 2002; Vandell and Ramanan 1992; Zaslow and Emig, 1997). The effects of maternal employment on children's development depend on the quality, extent, and timing of employment, with less complex jobs, longer hours, and employment in the child's first year of life often associated with unfavorable child outcomes (Brooks-Gunn, Han, and Waldfogel 2002; Harvey 1999; Parcel and Menaghan 1994).

Research on the effects of income consistently shows that poverty has a negative association with children's cognitive development (McLoyd, Aikens, and Burton 2006). Nevertheless, debates continue about the causal role of income per se, as opposed to other correlates of poverty, and about whether increased income can reduce the detrimental effects of poverty (Blau 1999; Bradley and Corwyn 2002; Duncan and Brooks-Gunn 1997; Duncan et al. 1998; Mayer 1997; McLoyd 1998; McLoyd et al. 2006; Morris and Gennetian 2002).

The effects of both employment and income may differ across child age groups. Some studies point to the particular vulnerability of infants under one year old whose mothers are in the labor force full time (Brooks-Gunn et al. 2002; Waldfogel 2006). The limited evidence for low-income adolescents suggests no marked effect of maternal employment on delinquency and substance abuse (Gottfried and Gottfried 1994; Hillman and Sawilowsky 1991; Paulson, 1994; Vander Ven et al. 2001), positive associations with some aspects of socioemotional development (Chase-Lansdale et al. 2003; Muller 1995; Richards and Duckett 1994), and some negative consequences for school achievement (Bogenschneider and Steinberg 1994). In one low-income sample studied in the 1950s, boys with employed mothers received less supervision and engaged in more delinquency than did those whose mothers were not employed (Sampson and Laub 1994). A National Academy of Science panel concluded that limited opportunities for meaningful and enriching outside activities contribute to some of the negative effects for adolescents (Smolensky and Gootman 2001).

The effects of income may also vary across stages of childhood. Although the patterns are not entirely consistent across studies, it appears that poverty has larger effects in the early years than in adolescence. Some investigations show that associations between income and achievement or later educational attainment are strongest for preschool children (Duncan and Brooks-Gunn 1997; Duncan et al. 1998; Votruba-Drzal 2006), but others show that poverty in the elementary school years predicts achievement at least as well as earlier poverty (NICHD Early Child Care Research Network [ECCRN] 2006). One reason for the relatively large effects in the preschool years is that income and poverty have particularly strong effects on the quality of the home environment (Votruba-Drzal 2003, 2006). Increases in family income produced by the Income Maintenance experiments had some positive effects on the school performance of elementary school children but not on the performance of adolescents (Salkind and Haskins 1982). All agree, however, that children living in chronic poverty are more likely to have low achievement than are those in transitory poverty at any age (McLoyd et al. 2006; NICHD ECCRN 2006).

III. The Experiments Used for This Analysis

The analyses conducted under the Next Generation Project are based on seven random assignment studies that together evaluate the effects of 13 employment-based welfare and antipoverty programs in the United States and two Canadian provinces.[2] They provide information on over 30,000 low-income children, primarily from single-parent families. All of them began in the late 1980s and early to mid-1990s (prior to 1996) and were designed to estimate the effects on low-income families and children of programs designed to increase parental employment. Many of these evaluations were implemented under waivers of the rules governing Aid to Families with Dependent Children (AFDC), the welfare system that was replaced in 1996 by Temporary Assistance for Needy Families (TANF). Although all of the studies were underway by 1996, they tested many program features that have since been adopted by the states under TANF. Appendix Table 7.1 provides further detail on the individual studies.

The great contribution of these studies derives from their random assignment designs—assigning participants to a program group that received an experimental policy package or to a control group that continued under the existing policies. In all but one study, parents were applying for welfare or renewing eligibility when they were randomly assigned. The exception is

---

[2] The number of studies and the number of programs are not the same because several studies, such as the National Evaluation of Welfare-to-Work Strategies, were implemented in multiple sites and had multiple experimental research groups within each site.

the New Hope program, for which all low-income adults living in two Milwaukee neighborhoods could volunteer; both program and control group parents remained eligible for public benefits and were subject to welfare rules.

Although various packages of policies were tested, we highlight the following policy dimensions: (1) *earnings supplements,* which are designed to make work pay by providing cash supplements outside the welfare system or allowing parents to keep part of their welfare grant as their earnings increase; (2) *mandatory employment services and time limits,* which attempt to boost work through the use of services, sanctions, and time limits; the service component of these programs offers education, training, and job search assistance and makes participation in those activities mandatory; (3) *expanded child care assistance,* which is designed to enhance access to subsidies and child care information by offering such services as resource and referral, encouragement of formal care, higher income-eligibility limits, direct payment to providers, and reduced bureaucratic barriers (Gennetian et al. 2004).

Random assignment provides a strong foundation for assessing causal impacts of welfare and employment policy packages. At the same time, the treatments and locations in these experiments represent neither the full range of TANF programs currently implemented by states nor the variety of macroeconomic conditions—both good and bad—that states currently face or are likely to face in the next decade. All of the Next Generation Study programs were developed prior to passage of the Personal Responsibility and Work Opportunity Reconciliation Act (PRWORA) in 1996. Some investigations were designed in response to the 1988 Family Support Act; states chose to perform others in anticipation of the federal welfare law changes. A number of studies included earnings disregards, although in several cases the generosity of the supplements exceeded that of post-1996 state policies. Several had mandatory employment services, but only two had time limits. Several offered some enhanced child care services that are currently available in most states (e.g., vouchers to pay providers), but only one (New Hope) included several enhancements in combination.[3] Although they do not represent all of the policy changes brought about by the 1996 law, the diversity of the programs provides an opportunity to test how variations in

---

[3]   Florida's Family Transition Program did have two components intended to directly affect children: It required parents to ensure that their children were attending school regularly and to speak with their children's teachers at least once each grading period; in addition, parents of preschoolers had to provide proof of immunizations. However, neither of these components appeared to change parental behavior (see Bloom et al. 2000).

policies affect children's development. In short, the Next Generation studies are strong in internal validity but weaker in external validity for the current policy context, a point to which we return in the concluding section. Moreover, with the exception of New Hope, these studies do not tell us about the effects of policies on those who do not apply for or use the welfare system.

To estimate average effects across studies, we pooled data from all of the studies and analyzed differences between the program and control groups on follow-up measures using ordinary least squares (OLS) regression analyses.[4] We report the *impact* of the programs as the difference between the program and control group levels, controlling for a small set of baseline demographic characteristics of families (employment, earnings, and welfare receipt in the year prior to baseline, mother's education [high school degree or equivalent], mother's marital status, number of children in the family, age of the youngest child, mother's race/ethnicity, and whether the parents were less than 18 years old at the time of the child's birth). Our sample includes 31,266 child observations taken from 17,489 children (some children were assessed with multiple measures at multiple follow-up points) living in 12,845 primarily single-parent families in the seven studies. Children ranged in age from 2 to 15 at the point of random assignment, but in most studies the focal children were between 2 and 10 years old (hereafter called "younger children"). Follow-up assessments were collected as early as two years later and as late as four years later, with several studies doing a second follow-up between four and seven years after random assignment. Most younger children were of school age at follow-up. For them the measures of achievement varied, including parent reports, standardized tests, and teacher reports, with some studies having more than one type of measure.[5] Some parent-report data were also collected for nonfocal children. Findings described here for adolescents are derived primarily from these parent reports of achievement, school progress, and school behavior, although the findings are similar when analyses are conducted separately on student test assessments.

---

[4]   All seven studies were conducted by MDRC and gathered data using virtually identical methods. An alternative approach to synthesis is to apply meta-analytic techniques (Lipsey and Wilson 1996) to impacts estimated from the individual studies. The overall results from pooling are identical to those obtained by meta-analysis, and pooling provides considerably more flexibility for estimating the kinds of age-of-child interactions that are central to our research.

[5]   In most studies, children's behavior problems and parent-reported health were also measured, but we limit this chapter to an examination of achievement.

A. Differences in Effects by Child Age

We classify children by their age *at the point of their parents' random assignment* to program and control groups rather than by their age at the follow-up assessment. Age at random assignment conforms to the hypothesis that there may be developmental differences in how children experience the intervention, especially at its onset. The point in development when we observe children's achievement is less important (except to the extent that the effects of an intervention may change as the time interval between the intervention and the follow-up increases). In the Next Generation studies, intervention impacts on employment and earnings typically emerged shortly after random assignment. Thus, random assignment marks the time at which children begin to experience the policy-induced changes in economic behavior on the part of their parents.

The effects of policies differed across the childhood age span, with positive effects on the achievement of preschool-age children and negative effects of the same policies on children entering adolescence, according to analyses of the pooled data (Morris, Duncan, and Clark-Kauffman 2005).[6] More specifically, for young children, the analyses pointed to one particularly sensitive transition period—from the preschool years to middle childhood and elementary school (children ages four to five years old at baseline, who enter elementary school during the follow-up period). The program effect on those children represents 7 percent of a standard deviation increase in child achievement, as measured two to five years after parents entered the programs. This is equivalent in magnitude to slightly more than a single point on a typical standardized achievement test with a standard deviation of 15.

For younger preschool children, ages 2 to 3 years old, and for middle childhood children, who were 6 to 9 years old when their parents were randomly assigned, we see less consistent positive effects. At the same time, for children aged 10 to 11 years at random assignment, there are negative effects, a finding that echoes a synthesis of findings for a roughly similar age group by Gennetian et al. (2004). The latter age group is going through

[6] We focused on children's achievement in school in these analyses because that information was collected consistently across a large age range of children, including children between the ages of 2 and 15 at the point of random assignment, who were then assessed two to five years later. Additional analyses have indicated that these differences in effects across children's age groups cannot be attributed to variations in family characteristics that coincide with having children in differing age groups (i.e., parents of older children may have longer histories of welfare receipt or otherwise face greater risk factors than parents of younger children).

another major transition from elementary school to middle school, as well as the beginning of puberty, when their parents enter the programs. Notably, these age-related differences cannot be attributed to family characteristics that differ for children of different ages.

The findings for young children are consistent with theoretical predictions about the developmental malleability of preschool children (Shonkoff and Phillips 2000) and about the susceptibility of the early childhood period to family influences, compared with those of peers and neighborhoods (Bronfenbrenner and Morris 1998, 2006; McCall 1981). Developmental theory also suggests that children in transition periods are particularly sensitive to environmental influences or changes (Graber and Brooks-Gunn 1996). Both the 4- to 5-year-olds and 10- to 11-year-olds are in developmental transition periods, but the effects of the welfare and employment programs go in opposite directions, suggesting that the experimental policies may lead to changes in the daily environments and experiences of young children that support their transitions and to changes in experience for early adolescents that fail to support the transitions they face.

B. Processes Accounting for Effects

In the following sections, we address questions about the processes leading to effects on child and adolescent achievement. We separate our discussion by age group because of the different pattern of effects for younger children and adolescents.

For younger children, we consider three major pathways—parent employment, family income, and child care—and comment on evidence about the roles of parent education and parenting. For adolescents, the potential pathways include features of parent employment such as number of hours worked and work schedule, income, the allocation of household responsibilities, out-of-school activities, and parent supervision. For each age group, we first group studies according to their impacts on the potential mediators and on child achievement to determine whether different policies had consistently different impacts on child achievement. For example, we examine whether or not studies that increased income the most also tended to increase achievement the most. Second, we apply a nonexperimental method (instrumental variables [IV] estimation) that takes advantage of both the large sample size and the policy variations available across studies to estimate the independent effects of key mediators of child achievement. The conclusion describes these findings in the context of other related research and draws implications for current welfare and income-security policies.

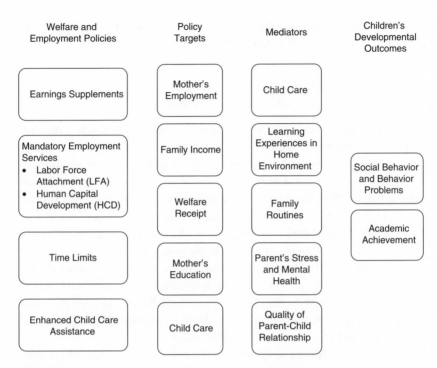

Figure 7.1. Conceptual Model for How Welfare and Employment Policies Might Affect Young Children's Developmental Outcomes
Notes: This is not intended to be a comprehensive model detailing all pathways between welfare and employment policies and outcomes for children. Direct, indirect, reciprocal, and moderating relations are not presented.

IV. Younger Children

Because parents rather than children are the direct targets of the programs, links between experimental policies and children's achievement are indirect, operating through changes in family resources, the home or child care environment, parent–child interactions, or parents' anxiety, stress, and mental health. A conceptual model of these mediating pathways based on nonexperimental literature is shown in Figure 7.1.

We first assess whether program effects on children can be linked to program-induced increases in parental employment and income. If the magnitude of program impacts on parents' employment is roughly proportional to the impacts on children, we might conclude that some of the benefits to children stem from increased employment. If developmental benefits are concentrated among programs with the largest impacts on family income, then the income pathway would be supported.

A. Income and Employment Effects: Comparing Variations across Studies

To assess income effects, we first compared achievement impacts on children whose parents participated in programs that had earnings supplements with effects on children whose parents participated in other program models (programs with mandatory employment services and a program with time limits, both without earnings supplements). In nonearnings supplement programs, parents' increased earnings were offset by declines in welfare payments, resulting in few gains in family income,[7] whereas programs with earnings supplements increased employment and income (Bloom and Michalopoulos 2001). Programs with earnings supplements increased family income by \$1,600 per year, on average; other programs increased income by a statistically insignificant \$240 per year. With the average level of annual income at \$11,854 in the control group, the former constitutes a substantial gain for families receiving earnings supplements.

Impacts on children's achievement do indeed vary across these program models, as shown in Figure 7.2. Positive impacts on children's school achievement are concentrated in those programs with generous earnings supplements. The nonearnings supplement programs had no statistically significant impacts on young children's achievement, either positive or negative. We find effects on young children (ages two to three and four to five) for earnings supplement programs of about 7 to 10 percent of a standard deviation improvement over the control group compared with a 3 to 4 percent standard deviation improvement over the control group in nonsupplement programs.

Concluding that benefits to children stem entirely from parents' income is premature, however, because earnings supplement programs not only increased income but also affected employment, child care, and receipt of public assistance. The comparative analysis across program models does not indicate the extent to which income alone was driving the benefits compared to a combination of income with employment and welfare receipt.

---

[7] These programs did not increase income because as parents transitioned from welfare to employment, they typically traded their welfare assistance for earnings. This corroborates the results found in nonexperimental analyses by Bollinger, Gonzalez, and Ziliak (Chapter Two, this volume) and Frogner, Moffitt, and Ribar (Chapter Four, this volume).

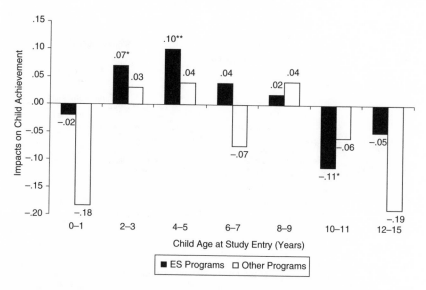

Figure 7.2. Individual Study Impacts on Children's Achievement by Age and by Program Type
Notes: Statistical significance levels are indicated as $*p < .05; **p < .01$.

B. Income and Employment Effects: Instrumental Variables Analysis

To isolate the contribution of increased income to young children's achievement, we adopted an instrumental variables analysis strategy that took advantage of both the large sample size and the policy variations across these studies. Key to the success of this approach is the fact that random assignment of parents to program and control groups serves as a source of variation in our predictor of interest (income) and that experimental treatment is unrelated to characteristics of families and children before they entered the programs (see Gennetian, Morris, et al. 2005 and Gennetian, Magnuson, and Morris 2008 for more detail on using this method with experimental data). We take advantage of the fact that different programs had different impacts on income, welfare, and employment to estimate the separate effects of income and employment on child achievement.[8]

The IV analyses show that program-induced income gains but not concurrent changes in parental employment and welfare receipt account

---

[8] These models pool data across studies and estimate the following achievement model:

$$Y_i = \alpha_1 \text{ Income}_i + \acute{X}_i \beta_Y + \acute{S}_i \gamma_Y + \xi_{2i} \tag{1}$$

(footnote cont...)

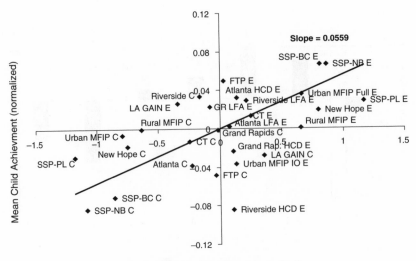

Figure 7.3. Individual Study Achievement Means by Income Means
Source: Morris, Duncan and Rodrigues (2006).
Notes: E = experimental group; C = Control group; FTP = Florida's Family Transition Program; LA-GAIN = Los Angeles Jobs-First Greater Avenues for Independence; SSP = Self Sufficiency Project; PL = Plus; BC = British Columbia; NB = New Brunswick; MFIP = Minnesota Family Investment Program; IO = Incentives Only; NEWWS = National Evaluation of Welfare-to-Work Strategies; LFA = Labor Force Attachment; HCD = Human Capital Development; GR = Grand Rapids; CT = Connecticut's Job's First.

for some of the observed improvements in school achievement (Morris, Duncan, and Rodrigues 2006). A visual presentation of what underlies the IV procedure is shown in Figure 7.3 (see Ludwig and Kling 2007). Each point represents deviations in mean income (in thousands of dollars) and achievement (in standard deviation units) for either the treatment or control groups in each of the programs. If income matters for child achievement, we would expect that the treatment group/site combinations with the biggest positive income deviations should also have the biggest positive

Y_i is achievement of the *i*th child, Income$_i$ is child *i*'s family income, $\mathbf{X}'_i$ is a vector of control variables. $\mathbf{S}'_i$ is a vector of 15 of the 16 site/program dummies. Income is predicted from

$$\text{Income}_i = \mathbf{X}'_i \, \beta_I + \mathbf{T}'_i \, \gamma_{11} + \mathbf{S}'_i \, \gamma_{12} + \xi_{3i} \tag{2}$$

where $\mathbf{T}'_i$ is a vector of 16 site/program-specific treatment dummies. The inclusion of site dummies in both equations (1) and (2) ensures that within-site differences between treatment and control groups drive the identification of the IV model. Additional endogenous variables, in particular employment and welfare receipt, can be added to this income-based model.

achievement deviations. When a trend line is fit through these points, the slope of the line (.06) is equal to the IV estimate of the effect of income on child achievement. Notably, IV analyses that include both employment and income show positive effects of income, but neutral effects of employment, on children's achievement.

To provide a sense of the magnitude of that income effect, our data show that a $1,000 increase in annual income sustained on average across two to five years of follow-up boosts child achievement by 6 percent of a standard deviation. Programs with earnings supplements increased family income for younger children by between $800 and nearly $2,200 per year, which corresponds to achievement effect sizes ranging from 5 to 12 percent of a standard deviation. By contrast, experimental studies of early preschool intervention programs offering very high levels of quality range from two-thirds to a whole standard deviation effect.

C. Child Care Effects

Child care, particularly center-based care arrangements, could also be a pathway through which programs affected achievement. Although all programs increased parents' employment and the use of paid child care (Gennetian, Crosby, et al. 2004), the type of child care affected depended on the program model and its provision of expanded child care assistance. Programs that included expanded child care assistance increased the use of center-based programs more than the use of home-based care arrangements (Crosby, Gennetian, and Huston 2005). By contrast, programs that did not offer such expanded assistance were more likely to increase home-based care than center-based care. In addition, by increasing income (as well as employment), programs with earnings supplements also increased by a few percentage points the use of center-based care arrangements compared to home-based care arrangements; the reverse is true for programs without such supplements.

Center-based care is defined as any licensed or regulated care that takes place in a group setting; it includes child care centers, Head Start, or other early education settings, as well as organized before- and after-school programs. Home-based care includes care by relatives or others in the child's own home or another person's home. We had no information about the quality of the care arrangements or the number of hours of care across the follow-up period. Regarding quality, we can infer from other work that center-based settings may be beneficial for low-income children because they are, on average, of higher quality than the home-based arrangements

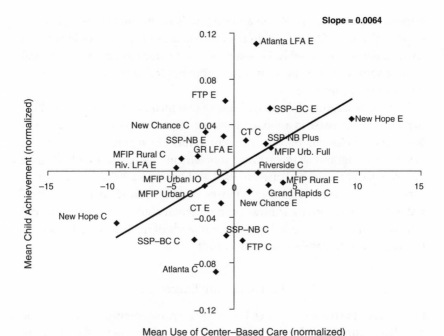

Figure 7.4. Individual Study Achievement Means by Use of Center-Based Care Means
Source: Gennetian, Crosby, Dowsett, Huston, and Alderson (2007).
Notes: E = experimental group; C = Control group; FTP = Florida's Family Transition Program; SSP = Self Sufficiency Project; BC = British Columbia; NB = New Brunswick; MFIP = Minnesota Family Investment Program; IO = Incentives Only; Urb = Urban; NEWWS = National Evaluation of Welfare-to-Work Strategies; LFA = Labor Force Attachment; Riv = Riverside; GR = Grand Rapids; CT = Connecticut's Job's First.

that low-income parents use (Coley, Chase-Lansdale, and Li Grining 2001; Dowsett et al. 2008; NICHD ECCRN 1997). There is also evidence of positive effects of center-based care on young children's school readiness (Loeb et al. 2004).[9]

Instrumental variables estimates leveraging differences in experimental impacts across studies show that the use of center-based care, as opposed to care in someone's home, during a child's preschool years has a positive

[9] That low-income families can generally access an organized care setting that is similar in quality to the care setting accessed by the families in these programs and that is of higher quality than home-based care settings is an underlying assumption in our analysis because we do not have information about the quality of care. Though developmental theories and research emphasize quality as the critical dimension determining whether child care will have positive or negative effects, the *type* of care also predicts academic skills independently of observed quality (see Fuller, Kagan, and Loeb 2002).

effect on school achievement in the early grades of elementary school, as shown in Figure 7.4. As in Figure 7.3, each point represents deviations in means on center-based child care use and child achievement (in standard deviation units) for either the treatment or control groups in each of the programs. The effect is small but significant; an increase in .10 of the probability of being exclusively in center-based care during the preschool years increases achievement by about 10 percent of a standard deviation. These analyses also show a positive effect of increased income, but once center-based care is included in the model, the positive income effect on children's achievement substantially decreases in magnitude, suggesting that some of the income effect may be a result of using center-based care (Gennetian et al. 2007). Because we cannot entirely separate program impacts on income and on center-based care, it seems reasonable to conclude that both, especially in combination, may contribute to improvements in children's achievement.

D. Parent Education, Parenting, and the Home Environment

Analyses similar to those described previously were conducted to test the effects of maternal participation in educational activities on children's achievement (see Gennetian, Magnuson, et al. 2008; Magnuson 2003). Here the analyses rely on variation in impacts across three sites in the National Evaluation of Welfare-to-Work Strategies program that tested two programs: a labor force attachment (LFA) approach focused on getting participants into jobs as quickly as possible and a human capital development (HCD) approach focused first on education and training and then on getting participants employed. Sample members in each site were randomly assigned to one of the two programs or to a control group that received AFDC.

Although one might expect that programs targeting parents' human capital would be beneficial for children, HCD program impacts on child achievement were not statistically significant across all three sites in which the program was evaluated in this study. Magnuson (2003) found that mothers in the HCD program stream acquired very little additional education—just over two months, on average—so the size of the human capital treatment was in fact very small. Magnuson's (2003) IV-based examination of variation in completed maternal schooling and child achievement showed bigger impacts, with every 10-month increase in maternal schooling being associated with an increase in child achievement of about a quarter of a standard deviation. This indicates that HCD programs for mothers have the potential to benefit children—but only if mothers spend time to acquire enough of it.

Changes in the home and parenting environments might also be pathways from the policies to outcomes for children. On the basis of earlier theory and literature (e.g., McLoyd et al. 2006; Votruba-Drzal 2003, 2006), we expected that increased income might improve the quality of learning experiences provided in the home, reduce parents' stress and depression, and improve the quality of parenting behavior. Surprisingly, across all of the Next Generation studies, there were few effects of any type of program on measures of parenting and the home environment, a point to which we return later.

Finally, one objective of welfare policy may be to affect marriage rates among single-parent families, and indeed, a few of the studies did slightly increase respondents' reports of marriage at the time of the two- to four-year follow-ups. The effects did not appear to be linked to the policy approach or program model (Gennetian and Knox 2003). And, in fact, analyses that test the relationship between experimentally induced increases in marriage and children's achievement show that marriage has no statistically detectable effect on children's outcomes. Even if these programs did produce effects on marriage, the fact that many of these marriages are likely to have resulted in the creation of stepfamilies raises questions about benefits to children, as existing nonexperimental evidence shows little difference in school performance for children in stepfamilies versus those in single-mother families (Gennetian 2005; Ginther and Pollack 2004; McLanahan and Sandefur 1994). In short, there is little evidence to suggest that any changes in marital status play a large role in affecting the outcomes of children.

E. The Duration of Impacts

In a few studies of earnings supplement programs, there were long-term effects on achievement. Young children in the Self Sufficiency Project showed sustained gains in achievement at both three and four and a half years after random assignment (Michalopoulos et al. 2002). Similarly, long-term follow-up of the Minnesota Family Investment Program showed positive effects on third- and fifth-grade reading among children who were preschoolers at study entry (Gennetian, Miller, and Smith 2005). Both five- and eight-year follow-ups of the New Hope program, when many children had reached adolescence, showed some sustained positive effects on parent reports of school progress and reading achievement (Huston et al. 2005, 2006).

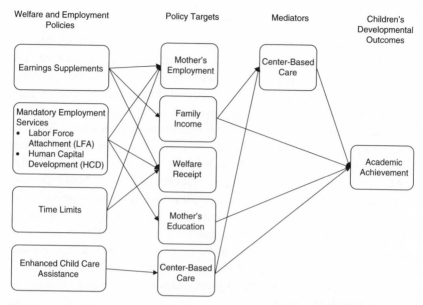

Figure 7.5. Model Illustrating Evidence on Direct and Mediating Relations Between Welfare and Employment Policies and Young Children's Academic Achievement

F. Young Children: A Summary

Taken together, we find that parents' income and center-based child care arrangements appear to be the key policy targets for explaining the beneficial effects of some welfare and employment policies on young children (Figure 7.5). Programs that increase income and the use of center-based child care are most likely to improve children's achievement measured a few years after program onset. There is little evidence from this sample that increases in employment or reductions in welfare, by themselves, produce detectable impacts on young children's achievement.[10] Programs targeting maternal human capital have the potential to improve the cognitive skills of children but only if mothers acquire enough of it. Among the mediators listed in Figure 7.5, center-based (but not home-based) child care stands out as the primary way in which a policy targeted to adults can improve the well-being of children. In effect, these programs allow parents to support their children's development by placing them in center-based care facilities.

---

[10] Notably, Kalil and Ziol-Guest (Chapter Nine, this volume) do find negative effects of welfare reform on the health of immigrant children.

V. Adolescents

Adolescents might be affected by welfare and employment policies through changes in families' financial resources, parental stress, the amount of time that parents spend away from the family, out-of-school activities, or exposure to new role models (Chase-Lansdale et al. 2003). Working parents may have less time and energy to spend on their children (e.g., to ensure that homework is completed and to communicate with teachers; Kurz 2002), to devote to parenting (Baumrind et al. 1991; Shumow, Vandell, and Posner 1998), or to monitor their children's behavior than they would if they did not work. Adolescents are too old for child care, but after-school programs and other structured out-of-school activities may provide supervision as well as opportunities for skill development. In addition to reducing opportunities for parents to monitor their children's activities and help them with schoolwork, spending less time at home may lead parents to expect adolescents to take on new adult tasks, such as caring for younger siblings, doing housework, shopping, cooking, or contributing to the family's income by working outside the home.

By contrast, increased family income may lead to increased investment in educational opportunities (e.g., specialized classes) or to residential change to a higher-quality neighborhood. Reduced parental monitoring or supervision of an adolescent because of increased employment may be balanced by increased time in high-quality supervised arrangements. If income gains are used to pay for tutoring, out-of-school activities, or relocation to a better neighborhood, which might improve school outcomes, they could help mitigate the co-occurring and potentially negative effects of reductions in the amount or changes in the quality of parent–adolescent interactions brought about by maternal employment. By the same reasoning, income losses (when welfare losses, for example, are not matched by earnings gains) could exacerbate some of the problems arising from maternal employment (such as lack of adult supervision or pressure on adolescents to work for pay) or even have direct adverse effects on school outcomes—for instance, if adolescents must go without school-related supplies or activities that promote academic achievement. Figure 7.6 presents a conceptual framework for adolescents.

A. Impacts across Studies

Overall, there were small but consistent detrimental effects on adolescent achievement regardless of the policy approach. The effects on children aged

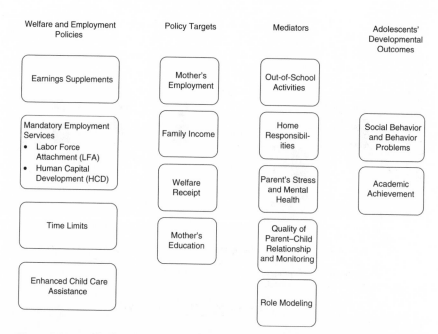

Figure 7.6. Conceptual Model for How Welfare and Employment Policies Might Affect Adolescents' Developmental Outcomes
Notes: This is not intended to be a comprehensive model detailing all pathways between welfare and employment policies and outcomes for children. Direct, indirect, reciprocal, and moderating relations are not presented.

11 and older are shown in Figure 7.2. In addition to these achievement effects, Gennetian, Crosby, et al. (2004) found significant effects on grade repetition and use of special educational services.

While for younger children the effects of welfare policies appeared to be related to the program model (and their differential effects on employment and income), this was not the case for adolescents: In all three program models, negative effects on adolescent school progress were observed. The programs with mandatory employment services alone—that generally increased parents' employment but not their income—increased receipt of special educational services. Programs with an earnings supplement—that generally increased parents' employment and income—increased school dropout rates. Finally, programs with a time limit decreased school performance. These adverse effects were significant within program type but were never significantly different from each other across program type. Even the pronounced adverse effect on school performance from programs with a time limit was not significantly different from the effect on

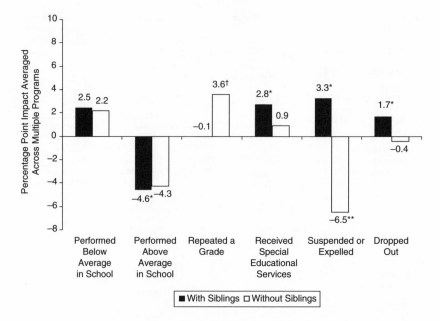

Figure 7.7. Impacts on School Outcomes for Adolescents with and without Siblings.
Notes: Statistical significance levels are indicated as *p < 0.05; **p < 0.01.

school performance from programs with mandates or earnings supplements. Because all three policies raised parents' average employment, it is likely that program effects on adolescent schooling were somehow linked to changes in parents' employment levels. Notably, we find these same effects from these experimental studies, which began prior to 1996, and from estimates from longitudinal data collected after 1996, suggesting that the findings are not sensitive to differing time periods (see Gennetian, Lopoo, and London 2008).

B. Potential Mediators

We considered several other possible mediators in analyses that aligned program impacts on outcomes such as income with program impacts on adolescent schooling. More specifically, we investigated the role of increased income, participation in out-of-school activities, changes in family structure or parenting, and frequency of residential moves. These analyses yielded little evidence that the factors tested mediated the program effects on adolescent outcomes overall, but there is support for the possible mediating role of out-of-school activities in New Hope, the one study in which such activities were measured extensively (Gennetian, Crosby, et al. 2004; Gennetian, Duncan, et al. 2004; Huston et al. 2005, 2006).

We found some evidence that increased responsibility for sibling care may have contributed to lowered adolescent school success, controlling for family size. Program effects on adolescents who had a younger sibling were compared to effects on adolescents who were the youngest child in the household. As shown in Figure 7.7, the detrimental effects of the programs were indeed larger and more consistent across schooling outcomes in the group of adolescents who had a younger sibling. For them, programs reduced the percentage who performed above average in school and increased the percentage who received special educational services, were suspended or expelled, and dropped out of school. Among adolescents with no younger siblings, in contrast, the programs had no significant effect on receipt of special educational services or dropping out and actually decreased the rate of suspension by nearly 7 percentage points.

These findings, in combination with ethnographic evidence, provide support for the hypothesis that increases in sibling care and potentially other home responsibilities are key mediating mechanisms.[11] In follow-up analyses using data on care arrangements, mothers' work schedules, and adolescent schooling from three experimental evaluations of U.S. state welfare reform programs, we investigated whether or not sibling caretaking is one way in which these programs affected adolescent achievement unfavorably (Hsueh and Gennetian 2006). In two of three state welfare experimental evaluations, increases in sibling caretaking and increases in nonstandard work schedules co-occurred with unfavorable effects on adolescent school performance. The third study, in Connecticut, also showed unfavorable program effects on adolescent achievement but no effect on sibling care arrangements. Although these analyses do not unequivocally rule out the hypothesis about sibling caretaking, they do suggest that sibling caretaking is probably one of multiple pathways affecting adolescent school performance in the context of these programs.

---

[11] One concern is that adolescents with co-resident younger siblings were also more likely to be in larger families than adolescents without younger siblings. Although it is plausible that larger families have fewer resources to invest in educationally enriching experiences, including after-school activities, analyses using data from a similar set of studies do not support the hypothesis that larger family size is confounding the effects we observe among adolescents with younger siblings (Gennetian 2004).

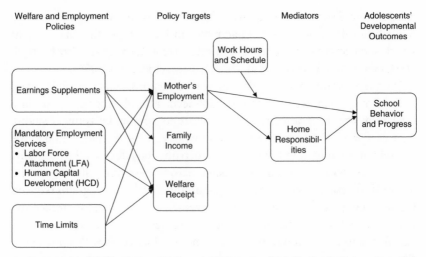

Figure 7.8. Model Illustrating Evidence on Direct and Mediating Relations Between Welfare and Employment Policies and Adolescents' Behavior and School Progress

C. Features of Work: IV Analyses

The analyses aligning experimental impacts across studies launched a series of investigations using IV techniques on the pooled experimental data in the same way we did in the analyses of young children. We exploit treatment-induced variation in parental employment to disentangle the effects of parents' work entry and hours on adolescents' school performance. In these analyses, we find that employment entry consistently shows an overall negative effect on adolescents' school performance (Hsueh, Gennetian, and Principe 2006), suggesting that the parental transition to work may be particularly disruptive for young adolescents who are also going through important developmental transitions.

D. Timing of the Intervention

The negative impacts on children who were young adolescents when their parents entered a study stand in contrast to the finding that positive impacts of New Hope last well into adolescence for children who were elementary-school age when their parents began the program (Huston et al. 2006). The difference suggests that the developmental period at which the program begins is important. It appears that there is something critical about changes in parents' economic behavior during early adolescence that contributes to negative effects on adolescents.

Whether small unfavorable effects on adolescents' school performance translate into sustained negative effects on future success in the labor market or educational attainment remains an open question. Findings from the Canadian Self-Sufficiency Project suggest that experimentally induced increases in minor delinquent behavior, such as drinking and smoking, as well as slight reductions in school performance at ages 14 to 17 are not linked to any subsequent effects on fertility, labor market behavior, or educational attainment (Michalopolous et al. 2002).

A summary of pathways for effects on adolescent achievement is presented in Figure 7.8. We caution that the number of studies and the number of measures of achievement are more limited for adolescents than for younger children. Moreover, many potentially important contexts were not measured. Within the limitations of the available data, our best evidence continues to point to increased maternal employment and the resulting increases in adolescents' home responsibilities such as sibling care as processes leading to interference with school participation and performance. Of course, changes in mothers' employment may generate a variety of other effects that we cannot address with these data.

VI. Open Questions and Caveats

Although these analyses provide a great deal of information, many questions remain. First, the experiments in our analyses include too few infants younger than a year old to analyze, but other research raises questions about possible negative effects of full-time employment on such young children (Waldfogel 2006). This is a highly relevant topic, as current law permits states to require mothers to participate in work-related activities such as employment, job training, and the like when their children are as young as three months old. A National Academy of Science panel specifically recommended that welfare policies should not require full-time maternal employment when children are less than a year old (Smolensky and Gootman 2001).

Second, these studies provide little information about changes in the expenditure patterns of families as a result of these programs. That is, the policies tested had the most positive effects on preschool-age children (from about two to five years old), and it appears that these positive effects are due in part to increased income. Yet, how did higher levels of family income affect younger children, especially given the fact that some of this income was probably used to pay for work-related expenses, including child care? These experimental studies have little information about consumption or expenditure patterns. The one pathway that is supported is center-based child care. Although we lack information on the quality of care children received or the number of hours they spent in care, other evidence shows positive associations of center-based care with achievement even with quality and hours controlled (NICHD ECCRN and Duncan, 2003).[12] Policies for working parents' child care assistance are typically separated from policies designed to use early educational settings to promote school readiness, even though the same children are affected by both. In fact, one analysis of these data shows that the experimental policies led to slight reductions in the use of Head Start (Chang et al. 2007). Research on integration of these services would inform both types of policy (Huston 2004).

Third, these studies raise questions about the mediating role of parenting: Contrary to our expectations, parents' psychological well-being and parenting practices (e.g., warmth, patterns of discipline) did not appear as a pathway for program effects on young children's achievement. One reason probably lies in the superficial measures of parenting (compared to observations of parenting), but the programs may not have had large impacts on these psychosocial aspects of parenting. If one defines parenting more broadly as "family management" (Duncan and Chase-Lansdale 2001), then parents' choices about child care, living environments, schools, and other environments for their children would be included. Increased resources might affect these choices. In fact, nonexperimental investigations suggest that investments in children's environments are better predictors of cognitive and academic skills than are parenting warmth and control (Yeung, Linver, and Brooks-Gunn 2002).

Fourth, although the overall impacts were neutral for children in the elementary school years at random assignment, several programs with wage supplements (e.g., New Hope, Minnesota Family Investment Program) did lead to improvements for this age group. In future research, we need more information about how middle childhood children spend their time when their parents go to work and about how policies promote (or fail to promote) school performance for these children.

Fifth, in this chapter we discuss only school achievement and performance as outcomes for children, but many of the studies contained measures of social behavior, emotional well-being, market work, and health. Some Next Generation papers describe these domains of development, but we have done less systematic analysis of them in part because the measures are less

---

[12] This study also shows that quality predicts children's cognitive performance, but there is no relation of intellectual and cognitive skills to the average number of hours the child has experienced in care.

satisfactory. Obviously, the impacts of policies on these areas of young people's development are important and deserve more research attention.

Finally, the policy experiments in the Next Generation studies took place during the 1990s, when unemployment was low and many jobs were available. Several major policy changes affecting working poor families were underway, including a considerable expansion of the Earned Income Tax Credit (EITC) and federal child care subsidies, as well as a decoupling of Medicaid from welfare. We do not know how specific programs may have interacted with local or national macroeconomic conditions or with other policies, nor do we know how different the results might have been in other economic and policy contexts.

VII. Conclusion

Employment and income support programs can affect children's school performance, but the amount and direction of influence depend on the child's age and on the work supports provided by the policy. Policies that increase employment and income positively affected the achievement of children who were preschoolers when their mothers increased their work effort. These effects were most apparent when policies provided work supports in the form of earnings supplements and expanded child care assistance. The resulting income and center-based care appear to be key pathways affecting children. Maternal education may play some role, but these programs did not substantially increase formal education—nor were they intended to do so. We did not find evidence for improved parent–child interactions, quality of the home environment, or maternal mental health. A partial reason may be poor measurement, but these programs may have had more effects on the family management aspects of parenting than on its psychosocial features.

By contrast, young adolescents fare poorly irrespective of the programs' key policy dimensions. Increased work and initial entry into work among these parents who are older and are likely to have been on welfare longer than parents with young children led to reductions in adolescents' school progress. That the unfavorable effects on adolescent schooling occurred for programs that required work, as well as for those that were voluntary, raises questions about the mediating mechanisms. It may be that employment per se does not harm adolescents if additional hours of employment do not translate one for one into reduced hours spent with adolescents. Chase-Lansdale et al. (2003) found only a small reduction in time spent with adolescents among mothers transitioning from welfare to work. The net of positive and negative effects of maternal employment may depend on how welfare and work programs are implemented, the circumstances of individual families, the types and schedules of the jobs, and the community context and institutional support. Nuanced features of employment—the type of work schedule, hours of employment, or quality of employment—may influence adolescent schooling.

Developmental differences may partly account for the age differences in impacts. Both children entering school and children going through puberty along with moving to middle school face important transitions that may leave them especially open to positive or disruptive changes in the family context. For younger children, work supports (specifically earnings supplements and child care/supervised activities) could also be developmental supports helping to increase school readiness and ease the transition to school. In contrast, it appears that there were few services to provide out-of-school care or supervised activities for children reaching early adolescence. By age 10 or older, most children are no longer going to organized child care settings; any child care tends to be home-based care of unknown quality. At the same time, children in this age range are rather immature to be on their own and especially to have responsibility for siblings. The National Academy of Science report on maternal employment identified an increase in the availability, hours, and quality of after-school programs for this age group as an important need. The New Hope program led to more participation in structured activities, which may have contributed to better achievement for this age group.

For older children and adolescents, extra income may be important because children in that age range are intensely aware of social comparisons with others, including the children in their schools; having resources for activities, equipment, and decent clothes may greatly affect their self-esteem and their willingness to participate in school. Perhaps the small increases in income attained by most families were not sufficient to make a real difference, or perhaps other factors simply outweighed any positive income effect. Sibling care may be part of the story, but we are missing a great deal of other information about how young adolescents spend their out-of-school time—including youth development activities, paid employment, and delinquent activity.

These findings can be compared with recent work examining the effects of employment transitions on a sample of low-income adolescents in three cities (Chase-Lansdale et al. 2003). In that study, parents' transitions to employment had few effects, positive or negative, on changes in the reading and math skills of very young children or adolescents, but adolescents whose parents had entered or remained in employment showed somewhat better mental health than those whose parents were unemployed. The Three-Cities Study differed from the Next Generation studies in design and measurement, making comparisons difficult, and employment transitions produced by an experimental policy may have different effects than those that occur nonexperimentally.

How well do the Next Generation studies represent the policy environment 10 years after the passage of PRWORA? The Next Generation studies include policies that are comparable to the most generous policies currently in effect. The maximum value of the federal EITC more than doubled during the 1990s and has continued to increase at a slower rate since then, providing a substantial earnings supplement for all low-income workers. In addition, some states offer an EITC, and most states have implemented an "enhanced earnings disregard" as part of their welfare strategy. The value of the enhanced earnings disregards varies considerably. A welfare recipient in Connecticut, for instance, can now continue receiving all of her welfare benefits as long as she earns less than the federal poverty threshold. Relative to how she would have fared under the AFDC system, this disregard provides her with about $500 more per month in income. And California allows welfare recipients who work to keep the first $225 of their monthly earnings without having their welfare benefits reduced; beyond that point, each additional dollar of earnings reduces their benefits by only half a dollar (rather than reducing benefits by about a dollar for every dollar of earnings, as under AFDC). Our studies examining the effects of generous supplement programs are probably quite applicable to these contexts. At the same time, some enhanced disregards are relatively small, sometimes as low as 20 percent (in Alabama, for example). In states with very low benefit levels (e.g., West Virginia, where the welfare benefit is only $253 and the earnings disregard is 40 percent), even a substantial earnings disregard translates into very little income. In these cases, our studies that increase employment but not income are likely to be the most relevant benchmark.

What about time limits and mandates? Only two of the studies examined included time limits, while 40 states now have time limits that result in loss of benefits (Bloom, Farrell, and Fink 2002). Moreover, nearly all states (except for a few that are more similar to the programs we evaluated) now sanction families who are noncompliant with program rules by closing the case or taking away the entire welfare benefit, whereas the studies examined here typically sanctioned parents by removing only the adult portion of the grant. In short, the differences between the studies we have examined and those in effect today are primarily in their focus on benefit reduction policies. These policies may lead to consequences for children of income loss and benefit termination that are not well documented in this body of work. Notably, a further examination of Florida's time limit policy did not suggest any harm to the children of families reaching welfare time limits and having their benefits reduced (Morris and Hendra under review), providing initial evidence that such negative effects may not be widespread.

As fewer parents receive welfare, policies affecting working poor families outside the welfare system assume greater importance for the future of children in low-income families. In these experiments, impacts on child achievement were consistently more positive in programs that provided work supports than in those that did not. The packages of work supports were diverse, ranging from generous earnings supplements provided alone to more comprehensive packages of earnings supplements, child care assistance, health insurance, and temporary community service jobs. Although work supports added costs, two of the programs with earnings supplements had costs within the range of some of the welfare reform packages implemented by states in response to the 1996 legislation. Relative to the AFDC program, the average yearly cost for a participant in a program with mandatory employment services ranged from savings of $255 to a cost of $1,595. The annual costs per participant of the earnings supplement programs ranged from $2,000 to $4,000 above the costs of the AFDC program. Yet, when you account for the benefit savings and increased tax revenue, the most targeted of these programs can almost pay for themselves.

These findings pose a choice for policymakers deciding which welfare reforms and poverty-reduction programs to support. They can increase parental employment and save government money with mandatory employment service programs but have little effect on the already low levels of school performance for children in low-income families. Or they can increase parental employment, raise family income, and increase government spending with earnings supplement and child care subsidy programs, with the likely result that young children will do better in school. Welfare and other policies for low-income families can affect and improve the well-being of children if states or the federal government choose to spend money on work supports within or outside the welfare system.

Our investigation of the mediating pathways was intended to identify targets of intervention. In that spirit, for younger children, center-based care seems to be a worthwhile policy target, either by encouraging parents to use such care through increased income or by encouraging that use through alternative policy levers. Early interventions (e.g., high-quality preschool

Appendix Table 7.1. *Descriptions of the studies*

Study	Sites	Generous earnings supplements	Mandatory employment services	Time limits	Expanded child care assistance	When study began and length of follow-up	Primary source(s)
		Key policy features tested					
Connecticut Jobs First Evaluation	New Haven and Manchester, CT	√	√	√		1996 36 months	Bloom et al. (2002)
Family Transition Program (FTP)	Escambia County, FL		√	√	√	1994 48 months	Bloom et al. (2000)
Minnesota Family Investment Program (MFIP)	Seven counties in Minnesota	√	√		√	1994 36 months	Gennetian and Miller (2000)
National Evaluation of Welfare-to-Work Strategies (NEWWS)	Atlanta, GA; Grand Rapids, MI; Riverside, CA; Portland, OR		√			1991 24 months 60 months	Hamilton et al. (2001); McGroder et al. (2000)
New Hope Project	Milwaukee, WI	√			√	1994 24 months 60 months	Bos et al. (1999)
Los Angeles Jobs—First Greater Avenues for Independence (GAIN)	Los Angeles County, CA		√			1996 24 months	Freedman et al. (2000)
Self-Sufficiency Project (SSP)	New Brunswick, British Columbia	√				1992 36 months 54 months	Morris and Michalopoulos (2000)

Notes: All sites used a random assignment design that consisted of one or more program groups and a control group. The control group in each case was the traditional welfare system in place at the time of the study (typically AFDC).

programs) for young children at risk of school failure form another policy stream with well-documented benefits for academic achievement (e.g.,
Karoly, Kilburn, and Cannon 2005). And, in fact, the effect sizes emerging
from studies of high-quality preschool programs are larger than those we
report here from earnings supplement policies. Perhaps coordinating welfare and employment policies with early intervention efforts would produce
the greatest benefits for children. For adolescents, supporting the needs
of the family system may be critical: If sibling care is part of the challenge,
then providing care for all children in the family may be important; after-
school programs for adolescents will not be sufficient.

We end by stressing the important value of leveraging experimental
studies not only to understand how policies that target parents can nurture or undermine the development of children, but also to reveal the ways
in which such policies affect children and thereby contribute to scientific
knowledge and the design of future social policies.

References

Baumrind, Diana, Jeanne Brooks-Gunn, Richard M. Lerner, and Anne C. Peterson.
1991. "Parenting Styles and Adolescent Development," in *The Encyclopedia of
Adolescence.* Jeanne Brooks-Gunn, Richard M. Lerner, and Anne C. Peterson, eds.
New York: Garland, 746–758.

Blau, David M. 1999. "The Effect of Income on Child Development." *The Review of
Economics and Statistics,* 81:261–276.

Bloom, Dan, Mary Farrell, and Barbara Fink, with Diana Adams-Ciardullo. 2002.
Welfare Time Limits: State Policies, Implementation, and Effects on Families. New
York: MDRC.

Bloom, Dan, James J. Kemple, Pamela Morris, Susan Scrivener, Nandita Verma, and
Richard Hendra, with Diana Adams-Ciardullo, David Seith, and Johanna Walter.
2000. *The Family Transition Program: Final Report on Florida's Initial Time-Limited
Welfare Program.* New York: MDRC.

Bloom, Dan, and Charles Michalopoulos. 2001. *How Welfare and Work Policies Affect
Employment and Income: A Synthesis of Research.* New York: MDRC.

Bogenschneider, Karen, and Lawrence Steinberg. 1994. "Maternal Employment and
Adolescent Academic Achievement: A Developmental Analysis." *Sociology of
Education,* 67:60–77.

Bos, Johannes, Aletha Huston, Robert Granger, Greg Duncan, Thomas Brock, and
Vonnie McLoyd. 1999. *New Hope for People with Low Incomes: Two-Year Results of
a Program to Reduce Poverty and Reform Welfare.* New York: MDRC.

Bradley, Robert H., and Robert Corwyn. 2002. "Socioeconomic Status and Child
Development." *Annual Review of Psychology,* 53:371–399.

Bronfenbrenner, Urie, and Pamela Morris. 1998. "The Ecology of Developmental
Processes," in *Theoretical Models of Human Development: Vol.I,.Handbook of Child*

Psychology, 5th ed. William Damon, series ed., and Richard M. Lerner, volume ed. New York: Wiley, 993–1028.

2006. "The Bioecological Model of Human Development," in *Theoretical Models of Human Development: Vol. I,. Handbook of Child Psychology,* 6th ed. Richard M. Lerner and William Damon, eds. New York: Wiley, 793–828.

Brooks-Gunn, Jeanne, Wen-Jui Han, and Jane Waldfogel. 2002. "Maternal Employment and Child Cognitive Outcomes in the First Three Years of Life: The NICHD Study of Early Child Care." *Child Development,* 73:1052–1072.

Chang, Young Eun, Aletha Huston, Danielle Crosby, and Lisa Gennetian. 2007. "The Effects of Welfare and Employment Programs on Children's Participation in Head Start." *Economics of Education Review,* 26:17–32.

Chase-Lansdale, P. Lindsay, Robert Moffitt, Brenda Lohman, Andrew Cherlin, Rebekah Coley, Laura Pittman, Jennifer Roff, and Elizabeth Votruba-Drzal. 2003. "Mothers' Transitions from Welfare to Work and the Well-Being of Preschoolers and Adolescents." *Science,* 299:1548–1552.

Coley, Rebekah L., P. Lindsay Chase-Lansdale, and Christine Li-Grining. 2001. "Child Care in the Era of Welfare Reform: Quality, Choices, and Preferences." Policy Brief No. 01–4, Report of *Welfare, Children, and Families: A Three-City Study.* Baltimore: Johns Hopkins University. Available at http://web.jhu.edu/threecitystudy/Publications/.

Crosby, Danielle A., Lisa A. Gennetian, and Aletha C. Huston. 2005. "Child Care Assistance Policies Can Affect the Use of Center-Based Care for Children in Low-Income Families." *Journal of Applied Developmental Science,* 92:86–106.

Dowsett, Chantelle, Aletha Huston, Amy Imes, Lisa Gennetian, and Desiree Principe. 2008. "Structural and Process Features in Three Types of Child Care for Children from High and Low Income Families." *Early Childhood Research Quarterly,* 23:69–93.

Duncan, Greg J., and Jeanne Brooks-Gunn, eds. 1997. *Consequences of Growing Up Poor.* New York: Russell Sage.

Duncan, Greg, and P. Lindsay Chase-Lansdale. 2001. *Welfare Reform and Child Well-Being.* Joint Center Poverty Research, Working Paper no. 217, Chicago: Northwestern University.

Duncan, Greg J., Wei-Jun Yeung, Jeanne Brooks-Gunn, and Judith R. Smith. 1998. "Does Poverty Affect the Life Chances of Children?" *American Sociological Review,* 63: 406–423.

Freedman, Stephen, Jean Tansey Knab, Lisa A. Gennetian, and David Navarro. 2000. *The Los Angeles Jobs-First GAIN Evaluation: Final Report on a Work First Program in a Major Urban Center.* New York: MDRC.

Fuller, Bruce, Sharon Kagan, and Susanna Loeb, with Judith Carroll, Jan McCarthy, Gege Kreicher, Bidemi Carrol, Ginger Cook, Yueh-Wen Chang, and Susan Sprachman. 2002. *New Lives for Poor Families? Mothers and Young Children Move Through Welfare Reform.* The University of California, Berkeley; Teacher's College, Columbia University; Stanford University; Yale University: The Growing Up in Poverty Project, Berkeley, CA: Policy Analysis for California Education.

Gennetian, Lisa A. 2004. "How Sibling Composition Affects Adolescents' Schooling Outcomes When Welfare Reform Policies Increase Maternal Employment." *Eastern Economic Journal,* 30:81–100.

Gennetian, Lisa. 2005. "One or Two Parents? Half or Step Siblings? The Effect of Family Composition on Cognitive Outcomes of Young Children." *Journal of Population Economics*, 18:415–436.

Gennetian, Lisa, Danielle Crosby, Chantelle Dowsett, Aletha Huston, and Desiree Alderson. 2007. *Maternal Employment, Early Care Settings, and the Achievement of Low-Income Children*. Next Generation Working Paper No. 30. New York: MDRC.

Gennetian, Lisa A., Danielle Crosby, Aletha C. Huston, and Edward D. Lowe. 2004. "How Child Care Assistance in Welfare and Employment Programs Can Support the Employment of Low-Income Families." *Journal of Policy Analysis and Management*, 23:723–743.

Gennetian, Lisa, Greg Duncan, Virginia Knox, Wanda G. Vargas, Elizabeth Clark-Kauffman, and Andrew London. 2004. "How Welfare Policies Can Affect Adolescents: A Synthesis of Evidence from Experimental Studies." *Journal of Research on Adolescence*, 14:399–423.

Gennetian, Lisa, and Virginia Knox. 2003. *Staying Single: The Effects of Welfare Reform Policies on Marriage and Cohabitation*. Next Generation Working Paper Series No. 13. New York: MDRC.

Gennetian, Lisa, Leonard Lopoo, and Andrew London. 2008. "Maternal Work Hours and Adolescents' School Outcomes Among Low-Income Families in Four Urban Counties." *Demography*, 45:31–53.

Gennetian, Lisa, Katherine Magnuson, and Pamela Morris. 2008. "From Statistical Associations to Causation: What Developmentalists Can Learn from Instrumental Variables Techniques Coupled with Experimental Data." *Developmental Psychology*, 44:381–394.

Gennetian, Lisa, and Cynthia Miller. 2000. *Reforming Welfare and Rewarding Work: Final Report on the Minnesota Family Investment Program: Vol. 2, Effects on Children*. New York: MDRC.

Gennetian, Lisa A., Cynthia Miller, and Jared Smith. 2005. *Turning Welfare into a Work Support: Six-Year Impacts on Parents and Children from the Minnesota Family Investment Program*. New York: MDRC.

Gennetian, Lisa A., Pamela Morris, Johannes Bos, and Howard Bloom. 2005. "Constructing Instrumental Variables from Experimental Data to Explore How Treatments Produce Effects," in *Learning More from Social Experiments: Evolving Analytic Approaches*. Howard Bloom, ed., New York: Russell Sage, 75–114.

Ginther, Donna K., and Robert A. Pollak. 2004. "Family Structure and Children's Educational Outcomes." *Demography*, 41:671–696.

Gottfried, Adele E., and Allen Gottfried. 1994. "Role of Maternal and Dual-Earner Employment Status in Children's Development," in *Redefining Families: Implications for Children's Development*. Adele E. Gottfried and Allen W. Gottfried, eds. New York: Plenum Press, 55–97.

Graber, Judy A., and Jeanne Brooks-Gunn. 1996. "Transitions and Turning Points: Navigating the Passage from Childhood Through Adolescence." *Developmental Psychology*, 32:768–776.

Hamilton, Gayle, Stephen Freedman, Lisa A. Gennetian, Charles Michalopoulos, Johanna Walter, Diana Adams-Ciardullo, Anna Gassman-Pines, Sharon McGroder, Martha Zaslow, Surjeet Ahluwalia, and Jennifer Brooks, with Electra Small and

Bryan Ricchetti. 2001. *How Effective Are Different Welfare-to-Work Approaches? Five-Year Adult and Child Impacts for Eleven Programs.* Washington, DC: U.S. Department of Health and Human Services, Office of the Assistant Secretary for Planning and Evaluation and Administration for Children and Families, and U.S. Department of Education.

Harvey, Elizabeth. 1999. "Short-Term and Long-Term Effects of Early Parental Employment on Children of the National Longitudinal Survey of Youth." *Developmental Psychology,* 35:445–459.

Hillman, Stephen B., and Shlomo S. Sawilowsky. 1991. "Maternal Employment and Early Adolescent Substance Use." *Adolescence,* 26:829–837.

Hsueh, JoAnn, and Lisa Gennetian. 2006. *Welfare Policies and Adolescents: Exploring the Roles of Sibling Care, Work Schedules, and Economic Resources.* MDRC, unpublished manuscript.

Hsueh, JoAnn, Lisa Gennetian, and Desiree Principe. 2006. *The Effects of Parents' Work Entry and Work Hours on Adolescent Achievement.* MDRC, unpublished manuscript.

Huston, Aletha. 2002. "Reforms and Child Development." *Future of Children,* 121:59–77.

Huston, Aletha C., Greg J. Duncan, Vonnie C. McLoyd, Danielle A. Crosby, Marika N. Ripke, Thomas S. Weisner, and Carolyn A. Eldred. 2005. "Impacts on Children of a Policy to Promote Employment and Reduce Poverty for Low-Income Parents: New Hope After Five Years." *Developmental Psychology,* 41:902–918.

Huston, Aletha C., Sylvia R. Epps, Mi-Suk Shim, Greg J. Duncan, Danielle A. Crosby, and Marika N. Ripke. 2006. "Effects of a Family Poverty Intervention Program Last from Middle Child-hood to Adolescence," in *Developmental Contexts in Middle Childhood: Bridges to Adolescence and Adulthood.* Aletha C. Huston and Marika N. Ripke, eds. New York: Cambridge University Press, 385–408.

Karoly, Lynn, M., Rebecca Kilburn, and Jill S. Cannon. 2005. *Early Childhood Interventions: Proven Results, Future Promise.* Santa Monica, CA: RAND.

Kurz, Demie. 2002. "Poor Mothers and the Care of Teenage Children," in *Child Care and Inequality: Re-Thinking Care Work for Children and Youth.* Francesca Cancian, Demie Kurz, Andrew London, Rebecca Reviere, and Mary Tuominen, eds. New York: Routledge, 23–36.

Lipsey, Mark, and David B. Wilson. 1996. *Tool Kit for Practical Meta-Analysis.* Nashville, TN: Vanderbilt University.

Loeb, Susanna, Bruce Fuller, Sharon Lynn Kagan, and Bidemi Carrol. 2004. "Child Care in Poor Communities: Early Learning Effects of Type, Quality, and Stability." *Child Development,* 75:47–65.

Ludwig, Jens, and Jeffrey R. Kling. 2007. "Is Crime Contagious?" *Journal of Law and Economics,* 50:491–518.

Magnuson, Katherine. 2003. *The Effect of Increases in Welfare Mothers' Education on Their Young Children's Academic and Behavioral Outcomes: Evidence from the National Evaluation of Welfare-to-Work Strategies Child Outcomes Study.* Institute for Research on Poverty, Discussion Paper no. 1274-03, Madison: University of Wisconsin.

Mayer, Susan E. 1997. *What Money Can't Buy: Family Income and Children's Life Chances.* Cambridge, MA: Harvard University Press.

McCall, Robert B. 1981. "Nature–Nurture and the Two Realms of Development: A Proposed Integration with Respect to Mental Development." *Child Development*, 52:1–12.

McGroder, Sharon M., Martha J. Zaslow, Kristin A. Moore, and Suzanne M. LeMenestrel. 2000. *The National Evaluation of Welfare-to-Work Strategies: Impacts on Young Children and Their Families Two Years After Enrollment. Findings from the Child Outcomes Study*. Washington, DC: U.S. Department of Health and Human Services.

McLanahan, Sara, and Gary D. Sandefur. 1994. *Growing Up with a Single Parent: What Hurts? What Helps?* Cambridge, MA: Harvard University Press.

McLoyd, Vonnie C. 1998. "Children in Poverty, Development, Public Policy, and Practice," in *Handbook of Child Psychology: Vol. 4, Child Psychology in Practice, 5th ed.* William Damon, series ed., Irving Sigel, and K. Ann Renninger, volume eds. New York: Wiley, 135–208.

McLoyd, Vonnie C., Nikki L. Aikens, and Linda M. Burton. 2006. "Childhood Poverty, Policy, and Practice," in *Handbook of Child Psychology: Vol. 4, Child Psychology in Practice, 6th ed.* William Damon and Richard W. Lerner, series eds., and K. Ann Renninger and Irving Sigel, volume eds. New York: Wiley, 700–775.

Michalopoulos, Charles, Doug Tattrie, Cynthia Miller, Philip K. Robins, Pamela Morris, David Gyarmati, Cindy Redcross, Kelly Foley, and Reuben Ford. 2002. *Making Work Pay: Final Report on the Self Sufficiency Project for Long-Term Welfare Recipients*. New York: MDRC.

Morris, Pamela, Greg J. Duncan, and Elizabeth Clark-Kauffman. 2005. "Child Well-Being in an Era of Welfare Reform: The Sensitivity of Transitions in Development to Policy Change." *Developmental Psychology*, 41:919–932.

Morris, Pamela, Greg Duncan, and Christopher Rodrigues. 2006. *Does Money Really Matter? Estimating Impacts of Family Income on Children's Achievement with Data from Social Policy Experiments*. MDRC, unpublished manuscript.

Morris, Pamela, and Lisa Gennetian. 2002. *Identifying Effects of Income on Children's Development: Integrating an Instrumental Variables Analytic Method with an Experimental Design*. New York: MDRC.

Morris, Pamela, and Richard Hendra. under review. "Losing the Safety Net: How Welfare Time Limits Affect Families and Children?" *Developmental Psychology*.

Morris, Pamela, and Charles Michalopoulos. 2000. *The Self Sufficiency Project at 36 Months: Effects on Children of a Program that Increased Employment and Income*. New York: MDRC.

Muller, Chandra. 1995. "Maternal Employment, Parent Involvement, and Mathematics Achievement." *Journal of Marriage and the Family*, 571:85–100.

Nichd Early Child Care Research Network. 1997. "Poverty and Patterns of Child Care," in *Consequences of Growing Up Poor*. Jeanne Brooks-Gunn and Greg Duncan, eds. New York: Russell Sage, 100–131.

Nichd Early Child Care Research Network. 2006. "Duration and Developmental Timing of Poverty and Children's Cognitive and Social Development from Birth Through Third Grade." *Child Development*, 76:795–810.

Nichd Early Child Care Research Network and Greg J. Duncan. 2003. "Modeling the Impacts of Child-Care Quality on Children's Preschool Cognitive Development." *Child Development*, 74:1454–1475.

Parcel, Toby L., and Elizabeth G. Menaghan. 1994. *Parents' Jobs and Children's Lives.* New York: Aldine de Gruyter.

Paulson, Sharon E. 1994. "Relations of Parenting Style and Paternal Involvement with Ninth Grade Students' Achievement." *Journal of Early Adolescence,* 14:250–267.

Richards, Maryse H., and Elena Duckett. 1994 "The Relationship of Maternal Employment to Early Adolescent Daily Experience with and without Parents." *Child Development,* 65:225–236.

Salkind, Neil J., and Ron Haskins. 1982. "Negative Income Tax: The Impact on Children from Low-Income Families." *Journal of Family Issues,* 3:165–180.

Sampson, Robert J., and John H. Laub. 1994. "Urban Poverty and the Family Context of Delinquency: A New Look at Structure and Process in a Classic Study." *Child Development,* 65:523–540.

Shonkoff, Jack P., and Deborah A. Phillips. 2000. *From Neurons to Neighborhoods: The Science of Early Childhood Development.* Washington, DC: National Academy Press.

Shumow, Lee, Deborah L. Vandell, and Jill K. Posner. 1998. "Harsh, Firm and Permissive Parenting in Low-Income Families: Relations to Children's Academic Achievement and Behavior Adjustment." *Journal of Family Issues,* 19:483–507.

Smolensky, Eugene, and Jennifer A. Gootman. 2001. *Working Families and Growing Kids.* Washington, DC: National Academies Press.

Vandell, Deborah L., and Janaki Ramanan. 1992. "Effects of Early and Recent Maternal Employment on Children from Low-Income Families." *Child Development,* 63:938–949.

Vander Ven, Thomas M., Francis T. Cullen, Mark A. Carrozza, and John Paul Wright. 2001. "Home Alone: The Impact of Maternal Employment on Delinquency." *Social Problems,* 48:236–257.

Votruba-Drzal, Elizabeth. 2003. "Income Changes and Cognitive Stimulation in Young Children's Home Environments." *Journal of Marriage and Family,* 65:341–355.

Votruba-Drzal, E. 2006. "Economic Disparities in Middle Childhood Development: Does Income Matter?" *Developmental Psychology,* 42:1154–1167.

Waldfogel, Jane. 2006. *What Children Need.* Cambridge, MA: Harvard University Press.

Yeung, Wei-Jun, Miriam R. Linver, and Jeanne Brooks-Gunn. 2002. "How Money Matters for Young Children's Development: Parental Investment and Family Processes." *Child Development,* 73:1861–1879.

Zaslow, Martha J., and Carol A. Emig. 1997. "When Low-Income Mothers Go to Work: Implications for Children." *Future of Children,* 71:110–115.

Zaslow, Martha J., Kristen A. Moore, Jennifer L. Brooks, Pamela A. Morris, Katheryn Tout, Zakia A. Redd, and Carol A. Emig. 2002. "Experimental Studies of Welfare Reform and Children." *Future of Children,* 121:79–95.

EIGHT

The Effects of Welfare and Child Support Policies on the Incidence of Marriage Following a Nonmarital Birth

Jean Knab, Irv Garfinkel, Sara McLanahan,
Emily Moiduddin, and Cynthia Osborne

I. Introduction

Researchers and policymakers have long been concerned that government policies may influence individual behavior in unintended ways. In particular, they worry that by providing mothers with an income that is independent of marriage, welfare and child support policies may discourage marriage and increase union dissolution. Economic theory is clear with respect to the marriage disincentives of welfare for single mothers (Becker 1981), but it is ambiguous with respect to the potential effects of child support policies on marriage. Whereas stronger child support enforcement reduces the costs of single motherhood for women, making marriage less attractive, it increases the costs for fathers, making marriage more attractive. Which effect dominates is an empirical question. Although empirical studies vary with respect to effect size and methods, the evidence compiled during the 1980s and early 1990s indicates that welfare generosity during this period had a small negative effect on marriage among mothers (Moffitt 1998), whereas stronger child support enforcement reduced single motherhood by reducing nonmarital childbearing (Aizer and McLanahan 2006; Case 1998; see Nixon 1997 for different findings; Plotnick et al. 2004),

A previous draft of this chapter was presented at the Ten Years After: Evaluating the Long-Term Effects of Welfare Reform on Children, Families, Welfare, and Work Conference organized by the University of Kentucky Center for Poverty Research, April 12–13, 2007, in Lexington. The authors are grateful to Bob Plotnick, Jim Ziliak, and other participants of the conference for their useful comments and to Austin Miller for helpful methodological advice. The Fragile Families and Child Wellbeing Study was supported by Grant Number R01HD36916 from the Eunice Kennedy Shriver National Institute of Child Health and Human Development (NICHD). The contents of the chapter are solely the responsibility of the authors and do not necessarily represent the official views of the NICHD.

though few researchers have pulled apart the decisions to give birth and to marry given a nonmarital conception.

In 1996, the Personal Responsibility and Work Opportunities Reconciliation Act (PRWORA) changed the parameters of welfare receipt and strengthened child support enforcement. Although under the new welfare regime states continued to provide modest cash benefits to poor single mothers, benefits are now constrained by time limits and work requirements that increase the costs of being a single mother relative to being a married mother. PRWORA also required states to relax their restrictions on two-parent families, making it easier for married and cohabiting couples to qualify for welfare benefits. Finally, PRWORA imposed new requirements on child support enforcement, rewarding states for raising their paternity establishment rates and making it harder for nonresident fathers to shirk their child support obligations. Taken together, these changes in welfare and child support policies are expected to reduce the marriage disincentives in welfare for mothers and to increase the costs of living in a separate household for fathers. Previous research provides inconsistent assessments of the impact on marriage and female headship of the recent changes brought about by PRWORA (e.g., Acs and Nelson 2004; Bitler, Gelbach, and Hoynes 2006; Carlson et al. 2004).

In this chapter, we use data from the Fragile Families and Child Wellbeing Study (Fragile Families Study) to examine the effects of welfare and child support policies on the incidence of marriage following a nonmarital birth. We examine the association between state welfare and child support policies and transition to marriage to the biological father of the focal child in the five years following a child's birth.

This chapter extends previous research in several ways. First, we examine the effects of welfare and child support policies on a group that is of great interest to policymakers—unmarried mothers who have recently had a child. Following this sample allows us to isolate the effects of the policies given a nonmarital birth, which are often confounded with fertility effects. Next, we distinguish between couples who are cohabiting and couples who are living apart at the time of the child's birth since both theory and prior empirical research suggest that these two groups of parents may respond differently to welfare and child support policies (Osborne 2005). Finally, we explore the effects of child support enforcement policies on marriage separately for couples where fathers have children with previous partners and those without other children to determine whether the effect of child support enforcement appears to be most relevant to the (future) support of the focal child or prior children.

The Fragile Families and Child Wellbeing data have characteristics that make these data attractive for studying the effects of welfare and child support policies on marriage. The study, which oversamples nonmarital births, provides extensive information on the population of women who are most likely to be affected by welfare and child support policies. Also, all of the births in the Fragile Families sample occurred between 1998 and 2000, so parents' decisions about marriage were made in the new era of welfare and child support enforcement. Finally, the cities in the Fragile Families sample were drawn via a stratified random sample that was designed to capture the extremes of welfare and child support policies and labor market conditions. See Reichman et al. (2001) for more detail on the study design.

The Fragile Families data also have limitations, however. State policies do not vary much during the five-year follow-up period, and we have limited within-state variation in policies to exploit. Therefore, we only have cross-sectional associations between policies and marriage. We cannot rule out the possibility that the state policies are proxies for other unobserved variables that vary across states and influence marriage among unmarried parents.

II. Theoretical Perspectives and Prior Research

According to economic theory (Becker 1981), generous welfare benefits should reduce incentives to marry and increase single motherhood by providing mothers with a source of income outside marriage. Welfare generosity extends beyond the value of cash benefits, however. Although most states have recently eliminated their categorical restrictions on two-parent families, the fact that welfare benefits are income-tested means that fathers' earnings are taxed at a very high rate, making it difficult for two-parent families to qualify for benefits (Carasso and Steuerle 2005; but see Ziliak 2007, who finds that effective tax rates declined by 50 percent in the post-PRWORA era). New welfare policies such as time limits and strict sanctions also make welfare less generous. These policies are expected to increase marriage among single mothers by making benefits less accessible and increasing the costs of living alone. Conversely, more lenient sanctions and time limit policies (i.e., more generous policies) may reduce incentives to marry compared with less generous policies.

Welfare (and child support) policies can impact marital decisions before or after a birth. Policies may discourage nonmarital conception (pure fertility effect) or encourage couples to marry following a nonmarital conception before the birth (marriage effect prebirth). Policies may also impact a couple's decision to marry following the birth of a child (marriage effect postbirth). The empirical literature often confounds some or all of these effects.

Overall, empirical research on the effect of welfare policies on mothers' fertility and marriage is mixed. Prereform econometric studies examining the effect of Aid to Families with Dependent Children (AFDC) benefit levels on these two outcomes generally found small, but significant, negative associations with marriage and positive associations with nonmarital fertility (Moffitt 1998). Although benefit levels have changed very little postreform, Temporary Assistance for Needy Families (TANF) ushered in a wave of new behavioral incentives, including sanctions and time limits, which may have more direct effects on marriage and fertility (Blank 2002). Econometric studies using waiver and post-TANF data find mixed results thus far (Acs and Nelson 2004; Chapter One, this volume). Fitzgerald and Ribar (2004) find little effect of welfare on headship or union transitions using longitudinal individual-level data (with strong local-level controls), whereas Schoeni and Blank (2000) find that stricter welfare policies increase marriage and reduce female family headship. Looking at aggregate-level data, Bitler et al. (2004) find that welfare reform was associated with less divorce and perhaps less marriage, depending on how they specify their models. Most recently, Graefe and Lichter (2008) use National Survey of Family Growth data from 1995 and 2002 and find that on the whole, welfare reform was not associated with changes in marriage among unwed mothers. However, they find a hint of a positive effect on marriage among the most disadvantaged mothers.

Researchers have also addressed how specific welfare provisions associated with waivers and TANF (e.g., time limits, sanctions, family caps, work exemptions) influence fertility. Blank (2002 and Chapter One, this volume) summarizes both econometric and experimental analyses of these specific policy effects and finds generally mixed results. Some studies find significant influences in expected directions on marriage and fertility (e.g., Fein 2001; Hu 2003; Miller et al. 2000). However, findings are just as likely to indicate that provisions have no influence (Acs 1996; Kaushal and Kaestner 2001) or have influences in unexpected directions (Kisker, Rangarajan, and Boller 1998). A very recent study by Graefe and Irving finds that stringent time limits are strongly associated with marriage among cohabiting couples (Graefe and Irving 2008). In this chapter, we will also examine results for cohabiting and noncohabiting couples separately.

According to economic theory, child support enforcement should affect mothers and fathers differently. For mothers, stronger enforcement should reduce the incentive to marry because, like welfare benefits, child support provides a source of income outside marriage. However, while a mother is on welfare, the child support often is not passed through to her; thus, the effect may be neutral for welfare-eligible mothers. Stronger child support enforcement also reduces the incentive for mothers to marry if their current partner has a child(ren) with a previous partner(s). This phenomenon, known as "multipartnered fertility," is very common among couples experiencing a nonmarital birth. In over 40 percent of couples experiencing a nonmarital birth, the father has had a child with a prior partner (Carlson and Furstenberg 2006). Partners may have formal or informal obligations to those children in a different household, which may decrease their attractiveness as marital partners. For fathers, stronger child support enforcement should increase the incentives of marriage because it increases the costs of divorce and possibly relationship dissolution among unmarried parents.

A significant body of literature finds evidence that child support policies reduce nonmarital childbearing using a variety of measures that capture a state's child support enforcement policies and its level of success in collecting payments (Aizer and McLanahan 2006; Garfinkel et al. 2003; Plotnick et al. 2004). For example, Huang, Kunz, and Garfinkel (2002) find that strict child support legislation and high expenditures on child support reduce nonmarital childbearing and increase marital childbearing; the latter finding is echoed by Aizer and McLanahan (2006), who show that increasing levels of child support expenditures by a state are associated with fewer nonmarital births. Others find that factors such as paternity establishment play a role in reducing nonmarital childbearing at the state level (Case 1998; Garfinkel et al. 2003) and among teens (Plotnick et al. 2004). Finally, Plotnick et al. (2004) find evidence that both legislation and collection success reduce nonmarital childbearing. Overall, this evidence suggests that stronger child support enforcement likely deters men from nonmarital fertility. Acs and Nelson (2004) find that stronger enforcement policies are associated with declines in single parenting and increases in dual parenting, but their analyses, like the others described previously, do not allow us to separate out the effects on fertililty and marriage following a nonmarital conception.

Child support policies may also affect the relationship decisions of parents following a nonmarital birth, but there is less research on this topic and much of it has been based on the Fragile Families data. Using data from the Fragile Families Study, Carlson et al. (2004) find that stronger child support enforcement reduces marriage among mothers and fathers in the year following a nonmarital birth. Consistent with this finding and using a subset of the Fragile Families sample, Mincy and Dupree (2001) find that child support enforcement slightly reduces mothers' plans to form a household with their child's biological father (cohabitation or marriage) and the actual formation of those households.

In the only experimental evaluation of child support influences to date, Cancian and Meyer (2007) find that Wisconsin's experimental child support policy allowing the full pass-through of support paid by nonresident fathers to mothers on TANF, as well as full disregard of that income in calculating cash assistance, has no influence on cohabitation or marriage between the mother and father. However, mothers in the experimental group cohabit at a lower rate with men who are not the father of their child than women in the control group receiving a partial pass-through. There is also evidence that stronger child support enforcement leads to a decline in remarriage for fathers (Bloom, Conrad, and Miller 1998). In sum, a higher proportion of women remain single with stronger child support enforcement. Taken as a whole, these studies suggest that the effects of stronger child support enforcement on marriage, remarriage, and cohabitation appear to be operating through the effects on mothers' independence via their higher income rather than on the stronger financial incentives for fathers to marry.

III. Data and Methods

We use data from the Fragile Families Study, a longitudinal birth cohort study of children born in large urban areas between 1998 and 2000. Fragile Families has a large sample of nonmarital births (and a comparison sample of married births) and significant diversity in welfare, child support, and labor market policies across 20 cities in 15 states. See Reichman et al. (2001) for more detail on the study design. The sample includes both biological parents of the child who were first interviewed at around the time of the child's birth, with follow-ups occurring at around the time of the child's first, third, and fifth birthdays.

At baseline, the Fragile Families sample included 1,186 married mothers and 3,712 unmarried mothers, whose response rates were 82 and 87 percent, respectively. In this chapter, we began with the sample of mothers unmarried at the time of the child's birth (3,712) and then excluded 518 mothers who were not born in the United States because Fragile Families does not have data on the immigrants' legal status and because welfare policies are applied differentially to legal immigrants, depending on the date of their arrival (as

well as differences in the treatment of immigrants across states). Because
we use covariates and outcomes measured at each wave, we excluded 743
mothers who did not respond to all three follow-up surveys (the one-,
three-, and five-year surveys). Results from sensitivity tests are similar if we
retain all mothers ever interviewed during the follow-up (and exclude certain covariates). Finally, we excluded 213 cases missing data on a covariate
(primarily on measures of the father's incarceration and fertility), yielding a
final sample of 2,176 mothers.

A. Outcome Measure

The outcome we examine is whether the mother ever married the child's
biological father in the five years following the child's birth. Relatively few
mothers have married a new partner. Results are robust to including those
marriages in the outcome measure.

B. Independent Variables

Welfare Generosity. The models include two indicators of welfare
generosity—the value of the cash benefits and the strictness of sanctions for
noncompliance. *Cash benefits* are represented in the models by the monthly
TANF benefit for a family of four taken from the University of Kentucky
Center for Poverty Research's national state-level economic data (available
at   http://www.ukcpr.org/EconomicData/UKCPRNationalDataSet_08–
05-07.xls). This variable is divided by $100 in the models. We also ran the
models with a measure of the amount of TANF a mother could expect for
her family size (of two, three, or four or more), and the results were consistent. We also present a model where we divide the value of the maximum cash benefits by the fair market rent in the metropolitan statistical
area (MSA) to get some additional variation within states and to adjust for
the cost of living across cities. Fair market rents were obtained from the
Department of Housing and Urban Development (available at http://www.
huduser.org). *Stringent sanctions* for noncompliance with work or other
welfare requirements are defined as those in which a state imposes immediate full-family sanctions or imposes gradual full-family sanctions with an
immediate 100 percent reduction in Food Stamp benefits or elimination of
Medicaid (Pavetti and Bloom 2001). We also ran an alternate set of models
that included additional measures of welfare including time limits and the
generosity of earnings disregards, as well as having a state Earned Income

Tax Credit (EITC). In Section IV, we discuss the results implied by the more extensive model.

Child Support Enforcement. The model includes a constructed measure of child support enforcement at the city level. This measure, the *child support payment ratio*, is constructed using year 2000 city-level census data by regressing the probability that an unmarried mother received any child support on the mother's race-ethnicity, age, education, nativity, parity, presence of a child under age six, state-level median male wage, and maximum combined TANF/Food Stamp benefit in the state. From this equation, the predicted aggregate city-level probability of receiving support is generated. The raw aggregate probability of receiving support is then divided by the predicted aggregate probability of receiving support for each city to get an estimate of how well a city does in collecting child support given the characteristics of the city's population. Finally, this measure is standardized. This measure was constructed by Nepomnyaschy and Garfinkel (2007).

C. Control Variables

All models include a set of individual controls measured at the time of the child's birth, unless otherwise noted. The controls are mother's age, age at first birth, number of children, education, race-ethnicity, relationship with the child's father (cohabiting or dating, with *nonromantic* as an omitted category), and depression (from the one-year follow-up). Depression is represented by a dummy variable where 1 indicates that the mother meets diagnostic criteria for depression based on the Composite International Diagnostic Interview Short Form (CIDI-SF) (Walters et al. 2002). We also include measures of whether the child's biological father had children from any prior relationships and whether he had ever been incarcerated (one-year).

In addition to city- and state-level measures of welfare generosity and stringency of child support enforcement, we tried to include the state's unemployment rate and a race-specific sex ratio. We found that the effects of welfare and child support policies on marriage are robust to their inclusion in the model. These results are not included in the text.

Finally, we ran models that include state fixed effects. Because there is practically no change over time in either the generosity of welfare benefits or the stringency of child support enforcement, the welfare and child support coefficients in the models with state fixed effects are driven only by city variation within states (which is limited).

D. Sample and City Characteristics

Table 8.1 presents the means of the dependent variables and the policy and contextual variables included in this analysis. Overall, about 18 percent of the unmarried couples had married by the time their child was five years old; however, the percentage of mothers that ever married the focal child's father between birth and the five-year interview ranged across cities from 6 to 34 percent. Marriage rates also differ considerably based on the parents' relationship status at the child's birth; roughly 27 percent of cohabiting couples marry within five years compared to only 10 percent of dating couples (not shown in Table 8.1).

The majority of mothers in the sample are black (62 percent), and approximately 21 percent have attended any college. The mean age of mothers is 24, and they average just over two children. Nearly one-half of the respondents were cohabiting at the time of the child's birth, 39 percent were dating, and approximately 13 percent were not romantically involved with the child's father. Fifteen percent of mothers reported symptoms of depression at the one-year interview. Roughly one-half of the fathers had children with a previous partner, and over one-third had ever been incarcerated.

Table 8.1 also shows the variation in welfare and child support policies across the 20 cities (in 15 states) observed in this analysis. There is considerable variation in maximum TANF benefits, ranging from a low of $230 per month to a high of $840 per month. One-half of the cities (in which 30 percent of the sample resided) were in states that imposed strict sanctions for welfare noncompliance. The child support payment ratio varies from 67 percent (i.e., cities that collect approximately 67 percent of the predicted child support dollars they should get based on their population's characteristics) to 159 percent. A standardized version of this variable is used in the multivariate models. And the value of the TANF benefit as a proportion of the fair market rent varied dramatically as well.

E. Analysis Plan

We examine the effects of policies on marriage using ordinary least squares (OLS) regression and controlling for a set of individual-, city-, and state-level characteristics. The regression results are weighted to account for the sample design (probability of selection, clustering, nonresponse at baseline) and attrition across the waves. Weighting the data makes the results representative of the 20 cities in the Fragile Families sample.

Table 8.1. *Sample and policy descriptives*

Key measures	Full sample		
Ever Married Bio Father by Five-Year Follow-up (%)	17.7		
Ever Married Any Partner by Five-Year Follow-up (%)	21.6		
White (%)	15.3		
Hispanic (%)	22.7		
Black or Other Race-Ethnicity (%)	62.0		
Mother's Age in Years (Mean)	23.9		
Mother Has Less Than HS Diploma (%)	37.3		
Mother Has HS Diploma (%)	41.5		
Mother Attended Any College (%)	21.2		
Mother's Number of Children (Mean)	2.3		
Cohabiting (%)	47.5		
Dating (%)	39.1		
Father Had Other Children (%)	48.6		
Father Ever in Jail (One Year) (%)	36.3		
Mother Depressed (One Year) (%)	14.6		
Mother's Age at First Birth (Mean)	19.9		
Sample Size	2,176		
For All 20 Cities (Weighted)	Min	Max	Mean[b]
Maximum TANF/$100 (Mean)	2.3	8.4	5.6
Strict Sanctions	0.0	1.0	0.3
C.S. Payment Ratio–unstandardized[a] (%)	66.5	158.9	98.4

Notes:
$N = 2,176$.
Results are weighted to account for sample design and attrition.
Characteristics of the mother and father at the time of the child's birth unless otherwise noted.
[a] A standardized version of this variable is used in the multivariate analysis.
[b] Mean experienced by all sample members.

IV. Results

Table 8.2 presents the full sample associations between welfare and child support policies on marriage. Model 1 presents the relationship between welfare and child support policies and marriage to the biological father controlling for individual-level characteristics. A greater maximum value of cash benefits is associated with less marriage. A $100, or 18 percent, increase in the

Table 8.2. *Associations between policies and marriage to the child's biological father by the time of the five-year follow-up*

	Model 1	Model 2	Model 3[b]	Model 4[b]
Maximum TANF/$100	−0.020*		−0.047	−0.002
Max TANF/Fair Market Rent/$100		−0.002*		
Strict Sanctions	0.044*	0.053*	−0.591**	−0.656**
C.S. Payment Ratio	−0.018*	0.000	−0.050*	−0.026
White	0.141**	0.144**	0.139**	0.138**
Hispanic	0.097*	0.095*	0.093^	0.092^
Mother's Age	−0.004	−0.005	−0.004	−0.004
Mother Has < HS Diploma	0.012	0.007	0.015	0.015
Mother Has at Least Some College	0.104*	0.103*	0.109*	0.109*
Mother's Number of Children	0.006	0.008	0.006	0.006
Cohabiting[a]	0.198**	0.198**	0.196**	0.195**
Dating[a]	0.071*	0.072*	0.073**	0.073*
Father Had Other Children	−0.048	−0.051	−0.046	−0.046
Father Ever in Jail	−0.099**	−0.099**	−0.103**	−0.103**
Mom Depressed (One Year)	0.034	0.037	0.031	0.031
Mother's Age at First Birth	0.006	0.006	0.005	0.005

Notes:

$N = 2,176$

$**p < 0.01$; $*p < 0.05$; $^p < 0.10$ two-tailed.

Results are weighted to account for sample design and attrition. OLS coefficients are presented. Characteristics of the mother and father at the time of the child's birth unless otherwise noted.

[a] Reference group is not romantically involved at the time of the child's birth.

[b] Model also includes state dummy variables.

maximum level of cash benefits is associated with a 2 percent reduction in marriage. In addition, stricter welfare sanctions are associated with increased marriage. Moving from a lenient or moderate sanctioning city to a strict sanctioning city (at mean benefit levels) is associated with a 4 percentage point increase in the likelihood of marrying during the five-year follow-up period. Considering the joint effects of both policies, these results imply that welfare generosity (i.e., higher benefits and weaker sanctions) is associated with a substantially lower incidence of marriage. In percentage terms, moving from a strict sanctioning environment with benefits of $500 per month to a more lenient sanctioning environment that has benefits of $600 per month would decrease the rate of marriage from 21 percent to 15 percent.

Stronger and more effective child support enforcement is also associated with lower rates of marriage. A one standard deviation increase in the child support payment rate ratio is associated with a 2 percent reduction in marriage during the five-year follow-up period. This finding is consistent with other research from the Fragile Families Study and research on remarriage. We explore the source of this effect later.

The individual-level variables, for the most part, behave as expected and are significant predictors of mothers' marriage. More educated mothers, white and Hispanic mothers (relative to black mothers), and mothers who were cohabiting or dating at the time of the child's birth (relative to non-romantic mothers) were all more likely to marry during the five-year follow up period. Mothers whose partner had ever been imprisoned were less likely to marry within five years. On the other hand, mother's age, age at first birth, number of children, depression, and number of children of the father are not significant predictors.

Model 2 replaces the measure of cash benefits with a variable that divides the cash benefits by the cost of fair market rent in the MSA in order to account for potential differences in the real value of welfare benefits across metropolitan areas. A value over 1 on this measure means that the cash benefit is greater than the fair market rent, and a value less than 1 means that the cash benefit is less than the fair market rent. The coefficient on the measure is significantly different from zero at the .01 level and the point estimate is −.002, indicating that a 10 percentage point increase in the real value of TANF is associated with a 2 percentage point decrease in marriage. This effect is nearly twice the size of the effect for TANF alone.

Note that in Model 2, where the TANF measure incorporates within-state variation, the child support enforcement coefficient goes to zero. This suggests that the estimated child support enforcement effect is not very robust.

In results not shown in the table, we included additional measures of state welfare policies in this model. Each operates as one would theoretically expect. More generous earnings disregards and having a state EITC, each of which would provide women with greater guaranteed income, are associated with lower rates of marriage. However, only the EITC coefficient is statistically significant. The coefficient on strict time limits is close to zero. Compared to a model with only the TANF benefit, the addition of all the variables passes an F test, but compared to the model with TANF plus sanctions, the additional variables are not significant. For simplicity, therefore, we report only the sanction results, but the reader should bear in mind that these results are also picking up the effect of other welfare state variables.

Table 8.3. *Associations between policies and marriage by the time of the five-year follow-up for key subgroups*

Subgroup	TANF/$100	Strict sanctions	Child support
Cohabiting (N = 1,035)	−0.013	0.137*	−0.052**
Dating (N = 812)	−0.023	−0.030	0.007
L.T. HS Diploma (N = 786)	−0.036**	0.061^	−0.018
High School (N = 793)	0.002	0.059	−0.023
Any College (N = 597)	−0.017	−0.049	−0.032^
Father Has Prior Children (N = 1,027)	−0.017	0.050*	−0.041**
Father Has No Prior Children (N = 1,149)	−0.015	0.042	−0.006

Notes: **$p < 0.01$; *$p < 0.05$; ^$p < 0.10$ two-tailed.
Results are weighted to account for sample design and attrition. OLS coefficients are presented.
Regression equation includes all variables included in Model 1 of Table 8.2.

Models 3 and 4 deal with unobserved state-level variables, including other state policies, that could be correlated with either welfare generosity or strength of enforcement, or both, and marriage of unmarried mothers. Therefore, Models 3 and 4 include dummies for each of the states in the sample. Because there is only trivial over-time variation within the five-year period in welfare generosity and child support enforcement, the welfare and child support coefficients are driven primarily by cross-city differences within states. There are only five more cities than states in the Fragile Families sample. The TANF benefit coefficients double and remain the same compared to those in Models 1 and 2, but, not surprisingly, neither is significantly different from zero. The coefficients on the sanction variable blow up 10-fold and change sign.

Similarly, adding state fixed effects strengthens the relationship between strong child support enforcement and marriage. The coefficient in Model 3 is two and one-half times the size of the coefficient in Model 1 and remains statistically significant. A one standard deviation increase in the child support payment rate ratio is associated with a 5 percent reduction in marriage during the five-year follow-up period. The coefficient in Model 4, while not significantly different from zero, does become negative and within the range of the coefficients in Models 1 and 3.

In sum, the point estimates from the fixed effects models are as large as or larger than those from the simple cross-sectional models. We have much less confidence in these results, however, because they are based on such a small sample of within-state city pairings and because the coefficients, which are already large compared to those reported in the previous literature, become unrealistically large.

Table 8.3 presents the results for subgroups (estimated in separate models) by relationship status at the child's birth, education, and father's prior fertility. We have reorganized the table so that the subgroups are in the rows and the policy variables are in the columns. All the models presented are identical to Model 1 in Table 8.2.

Rows 1 and 2 of Table 8.3 present the results for mothers who were cohabiting and dating at the time of their child's birth, respectively. Because cohabiting couples are more committed to one another and are already living together, marriage is a more salient option than it is for dating couples, where the options of breaking up or cohabiting are likely to be more salient. Thus, welfare and child support policies may have bigger effects on marriage for cohabiting than dating couples. While the TANF benefit level coefficients reject this hypothesis, both the sanctions and child support enforcement coefficients provide support for the hypothesis. The TANF coefficients are negative for both groups and larger for dating than cohabiting couples, but neither is significantly different from zero at conventional levels. The sanction and child support coefficients are large and statistically significant for cohabiting couples and have the wrong sign and zero for dating couples. The child support results are particularly striking, with a large, statistically significant effect at the .01 level for cohabitors and a tiny, statistically insignificant effect for dating couples. The sanction results are similar to those of Graefe and Irving (2008), who find a strong positive association between time limits and marriage among cohabitors but not among romantic couples. Indeed, if we exclude sanctions and include time limits, we also find a strong positive effect of stronger time limits on marriage among cohabitors. Clearly, as suggested previously, the sanctions variable is picking up more than just sanctions.

Rows 3, 4, and 5 present the results by education of the mother at the time of the child's birth. We expect that mothers who were most likely to be eligible for welfare (those with lower education) would be most affected by welfare policies. The biggest effects are for mothers in the lowest education group—those without a high school education—but surprisingly, there is practically no association between policies and marriage for the group of mothers with terminal high school degrees. The child support enforcement coefficients increase with education and approach statistical significance only among mothers with any college education. Perhaps enforcement has stronger effects on the more educated mothers because the fathers of their children have more ability to pay support and therefore strong enforcement provides more income to them, making them less dependent on future partners for their economic well-being.

In rows 6 and 7 we present results for couples in which the biological father had a child(ren) with a prior partner and couples in which the father had no children with a prior partner. While there is no reason to expect welfare generosity to vary by the father's multipartner fertility, the negative effects of child support on marriage should be larger for couples in which the father is potentially liable for paying child support for someone else's child. As described previously, strong enforcement reduces the incomes of fathers with such obligations, rendering them more unattractive marriage partners to mothers. The welfare generosity coefficients are nearly identical for the two groups. In stark contrast, consistent with our expectation, the child support coefficient for fathers with prior obligations is much larger (and highly significant) than the coefficient for fathers with no prior obligations, which is close to zero. That the negative effects on marriage of strong enforcement are concentrated among mothers whose partner has a prior obligation is a very interesting result, suggesting a different path than most investigators have explored.

V. Conclusion

This chapter examines the effects of welfare generosity and the stringency of child support enforcement on a couple's marriage over the five-year period following a nonmarital birth. The chapter uses data from the Fragile Families and Child Wellbeing Study, which is drawn from 20 large cities in 15 different states. We find support for the hypotheses that welfare generosity (i.e., higher cash benefits and more lenient sanctions) and strong child support enforcement are associated with lower rates of marriage. But we also find some support for the alternative.

In models without state fixed effects, we generally find large, negative, and statistically significant associations between marriage and welfare generosity and strict enforcement. As expected, these effects are larger for cohabiting couples who are closer to the marriage margin than for dating couples. The welfare effects are larger for the least-educated group, who are the most likely to be dependent on welfare, and the child support effects are confined to couples where the father had a preexisting potential child support obligation. Finally, despite very little variation over time or within state in welfare generosity and enforcement stringency, the fixed effects models do not wipe out these effects. The benefits level coefficient loses statistical significance because of an increase in standard errors, but the coefficients on TANF and child support remain the same or increase. However, the coefficients blow up 10-fold and change sign because our measure has no variation in sanction policies over time.

The findings are also, for the most part, robust to the inclusion of a significant number of individual-, city-, and state- level control variables and marriage to men who are not the biological father of the focal child.

But there is some countervailing evidence. In Model 2 compared to Model 1, where, rather than the TANF benefit level, we include the TANF benefit level divided by a city housing costs index, the already large effect size of TANF nearly doubles and the child support coefficient becomes zero. In the state fixed effects model, the sanction coefficients blow up. These results not only undermine the child support hypothesis, but raise questions about the sensitivity of all the coefficients to model specification.

Our analysis is limited by the fact that welfare and child support policies change very little over the observed five-year period (and, in truth, in any five-year period other than during a period of reform that brings with it other issues, such as generalizability). This renders the analysis effectively cross-sectional. Thus, our estimates of policy effects are based on between-city differences in policies rather than within-city changes in policies over time. We therefore cannot rule out the possibility that the effects attributed to welfare and child support policies are due to some unmeasured characteristics of the city other than these two sets of policies. In the fixed effects models, differences are coming off of only five within-state city pairs.

Examining the effects of welfare policies on marriage and other family-related behaviors was a popular research topic prior to and during the welfare reforms of the 1990s. Much less research has been done postreform and in the context of these new policies that seek to minimize the generosity of states' welfare benefits. Even less research has examined the impact of child support on marriage decisions given a nonmarital birth. Given the potential magnitude of these findings and the admitted limitations of the present analyses, future research should reexamine these questions using other datasets. It will be important to factor in not only better methodological techniques to control macro-level influences, but also the process by which an array of policies influence both mothers' and fathers' decisions to marry or remain single at the individual level.

References

Acs, G. 1996. "The Impact of Welfare on Young Mothers' Subsequent Childbearing Decisions." *Journal of Human Resources*, Fall: 898–915.

Acs, G., and S. Nelson. 2004. "Changes in Living Arrangements during the Late 1990s: Do Welfare Policies Matter?" *Journal of Policy Analysis and Management,* 23(2): 273–290.

Aizer, A., and S. McLanahan. 2006. "The Impact of Child Support on Fertility, Parental Investments and Child Well-Being." *Journal of Human Resources,* 41(1): 28–45.

Becker, G. 1981. *A Treatise on the Family.* Cambridge, MA: Harvard University Press.

Bitler, M. P., J. B. Gelbach, and H. W. Hoynes. 2006. "Welfare Reform and Children's Living Arrangements." *Journal of Human Resources,* 41(1): 1–27.

Bitler, M. P., J. B. Gelbach, H. W. Hoynes, and M. Zavodny. 2004. "The Impact of Welfare Reform on Marriage and Divorce." *Demography,* 41(2): 213–236.

Blank, R. M. 2002. "Evaluating Welfare Reform in the United States." *Journal of Economic Literature,* 40(4): 1105–1166.

Bloom, D. E., C. Conrad, and C. Miller. 1998. "Child Support and Father's Remarriage and Fertility," in *Fathers Under Fire: The Revolution in Child Support Enforcement.* I. Garfinkel, S. McLanahan, D. R. Meyer, and J. A. Seltzer, eds. New York: Russell Sage, 128–156.

Carasso, A., and C. E. Steuerle. 2005. "The Hefty Penalty on Marriage Facing Many Households with Children." *The Future of Children,* 15(2): 157–175.

Carlson, M., I. Garfinkel, S. McLanahan, R. Mincy, and W. Primus. 2004. "The Effects of Welfare and Child support Policies on Union Formation." *Population Research and Policy Review,* 23(5–6): 513–542.

Carlson, M. J., and F. F. Furstenberg. 2006. "The Prevalence and Correlates of Multipartnered Fertility Among Urban U.S. Parents." *Journal of Marriage and Family,* 68(3): 718–732.

Cancian, M., and D. R. Meyer. 2007. "The Effect of Child Support on Subsequent Marriage and Cohabitation." Presented at the annual meeting of the Population Association of America, New York.

Case, A. 1998. "The Effects of Stronger Child Support Enforcement of Non-marital Fertility," in *Fathers Under Fire: The Revolution in Child Support Enforcement.* I. Garfinkel, S. McLanahan, D. Meyer, and J. Seltzer, eds. New York: Russell Sage, 191–215.

Fein, D. J. 2001. "Will Welfare Reform Influence Marriage and Fertility? Early Evidence from the ABC Demonstration." *Evaluation and Program Planning,* 24(4): 427–444.

Fitzgerald, J. M., and D. C. Ribar. 2004. "Welfare Reform and Female Headship." *Demography,* 41(2): 189–212.

Garfinkel, I., C. C. Huang, S. S. McLanahan, and D. S. Gaylin. 2003. "The Roles of Child Support Enforcement and Welfare in Non-Marital Childbearing." *Journal of Population Economics,* 16(1): 55–70.

Graefe, D. R., and S. K. Irving. 2008. "Marriage among Welfare Recipients: Relationship Commitment Interacts with Welfare Policy." Paper presented at the annual meeting of the Population Association of America, New Orleans.

Graefe, D. R., and D. T. Lichter. 2008. "Marriage Patterns among Unwed Mothers: Before and After PRWORA." *Journal of Policy Analysis and Management,* 27(3): 479–497.

Hu, W. Y. 2003. "Marriage and Economic Incentives – Evidence from a Welfare Experiment." *Journal of Human Resources,* 38(4): 942–963.

Huang, C. C., J. Kunz, and I. Garfinkel. 2002. "The Effect of Child Support on Welfare Exits and Re-entries." *Journal of Policy Analysis and Management,* 21(4): 557–576.

Kisker, E. E., A. Rangarajan, and K. Boller. 1998. *"Moving into Adulthood: Were the Impacts of Mandatory Programs for Welfare-Dependent Teenaged Parents Sustained After Programs Ended?"* Princeton, NJ: Mathematica Policy Research.

Kaushal, N., and R. Kaestner. 2001. "From Welfare to Work: Has Welfare Reform Worked?" *Journal of Policy Analysis and Management,* 20(4): 699–719.

Miller, C., V. Knox, L. A. Gennetian, M. Dodoo, J. A. Hunter, and C. Redcross. 2000. *Reforming Welfare and Rewarding Work: Final Report on the Minnesota Family Investment Program.* New York: MDRC.

Mincy, R. B., and A. Dupree. 2001. "Welfare, Child Support, and Family Formation." *Children and Youth Services Review,* 23 (6/7): 577–601.

Moffitt, R. A. 1998. "The Effect of Welfare on Marriage and Fertility," in *Welfare, the Family, and Reproductive Behavior.* R. A. Moffitt, ed. Washington, DC: National Academy Press, 50–97.

Nepomnyaschy, L., and I. Garfinkel. 2007. "Child Support Enforcement and Fathers' Contributions to Their Nonmarital Children." Center for Research on Child Wellbeing Working Paper #2006–09-FF. Princeton, NJ: Princeton University.

Nixon, L. A. 1997. "The Effect of Child Support Enforcement on Marital Dissolution." *Journal of Human Resources,* 32(1): 159–181.

Osborne, C. 2005. "Marriage Following the Birth of a Child among Cohabiting and Visiting Parents." *Journal of Marriage and Family,* 67(1): 14–26.

Pavetti, L., and D. Bloom. 2001. "State Sanctions and Time Limits," in *The New World of Welfare.* R. M. Blank and R. Haskins, eds. Washington, DC: Brookings Institution Press, 245–269.

Plotnick, R., I. Garfinkel, S. S. McLanahan, and I. Ku. 2004. "Better Child Support Enforcement – Can It Reduce Teenage Premarital Childbearing?" *Journal of Family Issues,* 25(5): 634–657.

Reichman, N. E., J. O. Teitler, I. Garfinkel, and S. S. McLanahan. 2001. "Fragile Families: Sample and Design." *Children and Youth Services Review,* 23(4–5): 303–326.

Schoeni, R. F., and R. M. Blank. 2000. "What Has Welfare Reform Accomplished? Impacts on Welfare Participation, Employment, Income, Poverty, and Family Structure." NBER Working Paper Series. Cambridge, MA: National Bureau of Economic Research.

Walters, Ellen E., Ronald C. Kessler, Christopher B. Nelson, and Daniel Mroczek. 2002. "Scoring the World Health Organization's Composite International Diagnostic Interview Short Form (CIDI-SF)." World Health Organization. Available at http://www3.who.int/cidi/CIDISFScoringMemo12-03-02.pdf.

Ziliak, J. P. 2007. "Making Work Pay: Changes in Effective Tax Rates and Guarantees in U.S. Transfer Programs: 1983–2002." *Journal of Human Resources,* 42(3): 619–642.

NINE

Welfare Reform and Health among the Children of Immigrants

Ariel Kalil and Kathleen M. Ziol-Guest

I. Introduction

The 1996 federal welfare reform law introduced, among other things, broad restrictions on immigrants' eligibility for many health and social service programs, including cash welfare assistance (Temporary Assistance for Needy Families [TANF]), food stamps, and subsidized health insurance. Caseloads for welfare and other benefit programs have fallen dramatically in the wake of welfare reform (see the Introduction to this volume), but the declines have been steeper for immigrants than for native-born citizens (Fix and Passel 1999) even when immigrant families remain eligible for assistance. Indeed, most (80 percent) children in immigrant families, having been born here, are U.S. citizens, and are therefore eligible for government assistance on the same basis as all other U.S. citizens (Hernandez 2004). This phenomenon, which has been called the "chilling effect," is thought to reflect immigrants' confusion about their eligibility for assistance or their fear that benefit use will adversely affect their chances for citizenship or even their opportunity to reenter or stay in this county (Capps 2001; Fix and Passel 1999; Maloy et al. 2000). For example, parents who are not citizens may not be aware of their U.S.-born children's eligibility for important benefits or may face other administrative barriers to accessing programs after leaving welfare. This is a particular problem among low-income parents

Support for the first author was provided in part by a Changing Faces of America's Children Young Scholars Award from the Foundation for Child Development. Support for the second author was provided by the Robert Wood Johnson Foundation Health and Society Scholars program. We would like to thank Seth Sanders, Jim Ziliak, and conference participants at the University of Kentucky's Center for Poverty Research Conference "Ten Years After: Evaluating the Long-Term Effects of Welfare Reform on Work, Welfare, Children, and Families" for their helpful comments and suggestions. All remaining errors are the responsibility of the authors.

with low education, as this population has a high proportion of noncitizen parents (Hernandez 2004).

The developmental literature on the effects of recent welfare policy changes on children (see, e.g., Chapter Seven, this volume; Kalil and Dunifon, 2007) has had little to say about the well-being of young children in immigrant families. The literature on the effects of welfare reform on immigrant families has come primarily from the fields of economics, public policy, and sociology and has rarely examined effects on child well-being. Kalil and Crosby (2006) show that children of immigrant welfare leavers in Chicago fare significantly worse, in terms of their postwelfare health, than their peers in either native leaver families or immigrant families who continue to receive assistance. Kaushal and Kaestner (2007) report that welfare reform is associated with an increase in the proportion of low-educated foreign-born single mothers reporting delays in medical care or foregoing care due to its cost, but no impact on the health insurance, medical care utilization, or health of these mothers' children. The present study bridges various disciplines and seeks to contribute to the literature on the impact of welfare reform on children as well as that of welfare reform and immigrants.

Using data spanning a 10-year period (1994–2004) from multiple panels of the Survey of Income and Program Participation (SIPP), this study investigates the health of young children of low-income immigrants versus the children of natives over the period spanning welfare reform. Health is assessed with two indicators: parents' reports of children's physical health and access to care. We first examine basic over-time differences in children's health between the children of low-income immigrants (who are further distinguished by their parents' citizenship status) and those of natives. Given that virtually all of the children we examine here are native-born, and hence are citizens, significantly worse levels of their health compared to those of natives, especially if these gaps are more pronounced after welfare reform, provide some evidence to support the chilling effect hypothesis.

This study is the first, to our knowledge, to use the SIPP to examine the impact of welfare reform on children's health (by taking advantage of the little-used child health and well-being modules that appear in each SIPP panel) and one of only a handful of studies that has examined the impact of welfare reform on the children of immigrants. In doing so, it complements Chapter Six of this volume by Ham, Li, and Shore-Sheppard, who use the SIPP to examine the effect of welfare reform on the health insurance coverage of less-skilled single-mother families, including those headed by Hispanics.

II. Background

The children of immigrants are an important component of the U.S. population.[1] They are the fastest-growing segment of the U.S. population under age 15 and comprise 20 percent of all American children (25 percent of children under age six; Hernandez 2004). When considering immigrant children's use of federal programs, it is important to note that most (75 percent) children of foreign-born parents were themselves born in the United States and are therefore citizens. Indeed, this is true for 93 percent of immigrant children younger than age six (Capps, Fix, et al. 2004). As such, they are as eligible for public assistance as any native-born child of native-born parents. These "mixed-status" families—those with citizen and noncitizen members—represent a substantial segment of the population, comprising about 10 percent of all families with children.

A. Immigrants and Welfare Reform

The children of immigrants have received relatively little attention in the welfare reform research literature; however, there are several reasons to expect that their experiences after 1996 have differed in important ways from the experiences of children of U.S.-born parents. Above all, immigrants were the target of many of the most stringent federal reforms under the Personal Responsibility and Work Opportunity Reconciliation Act (PRWORA) (although many key federal features were later repealed at states' discretion). Prior to the reforms enacted in 1996, legal immigrants and their children were generally eligible for public benefits under the same terms as citizens, and eligibility for assistance was set at the federal, rather than the state, level (undocumented immigrants, in contrast, have never been eligible for public programs in most states, with the exception of emergency Medicaid[2] and public health services [e.g., vaccinations; see Fix and Haskins 2002 for an overview]). However, by the late 1990s, immigrant families faced a vastly different policy environment—one marked by a confusing and ever-changing set of rules concerning their eligibility to access social institutions and public assistance (Zimmerman and Tumlin 1999).

---

[1] Throughout this chapter, we refer to the "children of immigrants" as those children, both native and foreign-born, who have at least one foreign-born parent.

[2] The definition of emergency Medicaid was not changed from the previous definition as treatment only for medical conditions with acute symptoms that could place the patient's health in serious jeopardy, result in serious impairment to bodily functions, or cause dysfunction of a bodily organ or part.

Specifically, the federal welfare reform law introduced broad restrictions on immigrants' eligibility for many health and social service programs, including cash welfare assistance (TANF), food stamps, and subsidized health insurance. In determining eligibility, the reforms distinguish between "qualified" and "nonqualified" (though often legal) immigrants and between those who arrived "preenactment" versus "postenactment" (i.e., before and after August 22, 1996).

More specifically, PRWORA stipulated that the only individuals entitled to federal public benefits were U.S. citizens and other "qualified individuals" (who included lawful permanent residents [i.e., those with green cards] who had 10 years of Social Security earnings, refugees during their first few years in the United States, and noncitizens who had served or were serving in the U.S. military). Immigrants who entered the United States after PRWORA went into effect were barred completely from receiving programs for their first five years in the country, after which eligibility was at state option. Individuals already present as of August 22, 1996, had to demonstrate that they met the criteria (i.e., that they were qualified) or have their federal public benefits cut off (with the exception of emergency Medicaid and public health services). PRWORA originally also made most legal immigrants already residing in the United States ineligible for food stamps and Supplemental Security Income (SSI) until they attained citizenship.[3]

Second, the new federal law formalized the policies stipulating that undocumented immigrants and other nonqualified immigrants were ineligible for most state and local public benefits, although it allowed states to develop their own policies concerning the eligibility of qualified immigrants.

Third, new "deeming" policies were put in place in 1996, stating that every new immigrant arriving in the United States must have a sponsor who will sign an affidavit of support. The sponsor's income and/or resources are typically included in determining the immigrant's eligibility for public assistance. In theory, sponsors can be sued if they fail to fulfill their pledge to support their immigrant family member. The 1996 reforms expanded

[3] In order to naturalize, an immigrant is required to reside in the United States for five years, to pass a civics test, and to be able to speak, read, write, and understand the English language. In addition, the Immigration and Naturalization Service (INS) reviews the naturalization applicant's history and method of immigration. If any irregularities appear, the individual may not only be denied naturalization but may face deportation. INS policy also requires an affirmative clearance from the Federal Bureau of Investigation before an individual can be sworn in as a citizen. Assuming that an immigrant is qualified for naturalization, the wait until citizenship is granted is likely to be a year or more (Mautino 1999).

the deeming provisions to more federal programs, including food stamps, public health insurance, SSI, and TANF cash assistance. Moreover, the term for which deeming applies was extended and remains in effect until the immigrant naturalizes or provides evidence of 10 years of employment in the United States. Finally, the 1996 legislation, through PRWORA and the 1996 Illegal Immigrant Reform and Immigrant Responsibility Act (IIRAIRA), increased state and local involvement in immigration law enforcement.

Importantly, the 1996 reforms limiting immigrant eligibility for government assistance were predicated on projected savings. According to one estimate, denial of benefits to noncitizens and newly arriving immigrant families was expected to result in 44 percent of the net savings of PRWORA (Congressional Budget Office 1996; Singer 2001).

Some of the most stringent repeals of assistance in the federal law were later reinstated, and others were mitigated by state policy options. The Balanced Budget Act of 1997 largely restored SSI and Medicaid eligibility to those preenactment immigrants who were receiving benefits prior to 1996 (even if they did not meet the new definition of a qualified individual), and the Agriculture Research, Extension and Education Reform Act of 1998 restored food stamp benefits to a small share of the 940,000 legal preenactment immigrants (primarily working-age adults) who lost benefits after 1996 (out of 1.4 million legal immigrants receiving food stamps in 1996; Carmody and Dean 1998). These limited restorations primarily benefited about 200,000 immigrant children, elderly people, and people with disabilities. At the state level, nearly every state has opted to provide Medicaid and TANF assistance to all preenactment legal immigrants, but there is wide state variation in the eligibility of postenactment immigrants. Out of the six states with the largest immigrant populations (California, New York, Texas, Florida, Illinois, and New Jersey), only California offers substitute programs in all three areas of health, nutrition, and cash assistance for postenactment immigrants (Weil and Finegold 2002).

B. Immigrants' Use of Public Assistance Before and After Welfare Reform

Historically, immigrant mothers have been less likely than U.S.-born mothers to receive TANF or food stamps or to have private health insurance (Fix and Passel 1999). However, given their disproportionately higher levels of need, immigrants made up an increasingly large percentage of the welfare caseload in the years leading up the 1996 reforms (Bean, Van Hook, and Glick 1997; Borjas and Hilton 1996).

The literature on changes in public assistance receipt pre- and postreform has primarily examined changes in the makeup of welfare caseloads, using standard difference-in-difference techniques. In general, these studies have suggested that noncitizens experience a greater decline in their use of Aid to Families of Dependent Children (AFDC)/TANF, SSI, Medicaid coverage, and General Assistance than citizens, even when immigrant families remain eligible for assistance (Bollinger and Hagstrom 2008; Borjas 2004; Fix and Haskins 2002; Fix and Passell 1999; Haider et al. 2004; Ku and Blaney 2000; Lurie 2005; Van Hook and Balistreri 2006). In other words, the differential drops in program use are surprising because they exceed the number expected to have been affected by (i.e., made ineligible by) the policy changes (Fix and Passel 1999). For example, between 1996 and 2001, noncitizen participation in TANF dropped from 12.3 percent to 8.0 percent, and from 7.1 percent to 3.7percent in the Food Stamp Program; Food Stamp participation by citizen children with a noncitizen parent dropped 75 percent between 1994 and 1998 (Fix and Passell 1999). Following PRWORA enactment, eligible children of immigrant noncitizens experienced more persistent and higher levels of food insecurity than the children of citizens, and this in part reflects their lower rates of food stamp receipt (Van Hook and Balistreri 2006).

In general, research has shown that welfare leavers are at high risk of having no health insurance (e.g., Garrett and Hudman 2002); this lack of coverage may be more pronounced among immigrant leavers than among native-born leavers. For example, it has long been recognized that, conditional on eligibility, immigrant families are less likely to receive Medicaid than native families (Currie 2000); in 2000, 25 percent of citizen children with noncitizen parents lacked health insurance compared to 17 percent of children with citizen parents (Lessard and Ku 2003). A significant decline in health insurance coverage as a result of welfare reform has also been documented for citizen children of foreign-born mothers in low-income immigrant families relative to citizen children with U.S.-born mothers (Chapter Six, this volume; Kaushal and Kaestner 2005). Lurie (2005) finds substantial declines in insurance coverage among the citizen children of nonpermanent residents (but not among the citizen children of permanent residents) between 1996 and 2001. This suggests that parents with more precarious immigration statuses may be the most reluctant to take up programs in the wake of welfare reform (i.e., it is likely that a large share of the nonpermanent residents are in fact undocumented), despite their children's eligibility. In 1997, Congress passed the State Children's Health Insurance Program (SCHIP), which increased funding over 10 years to expand health insurance coverage for children in poor and near-poor families. While data show some decline in the number of uninsured children, Latino children remain more likely than other children to be uninsured and face other barriers to entering the health care system (Holahan, Dubay, and Kenney 2003).

C. What Are the Effects on Children's Development?

Very few studies have examined directly what the reforms and subsequent patterns of welfare use have meant for immigrant children (Lichter and Jayakody 2002). The literature on welfare reform has suggested that, in general, welfare leaving has had few associations, positive or negative, with child well-being (Kalil and Dunifon 2007). However, such average effects mask substantial heterogeneity among low-income families (Chapter Seven, this volume). Leaving welfare and other programs has been viewed as an indicator of positive adjustment among immigrants (e.g., indicating the ability to integrate into the American economy: Borjas 1998, 1999; Camarota 2001). On the other hand, those concerned with chilling effects reason that immigrants who can continue to access public resources are better off than those otherwise eligible immigrants who do not.

How might welfare reform be differentially associated with child well-being for the children of immigrants versus natives? First, to the extent that the chilling effect is real, it is reasonable to assume that low-income immigrants make less use of programs for which they are eligible than do their native counterparts. Lack of knowledge about or reluctance to access public programs may limit access to important services, and this could adversely affect children's health and well-being. Such barriers to participation could stem from individuals' own beliefs and knowledge about services or could also arise from the proliferation of misinformation on the part of agency staff (Maloy et al. 2000).

Of course, any observed differences in children's health could be a result of selection. Low-income immigrants could differ from their native counterparts in myriad ways, both observed and unobserved. These differences could affect both the reasons, different types of parents use public programs and how they care for their children's health. For example, a parent who is disorganized, who cannot provide a safe home environment, or who suffers from her own physical or mental health difficulties may be less likely to seek out assistance for her children, and this could also be reflected in the children's poorer health. We will use the pre– and post–August 1996 distinction as a natural experiment to better understand the causal impact of welfare reform on the children of immigrants. In other words, if gaps in health between low-income immigrant children and low-income native children are significantly larger in the post–welfare reform period, this will give us more confidence that the policy has had an impact.

D. The Importance of Early Childhood

Our study will examine the health of children ages six and younger. We do this for two reasons. First, we cannot determine with absolute certainty in the SIPP whether all children of a foreign-born parent were born in the United States (and hence are U.S. citizens eligible for public programs). However, this is likely to be true 93 percent of the time for children of foreign-born parents in this age group (Capps, Fix, et al. 2003), giving us more confidence that we can identify chilling effects of welfare reform. Second, there is good reason to think that any deleterious effects of limited access to or take-up of public programs, especially if they correlate with economic hardship, will have more pronounced effects on the well-being of younger children (Chapter Seven, this volume; Duncan and Brooks-Gunn 1997). A substantial number of studies document that family economic hardship has relatively more deleterious effects on preschool-age children, especially in families with low incomes, than on those in middle childhood or adolescence (Duncan and Brooks-Gunn 1997). For young children of immigrants, a lack of connection to child care programs or school-based health services could also exacerbate problems accessing health services through government assistance programs; on average, young immigrant children are less likely to be enrolled in early education and after-school programs compared to their native counterparts (Nord and Griffin 1999; Takanishi 2004). Preschool-age children are also less verbal and may be less fluent in English than older children.

III. Data and Methods

Data are drawn from the 1993, 1996, and 2001 panels of the SIPP. The SIPP, which is conducted by the Census Bureau, is a nationally representative sample of households whose (noninstitutionalized) members are interviewed at four-month intervals (each interview is considered a survey wave).

Each survey wave, the core, collects information on demographic characteristics, labor force participation, program participation, amounts and types of earned and unearned income received, and private health insurance from each individual in the household over the age of 15 (adult population).

Other questions, collected as part of the topical modules, produce in-depth information on specific subjects and are asked less frequently. This study uses data from both the core as well as several topical modules.

The SIPP uses rotation groups to field the survey; these groups are random subsamples of the full survey population of approximately equal size. Each month, the members of one rotation group are interviewed; thus, over the course of four months, all rotation groups are interviewed. The 1993 panel (which comprises our prereform observations) was first administered in February 1993; thus, 25 percent of the respondents were interviewed in February, March, April, and May. The 1996 panel was first administered in April 1996 and the 2001 panel in February 2001 (these comprise our postreform observations). The sample for our study is limited to low-income households (less than 200 percent of the poverty threshold for the family size) where a child under the age of six resides. These restrictions are imposed so that we have a sample most likely to be affected by welfare reform, and also so that we are as likely as possible to have a sample of young children who were born in the United States (and thus are themselves citizens). Children are categorized according to the citizenship status of their parents. We allow children to be added to (born into) sample families within SIPP panels (these children are given the existing citizenship status of the family; defined later), and children may contribute multiple observations within panels if they meet the age and income criteria for multiple waves.

A. Dependent Variables

The mother assessed the health of each child within the household as excellent, very good, good, fair, or poor. In 1993 these questions were posed in Waves 6 and 9; in 1996 in Waves 3, 6, 9, and 12; and in 2001 in Waves 3, 6, and 9. Responses originally ranged from one to five, with a higher value indicating poorer health. This variable is recoded to indicate "poor health" in the regression analyses. Following Currie and Stabile (2004), if the mother stated that the child is in "good," "fair," or "poor"health, the child is coded as being in "poor" health.

The household reference person is asked about postponement of medical care at the household level. Specifically, he or she is asked if in the past 12 months there has been a time when someone in the household needed to see a doctor or go to the hospital but didn't go.[4] This question is asked once

---

[4] No information on why the visit was postponed is collected.

in each SIPP panel, specifically in Wave 9 of 1993, Wave 8 of 1996, and Wave 8 of 2001. This variable is a dichotomous variable representing whether or not someone in the household had to postpone medical care.

B. Independent Variables

Children's immigrant status is obtained via the parents in the Wave 2 Migration Topical Module for each panel. The Migration Module is administered to household members who are age 15 or older; thus, children are classified according to the status of their parents, specifically distinguishing between three groups: children who have native-born (citizen) parents, children whose parents are naturalized citizens, and children who have noncitizen parents.[5] Children who reside with only one parent are classified according to the citizenship status of the resident parent. The majority of nonresident parents are not interviewed, and thus their citizenship status is not known. Children who reside with two parents are classified according to the citizenship status of both parents in the following way: (1) if both parents have the same status, the child is classified that way; (2) if one parent is a naturalized citizen and the other parent is native-born, the child is classified as the child of naturalized citizen parents; and (3) if either parent is a noncitizen, the child is classified as the child of a nonnaturalized parent.

We control for three child demographic characteristics (age, gender, and race) and a measure of health insurance status in the children's health analyses. Age is measured as a continuous variable measured in years at the time of assessment. Gender is measured as a dichotomous variable (boy is omitted). Race is measured as four mutually exclusive variables: white, black, Hispanic, and other (white is omitted). Finally, whether or not the child was covered by public health insurance or private health insurance at the time of assessment is controlled (no insurance coverage is omitted).

We control for several demographic characteristics of these households in all analyses. First, the age of the mother measured is entered as a continuous variable. Second, we control for the educational attainment of the mother with three dichotomous variables: not a high school graduate, a high school graduate, and more than high school (high school graduate is omitted). The mother's employment is measured with three dichotomous variables representing her work status in the month the outcome is measured. Mothers

---

[5] Information on permanent resident status was not part of the Migration Module in the 1993 SIPP panel; thus, this distinction is only permitted in the 1996 and 2001 modules covering the post–welfare reform years 1997–2004. For this reason and because sample sizes are small, this distinction will not be made in the analysis.

are classified as being (1) out of the labor force (i.e., not working and no time on layoff or looking for work); (2) in the labor force with no periods of unemployment in that month; or (3) in the labor force with some periods of unemployment in that month. Finally, the mother's marital status is captured with four mutually exclusive dichotomous variables: married, widowed, divorced/separated, and never married (omitted).

Household composition is assessed with two different variables. The first measure is the total number of children under the age of 18 residing in the household. The second measure is the total number of adults residing in the household, which can include own children who are older than 18. We also control for home ownership (coded 1 if yes, 0 otherwise), and we control for the log of monthly household income averaged over the four months prior to the interview (in 2005 dollars). Finally, all analyses include the state-level unemployment for the year in which the interview was administered, state fixed effects, and year-of-interview fixed effects.

IV. Results

Table 9.1 presents the weighted means and standard deviations of all variables in the analysis for the total sample, as well as by citizenship status. On average, children in these families are three years of age, with equal numbers of boys and girls. Forty-six percent of the children are white, 22 percent are black, and 28 percent are Hispanic. Among the children of nonnaturalized immigrants, 56 percent are of Mexican descent (data not shown). In contrast, among the children of naturalized citizens, only 24 percent are of Mexican descent (data not shown). The majority of these low-income children are covered by some health insurance. On average mothers are 30 years old and have no more than a high school degree, do not work, are married, and do not reside in homes that are owned. The average monthly income for these families is $1,800 (in 2005 dollars).

A. Children's Health Outcomes

Table 9.1 also presents the prevalence of poor health among children and postponement of doctor and hospital care among families. Twenty percent of these low-income children are rated in poor health by their mothers. These statistics differ, depending on immigrant status: Children of nonnaturalized parents are more likely (24 percent) than children of both native ($p < .001$) and naturalized parents ($p < .05$) to be in poor health. Recall that our definition of poor health includes children rated by their mothers as

Table 9.1. *Weighted descriptive statistics of sample*

	Total sample		Native	
	Mean or %	SD	Mean or %	SD
Child Characteristics				
Age	3.11	1.94	3.04	1.95
Boy	50.71%	–	51.19%	–
Race				
White	45.71%	–	56.80%	–
Black	21.47%	–	27.68%	–
Hispanic	28.06%	–	12.77%	–
Other	4.76%	–	2.75%	–
Health Insurance				
Public	48.10%	–	48.40%	–
Private	30.83%	–	33.88%	–
No Coverage	21.07%	–	17.72%	–
Household Characteristics				
Mother's Age	30.38	6.60	29.88	6.66
Mother's Educational Attainment				
No High School	30.77%	–	22.69%	–
High School Only	35.31%	–	38.87%	–
More Than High School	33.92%	–	38.45%	–
Mother's Work Status				
Works	37.79%	–	41.80%	–
Spent Some Time Unemployed	7.19%	–	7.64%	–
Out of the Labor Force	55.02%	–	50.56%	–
Mother's Marital Status				
Married	60.91%	–	54.74%	–
Divorced/Separated	0.72%	–	0.81%	–
Widowed	13.50%	–	14.92%	–
Never Married	24.87%	–	29.54%	–
Mother's Health Insurance				
Public	34.69%	–	36.52%	–

(continued)

Table 9.1. *Continued*

	Total sample		Native	
	Mean or %	SD	Mean or %	SD
Private	34.49%	–	37.83%	–
No Coverage	30.82%	–	25.65%	–
Number of Children < 18	2.60	1.52	2.57	1.56
Number of Adults	2.22	1.09	2.12	1.05
Own Home	42.53%	–	44.43%	–
Monthly Income	1,794.32	1,032.25	1,760.91	1,029.80
Median Monthly Income	1,758.31	–	1,731.34	–
State-Level Unemployment Rate	5.28	1.11	5.14	1.10
Health Outcomes				
Poor Health	20.31%	–	19.23%	–
Postponed Medical Care	10.98%	–	10.76%	–
Unweighted Person-Years	13,350		9,935	
Unweighted Persons	8,344		6,329	

	Naturalized		Not naturalized	
	Mean or %	SD	Mean or %	SD
Child Characteristics				
Age	3.33	1.94	3.28	1.89
Boy	47.06%	–	49.82%	–
Race				
White	28.85%	–	12.99%	–
Black	5.76%	–	4.22%	–
Hispanic	42.87%	–	74.54%	–
Other	22.51%	–	8.24%	–
Health Insurance				
Public	32.21%	–	49.81%	–
Private	37.12%	–	20.01%	–
No Coverage	30.67%	–	30.18%	–

Table 9.1. *Continued*

	Naturalized		Not naturalized	
	Mean or %	SD	Mean or %	SD
Household Characteristics				
Mother's Age	33.92	5.83	31.42	6.24
Mother's Educational Attainment				
No High School	33.08%	–	56.28%	–
High School Only	31.53%	–	24.53%	–
More Than High School	35.40%	–	19.20%	–
Mother's Work Status				
Works	37.25%	–	25.01%	–
Spent Some Time Unemployed	4.44%	–	6.24%	–
Out of the Labor Force	58.31%	–	68.75%	–
Mother's Marital Status				
Married	78.13%	–	77.80%	–
Divorced/Separated	0.12%	–	0.54%	–
Widowed	13.55%	–	8.96%	–
Never Married	8.19%	–	12.70%	–
Mother's Health Insurance				
Public	20.83%	–	31.17%	–
Private	43.40%	–	22.30%	–
No Coverage	35.77%	–	46.53%	–
Number of Children < 18	2.67	1.45	2.69	1.37
Number of Adults	2.57	1.14	2.48	1.13
Own Home	52.60%	–	34.78%	–
Monthly Income	1,901.79	1,157.97	1,883.36	1,011.43
Median Monthly Income	1,856.41	–	1,836.84	–
State-Level Unemployment Rate	5.64	1.08	5.68	1.05
Health Outcomes				
Poor Health	19.97%	–	23.79%	–
Postponed Medical Care	7.22%	–	12.50%	–
Unweighted Person-Years	*491*		*2,924*	
Unweighted Persons	*301*		*1,714*	

being in good, fair, or poor health. In actuality, very few children are rated as being in poor health (1 percent or less in each of the three groups; data not shown) or even in fair health (3 percent or less across groups; data not shown). Thus, our measure should be thought of as distinguishing children who are only in good health from those who are in very good or excellent health. Approximately 11 percent of families postponed medical care; for natives, naturalized citizens, and nonnaturalized citizens these figures are 11, 7, and 13 percent, respectively, on average across time.

Table 9.2 presents the weighted descriptive statistics for several control variables as well as the weighted proportions of the two outcome measures and a selected number of the control variables by citizen status and whether or not the child was assessed before or after welfare reform. There are several interesting differences to note. In the postreform period, fewer native mothers have less than a high school education ($p < .001$) and more have postsecondary education ($p < .001$). In contrast, immigrants (naturalized and nonnaturalized) in the postreform period are slightly less educated than their prereform counterparts (naturalized immigrants are more likely to have high school only [$p < .05$] and less likely to have some college [$p < .05$]; nonnaturalized immigrants are less likely to have some college [$p < .01$]). Postreform, native mothers are more likely to work ($p < .001$), but the same is not true of immigrant mothers. Immigrant mothers are more likely to be married in the postreform era than their counterparts in the prereform era ($p < .05$ for naturalized citizens and $p < .001$ for nonnaturalized citizens).

Nonnaturalized immigrant children, on average, are in worse health following welfare reform ($p < .02$), whereas native children are in better health ($p < .05$). Regarding the former, descriptive differences (not reported in the tables) suggest that the declines in children's health are being driven by fewer children being reported as in excellent health and instead being reported merely as in good health (data not shown). In other words, we do not see a large increase in the number of nonnaturalized immigrant children who are reported to be in fair or poor health on the original 5-point scale. Naturalized as well as nonnaturalized immigrant families are more likely to postpone medical care following welfare reform compared to similar naturalized ($p < .10$) and nonnaturalized ($p < .02$) immigrants before welfare reform.

Figure 9.1 presents the weighted proportions of children in poor health by immigrant status over time, and Figure 9.2 presents the weighted proportion of households where the reference person reported that someone postponed medical care by immigrant status over time.[6] Both figures suggest

---

[6] The 0 percent in the naturalized citizen group is a result of no postponement in this group in very small cell sizes.

Table 9.2. *Outcome variables and selected controls by immigrant status and time (weighted)*

| | Pre–welfare reform | | |
	Native	Naturalized	Not naturalized
Control Variables			
Mother's Educational Attainment			
No High School	28.11%	33.07%	52.68%
High School Only	38.98%	22.53%	22.86%
More Than High School	32.91%	44.40%	24.46%
Mother's Work Status			
Works	33.52%	40.36%	25.25%
Spent Some Time Unemployed	6.89%	0.00%	5.00%
Out of the Labor Force	59.59%	59.64%	69.75%
Mother's Marital Status			
Married	55.53%	70.01%	71.03%
Divorced/Separated	1.08%	0.00%	0.40%
Widowed	19.92%	20.15%	10.04%
Never Married	23.47%	9.84%	18.52%
Monthly Income	1503.48	1731.28	1693.93
Child's Health Insurance Coverage			
Public	54.30%	30.72%	54.20%
Private	27.61%	33.90%	18.59%
No Coverage	18.09%	35.38%	27.21%
Outcomes			
Health Status (Continuous Measure)	1.78	1.76	1.77
Poor Health	21.08%	16.00%	19.34%
Postpone Medical Care	13.70%	0.00%	5.70%
	Post–Welfare Reform		
	Native	Naturalized	Not naturalized
Control Variables			
Mother's Educational Attainment			
No High School	21.53%	33.08%	56.95%

(*continued*)

Table 9.2. *Continued*

	Post–welfare reform		
	Native	Naturalized	Not naturalized
High School Only	38.84%	34.00%	24.84%
More Than High School	39.63%	32.92%	18.21%
Mother's Work Status			
Works	43.57%	36.39%	24.97%
Spent Some Time Unemployed	7.79%	5.66%	6.47%
Out of the Labor Force	48.64%	57.95%	68.56%
Mother's Marital Status			
Married	54.57%	80.37%	79.07%
Divorced/Separated	0.75%	0.16%	0.56%
Widowed	13.85%	11.74%	8.76%
Never Married	30.83%	7.74%	11.61%
Monthly Income	1815.82	1948.66	1918.74
Child's Health Insurance Coverage			
Public	47.15%	32.62%	48.99%
Private	35.22%	38.00%	20.28%
No Coverage	17.63	29.38	30.73
Outcomes			
Health Status (Continuous Measure)	1.71	1.73	1.87
Poor Health	18.84%	21.06%	24.63%
Postpone Medical Care	10.00%	9.30%	14.08%

that nonnaturalized children and families have experienced increases in poor health and medical care postponement over the study period compared to native children and families.

B. Regression Analyses

Two separate regression models will be estimated for both of the health outcomes, (1) designed to understand basic differences in children's health between low-income children of immigrants and natives and (2) designed

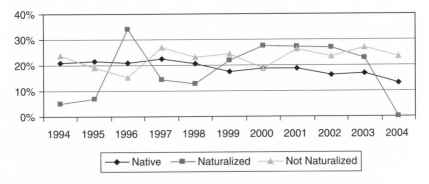

Figure 9.1. Percent of Children in Poor Health by Immigrant Status

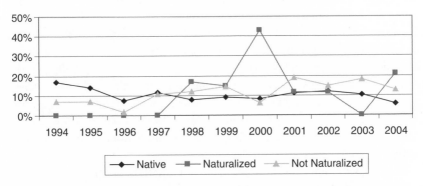

Figure 9.2. Percent of Households That Postponed Medical Care by Immigrant Status

to examine whether differences in children's health are more pronounced after enactment of PRWORA. First, regression models will be estimated to determine if low-income children of immigrants have different health outcomes than low-income children of natives. Specifically, we estimate the following equation:

$$h = \gamma_s + \delta_y + a_1 + a_2 Natural + a_3 NotNatural + a_j X + \varepsilon \qquad (1)$$

where h is the children's health outcome, γ denotes a set of state fixed effects, δ denotes a set of year fixed effects, *Natural* equals 1 if the child's parents are naturalized citizens, *NotNatural* equals 1 if the child's parents are nonnaturalized citizens (natives are the omitted group), X is a vector of demographic characteristics of the child and the household, a are the estimated coefficients, and ε is the error term.

Second, we use a difference-in-difference strategy to estimate the effect of welfare reform on children's health, specifically examining whether or not assessment prior to welfare reform and after welfare reform and citizenship status of the child's parents are associated with differences in health. Specifically, we will estimate the following equation:

$$h = \gamma_s + \delta_y + b_1 + b_2 Post + b_3 Natural + b_4 NotNatural + b_5 Post *$$
$$Natural + b_6 Post * NotNatural + b_j X + u \qquad (2)$$

Post equals 1 if the child's assessment occurred following welfare reform, and the other variables are defined as in equation (1). These models will be estimated using ordinary least squares (OLS), and the coefficients of interest are b_5 and b_6, which indicate whether the difference in the health outcome being measured for children with naturalized or nonnaturalized parents between children assessed before and after welfare reform is significantly different from the health outcomes among the children with native parents. Specifically, b_6 estimates $\{(h_{Post,NotNatural} - h_{Post,Native}) - (h_{Pre,NotNatural} - h_{Pre,Native})\}$, indicating the change in children's health due to welfare reform policies assuming that health did not change at different rates for other reasons.[7] In all regressions, we correct for the nonindependence of observations due to the presence of siblings and to children's contributing multiple observations within a panel.

Table 9.3 presents the findings from the analysis of children's health. Findings from Model 1 suggest that several characteristics are associated with children's poor health. White children are least likely to be reported as being in poor health. Children who are covered by public health insurance are 8 percentage points more likely to be in poor health than children who are uninsured, which possibly reflects that parents are more likely to obtain health insurance coverage for sick children or that there is adverse selection into public health insurance. Compared to children whose mothers are high school graduates, those whose mothers have less than a high school education are in poorer health and those whose mothers have more than a high school diploma are less likely to be in poor health. Mothers who are

---

[7] The difference-in-difference estimate may also be biased if the parallel trend assumption is violated. This may be particularly problematic among the naturalized citizen group, whose population may have been changing over this time period as a result of shifts in naturalization. Indeed, visual inspection of Figures 9.1 and 9.2 suggests that there were differences in the trends among naturalized citizens prior to welfare reform and that any significant differences found should be interpreted with caution.

Table 9.3. *Regression results: Child poor health (n = 13,350)*

	Model 1		Model 2	
	B	SE B	B	SE B
Child Characteristics				
Age	0.00	0.00	0.00	0.00
Boy	0.01	0.01	0.01	0.01
Black	0.05***	0.01	0.05***	0.01
Hispanic	0.04**	0.01	0.04**	0.01
Other	0.06*	0.02	0.06**	0.02
Covered by Public Health Insurance	0.08***	0.01	0.08***	0.01
Covered by Private Health Insurance	−0.01	0.01	−0.01	0.01
Household Characteristics				
Mother's Age	0.00**	0.00	0.00**	0.00
Mother No High School	0.03**	0.01	0.03**	0.01
Mother More Than High School	−0.03**	0.01	−0.03**	0.01
Mother Works	−0.01	0.01	−0.01	0.01
Mother Unemployed Part of Month	−0.01	0.02	−0.01	0.02
Mother Married	−0.01	0.01	−0.01	0.01
Mother Divorced/Separated	0.03*	0.02	0.03*	0.02
Mother Widowed	−0.04	0.04	−0.04	0.04
Number of Children < 18	0.00	0.00	0.00	0.00
Number of Adults	0.00	0.00	0.00	0.00
Own Home	−0.01	0.01	−0.01	0.01
Log Monthly Income	0.00	0.00	0.00	0.00
State-Level Unemployment Rate	−0.01	0.01	−0.01	0.01
Immigrant Status				
Naturalized Citizen	0.01	0.02	−0.04	0.04
Not Naturalized Citizen	0.02	0.01	−0.04	0.03
Difference-in-Difference				
Post–Welfare Reform	–	–	−0.04	0.03
Naturalized * Post–Welfare Reform	–	–	0.06	0.05

(continued)

Table 9.3. *Continued*

	Model 1		Model 2	
	B	SE B	B	SE B
Not Naturalized * Post–Welfare Reform	–	–	0.06*	0.03
Constant	0.01	0.11	0.04	0.10
F-Test	6.99***		6.84***	
R-square	0.05		0.05	

Note: Standard errors are adjusted for individuals contributing more than one observation to the analysis. All models also include state and year fixed effects. Regressions are weighted. $*p < .05$; $**p < .01$; $***p < .001$.

divorced or separated are more likely to report their children as being in poor health compared to mothers who have never married.

Model 2 presents the estimation from the difference-in-difference analyses, and the demographic findings reported from Model 1 are also significant in Model 2. Moreover, the interaction term between nonnaturalized citizen and the post–welfare reform period indicates that the probability of poor health is greater among children of nonnaturalized citizens compared to children of natives after welfare reform than it was in the prereform period. The gap between children of nonnaturalized citizens and children of natives in the post–welfare reform period is 6 percentage points larger than the prereform gap, or one-third larger than the baseline. The gap between children of naturalized citizens and children of natives in the postreform period is similar in magnitude, but it is measured imprecisely and is not statistically significant.

The pattern of results is similar if we use the original 5-point measure of child health as the outcome variable in a linear regression. Specifically, the interaction between nonnaturalized citizen and the post–welfare reform period is positive (recall that higher scores on the measure indicate worse health) and statistically significant ($p < .03$), whereas the interaction between naturalized citizen and the post–welfare reform period is not (results not shown).

Table 9.4 presents findings from the regression estimating equations (1) and (2) for household medical care postponement. Because this outcome is only available once in each panel and is only reported at the household level, it is conducted on individual households and does not control

Table 9.4. *Regression results: Household postponed medical care (n = 3,349)*

	Model 1		Model 2	
	B	SE B	B	SE B
Household Characteristics				
Mother's Age	0.00	1.62	0.00	0.00
Mother No High School	0.01	0.01	0.01	0.01
Mother More Than High School	−0.01	0.01	−0.01	0.01
Mother Works	0.01	0.01	0.01	0.01
Mother Unemployed Part of the Month	0.06*	0.02	0.06	0.02
Mother Married	0.01	0.02	0.01	0.02
Mother Divorced/Separated	0.00	0.02	0.00	0.02
Mother Widowed	0.10	0.06	0.09	0.06
Mother Covered by Public Health Insurance	−0.05**	0.02	−0.05	0.02
Mother Covered by Private Health Insurance	−0.09***	0.01	−0.09***	0.01
Number of Children < 18	0.00	0.00	0.00	0.00
Number of Adults	0.00	0.01	0.00	0.01
Own Home	−0.01	0.01	−0.01	0.01
Log Monthly Income	0.00	0.00	0.00	0.00
State-Level Unemployment Rate	−0.01	0.01	0.00	0.01
Immigrant Status				
Naturalized Citizen	−0.03	0.03	−0.12*	0.06
Not Naturalized Citizen	0.01	0.02	−0.07*	0.03
Difference-in-Difference				
Post–Welfare Reform	–	–	−0.01	0.04
Naturalized * Post–Welfare Reform	–	–	0.12	0.07
Not Naturalized * Post–Welfare Reform	–	–	0.09**	0.03
Constant	0.38**	0.14	0.37**	0.14
F-Test	2.29***		2.36***	
R-square	0.05		0.05	

Note: All models also include state and year fixed effects. *$p < .05$; **$p < .01$; ***$p < .001$.

for children's characteristics, but only for the mother's and household's characteristics. Results from Model 1 indicate that health insurance coverage is associated with a lower probability of postponement of medical care and that maternal unemployment is associated with a higher probability of postponement. Model 1 suggests that there are no significant differences, on average, in postponement of care depending on immigrant status.

The results in Model 2 show that there is no average impact of welfare reform on the likelihood of households' postponing needed medical care. Model 2, however, illustrates that whereas both naturalized and nonnaturalized citizens' households were much less likely to postpone medical care than the households of natives in the prereform period (recall, for example, the results shown in Table 9.2 indicating that in the prereform period, no naturalized citizen families postponed needed care), this pattern reverses after welfare reform. Nonnaturalized citizens' households increased postponement of necessary medical care by about 9 percentage points relative to natives following welfare reform. Naturalized citizens' households increased postponement of necessary medical care by an even greater amount, but this effect is measured imprecisely and is not statistically significant. That said, the effect size is quite large, and the lack of statistical significance is not surprising given the small samples.

V. Discussion

Immigrants, especially those from Mexico and other Latin American countries, often arrive in the United States with low levels of financial and human capital. At the same time, they tend to exhibit family forms (such as two-parent married household structures) and cultural values that may promote children's well-being. It has been suggested that public assistance is a potentially important form of investment for immigrant parents in building their children's human capital (Balistreri 2006; Hofferth 1999). The current policy environment, however, operates to restrict immigrants' access to federal health and welfare programs, particularly during their initial period of settlement in this country.

Over the past decade, the general policy conversation surrounding welfare has shifted from supports for unemployed parents to supports for low-income working parents. Immigrant families make up a substantial proportion of the working poor, and children in immigrant families in general face more challenges to healthy development than their native counterparts. Reforms enacted during the mid-1990s served to exclude many immigrant families from the supports that low-income families often rely on to care adequately for their children, and there are suggestions in the literature that policy reforms may have created additional barriers for families attempting to gain access to the resources they need, even when they remain eligible for such programs.

In line with prior work showing a greater decline in receipt of public programs over the period of welfare reform for immigrants versus natives, we found that the gap between the children of low-income noncitizens and the children of low-income natives in terms of children's health and family's access to care widened from the pre– to the post–welfare reform period. The effects were sizable. For example, a widening gap of 6 percentage points in children's poor health between the two groups over the period is meaningful when the average rate of poor health in the total low-income sample is about 20 percent.

Our regressions control for family income, wealth (in terms of home ownership), maternal employment, and health insurance. Thus, the differences in use of care and in children's health are not due to important average economic differences between the groups in the postreform period. Our results are therefore consistent with the hypothesis that families with noncitizen members face barriers, real or perceived, to using relevant programs in the wake of welfare reform. Moreover, we also see substantial increases in the number of children of naturalized citizens in poor health and in the number of naturalized citizen families who postponed medical care in the postreform period, although these estimates are noisier due to the smaller sample size. These results are consistent with those of Ham et al. (Chapter Six, this volume), who show a sizable reduction in Medicaid coverage among less-educated Hispanic immigrants in the postreform era. These authors also suggest that their results support the notion of a chilling effect.

We can only speculate why immigrant families with noncitizen parents might be more reluctant, or less able, to access relevant programs. Parents who are not citizens may not be aware of their U.S.-born children's eligibility for important benefits. It could also be that this group contains an over-representation of undocumented parents or family members, in which case fears of the Immigration and Naturalization Service could be a factor. Other studies suggest that immigrant parents may believe that seeking assistance for their eligible children will jeopardize their children's citizenship status or hinder other family members' efforts to obtain citizenship or legal status or their ability to reenter and stay in the United States (Capps 2001; Fix and Passel 1999; Maloy et al. 2000; Yoshikawa et al. 2005). One survey of low-income immigrants in New York City and Los Angeles in 1999–2000 found that half of the respondents answered two-thirds or more of the questions about eligibility incorrectly (Capps, Ku, and Fix 2002).

Other research suggests that some immigrants believe that receipt of benefits will result in their being labeled a "public charge" and prevent them from obtaining a green card, reentering the country, or reuniting with relatives. Some local area studies indicate that some immigration lawyers continue to advise their clients not to use public benefits to avoid this concern (Capps, Koralek, et al. 2004). In actuality, the specifics of the policy make it very unlikely that receipt of public benefits would affect an individual's ability to gain citizenship or act as a sponsor for new immigrants (National Immigration Law Center 1999).

Additional issues noted elsewhere include a lack of linguistically and culturally competent health care providers and a lack of outreach efforts to enroll eligible children and families in public health programs (Flores et al. 2002; Yu et al. 2005). There are many reasons to believe that the long-recognized barriers to immigrants' participation in public programs may be exacerbated in the post–welfare reform era, which have created misinformation, reluctance, and fear among some immigrants to use such programs.

Although we controlled for families' economic status, on average, the possibility exists that welfare reform affected families' work effort, income, and household configurations differently across different types of families. For example, welfare reform and its work requirements may be more of a perturbation of the family system to Latina mothers, who historically have cared for children at home and have not worked in the formal labor market. If the time costs imposed by maternal employment are especially detrimental in these families, this could explain the differences in the worsening of children's health between low-income children of noncitizens and natives over time. In this case, one might want to test three-way interactions between welfare reform, immigrant group, and maternal work effort. Unfortunately, our sample size cannot not support these tests, but an inspection of Table 9.2 reveals few differences in key variables across groups in the two time periods. For example, the work effort of noncitizen mothers changed very little across the period (whereas the work effort of native mothers increased). Still, there are many other dimensions of family life (including all aspects of the putative chilling effect) that are unobserved by us and could explain the differences we see here. One might also want to know if these results differ for those who live in states that have been more or less generous in their treatment of immigrants after reform, as those state efforts might spill over into their general treatment and outreach to the broader immigrant population.

It is also possible that these results reflect not a chilling effect of welfare reform, but rather a widening of the gap in children's health if new programs (such as SCHIP and Medicaid expansions) that were implemented in the late 1990s had differential impacts on young children in citizen versus immigrant households. For example, differences in outreach efforts could have resulted in these programs' reaching more native than immigrant families and better mitigating any declines in native children's health. Even if this were the case, however, it does not rule out the fact that immigrant families were more reluctant to access these programs in the wake of welfare reform.

VI. Conclusion

Notably, the sample of immigrant families participating in this study is likely to be relatively advantaged compared to more recently arrived immigrant groups. Given the likely citizenship status of their children, their eligibility for assistance would not have been affected in real terms by the welfare reforms.

Newly arrived families in the United States face many challenges, often navigating linguistic and cultural differences, the hazards of the low-wage labor market, and great financial hardship. Our results provide some evidence that young immigrant children may pay a price in a policy environment where some parents are barred from receiving assistance and many parents are worried about the consequences of using assistance to which they are entitled. This raises concerns about putting families in a vulnerable position during children's formative years and about the spillover effects of poor health in early life on subsequent steps in healthy development, such as school readiness (Currie 2005). Immigrants who have arrived since 1996 are barred from receiving federal assistance for at least their first five years in this country in many states. As the number of postreform immigrants quickly approaches the number of prereform immigrants, it is critical that more be known about how children in these families have fared.

If the particular barriers to immigrants' use of programs and support services can be identified, there may be a role for public policy to intervene. It may be necessary to develop or refine culturally sensitive outreach programs or develop other mechanisms that provide accurate information, encouragement, and assistance to help all families receive the support they need to ensure their children's healthy development.

References

Balistreri, Kelly S. 2006. "Welfare and the Children of Immigrants: Transmission of Dependence or Investment in the Future." Paper presented at the annual meetings of the Population Association of American.

Bean, Frank D., Jennifer Van Hook, and Jennifer E. Glick.1997. "Country of Origin, Type of Public Assistance, and Patterns of Welfare Recipiency among U.S. Immigrants and Natives." *Social Science Quarterly*, 78:432–451.

Bollinger, Christopher, and Paul Hagstrom. 2008. "Food Stamp Program Participation of Refugees and Immigrants." *Southern Economic Journal*, 74:665–692.

Borjas, George J. 1998. "Immigration and Welfare: A Review of the Evidence," in *The Debate in the United States Over Immigration*. Peter J. Duignan and L. H. Gann, eds. Stanford, CA: Hoover Institution Press, 121–144.

1999. "Immigration and Welfare Magnets." *Journal of Labor Economics*, 17:604–637.

2004. "Food Insecurity and Public Assistance." *Journal of Public Economics*, 88:1421–1443.

Borjas, George J., and Lynette Hilton. 1996. "Immigration and the Welfare State: Immigrant Participation in Means-Tested Entitlement Programs." *Quarterly Journal of Economics*, 111:575–604.

Camarota, Steven A. 2001. *Immigrants in the United States—2000: A Snapshot of America's Foreign-Born Population*. Washington, DC: Center for Immigration Studies.

Capps, Randy. 2001. *Hardship Among Children of Immigrants: Findings from the 1999 National Survey of America's Families, Series B, No. B-29*. Washington, DC: Urban Institute.

Capps, Randy, Michael Fix, Jeffrey S. Passel, Jason Ost, and Dan Perez-Lopez. 2003. *A Profile of the Low-Wage Immigrant Workforce*. Washington DC: Urban Institute.

Capps, Randy, Michael Fix, Jason Ost, Jane Reardon-Anderson, and Jeffrey S. Passel. 2004. *The Health and Well-Being of Young Children of Immigrants*. Washington, DC: Urban Institute.

Capps, Randy, Robin Koralek, Katherine Lotspeich, Michael Fix, Pamela Holcomb, and Jane Reardon-Anderson. 2004. *Assessing Implementation of the 2002 Farm Bill's Legal Immigrant Food Stamps Restorations*. Washington, DC: Urban Institute.

Capps, Randy, Leighton Ku, and Michael Fix. 2002. *How Immigrants Are Faring: Preliminary Evidence from Los Angeles and New York City*. Washington, DC: Urban Institute.

Carmody, Kelly, and Stacy Dean. 1998. *New Federal Food Stamp Restoration for Legal Immigrants: Implications and Implementation Issues*. Washington, DC: Center on Budget and Policy Priorities.

Congressional Budget Office. 1996. *Federal Budgetary Implications of the Personal Responsibility and Work Opportunity Reconciliation Act of 1996*. Washington, DC. Available at http://www.cbo.gov/gtpdocs/46xx/doc4664/1996Doc32.pdf.

Currie, Janet. 2000. "Do Children of Immigrants Make Different Use of Public Health Insurance?" in *Issues in the Economics of Immigration*. George J. Borjas, ed. Chicago: University of Chicago Press, 271–308.

2005. "Health Disparities and Gaps in School Readiness." *The Future of Children*, 15:117–138.

Currie, Janet, and Mark Stabile. 2004. "Socioeconomic Status and Health: Why Is the Relationship Stronger for Older Children?" *American Economic Review*, 93: 1813–1823.

Duncan, Greg J., and Jeanne Brooks-Gunn. 1997. *Consequences of Growing Up Poor*. New York: Russell Sage.

Fix, Michael and Haskins, Ron. 2002. *Welfare benefits for non-citizens.* Welfare reform and beyond. Policy Brief No. 15. Washington, D.C.: The Brookings Institution.

Fix, Michael, and Jeffrey S. Passel. 1999. *Trends in Noncitizens' and Citizens' Use of Public Benefits Following Welfare Reform.* Urban Institute Research Report. Washington, DC: The Urban Institute.

Fix, Michael, Wendy Zimmerman, and Jeffrey S. Passel. 2001. *The Integration of Immigrant Families in the United States.* Washington, DC: Urban Institute. Available at http://www.urban.org/UploadedPDF/immig_integration.pdf.

Flores, Glenn, Elena Fuentes-Afflick, Oxiris Barbot, Olivia Carter-Pokras, Luz Claudio, Mariaelena, Lara, Jennie A. McLaurin, Lee Pachter, Francisco Ramos Gomez, Fernando Mendoza, R. Burciaga Valdez, Antonia M. Villarruel, Ruth E. Zambrana, Robert Greenberg, and Michael Weitzman. 2002. "The Health of Latino Children: Urgent Priorities, Unanswered Questions, and a Research Agenda." *Journal of the American Medical Association,* 288:82–90.

Garrett, Bowen, and Julie Hudman. 2002. *Women Who Left Welfare: Health Care Coverage, Access and Use of Health Services.* Washington, DC: Kaiser Commission on Medicaid and the Uninsured. Available at http://www.kff.org/content/2002/4050/4050.pdf.

Haider, Steven, Robert F. Schoeni, Yuhua Bao, and Caroline Danielson. 2004. "Immigrants, Welfare Reform, and the Economy." *Journal of Policy Analysis and Management,* 23:745–764.

Hernandez, Donald J. 2004. "Demographic Change and the Life Circumstances of Immigrant Families." *The Future of Children,* 14:17–47.

Hofferth, Sandra L. 1999. "Receipt of Public Assistance by Mexican American and Cuban American Children in Native and Immigrant Families," in *Children of Immigrants: Health, Adjustment and Public Assistance.* Donald J. Hernandez, ed. Washington, DC: National Academies Press, 546–583.

Holahan, John, Lisa Dubay, and Genevieve M. Kenney. 2003. "Which Children Are Still Uninsured and Why." *The Future of Children,* 13:55–79.

Kaestner, Robert, and Neeraj Kaushal. 2005. "Welfare Reform and Health Insurance Coverage of Low-Income Families." *Journal of Health Economics,* 22:959–981.

Kalil, Ariel, and Danielle Crosby. 2006. "*Welfare Leaving and Health Trajectories Among the Children of Immigrants and Natives."* Paper presented at the annual meeting of the Population Association of America, Los Angeles.

Kalil, Ariel, and Rachel E. Dunifon. 2007. "Maternal Work and Welfare Use and Child Well-Being: Evidence from Six Years of Data from the Women's Employment Study." *Children and Youth Services Review,* 29:742–761.

Kaushal, Neeraj, and Robert Kaestner. 2005. "Welfare Reform and Health Insurance of Immigrants." *Health Services Research,* 40:697–722.

———. 2007. "Welfare Reform and Health of Immigrant Women and Their Children." *Journal of Immigrant Health,* 9:61–74.

Ku, Leighton, and Shannon Blaney. 2000. *Health Coverage for Legal Immigrant Children: New Census Data Highlight Importance of Restoring Medicaid and SCHIP Coverage.* Washington, DC: Center on Budget and Policy Priorities.

Lessard, Gabrielle, and Leighton Ku. 2003. "Gaps in Coverage for Children in Immigrant Families." *The Future of Children,* 13:100–115.

Lichter, Daniel T., and Rukamalie Jayakody. 2002. "Welfare Reform: How Do We Measure Success?" *Annual Review of Sociology*, 28:117–141.

Lurie, Ithai. 2005. "*Welfare Reform and the Loss of Health Insurance Coverage by Children of Immigrants*." Unpublished paper, Institute for Healthcare Studies, Northwestern University.

Maloy, Kathleen, Julie Darnell, Lea Nolan, Kyle A. Kenney, and Soeurette Cyprien. 2000. *Effect of the 1996 Welfare and Immigration Reform Laws on Immigrants' Ability and Willingness to Access Medicaid and Health Care Services: Findings from Four Metropolitan Sites*. Washington, DC: George Washington University, Center for Health Services Research and Policy.

Mautino, Kathrin S. 1999. "Welfare Reform—What Does It Do?" *Journal of Immigrant Health*, 1:3–7.

National Immigration Law Center. 1999. "Immigrant Eligibility for Public Benefits." Available at http://www.nilc.org/immspbs/special/imm_elig_for_pub_bens_aila_0305.pdf.

Nord, Christine W., and James A. Griffin. 1999. "Educational Profile of 3- to 8-Year Old Children of Immigrants," in *Children of Immigrants: Health, Adjustment, and Public Assistance*. D. Hernandez, ed. Washington, DC: National Academies Press, 348–409.

Singer, Audrey. 2001. "Living with Uncertainty: Welfare Reform and Latin American Immigrants in New York and Los Angeles." *Research Perspectives on Migration*, 3:21–22.

Takanishi, Ruby. 2004. *Leveling the Playing Field: Supporting Immigrant Children from Birth to Eight*. New York: Foundation for Child Development. Available at http://fcd-us.org/uploadDocs/RTPackard06_11_04.pdf.

Van Hook, Jennifer, and Kelly S. Balistreri. 2006. "Ineligible Parents, Eligible Children: Food Stamps Receipt, Allotments, and Food Insecurity among Children of Immigrants." *Social Science Research*, 35:228–251.

Weil, Alan, and Kenneth Feingold. 2002. *Welfare Reform: The Next Act*. Washington, DC: Urban Institute Press.

Yoshikawa, Hirokazu, Julieta Lugo-Gil, Ajay Chaudry, and Catherine Tamis-LeMonda. 2005. "*How Lower Income Immigrant Parents in New York City Learn about and Navigate U.S. Programs and Policies for Families and Children*." Paper presented at the biennial conference of the Society for Research in Child Development, Atlanta, GA.

Yu, Stella M., Zhihuan J. Huang, Renee H. Schwalberg, and Michael D. Kogan. 2005. "Parental Awareness of Health and Community Resources among Immigrant Families." *Maternal and Child Health Journal*, 9:27–34.

Zimmerman, Wendy, and Karen C. Tumlin. 1999. "*Patchwork Policies: State Assistance for Immigrants Under Welfare Reform*." Occasional Paper Number 24. Washington, DC: Urban Institute.

TEN

Mismatches and Unmet Need

Access to Social Services in Urban and Rural America

Scott W. Allard

I. Introduction

How do society and our communities assist low-income populations? Typically, welfare cash assistance, food stamps, Medicaid, and the Earned Income Tax Credit (EITC) are identified as primary sources of support for poor populations. These prominent antipoverty programs, however, are only a part of how society and communities help low-income populations. Social services that promote work activity and greater personal well-being (e.g., job training, adult education, child care, substance abuse or mental health services, temporary emergency assistance) have become primary methods for assisting low-income families. Whereas annual governmental spending on welfare cash assistance totals about $11 billion, government expenditures for just a limited number of job training and social service programs are about $34 billion each year (in $2006). If we include a host of mental health, substance abuse, emergency assistance, and housing programs, social service programs receive more than $100 billion in public funding each year—a far greater share of governmental safety net expenditures than many scholars and policymakers recognize (Allard 2009; Congressional Research Services 2003).

Social service programs have steadily expanded in the past several decades to address low-income workers' struggles with persistent human capital, physical health, mental health, child care, or transportation barriers

This project was supported by research grants from the Brookings Institution, Brown University, the Department of Housing and Urban Development (HUD), the University of Kentucky Center for Poverty Research, and the Rural Poverty Research Center, and by support from the Institute for Research on Poverty at the University of Wisconsin-Madison and the Institute for Policy Research at Northwestern University. The author thanks Donna Pavetti for comments on a previous draft.

to employment. For example, about 40 percent of the women receiving welfare in 2002 experienced multiple barriers to employment including low educational attainment, physical health problems, a child with a disability, and mental health problems (Zedlewski 2003). Given such needs, it is not surprising that many poor households draw assistance from social service agencies at some point. A 2006 study of low-income populations in and around Pittsburgh concluded that 43 percent of individuals from high-poverty neighborhoods received help from a social service agency in the previous year (Gutiérrez-Mayka and Bernd 2006). Increasingly, social service programs occupy the void left by retrenchment of more commonly identified public assistance programs. For instance, as highlighted in the Introduction to this volume, welfare caseloads have declined by more than 60 percent since 1996. Many former recipients often seek help from or are referred to social service agencies for assistance with basic material needs or job searches. Edin and Lein (1997) find that 22 percent of working poor single mothers received temporary emergency or in-kind assistance from public and nonprofit agencies that totaled approximately $165 per month. In another study, the authors found that poor single mothers contacted over a dozen separate nonprofit organizations for help with different needs in a given year (Edin and Lein 1998).

Providing social services poses different challenges than does the delivery of cash assistance. Unlike cash assistance programs, social services often cannot be delivered to clients in their homes or transferred electronically to an individual. Instead, poor persons participating in social service programs must make regular visits to local agencies and incorporate these visits into complex daily commutes between home, work, and child care, often without adequate access to an automobile or public transportation. While most social service programs are funded by government agencies and grant programs, programs generally are delivered to persons in need through private nonprofit service organizations and, to a lesser extent, through private for-profit organizations (Allard 2009; Marwell 2004). Nonprofit service organizations, therefore, are critical conduits through which the poor link to the safety net. Also, unlike cash assistance programs that may carry an entitlement or a guarantee of assistance to those who are eligible, low-income populations typically have no entitlement to social service programs: State and local governments have great discretion over what social service programs to fund; local private service organizations choose the programs and areas in which to operate.

For these reasons, spatial access to service providers should be an important determinant of whether low-income populations receive assistance or utilize programs. Living closer to service agencies should reduce commuting costs and challenges, increasing the likelihood that low-income persons are able to participate in and complete social service programs. Apart from a lower commuting burden, persons seeking help are more likely to have information or to be referred to agencies in the immediate area. Agencies located within the neighborhood or community are likely to be more trusted or to have a better understanding of residents' needs than providers located far away. Although few studies connect social service accessibility and utilization, there is some evidence that proximity to providers affects individual behavior. One study finds that welfare recipients with mental health and/or substance abuse problems in Detroit who lived closer to service providers were more likely to utilize services than those living farther away (Allard, Tolman, and Rosen 2003).[1] Qualitative interviews in Philadelphia reveal that low-income women are more likely to favor service providers nearby and providers in safe communities over those far away and those located in particularly dangerous areas of their neighborhoods (Kissane 2003).

The availability and stability of program funding are closely related to how accessible services may be at the street level. Unpredictable or volatile revenue streams will make it difficult for agencies to maintain consistent programming or staffing, which are necessary to complete implementation of program cycles and to adequately assist persons in need. Although there may be the perception that public and private support for social service programs does not change appreciably, local service agencies experience substantial changes in the mix of revenues from year to year. In fact, social service program funding is most likely to be cut during periods of economic recession and tight budgets. Agencies often are challenged to cope with fewer program resources just at the time when demand for assistance is on the rise. Providers that cannot secure steady or reliable revenue flows will be forced to reduce program offerings and limit the number of people served.

Several research questions about the provision of social service programs emerge as we weigh these changes to the safety net. Where do our communities provide assistance to poor and near-poor households? Do gaps or mismatches in access to social services exist in our communities? How do providers finance services for low-income populations, and how often do providers experience shifts in their revenue streams? How often do cuts in funding lead to instabilities or inconsistencies in service delivery?

---

[1] For instance, the authors find that a white recipient at risk for mental health problems with access to providers double the metropolitan mean would be 25 percent more likely to utilize services than the same respondent with mean access to providers.

To begin to answer these questions, this chapter examines data from the Multi-City Survey of Social Service Providers and the Rural Survey of Social Service Providers, which interviewed program managers and executive directors from public, nonprofit, and for-profit service organizations in seven different urban and rural sites. Using these unique survey data, I find that service agencies are not located proximate to low-income populations and that low-income persons seeking help may often have to travel long distances to receive it. Moreover, I find that service agencies experience substantial volatility in funding and operations from year to year, which compromises their ability to deliver consistent assistance to the poor. Combined, these findings have implications for safety net policies in the future.

II. The Social Service Eclipse of Cash Assistance

Even though cash assistance programs, particularly welfare programs, were a prominent and rapidly growing component of the safety net during the last third of the twentieth century, these programs have receded in recent years (see Chapter One, this volume, for a summary of research on the causes of the decline). In addition to welfare caseload reduction, there has been a significant shift in the nature of welfare assistance itself. Federal and state Temporary Assistance for Needy Families (TANF) expenditures today consist of both cash and noncash forms of assistance. Cash assistance is defined by law as recurring monthly welfare checks. Noncash TANF assistance, defined legally as "nonassistance," includes short-term child care, job search assistance, mental health services, substance-abuse treatment, domestic violence counseling, and income support intended to support work activity and help recipients overcome barriers to employment. Complementing the dramatic decrease in the number of welfare recipients in the past decade has been a historic shift in the emphasis of welfare aid away from cash to noncash forms of assistance. From 1997 to 2004, the percentage of federal welfare dollars devoted to cash assistance fell from 77 percent to 33 percent. At the same time, the percentage of federal welfare dollars going to nonassistance increased from 23 percent in to 58 percent (U.S. Department of Health and Human Services 2007).

States also have taken advantage of the option to transfer TANF funds to the Child Care and Development Block Grant (CCDBG) and the Social Services Block Grant (SSBG), which provide supports and services to working poor families. When transfers to the CCDBG and SSBG are included, 65 percent of federal TANF monies were spent on social services in 2004. While federal and state TANF expenditures for cash assistance amounted to

$11 billion in 2004 (in $2006), TANF-funded social services and transfers to other service programs totaled almost $18 billion in that same year (in $2006; Allard 2007; U.S. Department of Health and Human Services 2007). Rather than relying on welfare checks, the system now uses a wide range of tools to transform individual behavior, increase work readiness, and promote economic self-sufficiency.

In comparison to the contraction of welfare cash assistance in the 1990s, funding for means-tested social service programs addressing basic material needs or seeking to improve personal well-being has increased steadily in the past three decades. Prior to the War on Poverty, very little governmental funding was targeted at social service programs that provided substance abuse or mental health services, food pantries, emergency assistance, child care assistance, employment services, adult education, housing assistance, or transportation assistance to low-income populations (Smith and Lipsky 1993).[2] Expansion of public funding for social service programs began with growth in the public welfare titles of the Social Security Act (SSA) during the late 1960s and the creation of dozens of new federal social service grant programs in subsequent years.[3] Even though it omits expenditures for adult education, substance abuse and mental health treatment, community development, and food, housing, and energy assistance programs supported by federal, state, and local governments, Congressional Research Services estimates that government expenditures for job training, child care programs, and the SSBG increased from $19 billion in 1975 to approximately $34 billion in 2002 (in $2006; Congressional Research Services 2003).[4]

---

[2] For instance, federal social service expenditures totaled about $124 million in 1954, with state and local social service program expenditures reaching $600 million (expenditures are not corrected for inflation); see Smith and Lipsky (1993, pp. 51–53).

[3] Social services began to receive substantial support from Title IV-A of the Social Security Act (SSA) in the late 1960s and early 1970s. Eventually, these funds were transferred to Title XX of the SSA and then consolidated into the Social Services Block Grant (SSBG) in 1981. Later, programs such as the Comprehensive Employment and Training Act (CETA), the Job Training Partnership Act (JTPA), and the Workforce Investment Act (WIA) would fund tens of billions of dollars in employment services to low-income youth and adults. The Community Services Block Grant (CSBG), the Community Development Block Grant (CDBG), and the Substance Abuse and Mental Health Services Administration (SAMHSA) have administered billions of dollars in grants and contracts to social service agencies. Medicaid also has provided states and communities with several billion dollars in fees and reimbursements for substance abuse and mental health programs in recent years, particularly programs that help expectant mothers or women who have recently given birth. See Smith and Lipsky (1993); U.S. House of Representatives, House Committee on Ways and Means (2004, pp. 277–304).

[4] Of this $34 billion in social service spending in 2002, about $8 billion (in $2006) was child care assistance through the Child Care Development Block Grant (CCDBG) or TANF.

Many publicly funded social service programs are delivered on the ground by local nonprofit service organizations. As government funding for these programs has increased since 1970, therefore, the number of nonprofit service agencies and the total revenues of the nonprofit service sector also have increased. For example, one study concludes that the number of nonprofit human service providers increased by 47 percent from 1989 to 1996 (Boris 1999). Growth of the nonprofit human service sector appears to have quickened more recently; the number of human service nonprofit agencies in large metropolitan areas increased by 41 percent from 1992 to 1996 (Twombly 2001). Another study finds that public funding of nonprofit social service organizations increased by 200 percent from 1977 to 1997 in real dollars (Salamon 2003). Nonprofit human service and job training agencies filing as tax-exempt entities with the Internal Revenue Service (IRS) increased by about 65 percent between 1990 and 2003, totaling almost 40,000 agencies nationwide. Total revenues for these nonprofit organizations increased to $80 billion by 2003 (in $2006).[5] At the same time, there has been a rise in for-profit organizations' social service provision, mostly in the areas of mental health, substance abuse, and employment.

The rising prominence of social service programs versus cash assistance programs within the safety net has a number of implications for the way society and communities assist low-income families. The ability of a social service–based safety net to promote economic self-sufficiency and improve the well-being of low-income families hinges on how well services are delivered to those in need. Unlike cash assistance programs, participation in a social service program is highly contingent upon place. Social services cannot be mailed or transferred electronically to an individual. Instead, poor persons must often visit a social service agency to receive assistance, complete a set of classes, and attend sessions or meetings. In the context of social service–based forms of assistance, therefore, issues of spatial accessibility to providers are of the greatest importance.

Although we proceed as if social service provision is equitable from place to place and from community to community, access to social service agencies in actuality varies both across and within communities. There is no entitlement

Since social service programs receive funding from many different federal, state, and local agencies, it is difficult to derive an accurate estimate of public social service expenditures; see Allard (2009). While these data are the best available on annual social service spending, therefore, they dramatically understate the size and scope of public social service financing.

[5] Findings on the size of the nonprofit human service and job training sector come from my estimates based on data from the National Center for Charitable Statistics, excluding nonprofits unlikely to serve low-income working-age adults.

to social service assistance among low-income populations, and communities are not obligated to provide particular social service programs. Some communities have access to many organizations, others to few. Variation in access to social service agencies is in part a function of where providers choose to locate. The availability of grants and contracts may lead agencies to locate within particular neighborhoods, municipalities, or counties. Some agencies may choose to be closer to concentrations of low-income individuals in order to achieve economies of scale for service delivery; others may prefer to be near potential private donors, clients who generate fee revenue, or partnering service organizations. Service providers may find location options constrained due to lack of adequate facilities in other areas, difficulty of finding professional staff, or insufficient funds to relocate or acquire new facilities.

Proximity to service providers matters for several reasons. Poor persons are more likely to have information about agencies operating in their immediate community or neighborhood than about agencies located farther away. Similarly, caseworkers are likely to inform low-income individuals about programs and resources located nearby. Agencies located in one's immediate neighborhood or community may be more trusted than those located farther away, which should increase the likelihood of seeking help from nearby agencies. Proximity to providers also reduces the burden of commuting. Regular visits to a provider must be incorporated into daily commutes between work and child care. Greater distances complicate commutes and increase the travel costs of program participation, which in turn hampers the ability of an individual to receive help. Limitations of public transportation in many high-poverty areas and low rates of automobile ownership among low-income households make it even more important that providers are located nearby. Ensuring that low-income populations have adequate spatial access to social service providers is critical, therefore, as inadequate availability or accessibility of social services is tantamount to being denied aid in a service-based welfare system or safety net.

We also should be concerned with whether social service agencies are stable or predictable sources of support for low-income populations. Stability and predictability of service delivery are largely a function of the consistency and reliability of service funding. Funding dictates staffing, resources, facilities, available programs, the number of clients served, and the length of time clients spend on waiting lists. Increased funding enables service providers to expand the range of services offered or increase the number of clients served. Lost funding can force agencies to pare back programs, staffing, numbers of clients served, and hours of operation. At the extreme, loss of an entire contract or grant can jeopardize the very existence of a service organization.

The basic character of social service program funding exposes both public and private agencies to consistently shifting revenue flows. Social service programs must compete with changes in public priorities, the agendas of private charities, and other discretionary elements of public budgets. Most service programs carry no entitlement status and are vulnerable to budget cuts or shuffling of funds to new priorities. Public and private funding also contracts when the economy lags, tax revenues dip, and deficits rise. Funding for the social service components of the safety net, therefore, is cyclical and likely to contract just at the moment when need rises. Beyond their impact on government agencies and programs, cuts in public funding for social services have a ripple effect through the nonprofit community that delivers so many programs at the street level and has become increasingly dependent upon public revenues for operations (Allard 2009; DeVita 1999; Wolff 1999).

Even though we may have intuitions about mismatches and instabilities within the contemporary service-based elements of the antipoverty safety net, there is relatively little data or research examining how we provide programs at the neighborhood level. Because social service programs are funded by thousands of government and private revenue sources and delivered by thousands of different public and private agencies across the country, there is no one agency responsible for tracking the location of programs or one data clearinghouse collecting information about program funding. Most often, scholars and policymakers are left to draw inferences from IRS data derived from tax-exempt filings of nonprofit agencies, which cannot easily be used to generate insight into street-level variation in the accessibility and stability of the safety net. As a result, even though social service programs likely receive more than $150 billion in public and private funding each year, we have very little information about what services are available, who provides these services, and who is being served.

III. Social Service Provision in Urban and Rural America

To provide a snapshot of social service provision in urban and rural communities, I analyze data from two surveys conducted with executives and managers of public and private social service agencies between November 2004 and August 2006: the Multi-City Survey of Social Service Providers (MSSSP) and the Rural Survey of Social Service Providers (RSSSP). The MSSSP conducted telephone survey interviews in Chicago/Cook County, Los Angeles/Los Angeles County, and metropolitan Washington, D.C.; the RSSSP completed similar surveys in southeastern Kentucky, south-central Georgia, southeastern New Mexico, and the border counties of

Oregon-California. Respondents to each survey were asked to provide detailed information on services provided, clients served, funding, location, and organizational characteristics from a range of governmental and non-profit service providers. The analyses reported here are based on the 1,750 government, nonprofit, or for-profit agencies (1,349 in the MSSSP, 401 in the RSSSP) that provided at least one of the following services to low-income persons at the time of the interview: outpatient mental health services, out-patient substance abuse services, adult education, employment assistance, emergency assistance, food assistance. See the Technical Appendix at the end of the chapter for more detail about these two surveys.

Who provides help in our communities? The majority of providers deliv-ering social service programs on the ground in these diverse urban and rural communities are nonprofit organizations. Anywhere from 52 percent of agencies in rural New Mexico to 73 percent of agencies in metropolitan Washington, D.C., identify themselves as nonprofit organizations (see the top panel of Table 10.1). Government agencies are prominent in these local safety nets as well, accounting for about 25 to 40 percent of all service agen-cies interviewed. It does appear, however, that government agencies com-prise a larger share of help-giving organizations in rural safety nets than in urban safety nets. For example, roughly 40 percent of service organizations in Kentucky, Georgia, and New Mexico are government agencies, com-pared to less than 25 percent of providers in Chicago and Washington, D.C. Secular nonprofits comprise about 40 to 50 percent of agencies interviewed in the three cities. A much smaller share of providers in three of the four rural areas self-identify as secular nonprofit organizations. Religious non-profits play a prominent role in both urban and rural safety nets, account-ing for about one-fifth to one-third of service agencies interviewed in six of the seven sites. The share of religious nonprofits was notably higher in rural Kentucky and Georgia, as well as in Washington, D.C. (37 percent, 33 per-cent, and 30 percent respectively), than in the other study sites. Perhaps surprisingly, given the privatized nature of the contemporary service-based safety net, only a very small percentage of agencies in these seven urban and rural communities were for-profit organizations.

Median monthly caseload totals provide additional insight into the character and capacity of local service providers. In almost every site, the median government agency maintains a much larger caseload than private nonprofit or for-profit organizations. For instance, the median government agency in Washington, D.C., maintains a monthly caseload that is more than five times that of the median religious nonprofit agency (500 versus 85 clients, respectively). Similar patterns are present in the four rural locations,

Table 10.1. *Characteristics of service providers in the MSSSP and RSSSP*

	MSSSP			RSSSP			
	Chicago	Los Angeles	Washington, D.C.	Kentucky	Georgia	New Mexico	California/Oregon
Governmental	24.5	36.6	24.4	37.0	36.8	43.1	30.3
Median Monthly Caseload	598	560	500	175	200	300	300
Secular Nonprofit	49.4	40.7	42.7	24.0	24.6	29.2	47.3
Median Monthly Caseload	200	150	150	200	50	160	75
Religious Nonprofit	20.3	18.6	30.4	37.0	33.3	23.1	13.9
Median Monthly Caseload	200	200	85	40	23	200	200
For-Profit	5.8	4.2	2.6	2.0	5.3	4.6	8.5
Median Monthly Caseload	60	170	53	7	40	40	55
Services Offered							
Mental Health	43.4	31.5	28.2	17.5	20.7	19.4	40.1
Substance Abuse	35.6	36.0	23.6	21.4	31.0	19.4	30.8
Adult Education/GED	26.1	41.5	42.9	34.0	39.7	28.8	29.2
Employment Services	48.3	49.4	57.0	48.5	50.9	50.8	38.2
Emergency Assistance	41.8	23.8	39.8	31.1	29.3	14.9	20.6
Food Assistance	44.9	46.3	56.2	73.8	58.6	50.8	48.8
N	421	540	388	103	59	67	172

Note: Reported numbers are column percentages of all service organizations.

Sources: Multi-City Survey of Social Service Providers and Rural Survey of Social Service Providers.

where the typical government provider serves many more low-income clients in a month than do nonprofit or for-profit organizations. While the median government agency in the MSSSP is larger than that in the RSSSP, there are no consistent urban–rural differences in median monthly caseloads for nonprofit service organizations. It should be noted, however, that religious nonprofits in southeastern Kentucky and south-central Georgia are much smaller than their counterparts in the West or in urban settings. For instance, the median religious nonprofit in rural Kentucky serves 40 clients per month, compared to median monthly caseloads of 200 among religious providers elsewhere.

What do local safety nets offer to those in need? Although service providers were examined in seven very different settings, the bundle of services offered in each community appears to be quite similar. Employment services are offered by about one-half of all agencies (see the bottom panel of Table 10.1). Temporary or emergency food assistance is also common among providers operating in different urban and rural settings. Although not always statistically significant, some differences in service provision do emerge in Table 10.1. For instance, adult education, outpatient mental health, and outpatient substance abuse services are more common among providers in urban locales than in rural areas. More than 40 percent of agencies in Los Angeles and Washington, D.C., offer adult education services, compared to about 30 percent of agencies in the rural western sites. Approximately 20 percent of agencies in three of the four rural areas offer outpatient mental health services, compared to 28 percent of providers in Washington, D.C., and 43 percent of providers in Chicago.

Some of the observed differences in caseloads and social service offerings across these urban and rural areas are tied to differences in resource availability. Larger caseloads reflect greater resources for programs and assistance, as well as the obligation of public agencies to provide programs or services to a wide range of individuals. In contrast, lower client capacities indicate the presence of few public resources and limited numbers of well-financed nonprofit service organizations. Consistent with these conclusions, the top panel of Table 10.2 indicates that local safety nets in the urban areas and in the border area of rural California-Oregon consist predominantly of agencies with annual budgets greater than $200,000. In fact, more than one-third of the agencies in these areas report annual budgets of over $1 million. Local safety nets in rural Kentucky, Georgia, and New Mexico consist mostly of organizations with quite modest annual budgets. Roughly one-half to two-thirds of the agencies in these three rural regions report budgets below $200,000.

Table 10.2. *Characteristics of service providers in the MSSSP and RSSSP*

	MSSSP				RSSSP			
	Chicago	Los Angeles	Washington, D.C.	Kentucky	Georgia	New Mexico	California/ Oregon
Size of Annual Budget							
More Than $1 Million	59.6	43.7	35.2	19.8	21.6	28.6	34.7
$1 Million–$200,000	27.2	31.0	38.3	16.3	17.7	24.5	31.3
$200,000–$50,000	9.2	14.7	18.5	31.4	35.3	20.4	20.1
Less Than $50,000	4.0	10.6	8.0	32.6	25.5	26.5	13.9
More Than One-Half of Clients							
Are Women	60.3	58.4	67.8	78.4	73.7	75.4	66.1
Are African American	45.5	11.2	44.9	0.0	37.5	0.0	0.0
Are Hispanic	10.1	41.4	20.7	0.0	0.0	48.5	4.2
Receive Welfare	27.3	20.0	22.1	35.5	35.3	38.7	31.1
Live within Three Miles	64.1	64.8	60.4	na	na	na	na
Live in the County	na	na	na	90.8	79.6	96.8	97.6

Note: Reported numbers are column percentages of all service organizations.
na: Survey question not asked.
Sources: Multi-City Survey of Social Service Providers and Rural Survey of Social Service Providers.

Whom do local safety nets target for assistance? It appears that social service providers target most of their efforts at poor women. From 60 percent to almost 80 percent of providers in these urban and rural settings maintain caseloads that are majority female (see the bottom panel of Table 10.2). This likely reflects the tendency of social policy to focus on women and those caring for children, but it is a striking reminder of how marginalized poor men are within urban and rural communities. Reflecting the broad needs of working poor families today and the retrenchment of the welfare system in recent years, roughly one-fifth to one-third of providers maintain caseloads composed predominantly of welfare recipients. It is telling, however, that when asked about changes in demand from welfare recipients, about 30 percent of all providers in both urban and rural areas report serving larger numbers of welfare recipients than in previous years (figures not shown in Table 10.2). Caseloads also appear to be drawn from the immediate community. About 65 percent of providers in the MSSSP sites maintain client caseloads that are mostly located within three miles of the agency. Although it is difficult to apply a three-mile rule to rural agencies that serve populations dispersed across vast areas, nearly all rural providers report that a majority of their clients live within the same county.

IV. Barriers to Service Receipt

Policymakers and researchers often proceed as if the failure of clients to participate in a program reflects personal choice. However, because social service programs often require clients to attend regular, repeated sessions and navigate complex administrative bureaucracies, factors commonly identified as barriers to employment (e.g., poor health, physical disability, mental health problems, lack of transportation resources, low literacy) may also affect patterns of service utilization. To explore the factors that may inhibit successful completion of social service programs, the RSSSP asked rural service providers about barriers to service receipt frequently observed by agency staff. The results are presented in Table 10.3.

Difficulty arranging child care is one of the most prevalent barriers to service receipt in all four rural regions. Roughly 30 percent of providers in each rural locale (41 percent of providers in Oregon-California border counties) identified child care as a frequent problem that clients face when trying to attend treatment sessions or make appointments. Reflecting the transportation challenges in rural areas, transportation barriers to service receipt also were prominently reported by agencies in all four rural sites. For instance, one-third of providers in the border counties of California and Oregon and

Table 10.3. *Perceived barriers to social service receipt in the RSSSP*

Barriers to service receipt that clients frequently encounter	Kentucky	Georgia	New Mexico	California/ Oregon
Difficulty Arranging Child Care	34.0	27.5	29.2	40.7
Problems with Transportation	45.5	22.8	18.5	33.7
Difficulty Keeping Appointments Due to Substance or Alcohol Abuse	27.3	22.0	27.8	34.4
Physical Health Problems or Illness	20.8	22.2	15.9	31.3
Fear of Stigma or Personal Concerns	9.0	13.2	19.1	27.1
Difficult to Make Appointment Due to Work Schedule	5.0	11.3	16.9	22.7
Low Literacy or Difficulty Completing Paperwork	19.6	17.5	18.5	16.2
Domestic Violence	5.5	2.0	12.3	10.7

Note: Reported numbers are column percentages of all service organizations.
Source: Rural Survey of Social Service Providers.

46 percent of providers in southeastern Kentucky identify transportation problems as the most common barrier to service receipt. Interestingly, transportation barriers appear to be greater in Kentucky, Oregon, and California, perhaps an indication that automobile transportation is more essential in rural areas with challenging mountainous topography.

Substance or alcohol abuse also is a frequent barrier to service receipt, reported by about 25 percent of providers in Georgia, Kentucky, and New Mexico and by 34 percent of providers along the border of California and Oregon. More than 20 percent of providers in three of the four rural sites indicated that physical health problems were a common barrier or obstacle to service receipt. Low literacy or difficulty completing paperwork was found to be a frequent barrier to service receipt by slightly less than 20 percent of rural agencies. Finally, although the prevalence is low compared to other types of barriers to service receipt, domestic violence appears to play a nontrivial role among the rural poor.

These data suggest that poor persons seeking help face challenges similar to those experienced when seeking employment. Many service providers, particularly those with few resources or a narrow programmatic mission, may be ill-equipped to address these different and likely multiple barriers to service utilization. Because social services are central to our local safety nets and critical to accessing other types of social benefits, however, communities should undertake more comprehensive examinations of the factors limiting service receipt among the poor.

V. Poor Persons' Access to Services

To assess whether services are properly matched to the geographic location of poor populations, I calculate service accessibility scores for residential census tracts in Chicago, Los Angeles, and Washington, D.C. These scores weight for capacity by summing the number of clients served by agencies within three miles of a tract and dividing that sum by the number of poor persons within three miles to capture potential demand for assistance. Scores are divided by the metropolitan mean to allow for comparisons across census tracts. I calculate three separate access scores, which reflect accessibility of basic needs assistance (e.g., emergency cash or food assistance), mental health and substance abuse services, and employment services (e.g., job training, job placement, adult education). All things being equal, it is assumed that services are more readily accessible if a person seeking help is located near an agency that offers relevant services, has resources available, and is not overwhelmed by demand for assistance from the surrounding community. See the Technical Appendix for more details about these service access scores.

The service accessibility scores reported here can be interpreted to make comparisons between a residential tract and the metropolitan average, Residential Tract or Neighborhood A, with an access score of 1.10 for employment services, located within three miles, has 10 percent more employment service opportunities than the metropolitan mean tract; Residential Tract or Neighborhood B, with an access score of 0.90, is located near 10 percent fewer employment service opportunities than the metropolitan mean tract. Access scores can also be used to reflect the magnitude of differences in access between two neighborhoods or two types of census tracts. For instance, if Neighborhood A has an access score of 1.10 and Neighborhood B has an access score of 0.90, then it can be said that Neighborhood A has access to 22 percent more opportunities than Neighborhood B (1.10 ÷ 0.90 = 1.22). If providers are equitably located or distributed,

Table 10.4. *Access to social service providers by poverty rate*

	Access to employment services	Access to mental health and substance abuse services	Access to basic needs assistance
Chicago			
Poverty Rate 0 to 10%	1.16[a,b,c]	1.36[a,b,c]	1.23[a,b,c]
Poverty Rate 11 to 20%	0.88[a]	0.79[a]	0.78[a]
Poverty Rate 21 to 40%	0.84[b]	0.60[b]	0.79[b]
Poverty Rate +40%	0.85[c]	0.63[c]	0.84[c]
Los Angeles			
Poverty Rate 0 to 10%	1.28[a,b,c]	1.35[a,b,c]	1.14[a]
Poverty Rate 11 to 20%	0.99[a]	0.83[a]	0.95
Poverty Rate 21 to 40%	0.77[b]	0.77[b]	0.91[a]
Poverty Rate +40%	0.63[c]	0.86[c]	0.88
Washington, D.C.			
Poverty Rate 0 to 10%	1.03	0.95	0.97
Poverty Rate 11 to 20%	0.88	1.05	1.14
Poverty Rate 21 to 40%	1.06	1.36	1.04
Poverty Rate +40%	0.80	1.00	0.72

[a,b,c] Notations identify sets of paired cells where the mean difference in service access is significant at the .10 level or below.

Sources: Multi-City Survey of Social Service Providers and Rural Survey of Social Service Providers, 2000 Census.

then service accessibility scores should be close to 1 and will be comparable across different neighborhoods. Mismatches in service accessibility or availability will exist when high-poverty areas have access scores well below 1. Tables 10.4 and 10.5 chart service accessibility scores for low-poverty (0 to 10 percent), moderate-poverty (11 to 20 percent), high-poverty (21 to 40 percent), and extreme high-poverty (+40 percent) tracts in each city, as well as across tracts with low (0 to 25 percent) versus high percentages (+75 percent) of blacks, Hispanics, and whites.

High-poverty neighborhoods tend to have less access to social services than low-poverty neighborhoods, particularly in Chicago and Los Angeles. For example, low-poverty tracts in Chicago have access to about 40 percent more employment service opportunities than high- and extreme high-poverty tracts (see the first column of Table 10.4, 1.16 versus 0.84 and 0.85, respectively). Low-poverty tracts in Chicago have access to twice as many mental health and substance abuse services as high-poverty tracts. Perhaps even more surprising, low-poverty tracts in Chicago have access to about 50 percent greater access to basic needs services than high-poverty tracts. Very similar patterns are apparent in Los Angeles, where low-poverty tracts have about twice as much access to employment services as high-poverty and extreme high-poverty tracts (1.28 versus 0.77 and 0.63, respectively). Across several different measures, both Chicago and Los Angeles exhibit evidence of mismatches in service accessibility across low- and high-poverty areas.

Although metropolitan Washington, D.C., displays the same basic relationships between poverty and service accessibility, there are no statistically significant differences in access scores across low- and high-poverty census tracts. This is due in large part to the concentration of poverty within a few neighborhoods and the compact nature of the urban geography in the District of Columbia, where a three-mile radius brings many high-poverty tracts within three miles of a service provider. As a result, we should expect providers to be more equitably distributed within compact cities like Washington, D.C., and less equitably distributed across more sprawling cities like Chicago and Los Angeles. Nevertheless, 50 percent of all tracts in Washington, D.C., with a poverty rate of over 20 percent are in areas of the city that have access scores for basic needs and employment services of .75 or lower (figures not shown here). Despite few differences at the mean, therefore, many high-poverty neighborhoods in Washington, D.C., either are distant from service providers or contain demand for assistance that far exceeds the capacity of providers located nearby.

There is evidence of racial variation in service accessibility as well. Neighborhoods with high percentages of black and Hispanic residents have far less access to social service providers than neighborhoods that have a small percentage of minority residents or are predominantly white (see Table 10.5). In Washington, D.C., tracts where more than 75 percent of the residents are black have half as much access to employment services as tracts where fewer than 25 percent are black (0.54 versus 1.24, respectively). Likewise, tracts with a small percentage of blacks in Chicago have access to about 70 percent more employment service opportunities than tracts where at least three-quarters of the population is black (1.17 versus 0.68, respectively). In most instances, predominantly Hispanic tracts in Los Angeles and Chicago have access to about 50 percent fewer service opportunities than tracts with a small percentage of Hispanics. Not only is the safety net mismatched by need and poverty, therefore, but living

Table 10.5. *Access to social service providers by racial composition*

	Access to employment services	Access to mental health and substance abuse services	Access to basic needs assistance
Chicago			
Percent Black 0 to 25%	1.17[a]	1.25[a]	1.15[a]
Percent Black +75%	0.68[a]	0.55[a]	0.64[a]
Percent Hispanic 0 to 25%	1.07[b]	1.09[b]	1.10[b]
Percent Hispanic +75%	0.72[b]	0.55[b]	0.63[b]
Percent White 0 to 25%	0.72[c]	0.56[c]	0.68[c]
Percent White +75%	1.28[c]	1.57[c]	1.26[c]
Los Angeles			
Percent Black 0 to 25%	1.05	1.02	1.03
Percent Black +75%	0.50	0.85	0.66
Percent Hispanic 0 to 25%	1.20[a]	1.30[a]	1.22[a]
Percent Hispanic +75%	0.82[a]	0.57[a]	0.89[a]
Percent White 0 to 25%	0.72	0.68[b]	0.71[b]
Percent White +75%	0.96	1.27[b]	1.27[b]
Washington, D.C.			
Percent Black 0 to 25%	1.24[a]	1.22[a]	1.17[a]
Percent Black +75%	0.54[a]	0.64[a]	0.60[a]
Percent White 0 to 25%	0.58[b]	0.67[b]	0.64[b]
Percent White +75%	1.48[b]	1.47[b]	1.35[b]

[a,b,c] Notations identify sets of paired cells where the mean difference in service access is significant at the .10 level or below.

Sources: Multi-City Survey of Social Service Providers and Rural Survey of Social Service Providers, 2000 Census.

in neighborhoods highly segregated by race also significantly diminishes access to the safety net.

Service accessibility has a different meaning in rural places. Simply assessing which providers are within three miles may not be very meaningful given the great distances one might have to commute between towns or to a county seat. Providers in one town or county seat may be willing to serve populations outside that location, but most rural towns are a considerable distance apart. These distances limit the extent to which the absence of a particular program or provider can be remedied simply by traveling to a neighboring town or community, where that program or provider may be located. Moreover, the dispersal of population and the low densities of potential clients outside of main town areas may prevent service providers from locating outside of county seats or population centers, even if unmet needs are recognized in more isolated portions of a rural community. In rural places, therefore, having access to a reliable automobile and/or living in a population center may be even more critical determinants of service access than in urban places.

As survey respondents indicated, most low-income persons in rural areas must travel for about 15 minutes by automobile to an agency to receive assistance. The mean travel times for clients were 18 minutes in southeastern Kentucky, 14 minutes in south-central Georgia, 17 minutes in the Oregon-California border counties, and 13 minutes in southeastern New Mexico. Consistent across all four rural sites, about three-quarters of providers reported that clients traveled an average of 10 to 20 minutes by car to receive assistance. Fifteen percent of all rural providers indicated that the average travel time by car was more than 20 minutes. For most clients in rural areas, even 10 to 20 minutes of automobile travel often translates into significant distances that must be covered to receive help. Keeping in mind that many low-income adults in these rural regions have little or no access to automobile transportation, travel distances of 5 or 10 miles will be difficult for many poor persons seeking help from local service agencies.

VI. Funding Social Service Agencies

Understanding the manner in which social service agencies finance programs should be the key to understanding mismatches and identifying volatility in service provision. Because government agencies draw funding from public sources, I explore variation in the revenue sources of private nonprofit and for-profit service organizations. Nonprofit and for-profit organizations typically receive funding from three key sources: government grants or contracts, Medicaid reimbursements, and earned revenues. In addition, nonprofit organizations often receive funding through grants and contracts from other nonprofit organizations or foundations, as well as receive support from private individual donors. Beyond sources of funding, it is important to understand the degree to which private agencies rely upon a single source of revenue. When agencies are dependent on a given revenue source, they become vulnerable and unstable when funding from that source is lost. For the purposes of these analyses, therefore, I classify agencies as dependent or heavily reliant upon a particular revenue source if they receive at least half of their total revenue from a given source.[6]

Fitting with changes in safety net financing over the past 40 years, government grants and contracts are the most critical source of funding for private social service organizations. Nearly two-thirds of all private service providers in both urban and rural areas report receiving federal, state, and/or local government funds in the most recent fiscal year (see the top panel of Table 10.6). Receipt of public funding appears to vary with state and local government expenditures for social service programs. More than 80 percent of private agencies in Chicago and 75 percent of private agencies along the Oregon-California border report receiving government funds, which should be expected given the size of social welfare expenditures in those states. Consistent with the State of Georgia's history of limited government support for antipoverty programs, only 43 percent of private service organizations in rural Georgia report receiving public funds.

Private nonprofit and for-profit service providers receiving public funds are quite dependent upon those funds, as government funding comprises more than 50 percent of total revenues for about half of all service providers receiving public funding. Organizations dependent upon government grants and contracts are larger organizations (with budgets of over $1 million) that typically offer resource- or capacity-intensive services such as substance abuse, adult education, or employment services to low-income individuals.

Many nonprofit and for-profit agencies that bundle basic health care, maternal health programs, and mental health services with other types of support services can be eligible for Medicaid reimbursement of qualifying procedures (Mark et al. 2005; Smith 2002).[7] Yet, limited data on how private agencies draw upon Medicaid make it difficult to generate accurate assessments of how important Medicaid is to social service providers. Data here indicate that Medicaid is an important source of funding for a small share of private agencies. The share of nonprofit and for-profit providers reporting program revenues from Medicaid varies from less than 15 percent in rural Kentucky and Georgia to almost 40 percent in Chicago. While few rural agencies report receiving Medicaid reimbursements, it is a particularly key source of funding for those that do. About half of all private agencies in the RSSSP receiving Medicaid depend on those revenues for at least 50 percent

---

[6] Each survey asked providers whether they received funds from a particular source and then to estimate the share of total funding from that source.

[7] Salamon (2003) states that 70 percent of federal assistance to nonprofits came in the form of fees or subsidies for services, much of it through Medicaid and Medicare.

Table 10.6. Sources of support for private nonprofit and for-profit social service providers in the MSSSP and RSSSP

	MSSSP			RSSSP			
	Chicago	Los Angeles	Washington, D.C.	Kentucky	Georgia	New Mexico	California/ Oregon
% of All Private Agencies Receiving …							
Government Grants or Contracts	81.8	67.9	62.0	60.9	43.2	54.1	75.8
+50% of Revenues	58.0	50.0	40.8	46.0	57.1	38.9	54.0
Receive Medicaid Reimbursements	39.4	19.4	16.8	13.9	13.5	32.4	28.0
+50% of Revenues	21.4	39.3	21.7	57.1	25.0	45.5	45.8
Receive Earned Revenues	37.1	32.3	39.0	24.6	21.9	32.4	37.3
+50% of Revenues	20.0	28.2	22.2	21.4	28.6	8.3	31.3
% of Private Nonprofit Agencies Receiving …							
Nonprofit Grants	76.7	62.1	75.9	45.9	25.0	50.0	63.6
+50% of Revenues	13.0	11.3	16.5	14.3	16.7	31.3	14.6
Receive Private Giving	80.2	71.6	87.9	85.5	70.0	74.3	58.9
+50% of Revenues	6.4	22.1	14.1	41.2	79.0	32.0	25.9

Note: Reported numbers are column percentages of private nonprofit and for-profit service organizations.
Sources: Multi-City Survey of Social Service Providers and Rural Survey of Social Service Providers.

of their total organizational revenues, compared to less than one-quarter of private agencies in the MSSSP.

Similarly, nonprofit and for-profit organizations often draw upon earned revenues from fees for services. As the middle panels in Table 10.6 indicate, earned revenue is much more common among private nonprofit and for-profit organizations than is Medicaid reimbursement. From one-fifth to one-third of nonprofit and for-profit providers in the MSSSP and RSSSP report earned revenue. As is the case for Medicaid, these agencies tend to specialize in mental health and substance abuse services. Only a fraction of those agencies receiving earned revenues—generally around 20 to 30 percent—are dependent on those revenues for more than 50 percent of their total budget.

Nonprofit agencies frequently draw upon two additional sources of revenue: grants and contracts from nonprofit organizations and private philanthropy. As is seen in the bottom rows of Table 10.6, most private nonprofits in this study receive support from other nonprofits and/or from private donors. Yet, these sources account for only a small share of total organizational revenues in most instances. For example, 76 percent of nonprofit service organizations in Washington, D.C., report revenue from nonprofit organizations or foundations, with 88 percent receiving revenue from private giving. Receipt of nonprofit grants or philanthropy and private giving is comparable across nonprofits in Chicago and Los Angeles, as well as in the four rural regions. Neither urban nor rural nonprofit agencies are very likely to be dependent upon nonprofit or foundation grants, and urban nonprofits do not rely heavily upon private giving. Private donations constitute more than 50 percent of total revenue for one-quarter to three-quarters of nonprofit service organizations in the four rural regions.

VII. Volatility of Service Delivery

In addition to identifying the prevalence of funding from various revenue streams, we should be interested in the volatility of funding and the frequency with which funding streams are cut or reduced. Volatility in funding will impair a program's ability to provide consistent and quality services to low-income populations. Of particular concern are cuts to a primary or key source of revenue. Since program funding has an inherent discrete or "blockiness" quality, programs often are funded in full or not at all. Any loss or increase in a primary revenue source will have a significant impact upon how an agency operates. Lost funding creates obvious challenges for service agencies, particularly if organizations cultivate few other funding sources and cannot find substitute revenues readily. Beyond seeking replacement funds, agencies may have to choose whether to reduce staff, lower program costs, or trim client caseloads in order to fit program activities within a more constrained budget. Because funding volatility is a problem for all types of social service agencies, Table 10.7 examines funding and program volatility across public and private social service agencies.

When looking at increases and decreases in funding sources in the three years prior to the survey, both urban and rural service providers show substantial volatility or change in the composition of agency funding. Although the figures vary by site, about 30 percent to 50 percent of providers in each site report a decrease in at least one funding source over the previous three years. Comparable percentages of agencies report an increase in a given revenue source over the three years prior to the survey. While the MSSSP and RSSSP do not contain enough detail about funding to determine whether increases and decreases in funding leave agencies with a net positive or negative budgetary position, it does appear that many agencies reporting lost funds from one source do not replace those funds with increased funding from another source. Of the agencies reporting a funding cut in the previous three years, 61 percent of urban providers and 75 percent of rural providers did not experience an increase in other funding sources during that time (figures not shown in Table 10.7). Rural service agencies in the Southeast appear to have been hardest hit in recent years; 84 percent of agencies in Georgia and Kentucky that report a recent funding decrease do not report a funding increase during the same time period.

Further highlighting the volatility of program funding, a significant share of public and private service agencies reported a decrease in a key or primary source of funding in the three years prior to the survey. Almost one-quarter of all providers in Los Angeles (24 percent) and Chicago (22 percent) saw a decrease in funding from a primary revenue stream; 12 percent of providers in Washington, D.C., had the same experience. Roughly 20 percent to 40 percent of rural service agencies report a decrease in a primary revenue source within the previous three years.

Any cut in program funding will have an immediate effect upon service providers. Lost funds will create fiscal uncertainty and instability within agencies, forcing many to make immediate modifications to service provision. Accordingly, providers were asked whether recent funding problems had forced changes to service delivery: reductions in staffing levels, reductions in services offered, reductions in the number of clients served, or temporary closure of their facility. Far from operating stable programs from year to year, it appears that providers in both urban and rural areas

Table 10.7. *Funding and program instability among public and private social service providers in the MSSSP and RSSSP*

	MSSSP			RSSSP			
	Chicago	Los Angeles	Washington, D.C.	Kentucky	Georgia	New Mexico	California/Oregon
In the Previous Three Years …							
Decrease in Any Revenue Source	43.9	38.9	29.6	52.4	42.4	37.3	54.1
Increase in Any Revenue Source	43.9	33.0	50.0	28.2	25.4	40.3	40.7
Decrease in Primary Revenue Source	22.1	23.5	12.4	38.8	20.3	20.9	32.0
If Experienced Decrease in Any Revenue Source …							
Reductions in Services Offered	47.8	52.9	35.7	38.9	56.0	48.0	55.9
Reductions in Number of Clients	35.3	43.8	31.3	22.2	44.0	36.0	47.8
Reductions in Staff	63.8	63.6	45.2	38.9	64.0	60.0	64.5
Reductions in Hours of Operation	na	na	na	14.8	32.0	12.0	23.7
Temporarily Shut Down Site	5.0	5.7	8.7	5.6	24.0	8.0	5.4

Note: Reported numbers are column percentages of all public and private service organizations.
na: Survey question not asked.
Sources: Multi-City Survey of Social Service Providers and Rural Survey of Social Service Providers.

experience substantial volatility in service provision. For instance, 71 percent of urban service providers and 76 percent of rural agencies experiencing a decrease in funding report reducing staff, reducing services, reducing the number of clients served, or temporarily halting operations in response (figures not shown in Table 10.7).

Reducing staff was the most common strategy for coping with funding cuts. About one-half of all providers in Washington, D.C., and nearly two-thirds of all providers in Chicago and Los Angeles retained fewer staff as a result of funding problems, perhaps trying to provide the same level of assistance with fewer personnel. Roughly two-thirds of all rural providers also trimmed staff in response to funding cuts. Given that service organizations are typically understaffed, particularly in rural areas, the loss of staff members is likely to shrink the organization's capacity to serve. Cuts in staff mean longer waiting times for program applicants, more burdensome caseloads for staff, and less time for staff to work with clients or assess their needs. A nearly equal share of public and private organizations report simply reducing services offered to low-income clients as a result of funding cuts. More than 50 percent of providers in Los Angeles, Georgia, and the border counties between California and Oregon indicated that they reduced services to cope with lost revenue. Slightly fewer providers indicated reductions in the number of clients served. For instance, roughly one-third of providers in Chicago, Washington, D.C., and New Mexico reduced the number of clients served following funding cuts.

With the exception of Georgia, less than 10 percent of agencies in both urban and rural areas report temporary closures in response to decreases in funding. Taken alone, this may seem like a small reduction in service capacity across our communities. Initial phone calls to agencies drawn from community directories, however, indicated that 10 percent to 15 percent of the agencies listed in the most current community service directories were no longer operational. Combining the prevalence of temporary closures with organizations that were not in operation at the time of the survey, it is apparent that a sizable share of the service capacity within local safety nets faces difficulty operating successfully from month to month and from year to year.

Finally, although not reported here, accessibility scores reflecting proximity to different service delivery reduction strategies in urban areas indicate that high-poverty tracts were proximate to three to nine times as many providers reducing service delivery as a result of funding cuts as low-poverty tracts. For instance, high-poverty tracts in Washington, D.C., had access to nearby six times as many service providers that reduced staff to cope with funding cuts as low-poverty tracts. High-poverty tracts in Chicago had access to three times as many providers reducing the number of services in response to funding cuts as low-poverty tracts. Even more dramatic, high-poverty tracts in Los Angeles had twice as much access to providers that temporarily shut down due to funding cuts as the average tract and almost nine times as much access to providers with temporary shutdowns as low-poverty tracts. Volatility in the contemporary safety net appears to have a particularly negative effect on already hard-pressed and disadvantaged communities.

VIII. Discussion

Examining social service provision in seven different urban and rural locations, I find evidence of striking spatial mismatches and volatility in the contemporary safety net. Far from simply being interesting academically, these features of our safety net have important implications for working poor families and the policy tools we develop to reduce poverty.

First, inequality in access to the safety net likely compounds other place-based inequalities we observe in communities today. Poor-quality schools, substandard housing, inadequate transportation resources, and limited access to job opportunities all have spatial relationships similar to those found here for service provision. It is an ironic reality that the social service programs designed to reduce the impact or prevalence of these social problems also are mismatched from communities in need. Insufficient distribution of social assistance and service providers should undermine the success of safety net programs, the efficiency with which the safety net operates, and the ability to promote better outcomes among the poor. Policymakers, community leaders, and scholars should not be surprised, therefore, that low-income, low-skilled workers have persistent difficulty achieving greater economic self-sufficiency and trajectories. Today's safety net simply reinforces the obstacles to opportunity that low-income populations confront in other aspects of their everyday lives.

The mismatches and instabilities in service provision observed here are the cumulative products of many separate and disconnected decisions that government, nonprofits, and individuals make about which programs, populations, and agencies to support. Although all operate with the mission to reduce poverty and improve well-being, neither public agencies, program funders, nor private service organizations operate with a systemic view of how the geography of social assistance matches the geography of need in their community. The challenge for policymakers and community leaders is to identify strategies that will reduce the gaps between safety net assistance and those in need.

Improved access to the safety net can be achieved by building information systems that better link persons in need with community resources and service providers. Public and private agencies should invest resources to better understand individual-level and structural barriers to social service utilization. Even effort to simply map service provision against the location or changing location of poor populations should highlight inefficiencies and areas of underprovision. Complementing these efforts, communities could seek to improve the information available about services located near high-poverty neighborhoods. Well-maintained 2-1-1 telephone systems that would link persons in need to relevant nearby community service agencies may be critical in improving the flow of information. Updated Web-based community directories of service providers also may help clients find help nearby. Improving data-sharing relationships between public and private agencies will help to better identify client needs, track client referrals, and understand patterns of service utilization.

In fact, one reason the mismatches and volatilities in the safety net have gone unnoticed is that there is little policy research linking social service provision, community-based organizations, and individual outcomes. Greater scholarly attention should be given to understanding the bundle of services and supports that states and communities provide to low-income populations and how that bundle of assistance relates to changes in well-being. This requires a shift not only in orientation, but also in data collection. Many of the large datasets used to study poverty in America are not designed to address issues of service utilization, nor are they geographically representative of a particular region, state, or city. A better understanding of why certain individuals seek assistance, follow up on referrals, or fail to complete programs will improve how local service agencies provide assistance to low-income populations.

Communities should begin to consider more aggressive metropolitan or regional planning for the delivery of antipoverty assistance and social services. Rather than allocate funds by program, organization, or municipality, funding should flow to areas with the greatest need. Multiyear guaranteed grants or contracts can be awarded on the condition that providers locate within certain neighborhoods or areas. Public agencies can attempt to match private funds targeted at underserved areas, rewarding community-based service providers who seek to operate among the hardest-to-serve areas and raising revenues from nongovernmental sources. One-stop facilities can be expanded to provider low-overhead space to a wider range of service providers.

Reallocating resources will not come without controversy. Since there are few places where the resources are adequate to meet needs, no community will feel that there are excess funds to share. Not In My Backyard (NIMBY) sentiment may lead other communities to resist becoming the destination for a particular service provider. Reallocation of resources may run counter to the missions of foundations and umbrella organizations to distribute funds widely in communities. Distribution of public funds is likely to be heavily rooted in subtle forms of patronage. Donors do not easily see how their giving would be better invested in neighborhoods to which they have little connection and for causes that seem distant from their everyday lives. Shifting how we fund and target social service programs, therefore, will require the collaboration of both the nonprofit and public service sectors.

The United Way of Greater Toronto (UWGT) provides a recent example of how communities can work together to address mismatches in service provision. Over the past few years, the UWGT has shifted its mission to respond to increasing poverty in the inner-tier suburbs of Toronto and the presence of few service providers in those communities. Through the Strong Neighbourhoods Task Force, the UWGT has begun to target millions of dollars in resources at 13 neighborhoods with rising needs but few agencies that provide social services. Funds from UWGT will support the creation of community hub facilities delivering services and programs to previously underserved low-income populations in metropolitan Toronto. In addition to generating private funding for this initiative, the UWGT has sought to improve collaboration among federal, provincial, and local government agencies and area nonprofits to better address the needs of high-poverty areas outside central city Toronto (Gray 2005; United Way of Greater Toronto 2004, 2005).

States and communities should also consider new strategies for providing service agencies with resources to acquire new facilities and relocate to be closer to populations in need. Programs that allow nonprofits to renovate and/or acquire space in underserved communities can help nonprofits overcome the resource hurdles to relocating to or expanding within high-poverty neighborhoods. One example is the IFF (formerly the Illinois Facilities Fund), a nonprofit organization that offers financial and technical assistance to help nonprofit service providers secure proper facilities and plan for future facility needs. By addressing the space needs of agencies, IFF helps nonprofits better position themselves in the service delivery marketplace (Illinois Facilities Fund 2006). Nonprofits like IFF can be self-supporting through fees and loan payments, making them a low-cost approach to strengthening the nonprofit service sector and reducing mismatches in assistance.

Complementing governmental support of social service agencies, communities should increase private support for programs that help low-income populations. Given the resource dependency of many service agencies, communities should support efforts by nonprofits to cultivate more diverse and durable revenue sources. Increasing volunteerism within nonprofit service organizations may also help to strengthen these organizations. Although volunteers cannot provide direct services in all instances, they can help maintain facilities or perform basic administrative tasks, allowing many nonprofit service agencies to dedicate staff and financial resources to service delivery. Volunteers also can help nonprofits develop client outreach efforts or conduct fund-raising campaigns, which will strengthen nonprofit service organizations and increase their service capacity in the long term. For their part, local foundations and funders can provide information to private donors about community needs, program outcomes, and places where private donations are most needed. Such information can connect private donors to important causes and needs that otherwise might go overlooked (Wolpert 1999).

Finally, it is important for government to maintain its commitment to social service programs, especially during hard economic times. Service providers, particularly nonprofit organizations, are the critical threads that tie together our local safety nets and determine how communities assist poor populations. Nonprofit service organizations emerge to address unmet needs in communities and to provide help to those who fall between the cracks of public assistance programs. The economic circumstances today—rising costs of living, declining availability of good jobs for low-skilled workers, widening income inequality, high rates of poverty in cities and suburbs—suggest that community-based service organizations will face even greater demands for assistance in the coming years. Retrenchment of public safety net programs will make local nonprofits even more integral sources of support for the poor. Yet, because nonprofits are dependent on public funds, these cuts in public social service programs will have powerful ripple effects throughout local safety nets. Nonprofits losing public funding will find it difficult to maintain programs and remain operational. Decreases in governmental social service funding will increase the vulnerability and volatility of the nonprofit service sector rather than enhance private commitments to the safety net. Because of the fragmented nature of social service provision, however, we have given less thought to whether the safety net is well equipped to meet changing demands for assistance. Community leaders, policymakers, and scholars therefore should engage issues of social service accessibility and stability to ensure that the safety net meets current needs and future challenges.

Technical Appendix: THE MSSSP AND RSSSP

The MSSSP and RSSSP are telephone surveys of executives and managers from more than 2,200 social service providers in three cities (Chicago, Los Angeles, Washington, D.C.) and four high-poverty rural areas. The RSSSP was completed in four high-poverty multicounty rural regions: south-central Georgia (Atkinson, Bacon, Ben Hill, Berrien, Coffee, Jeff Davis, Pierce, and Ware counties), southeastern Kentucky (Bell, Clay, Harlan, Jackson, Knox, Laurel, Rockcastle, and Whitley counties), south-central New Mexico (Chaves, Curry, Debaca, Eddy, Lea, and Roosevelt counties), and along the border of California and Oregon (Del Norte, Modoc, and Siskiyou counties in California; Coos, Curry, Douglas, Jackson, Josephine, Klamath, and Lake counties in Oregon). Respondents were drawn from community directories, social service directories, county agency referral lists, telephone books, and Internet searches. Providers included in the survey operated in a number of service areas (welfare to work, job training, mental health, substance abuse, adult education, emergency assistance). Agencies that provided services on-site to low-income populations broadly defined were contacted to complete a longer telephone survey.

The MSSSP database contained 2,953 agencies eligible for the longer survey. Between November 2004 and August 2005, a survey team contacted each of the 2,953 eligible agencies using a five-callback minimum rule. Efforts to complete the longer telephone survey identified 770 agencies not eligible for the survey. Telephone surveys were then completed with 1,487 of the remaining 2,183 social service providers, for a response rate of 68 percent. The RSSSP database contained 1,270 agencies and churches eligible for the telephone survey. Again, 186 agencies were deemed ineligible for the survey as efforts to complete the longer telephone survey progressed. Surveys were completed with 724 of the remaining 1,084 social service providers between November 2005 and August 2006, for a response rate of 66.8 percent.

Calculating Service Accessibility Scores for the MSSSP

Service accessibility scores are calculated for each census tract in the three study sites. Scores are calculated by first summing the total number of clients served by agencies within three miles of each residential census tract. This figure provides a sense of the supply of services or the capacity of service agencies within three miles of a given tract or neighborhood. To account for potential demand for services, I calculate the number of individuals with income below the poverty line within three miles of each residential tract. A radius of three miles is selected because interviews with social service program managers indicate that clients typically are not expected to commute more than a few miles to a social service provider.

With these data, I calculate a set of demand-, distance-, and organizational-weighted service accessibility scores as follows:

$$IA_i = \Sigma(W_j) \div \Sigma(P_j) \quad \text{for } d_{ij} = 0 \text{ to } d_{ij} = 3 \tag{1}$$

where IA_i is a particular initial access score. W_j reflects the number of clients served in a typical month. I sum the number of clients served (W_j) and the number of poor persons (P_j) across tracts j within a three-mile radius (d_{ij}) of tract i. To make service accessibility scores more readily interpretable, I divide each tract's score for a given access measure IA_i by the metropolitan area mean score for that particular access measure. Thus, the scores reported in the tables here reflect service accessibility for a given tract with respect to the mean tract in the area.

$$A_i = LIA_i \div \text{Metropolitan Mean of } LIA_i \text{ across } j \text{ tracts} \tag{2}$$

References

Allard, Scott W. 2007. "The Changing Face of Welfare During the Bush Administration." *Publius: The Journal of Federalism*, 37(3): 304–332.

———. 2009. *Out of Reach: Place, Poverty, and the New American Welfare State*. New Haven, CT: Yale University Press.

Allard, Scott W., Richard Tolman, and Daniel Rosen. 2003. "Proximity to Service Providers and Service Utilization among Welfare Recipients: The Interaction of Place and Race." *Journal of Policy Analysis and Management*, 22(4): 599–613.

Boris, Elizabeth T. 1999. "The Nonprofit Sector in the 1990s," in *Philanthropy and the Nonprofit Sector in a Changing America*. Charles T. Clotfelter and Thomas Ehrlich, eds. Bloomington: Indiana University Press, 1–33.

Congressional Research Services. 2003. "Cash and Noncash Benefits for Persons with Limited Income: Eligibility Rules, Recipient and Expenditure Data, FY2000–FY2002." Report # RL32233, Washington, DC: Library of Congress.

DeVita, Carol J. 1999. "Nonprofits and Devolution: What Do We Know?" in *Nonprofits and Government: Collaboration and Conflict*. Elizabeth T. Boris and C. Eugene Steuerle, eds. Washington, DC: Urban Institute Press, 214–233

Edin, Kathryn, and Laura Lein. 1997. *Making Ends Meet*. New York: Russell Sage.

———. 1998. "The Private Safety Net: The Role of Charitable Organizations in the Lives of the Poor." *Housing Policy Debate*, 9(4): 541–573.

Gray, Jeff. 2005. "Report Finds Shortchanged Neighbourhoods; Nine Areas with Many New Immigrants and the Very Poor Lack Social Services." *The Globe and Mail (Canada)*, July 1, p. A9.

Gutiérrez-Mayka, Marcela, and Elisa Bernd. 2006. *How Is the Region Doing? Human Service Use and Service Availability in Allegheny County, PA.* The Forbes Funds. Available at http://www.forbesfunds.org/docs/2006Tropman_study2.pdf.

Illinois Facilities Fund. 2006. *Annual Report 2004–2005.* Available at http://www.iff.org/resources/content/2/6/images/2006annualrep.pdf.

Kissane, Rebecca Joyce. 2003. "What's Need Got to Do with It? Barriers to Use of Nonprofit Social Services." *Journal of Sociology and Social Welfare*, 30(2): 127–148.

Mark, Tami L., Rosanna M. Coffey, Rita Vandivort-Warren, Hendrick J. Harwood, Edward C. King, and the MHSA Spending Estimates Team. 2005. U.S. Spending for Mental Health and Substance Abuse Treatment, *1991–2001. Health Affairs* Web Exclusive, March 29.

Marwell, Nicole P. 2004. "Privatizing the Welfare State: Nonprofit Community-Based Organizations as Political Actors." *American Sociological Review*, 69: 265–291.

Salamon, Lester M. 2003. *The Resilient Sector: The State of Nonprofit America.* Washington, DC: The Brookings Institution.

Smith, Steven Rathgeb. 2002. "Social Services," in *State of Nonprofit America.* Lester M. Salamon, ed. Washington, DC: The Brookings Institution, 149–186.

Smith, Steven Rathgeb, and Michael Lipsky. 1993. *Nonprofits for Hire.* Cambridge, MA: Harvard University Press.

Twombly, Eric C. 2001. *Human Service Nonprofits in Metropolitan Areas during Devolution and Welfare Reform.* Washington, DC: Urban Institute, Center on Nonprofits and Philanthropy, Charting Civil Society, No. 10.

United Way of Greater Toronto. 2004. *Poverty by Postal Code.* Available at http://www.uwgt.org/who_we_help/pdfs/PovertybyPostalCodeFinal.pdf.

United Way of Greater Toronto. 2005. *Strong Neighbourhoods.* Available at http://www.uwgt.org/who_we_help/pdfs/SNTF-web_report.pdf.

U.S. Department of Health and Human Services. 2007. *TANF Financial Data.* Available at http://www.acf.hhs.gov/programs/ofs/data/index.html and links.

U.S. House of Representatives, House Committee on Ways and Means. 2004 *Green Book.* Washington, DC: U.S. Government Printing Office.

Wolff, Edward. 1999. "The Economy and Philanthropy," in *Philanthropy and the Nonprofit Sector in a Changing America.* Charles T. Clotfelter and Thomas Ehrlich, eds. Bloomington: Indiana University Press, 73–98

Wolpert, Julian. 1999. "Communities, Networks, and the Future of Philanthropy," in *Philanthropy and the Nonprofit Sector in a Changing America.* Charles T. Clotfelter and Thomas Ehrlich, eds. Bloomington: Indiana University Press, 231–247

Zedlewski, Sheila R. 2003. *Work and Barriers to Work among Welfare Recipients in 2002.* Washington, DC: The Urban Institute, Snapshots of America's Families, No. 3.

Index